# COLLECTION
# AND CONTAINER
# CLASSES IN C++

# COLLECTION AND CONTAINER CLASSES IN C++

## CAMERON HUGHES

## TRACEY HUGHES

WILEY COMPUTER PUBLISHING

JOHN WILEY & SONS, INC.

*New York   Chichester   Brisbane   Toronto   Singapore*

Publisher: Katherine Schowalter
Senior Editor: Marjorie Spencer
Managing Editor: Robert S. Aronds
Electronic Products, Associate Editor: Mike Green
Text Design & Composition: Irving Perkins Associates & Pagesetters

Designations used by companies to distinguish their products are often claimed as trademarks. In all instances where John Wiley & Sons, Inc. is aware of a claim, the product names appear in initial capital or all capital letters. Readers, however, should contact the appropriate companies for more complete information regarding trademarks and registration.

This text is printed on acid-free paper.

This publication is designed to provide accurate and authoritative information in regard to the subject matter covered. It is sold with the understanding that the publisher is not engaged in rendering legal, accounting, or other professional service. If legal advice or other expert assistance is required, the services of a competent professional person should be sought.

*Library of Congress Cataloging-in-Publication Data:*

Hughes, Cameron, 1960–
 Collection & container classes in C++ / Cameron Hughes, Tracey Hughes.
  p. cm.
 Includes bibliographical references.
 ISBN 0-471-14337-5 (paper/disk : alk. paper)
 1. Object-oriented programming (Computer science) 2. C++
(Computer program language) I. Hughes, Tracey.
 QA76.64.H825 1996
 005.1—dc20                95-50871
                           CIP

Printed in the United States of America
10 9 8 7 6 5 4 3 2 1

# Contents

## CHAPTER 2 OBJECTS IN C++      24

## CHAPTER 4 THE STANDARD TEMPLATE LIBRARY                                             127

## CHAPTER 5 THE OBJECT-ORIENTED SET    178

## CHAPTER 6 OBJECT-BASED SEQUENCES                                  244

# PREFACE

THE C++ language has become the industry standard for object-oriented development. The C++ language supports software development efforts of all sizes. Projects ranging from single-program single-developer to multimodule systems containing hundreds of thousands of lines of code implemented by teams of developers can all be developed efficiently and effectively in the C++ language. C++'s support for the *object metaphor* has been a driving force in the wide acceptance of object-oriented programming and object-oriented design techniques. Now that there is an ISO/ANSI standard for C++, *objects* are here to stay.

Objects are models. Objects can represent persons, places, things, or ideas. The number and kind of objects in a C++ application are virtually unlimited. Once the developer realizes the power of object-oriented programming, the objects in the developer's application start to multiply. Object storage and multiple object organization and manipulation become major issues. Techniques for referring to and controlling group of objects stored in internal computer memory or groups of objects stored in files become mandatory.

*Collection and Container Classes in C++* provides the developer with a detailed explanation of the constructs and techniques used to manage and organize groups of objects. We describe how container classes can be used to store groups of objects in computer memory. We demonstrate how persistent containers can be used to store collections of objects on external storage media. This book shows how traditional algorithms and data structures are related to collection and container classes. *Collection and Container Classes in C++* also provides an in-depth look at STL (Standard Template Library), which has been accepted as a part of the ANSI/ISO C++ standard. There are examples demonstrating how STL containers are used and accessed. Finally, there are numerous code examples and applications that demonstrate how collections and containers are designed, how they work, and when to use them.

## STANDARD TEMPLATE LIBRARY (STL)

This book contains the STL specification written by Alexander Stepanov anad Meng Lee. The disk that accompanies this book contains a complete working copy of the STL library. There are numerous examples in Chapters 4 through 8 that contain demonstrations of how to declare and use STL containers and algorithms.

## NIH COLLECTION AND CONTAINER CLASS LIBRARY

The National Institute of Health Collection and Container Class Library is discussed in Chapter 3. The NIH's collections and containers are object based. Although intended for UNIX, the reader can gain insight into object-based collections and containers and can contrast the STL template-based containers.

## WHO IS THIS BOOK FOR?

A mild acquaintance with the C++ programming language is assumed. Chapter 2 gives an overview of C++'s support for object orientation. Chapter 2 can also be used to review the basic object-oriented constructs of the C++ language. This book is for C++ programmers and developers who want to gain an understanding of the collection and container class concepts and the Standard Template Library containers that are available in the C++ language. This book covers the collection and container classes from the very beginning to an intermediate level. No prior experience with collection or container classes is assumed.

## ENVIRONMENTS

The examples and applications in this book have been designed using the standard C++ language. The collection and container examples in Chapters 6 through 10 can be compiled by any C++ compiler that supports the ANSI/ISO C++ standard. The application examples that are on the disk that accompanies this book can be run on any IBM PC compatible that is running Windows 3.0 and later, OS/2 2.0 and later, or Windows 95. Most of the examples in this book can be run as is in UNIX, VMS, and MSDOS environments. The examples that make use of OS/2's Presentation Manager and the Windows API can be easily modified to run in UNIX, VMS, or MSDOS console modes.

## STYLE OF CHAPTERS

Each chapter consists of practical discussions and examples. Diagrams and tables are used to aid in explaining and organizing difficult topics. Some of the chapters contain ancillary information that can be used to gain a more advanced understanding of the collection and container class theory. This information is contained in discussion side-bars and is not necessary to understand the material in this chapters. Chapters 5, 6, and 8 have application sidebars.

## Discussion Sidebars

The discussion sidebar will contain information that is used to explain computer science foundations for the collection and container classes. Discussion sidebars are self-contained and can be read at any time.

## Application Sidebars

Application sidebars present a complete computer application and an in-depth discussion of how the collection and container classes were used in the application. While the application sidebars are not necessary to understand the material in the chapter, they provide detailed explanation of each topic as well as some application-specific uses of the collection and container classes. The programs that are discussed in the application sidebars are all contained on the disk that accompanies this book. There is a compiled version for each application program. The application sidebar for Chapter 8 includes an application that runs under OS/2 Presentation Manager and Windows. The application sidebars for Chapters 5 and 6 can be run in console mode in the UNIX, VMS, or MSDOS environments. The complete source code for all the applications can also be found on the disk.

Although the application sidebars are not necessary to understand the material in the chapter, the material in the chapter is necessary to understand the application sidebars, and should be read as a prerequisite.

## CLASS RELATIONSHIP DIAGRAMS

This book utilizes the class relationship diagrams to describe the relationships between families of related classes and collection and container class hierarchies. A detailed explanation of class relationship diagrams can be found in Chapter 2.

## COMPILATION, TESTING, AND CODE RELIABILITY

All code in this book was compiled using IBM's CSET++ for OS/2 and Borland's C++ for Windows 95, NT, and C++ for OS/2. Many of the examples were also compiled using GNU C++. Although all the examples and applications in this book were tested to ensure correctness we make no warranties that the programs contained in this book are free of defect or error, or are consistent with any particular standard of merchantability, or that they will meet your requirement for any particular application. They should not be relied on for solving a problem whose incorrect solution could result in injury to person or loss of property. The authors and publishers disclaim all liability for direct or consequential damages resulting from use of the examples or applications presented in this book and contained on the disk accompanying this book.

# ACKNOWLEDGMENTS

WE WOULD like to give special thanks to all of our family, friends, and associates for enduring our frequent short hellos and premature good-byes.

This book is dedicated to Rahamel, Cherub, Lael, Robby, Anthony, Chrystal, Shantel, Aaron, Nicole, Michael, Victor, Rachel, Little Mike, Scottie, Jeremiah, Joshua, and all those who participate in our annual science fair.

# COLLECTION AND CONTAINER CLASSES IN C++

CHAPTER 1

# OBJECT-ORIENTED SOFTWARE DEVELOPMENT

## SOFTWARE DEVELOPMENT

Software development is the process of translating concepts, ideas, patterns of work, rules, algorithms, or formulas into sets of instructions and data that can be executed or manipulated by a computer. There are almost as many approaches to software development as there are software developers. There are always attempts to classify software development, to reduce it to a single comprehensible process. There have been attempts to restrict software development to the scientific method. It is sometimes adopted as an engineering discipline. When the complexity of the software requirements increases without bound then the development of software suddenly becomes an art! While these attempts at categorization are occasionally successful they are never long lasting. The constant change in how software is used, what it does, who develops it, and what kinds of devices it runs on make a characterization of the software development process difficult at best.

Each attempt at defining or refining the software development process introduces a new set of developmental models. From the new models follow new terminology, new techniques, and new computer languages, design tools, and programming paradigms. If the developmental model has wide application, and is easily understood, and is easily communicated, and can be effectively implemented, then it is accepted by the software developer community. The new model becomes another approach to software development.

Although the software development process cannot be strictly classified as an art, science, or engineering discipline, it can and often does employ elements of all three. Table 1.1 lists the categories that the software development process is usually placed in. Note that the characteristics of the software development process have a number of similarities with other fields inasmuch as it could be considered an exercise in those

**1**

**Table 1.1   The characteristics of the software development process.**

| Fields | Characteristic Similarities of Fields and Software Development |
|---|---|
| **Engineering Discipline** | * The need of a strong mathematical background.<br>* Extensive use of modeling oriented toward design.<br>* The use of tools and techniques to assist in the design phase.<br>* Extensive use of testing a system.<br>* The use of proven concepts, abstractions, techniques, and mechanisms in the structure of new systems.<br>* The use of already-existing parts in the construction of systems.<br>* The use of design methods to assist in the creation of a path from system requirements to implementation.<br>* The use of schematics or blueprints in the design of a system.<br>* Charting. |
| **Scientific Discipline** | * The need of a strong mathematical background.<br>* Extensive use of modeling oriented toward interpretation of reality.<br>* The use of the scientific method.<br>* The accumulation of a body of knowledge referred to as computer science. |
| **Artistic Endeavor** | * The use of creativity.<br>* The use of imagination.<br>* Aesthetics.<br>* Talent. |
| **Mathematical Discipline** | * The use of mathematical structures and concepts.<br>* The need of a mathematical background.<br>* The use of mathematical notation to express computer science concepts. |
| **Craft** | * Skill.<br>* Experience.<br>* Specific education.<br>* Apprenticeships.<br>* Vocation.<br>* Mentoring. |

fields. Those fields includes science, mathematics, art, and engineering disciplines. In this sense software development looks more like a craft. And software development models look more like mental paradigms of skilled artisans. We proceed under the assumption that there is no single right way to develop software, but instead many right ways. The particular approach chosen will usually be dictated more by aesthetics and the personality of the institution, team, or individual than any other factor.

In this book we explore object-oriented software development methods that involve the usage of collection and container classes. The collection and container classes are implemented using the C++ language. The C++ language has become the de facto standard for object-oriented programming. While C++ is a general purpose language and can be used for all types of programming, we focus primarily on the features it has that support object-centered programming. That is programming where the basic unit of modularity is the *object*. In this book when we refer to an object we mean the runtime version of a *class*. A class is a software construct that models a person, place, thing, or idea. A class exists as a declaration, definition, or description. A class can exist on a piece of paper as part of a design. An object is a class that has been implemented in software and can exist only in software. An object is an instance of a class. For example, an engineer's blueprint may describe a car or line of cars. However, the blueprint serves only as a description or plan for a car; it is not the car. The car is manufactured on the assembly line and is an *instance* of the engineer's blueprint. Classes are related to objects in this way. Classes are descriptions of objects, not the objects themselves. Objects are actual instances of classes.

Collections and containers are types of objects that are used to manage groups or collections of other objects. Collection and container objects get their name from their usage. They are software constructs that can group together or contain multiple objects. The containers act as *generic holders*, making it possible to store, retrieve, manipulate, and access groups of objects. The containers can hold collections of objects of all types, both built in and user defined. These collections can be heterogeneous (consisting of groups of mixed objects) or homogenous (consisting of groups of the same type of object). The collection and container classes in C++ extend the object-oriented development model to include support for super classes and metastructures. We explore the concepts of super classes and metastructures in Chapter 3.

The object-oriented software development model using C++ consists of three fundamental processes:

1. Object-oriented analysis
2. Object-oriented design
3. Object-oriented programming

There are many formal methods that extend these processes with other processes, that is, object-oriented testing or detailed object design. Also, each process can be divided into subprocesses. For example, Jacobson et al. (1992, 18) present possibilities for analysis decomposition as enterprise analysis, change analysis, requirements analysis, and a robustness analysis. The textbook order of the analysis, design, and programming processes suggests that object-oriented software development should begin with analysis and from analysis proceed to design. Figure 1.1 shows a typical progression of an object-oriented development life cycle (OODLC). Once the design is finished, then the programming should begin. This type of ordering is referred to as a *software development life cycle* because it tracks each phase of a software development effort. Software development life cycles are the subject of much discussion and debate. This is partly because the development cycle chosen is critical to the success of a project, and partly because a life cycle that works nicely for one type of software effort may not work at all for another

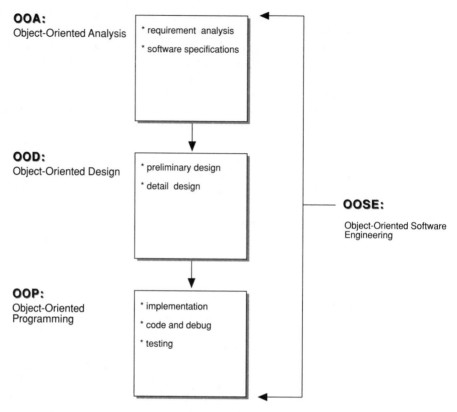

**Figure 1.1** The object development life cycle.

type. For instance, many corporate developers use different software development life cycles than software manufacturers use. The corporate life cycle may include extensive feasibility analysis and the software manufacturer may not be concerned with feasibility, or vice versa.

In this book we are concerned more with the relationships between the processes than the order the processes should follow. Although the order of the processes may be fixed when software development is approached as a scientific or engineering discipline, the order is dynamic in the practice of software development as a craft. We have found that in practice the relationships between the development processes are transitive, symmetrical, and reflexive. The development processes are *transitive* because the analysis process shapes the design process, the design process shapes the development process, and the transitive nature of the relationship implies that the analysis process shapes the development process. The development processes are *symmetrical* because there is impact feedback between each process. For instance, the analysis process gives information to the design process. The design process may use this information to describe an object-oriented model of the proposed system. On the other hand, the design process can give information back to the analysis process causing the need for further or perhaps different analysis conclusions. The development processes are *reflexive* because each process is recursive and may impact itself. For example, details discovered during the design process may call for a change in the original design. Figure 1.2 shows the relationships between the different processes in the OODLC. The difficulty of implementing a design during the programming process may call for a different implementation.

These relationships indicate that software development as a craft does not proceed in simple cycles but rather as a set of interrelated, interdependent processes that are reentrant and can occur in a parallel, recursive, iterative, or sequential order. The C++ environment contains the flexibility to meet these dynamic requirements. C++ contains the class, inheritance, and polymorphic constructs to support the full object paradigm. The object-oriented software development process using C++ is further enhanced by three powerful *class-centered* concepts:

1. Class libraries
2. Collections and containers
3. Application frameworks

In this chapter we explain what object-oriented software development is. We explain how object-oriented software development in C++ is supported by class libraries, collections and containers, and application frameworks. We describe the relationships between collections, containers, application frameworks, and class libraries and how these components fit into object-oriented analysis, object-oriented design, and finally, object-oriented programming.

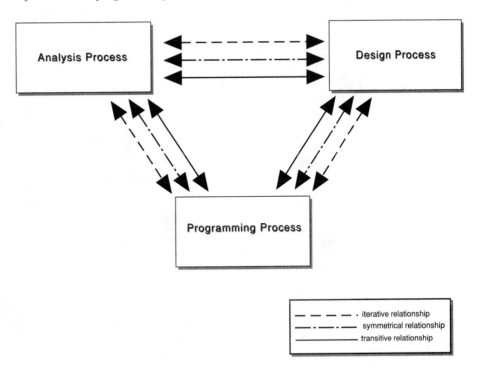

**Figure 1.2** The relationship between analysis, design, and programming can be iterative, transitive, or symmetrical.

## OBJECT-ORIENTED ANALYSIS

Object-oriented analysis is an inside-out, outside-in process of discovery. Object-oriented analysis has one fundamental goal, and at least two consequences. The fundamental goal of object-oriented analysis is to discover or recognize the objects that a process, scenario, system, or instance consists of and how those objects are related and interact. A pure object-oriented analysis will describe a process, scenario, system, or instance totally as a collection of objects acting and interacting. For example, we want to devise a system where an intelligent e-mail agent is to deliver an e-mail message to some user on the Internet using the shortest path and time spans possible (see Figure 1.3). A cursory object-oriented analysis would identify the following objects:

An e-mail message
An intelligent e-mail agent
The Internet
A generic user
Paths
Distances
Duration

Our proposed system in its simplest form would consist only of these objects acting and interacting. This simplified analysis has at least two fundamental consequences:

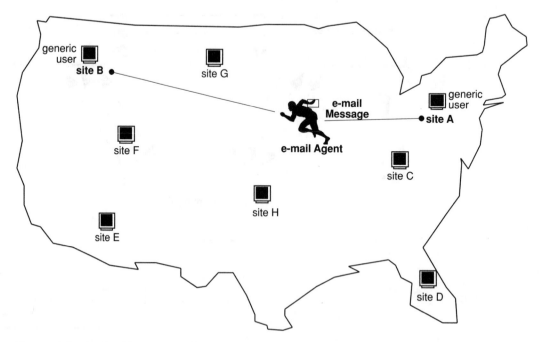

**Figure 1.3** An intelligent e-mail agent carries an e-mail message from one generic user to another using the shortest path in the least amount of time.

1. The system is broken down into more manageable parts.
2. The identified objects and their relationships form the begining of design requirements.

The function of this cursory object-oriented analysis can be restated as three general principles of analysis:

1. Understand the system under consideration (identify the objects, their relationships and interactions).
2. Reduce the system to a comprehensible and approachable form (describe the
   system totally in terms of objects acting and interacting).
3. Use the reduced description of the system as requirements for the object-oriented
   design.

An object-oriented analysis can be pure or hybrid. A pure object-oriented analysis will lead to a piece of software with an object-oriented architecture. A hybrid analysis will describe the process, scenario, system, or instance as only partially consisting of objects. In a hybrid analysis, other approaches such as structured analysis or data analyses are used to form a complete picture of what is to be committed to software. Hybrid analysis supports hybrid software development. A piece of software may contain objects and not have an object-oriented architecture. This piece of software would be considered hybrid.

## Inside-Out, Outside-In Analysis

One of the consequences of object-oriented analysis is *system decomposition*. Decomposi-tion breaks a system down into more manageable or comprehensible parts. *Inside-out, outside-in analysis* is a form of decomposition. Inside-out, outside-in analysis looks for any apparent objects in a process, scenario, system, or instance. Once any objects are identi-fied, the relationships between those objects are investigated. The investigation of the rela-tionships between objects usually leads to the discovery of new objects as well as a deeper understanding of previously found objects. This process is both deductive and recursive. Figure 1.4 depicts the flowcharts of the inside-out, outside-in models of analysis. The goal is to find all the objects that the process, scenario, system, or instance implies. Simply stated: Find one object, then find any relationships or other objects that object suggests should be present. Once all the objects have been deduced the system has been totally decomposed.

*Inside-out, outside-in analysis* is in contrast to top-down or bottom-up analysis. The system under consideration is the focal point in top-down or bottom-up analysis. The object and its internal and external relationships are the main considerations for inside-out, outside-in analysis. The distinguishing feature of inside-out, outside-in analysis is the focus on the object as opposed to the system. The inside-out aspect of the analysis determines how the object acts with and reacts to the outside world. The outside-in component discovers what the object requires to be totally encapsulated. This process lends itself to deeper understanding of object interfaces, object relationships, and object composition. Any consideration to the system as a whole is completely secondary. In fact, if a pure object-oriented analysis is done properly the system is already present in a subset of the relationships between the objects.

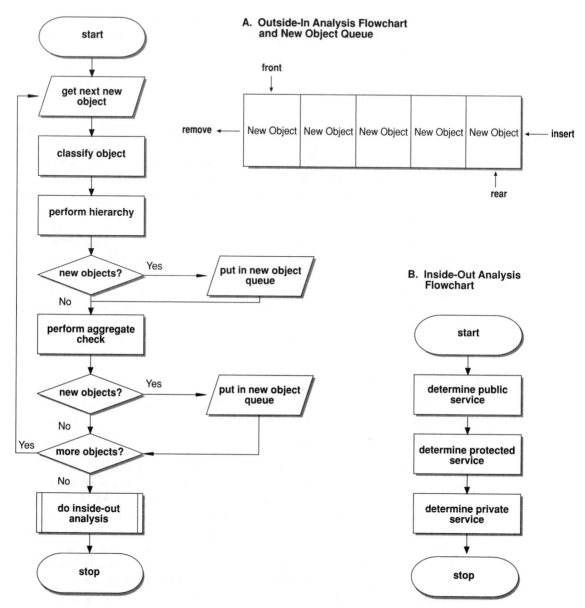

**Figure 1.4**   Flowcharts for the inside-out and outside-in models of analysis.

## Why Do Analysis?

Analysis, object oriented or otherwise, is done to gain a complete *understanding* of the scenario under consideration. Unless there is a thorough understanding of the mission that the software is to perform, the software development effort is in jeopardy before it even begins. A basic understanding of the scenario or system can be measured by complete and detailed answers to the following questions:

1. Who are the users of the system?
2. What is the system supposed to do or be?
3. In what ways are the users going to use the system?
4. When is the system to be completed?
5. Why do the users need or want the system?

Although these questions are simplistic and should be obvious, failure to answer all of them in complete detail continues to be one of the largest reasons why software development efforts fail. Understanding is the first reason for doing analysis.

After the scenario or system is understood another important determination can be made. That is, can the system be implemented in software? Making this determination is critical and similar to why existence theorems are used in mathematics. The mathematician uses an existence theorem to determine first if an answer exists to a complicated math problem before any effort is expended in trying to find the answer. Software may be requested for a scenario that cannot be implemented on a computer. A thorough analysis can make this determination and save everyone the trouble.

Another important reason for doing analysis is to determine the scale of the software development effort. Some complex software development efforts at the onset seem deceptively small and simple, while others appear to be large and complex but turn out to be one-person projects. Don't call an army when a soldier will do. On the other hand, if the job seems too simple to be true, it's probably not. The scale of a system may also prevent it from being designed. Although any given portion of the system is capable of being implemented on a computer, the sheer magnitude of the development effort may be prohibitive. Figure 1.5 is a graph showing complexity versus size in any given project. This kind of graph can be used to measure the *scale* of a project. The project may be large and not complex. The project may be small and very complex. Thorough analysis can discover the scale of the software development effort.

Along with discovering the scale of the system the analysis can determine system complexity. It is entirely possible for a system that has been broken down into comprehensible parts to still be considerably complex. For example, the space shuttle is not only one of the most well-understood systems ever developed, it happens to be also one of the most complex systems ever developed. An understanding of the complexity of the system can help to determine what type of talent, ability, creativity, education, and skill will be required to design and implement the piece of software. Many theoreticians would probably move to place this kind of evaluation in some other level of the development life cycle. However, from a practical point of view we have found that the earlier in the process complexity issues are discovered and dealt with, the better off are the remaining processes in the software development effort.

Analysis serves to break a scenario or system down into comprehensible parts. Object-oriented analysis decomposes a system or scenario into a collection of objects, their relationships, and their meanings. It is important to know what an object means to the overall system. That is, the analysis must map object semantics to domain vocabulary.

Finally, the conclusions of the analysis process can be used to form the system requirements. The system requirements provide the direction for the system design. Without system requirements system design is guesswork. The success of any system

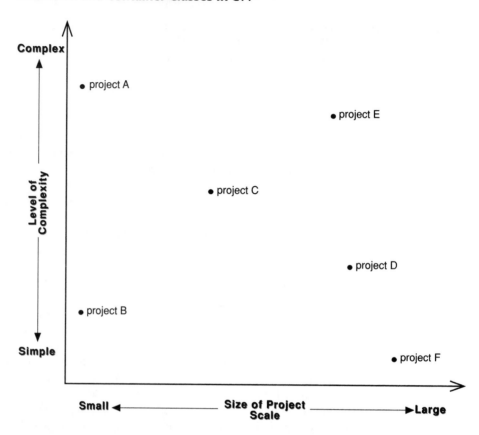

**Figure 1.5** This graph demonstrates the complexity and size ratio scale of a project. The complexity is measured from simple to complex on the *y*-axis and the size is measured from small to large on the *x*-axis. A project can be large and complex (project E) or small and simple (project B). A project can be small and complex (project A), large and simple (project F), or many grades in between.

that does not have the benefit of direction from requirements is mingled with chance and serendipity. Requirements are extracted from the system analysis.

## What Can Be Analyzed for the Existence of Objects?

Object-oriented analysis is not restricted by scale. Object-oriented analysis can be done on large complex manual systems, or on a small existing software system. A sequence of possible future events can be analyzed for objects. A procedure, function, or algorithm can be searched and evaluated for the existence of objects. In fact, upon close scrutiny objects can be found anywhere!

# OBJECT-ORIENTED SOFTWARE DESIGN

Object-oriented software design (OOSD) is a large discipline, with many subdisciplines. Entire books have been written about software design. We can only hope to introduce some of the more important areas of OOSD in this chapter. For a detailed introductory treatment of OOSD, see Booch (1994, 169–290) or Ivar Jacobson et al.'s *Object-Oriented Software Engineering* (1992).

We are concerned with how collection and container classes can be used in OOSD to support an object-oriented development effort. Using collection and container classes at the design level provides an easier transition when transforming design objects into implementation objects. Before we can discuss how collection and container classes can impact OOSD, we will review some of the basic concepts.

## What Is Object-Oriented Software Design?

Software design is the process of translating software requirements into software blueprints, architecture, and specification. The software design is an abstract model representing what the software will do and be. Object-oriented software design is the process of translating software requirements into a blueprint where objects model each aspect of the system to be developed. In other methodologies the design is driven by the flow of control in a system, or by the movement of data in a system. In object-oriented design the blueprint is centered around the structure and hierarchy of collections of objects, their relationships and interactions.

One of the main objectives of the design process is to transform the system requirements into a blueprint or architecture that describes and defines software that can meet those requirements. In an extreme oversimplification of the design process we could imagine the design process as a box with two ends. System requirements go in one end and design elements come out the other. A transformation takes place inside the box and system requirements undergo a decomposition or recomposing and recording process. In a very basic approach there would be one design element for every system requirement. However, in real system design there is normally not a one-to-one correspondence between requirements and design elements. In many cases, one system requirement may be transformed into multiple design elements, or one design element may capture multiple system requirements. Figures 1.6 a, b, and c show the flow of transformation from system requirements to design elements. This is one of the primary reasons that a cookbook approach to designing software systems has failed to appear. If each system requirement had a single corresponding design element then there would be a functional relationship between system requirements and system design. This would greatly simplify software design. However, there is no functional relationship (one-to-one correspondence) between system requirements and software design. Instead the relationship between system requirements and software design can be described as one-to-many or many-to-one.

The transformation of system requirements to software design must produce at least two items: (1) a description of the software architecture, and (2) description artifacts.

The complete and thorough description of the software architecture is essential for the programming process to be successful. However, unless this description has been

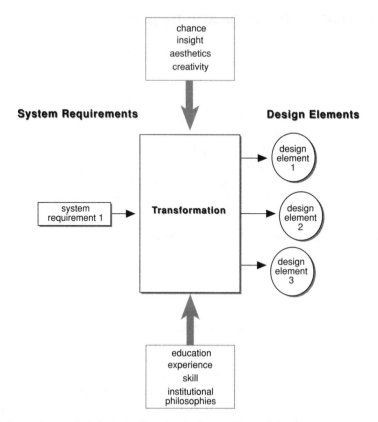

**Figure 1.6A**   System requirements are transformed into design elements. The transformation is affected by chance, insight, aesthetics, and creativity impacting the transformation from the top, and skill, education, experience, and institutional philosophies impacting the transformation from the bottom. A single system requirement can be transformed into many design elements.

recorded by some means, it cannot be measured objectively for its completeness or thoroughness. The communication of a design that has only a mental blueprint is difficult at best. That is, description artifacts are a necessary byproduct of the design process. These artifacts may include anything from block diagrams, Input Process Output (IPO) charts, Hierarchical Input Process Output (HIPO) charts, pseudocode, flowcharts, data flow diagrams, and data dictionaries to class relationship diagrams, class specification sheets, object interaction charts, finite state diagrams, and use case descriptions. The important point here is that if there are no measurable, testable, verifiable description artifacts then the transformation from requirements to design is incomplete.

For object-oriented systems the software design process will produce a software architecture that is divided into modules. The architecture is broken down into modules to help manage system requirement complexity. In object-oriented design the class is the basic unit of modularity. The class serves as the organizing unit of description in an object-oriented design. This means that all system components can be described in terms of their relationships to classes or groups of classes.

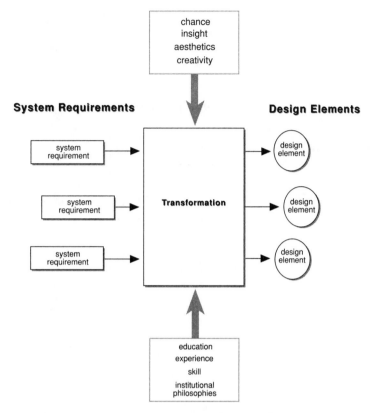

**Figure 1.6B** Many system requirements can be transformed into many design elements.

During the process of transformation of requirement elements to design elements, the advantages of OOSD become apparent. Using OOSD, persons, places, things, or ideas from the application domain can be modeled or simulated as classes or patterns of classes. In effect, the designer is able to devise a software version of the domain scenario. The notion of modeling and simulation are at the core of OOSD. Further, modeling and simulation as foundations of OOSD set the stage for comprehensible and manageable system evolution and system testing. The closer the classes model or simulate the domains they represent, the more approachable reliable system test plans become and the easier it is to anticipate system change. Insofar as the domain is understood, domain behavior, characteristics, attributes, and anomalies are known and can be predicted. When the software design is truly representative of the application domain, then the characteristics and behavior of those components of the software that model the domain can be mapped to the application domain counterparts. Likewise the characteristics and behavior in the application domain can be mapped to the software.

When we use the term *modeling* in reference to OOSD we are referring to the process of designing software representations of real-world notions. The representations may be simplified versions of their real-world counterparts, or there may be an *isomorphic* relationship between the software representation and the real-world entity that the software

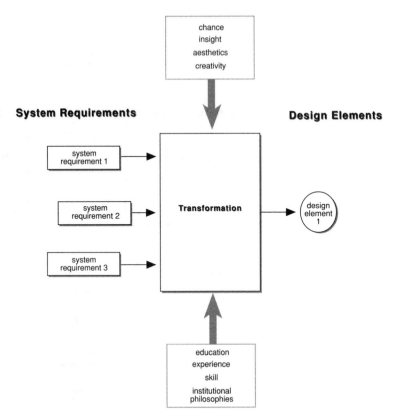

**Figure 1.6C** Many system requirements can be transformed into a single design element.

models. That is, the software may for all intentional purposes completely duplicate each element of what it is modeling both in behavior and characteristic. Figure 1.7 shows a classification of some of the common types of models that a designer may encounter. The classes that are designed in OOSD models are really mathematical models and notions. They fall under the categories of discrete structures, mathematical systems, Abstract Data Types (ADTs), groups, and fields.

In many cases an object-oriented system is being designed to replace some manual system. In these cases the object-oriented system reproduces, imitates, or simulates in software the system that it is replacing. The model that the designer constructs must capture the essential characteristics and behavior of the manual system in its entirety. OOSD allows the designer to represent each component of the system as a characteristic of a class or pattern of classes. Unfortunately, there is no one way to go about modeling or simulating during the design. Experience, aesthetics, and perspective will be the major contributors to any modeling or simulation approach chosen. However, we can say that a thorough understanding of the system or scenario to be represented is required in order to construct a viable software model.

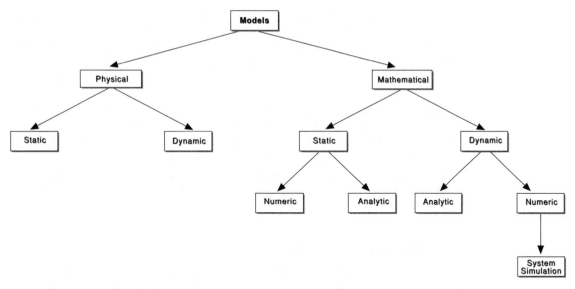

**Figure 1.7** Types of models.

## What Must Be Considered during Design?

There are at least five models of the system that must be considered during the design process:

1. The user model
2. The requirements model
3. The implementation model
4. The test model
5. The documentation model

For a detailed treatment of the user model, requirements model, implementation model, and test model see Ivar Jacobson et al.'s book, *Object-Oriented Software Engineering* (1992).

### THE USER MODEL

The design of a piece of software is not complete unless it includes functionality that addresses every level of user of the system to be implemented. The identification of who the users of the proposed system are and how they will use the system is one of the fundamental tasks of the analysis process. Most systems have multiple levels of users. Most systems can perform more than one task. A particular user level plus a particular type of system use represents one *usage possibility*. Ivar Jacobson refers to this as a *use case* (Jacobson et al. 1992, 129). We can use the Fundamental Principle of Counting to determine how many use cases we have. Basically the Fundamental Principle of Counting states that if process $a_1$ can be done in $n_1$ ways, and process $a_2$ can be done in $n_2$ ways, and process $a_3$ can be done in $n_3$ ways, . . . , and process $a_m$ can be done in $n_m$ ways, then the number of ways the processes can occur is $n_1 \times n_2 \times n_3 \ldots n_m$. Using The Fundamental Principle of Counting, if $A$ represents the set of all types of users of the system, and $B$ represents all the ways the system can be used, and $m = |A|$ and $n = |B|$ then the number of use cases is $n^m$. Let us say that we have five types of users of a system, and we have nine unique ways that each user can interact with the system; then the number of use cases for these systems is $9^5$ or 59,049 use cases. Of course, in determining all the ways the system can be used we are only referring to legitimate ways of using the system as specified in the requirement specification. At this point we are not trying to capture all the ways that the software can be misused or ways that the designers or requesters have not specified. That level of system use should be considered in the testing model. The designer must provide a system design for every valid use case.

## The Requirements Model

The requirements model focuses primarily on the use cases and the requirement specifications. In order for a design to pass requirement audits every requirement element must be traceable to a design component or components. A requirement audit examines the design to determine if every requirement element is represented in the design. For instance, if the design calls for the system to accept synchronous input from a modem and support fax capabilities then an audit of the design will determine if in fact these requirement elements are accounted for. This is another important reason why the design must ultimately be put in a form that can be easily communicated and verified. For most medium to large-scale projects, the design will be examined by multiple people. The use of the design description artifacts is normally iterative. The design is usually visited and revisited even long after the system has been delivered in order to effectively manage changes that are to be made to the system. Without clear and accurate description artifacts the design process is not reliable. This marks the importance of the design as a communication tool. Traceability is one of the hallmarks of a good design. In this case traceability is needed in only one direction. It is not necessary that every design element or component have originated from user or system requirements. However, it is necessary that every user or system requirement is represented in the design.

It is during the design process that the system requirements must be transformed into components that can be implemented in software. In OOSD, chunks of the application domain are modeled as classes or patterns of classes that can be realized in an object-oriented language. In this way the design process serves as a reality check. If there are requirements that are impossible or impractical to implement as software, those requirements must be reevaluated and restated, or removed. This is usually a give-and-take process where the designer(s) engage in the art of negotiation.

## The Implementation Model

In the implementation model environment specifics are considered. The following are some of the types of specifics that are addressed in the implementation model:

What is the target environment(s)?

What are the memory and speed constraints of the hardware platform(s)?

What will the memory and speed demands of the proposed system be?

What language(s) is the system to be developed in?

What testing and debugging tools are available?

What source code management and revision facilities will be used?

Is the source code to adhere to software standards (i.e., ISO/ANSI)?

What is the projected size (number of modules, lines of code) of the software?

According to Jacobson (1992, 144), "The implementation model consists of the annotated source code." In the implementation model the design elements are transformed into software components. Note that during the transformation of requirements to design the requirement elements enjoyed a one-to-many or many-to-one relationship with the design elements. This is also the case when translating design elements into actual software components. One software component may represent multiple design components, and one design component may require multiple software components. Just as there is a required traceability from the requirement specification to the design specification there is a required traceability from the design specification to the software component implementation. As was the case from requirement to design, the traceability from design to component only needs to be a one-way dependency. That is, every element from the design must be found in the software components, but every software component does not have to be traced back to the design. Why is this so? Well, a closer look at the types of classes that will be required in the implementation model reveals that there will be many utility classes, software development support classes, debugging components, and so on that are not parts of the design but will have to be built in order to successfully complete the project.

In the implementation model the designer should also consider whether the system requires any concurrency, or whether multithreading issues need to be addressed. The behavior of the system if it is to be deployed in a networked or distributed environment should be considered. Many systems operate with some form of Database Management System (DBMS). File handling performance and external storage access must be considered in the implementation model. Memory models should be decided upon in this model; that is, will the system implement a proprietary memory management scheme or will the operating system's virtual paging be used? Also, compatibility issues must be considered. Is this system an upgrade of a previous system? Will this system have to be compatible with future systems? Does this system need to be upwardly or downwardly compatible? If so, how will this be achieved? The implementation model must also address code portability standards. Namely, how can the system be designed so that operating-specific, and compiler- or interpreter-specific language extensions are isolated or readily separable from the domain components? Another important area is project file management. Should the modules be managed by some compiler-specific project manager that saves project information in some proprietary format, or should more widely accepted *make* project management schemes be employed?

These are just a few of the basic questions and issues that should be addressed in the implementation model. The designer must set the ground rules for system implementation in this model. This means that every relevant aspect of the target environment must be addressed. As a part of the implementation model the types and caliber of developers should be considered. In an ideal situation the designer(s) have access to unlimited talent, skill, experience, and education in the developer pool. In most situations this is not the case, and the caliber of the developers must be considered in the implementation model. It is not productive to come up with a design that cannot be implemented by the developers that are available. In some cases the designer and the developer are one and the same. In these cases, extra care must be taken to separate each model properly and to approach each aspect of the software development life cycle as objectively as possible.

## THE TEST MODEL

The test model is used for system verification. Here the importance of good modeling and simulation techniques is magnified. If the software components are good representations of their real-world notions, then understanding of the characteristics and behaviors of the real-world notions can be applied to the software counterparts. This has important implications for the test model. In order for a test plan to be successful the results of the testing must be known in advance. Specifically, the designer must specify what tests are to be run, how the tests are to be run, and what the expected results should be. If the software components are good models or simulations of their real-world counterparts, then the designer is aided in knowing what to expect from the class components in the system. For instance, if a system has been designed to model a bank, and the system captures the major characteristics of the bank, then withdrawals at midnight are not allowed, unless they happen at an ATM machine! Obviously this is a simplistic example. The point here is that the designer can take advantage of domain knowledge when creating the test model. The parameters, limits, system normalities, and system absurdities are easier to identify in the domain than they are in the software. However, if they are identified in the domain they can be more readily addressed in the class components that model the domain.

The testing model should provide testing specifications. These testing specifications should at the very minimum be use case driven. This means that for every legitimate use case in the system there should be verification testing and validation testing that provides assurance that the system does what it should do when the various types of users use the system in legitimate ways.

## THE DOCUMENTATION MODEL

Constructing plans for the types and scope of system documentation in the design model is effective. Especially during the design of user-level documentation. When user-level documentation is designed during the design phase rather than after the software has been implemented, the use cases are further verified. If the design of the user documentation is a true and accurate picture of the elements that are in the design, then a thorough audit of the user documentation can uncover use cases that were missed or, what is more important, uncover requirements that never became use cases but should have become use cases. Another important advantage of designing and in some cases implementing the system documentation in the design model is the value of communicating with everyone involved on a project. By attacking the scope of the system documentation any shortcomings will be uncovered. The range of system documentation should be identified as early in the design process as possible: what documentation tools will be used, what format will the reports be in, what is the least acceptable level of detail in a document, what is the greatest level of detail required, how it should be distributed, and how it will be named, referenced, and archived. The better both system documentation designs and user documentation designs are, the higher the chance for a successful software development project.

## Object-Oriented Software Design and Class Reuse

One of the important adages in software development is "don't reinvent the wheel." If the functionality that is needed already exists, then use it. The goals here are to:

Minimize software development time.
Reduce the amount of code that needs testing.
Reduce the amount of time spent learning complicated algorithms and procedures.
Reduce the amount of time spent searching for solutions.
Build on code that already works.

The technique of using the same code in different projects or even more than once in the same project is called code *reuse*. There are many ways that a developer can reuse code. One of the basic techniques of code reuse is to use procedures or functions. Procedures and functions place a set of operations in one unit. The unit can be used at different places in one program, or by different programs without the need of rewriting the operations. Another simple way for a developer to reuse code is to take advantage of the hundreds of algorithms that have been published. In many cases these algorithms need only minor revisions before they can be put to productive use. The use of code libraries is a major form of code reuse. A code library is a collection of useful, tested, documented functions and procedures. Code libraries come in many flavors:

Mathematical libraries
User interface libraries
File management libraries
Memory management libraries
Graphics libraries
Utility libraries
Task and coroutine libraries
Operating system API libraries
Domain specific libraries

The library is one of the most effective forms of code reuse. There are code libraries available that address a wide range of applications. The developer can use the code in these libraries without having to understand how all the code works, or what internal representation techniques were used. Good code libraries have been well tested and documented. The developer can use functions or procedures from a code library and be spared the process of reinventing the wheel.

The notion of code reuse can also be used in object-oriented software design. C++

supports a number of software components that facilitate code reuse, such as: frameworks, class libraries, collections and containers, and classes. The major difference between these components and function or procedure libraries is that these components are object oriented. This means that not only is the developer spared from having to reinvent the wheel, but the developer can enhance the performance of the wheel using object-oriented techniques. These components provide the developer and designer with the entire object metaphor. Therefore the developer can take advantage of inheritance, polymorphism, and encapsulation when using these components. Through inheritance the developer or designer can redefine or specialize the behavior of these components without having to start from scratch. They do not need to make any changes in the original source code for these components because these components support the notion of encapsulation and information hiding. This is in contrast to traditional procedure or function libraries. The developer must make changes to original source code when using traditional procedure or function libraries and would like to modify the behavior of any given procedure and function. This is risky business because the developer has to gain a thorough understanding of the internal workings of the function or procedure to be changed as well as any other procedure and function that uses the changed code. After any changes are made the entire library will have to be tested. Any change to the source code could introduce subtle bugs that may not show up immediately after the change. If these bugs surface at some later time the developer cannot be sure whether there was a problem originally with the library or whether the bugs were introduced because of the changes that were made to the source code. These issues are avoided using object-oriented components and the inheritance feature of C++. We review the support that C++ has for the object metaphor in Chapter 2.

## APPLICATION FRAMEWORKS

Major code reuse is obtained by using *application frameworks*. Application frameworks are generic object-oriented applications. The application framework serves as a pattern for an entire application. It embodies the fundamental structure or skeleton that the application will have without providing the application details. The developer and designer are relieved of the responsibility of deciding upon the architecture of the application because the application framework supplies them with a software component blueprint that specifies predefined relationships between the major classes in the application. This may sound restricting but fear not, because the application framework broadly defines an entire class of applications with a wide range of genericity. The applications that are committed to a framework are usually well defined and well understood. Furthermore, because they model the application at its most abstract level, application frameworks tend to provide the developer with open but deterministic structures. This implies that if the system that the developer is implementing can be classified as one of these well-defined applications then it is likely that the system will have a structure that is very similar to the predefined patterns and relationships that the application framework provides.

Application frameworks are built using C++ classes. The highest-level classes in an application framework represent the generic functionality of the application that is being modeled. These classes normally have very fat interfaces (see Stroustrup 1991, 455).

This means that they are so generic that they are difficult to classify. When application frameworks are used during the design process, design efforts are greatly simplified. The designer can move on from overall structure to component specifics. Because application frameworks normally represent well-defined applications, the success of a software development effort that employs application frameworks is increased.

## CLASS LIBRARIES

Class libraries are also important in code reuse schemes. Class libraries are collections of useful and general classes that are normally grouped by categories. Just as with function and procedure libraries, C++ class libraries come in many flavors:

Mathematical class libraries
User interface class libraries
File management class libraries
Memory management class libraries
Graphics class libraries
Utility class libraries
Task and coroutine class libraries
Operating system API class libraries
Domain-specific class libraries

There is a distinction between class libraries and application frameworks. Whereas a class library can be used for virtually anything that it can be applied to, an application framework is a collection of classes that has a predefined structure and represents an application. The relationships between the classes in an application framework are set and the use of the application framework is restricted to the family of applications that it represents. The classes in a class library may not be related at all except for category, and the patterns of their use cannot be predicted. For instance, in a mathematical class library there may be triangle classes and polynomial classes. Although a relationship can be invented there is no predefined relationship. Also, the polynomial class or the triangle class could be used for any application and in any manner that is appropriate. This is not true for the application framework. Although the application framework represents a broad family of applications, the components of the applications have a predefined relationship and are meant to work together based on predesigned assumptions. Class libraries are collections of classes and application frameworks are collections of classes. Class libraries can be used in a wider range of ways than application frameworks may be used.

As with the other object-oriented components that C++ supports, the class library can be extended through inheritance. This gives the developer a powerful model for reuse. The developer has the option of using the class library as is and gaining the benefits of code reuse or can extend the class library's functionality by deriving new classes and specializing the behavior for those new classes. Because the class library supports the object metaphor, the developer does not have to be concerned about the internal implementation of the classes. The developer does not have to change the source code in a class library to extend its functionality.

## COLLECTIONS AND CONTAINERS

Collections and containers are objects that act as *generic holders* for other groups of objects. Collection and container classes may be only a part of a class library, or a class library may consist of only collection and container classes. Although application frameworks normally utilize collections and containers, collections and containers are not application frameworks. Collections and containers are general purpose grouping structures. The developer or designer can use collections and containers to manipulate groups of heterogeneous or homogeneous objects. Collections and containers are used to manage a group of objects in the same way that traditional arrays are used to manage traditional data types such as integers or characters.

Collections and containers are objects. This means that the benefits of inheritance, polymorphism, and encapsulation can all be applied to collections and containers. Many of these structures are object-oriented versions of stacks, queues, dequeues, sets, multisets, lists, associative arrays, graphs, and trees. However, the possibilities for collection and container design go far beyond these data structures. We've come across garages, banks, cells, crowds, villages, groups, rings, fields, transfinite sets, cabinets, and so forth.

This book is about collections and containers and how they are implemented in the C++ language. We will have much to say about the various possibilities for collections and containers in the chapters that follow. The relationships between collections, containers, and object-oriented designs relate to organization and modeling. When the designer needs to consistently refer to multiple objects as a unit, then the specification of a collection or container class is appropriate. When the designer needs to model some real-world object that will ultimately contain groups or collections of other objects, then the designer can specify a collection or container class. The designer can specify these collections or containers by name in the design because many of the collections and containers that can be implemented in C++ are well known. If the design calls for a stack component, then the designer can specify a stack component. If the design requires a vector component then the designer can specify a vector component. Because object-oriented design is usually meant to be implemented by languages that support the object metaphor, the designer can use the

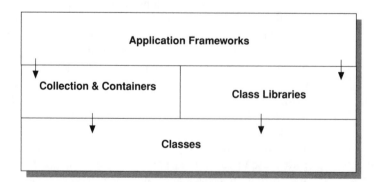

**Figure 1.8**  The object-oriented baseline is comprised of reusable components. The application framework is comprised of class libraries and collection and containers. They are both comprised of classes.

notion of preexisting objects in the design specification. The designer may refer to application frameworks, class libraries, or collection and container classes as design components. Since application frameworks, class libraries, and collection and container classes are standard parts of most object-oriented development environments, the designer can assume their existence and specify their inclusion in a design.

C++ has the object metaphor that supports collections and containers as well as the template facility that supports genericity. Because C++ supports the notions of object orientation and genericity, there is an abundance of application frameworks, class libraries, and container classes available in the C++ environment. Figure 1.8 shows the relationships between the major reusable components and application frameworks. Using these types of components the designer and the developer can take advantage of both *vertical* and *horizontal* code reuse. In general, inheritance supports vertical object-based container structures and genericity supports horizontal template-based container structures. These two approaches to developing and designing collections and containers represent opposite extremes in object-oriented code reuse. We shall discuss both approaches in this book.

CHAPTER 2

# OBJECTS IN C++

THIS CHAPTER is a review of the basic concepts of object-oriented programming that are discussed in this book. In this chapter, we will discuss the support C++ has for object-oriented programming. Our review will include:

Basic concepts of object-oriented programming
Terms used in object-oriented programming
Class types
Coding syntax

For a detailed discussion, see Stroustrup *The C++ Programming Language* (1991).

## WHAT ARE CLASSES?

A class is an encapsulation of characteristics and behaviors that define some person, place, thing, or idea. Classes place objects or concepts into groups. Each member of the group shares a set of common attributes. These attributes define the group. If X represents the collection of all possible characteristics and behaviors, then a class is a subset of X that includes certain attributes while excluding others. It is the exclusion of some attributes and the inclusion of other attributes that makes a class unique. These attributes serve to distinguish one class from another. These classes can be very broad to highly specific. They can be artificial or natural classes that occur in real-world situations. The concept of classes can be represented in C++ in three ways: as an abstract data type, as a generalization or category of objects, and as a model.

### Classes as Abstract Data Types

Classes can be used to represent *abstract data types*. A data type is a collection of data values and a set of operations that manipulates that data. An abstract data type defines the basic concepts of the data type. Both built-in data types and user-defined types have this level of abstraction. The abstract data type describes the properties and the available services provided by the structure to the outside world. The operations or services and the set of data values are bound together to create a single unit called the *class*. User-defined types can be created by using the class construct. The class embodies the layout of the data type. The class defines all the code for any behavior and/or operations expected to be performed on the set of data values. For example, the class **binary-_number** is an abstraction of a binary number. A binary number is based on the base two number system. The base two number system has two digits, 1 and 0. They are called *bits* (from the terms *binary digits*). The binary number is expressed as a series of bits. The series of bits have a decimal equivalent. The binary number 110 is the base two representation of the decimal number 6. The binary number data abstraction class would describe all the operations that can be performed on a binary number. The following is an example of the technique we use for outlining a class abstraction.

**Class Name:** binary_number

**Description:** The binary number class is an encapsulation of the operations that can be performed on a binary number. A binary number is a series of bits (0's, 1's). The series is a number that has a decimal, hexadecimal, and octal equivalent. The services of the class include conversion facilities, arithmetic operations, logical operations, and assignment.

**Data:** Binary Number—the binary number and its decimal equivalent

**Services/Operations:**

| | |
|---|---|
| *Addition* | —the addition of binary numbers |
| *Subtraction* | —the subtraction of binary numbers |
| *Multiplication* | —the multiplication of binary numbers |
| *Twos Complement* | —the binary number converted to its negative |
| *Ones Complement* | —the binary number converted to its ones complement |
| *Less Than* ($<$) | —the comparison of a binary numbers |
| *Greater Than* ($>$) | —the comparison of binary numbers |
| *Equality* ($==$) | —the comparison of binary numbers |
| *Less Than or Equal* ($<=$) | —the comparison of binary numbers |
| *Greater Than or Equal* ($>=$) | —the comparison of binary numbers |
| *Not Equal* ($<>$) | —the comparison of binary numbers |
| *Assignment* ($=$) | —the assignment of a binary number to a variable |
| *Output* | —sending the binary number to an output device |

This abstraction describes the class **binary_number** and its data and services available outside the class. The outside view of the class is the focus of the abstraction. The specific details of the implementation of the services are immaterial to the user and are hidden. It is not necessary for the user of the class to know the specific details of the implementation to use the class. The user-defined classes can be used in the same manner as the built-in data types.

## Classes as Categories

Classes can be used to generalize a group of objects. The class incorporates the behavior and characteristics of a certain group of objects. The class represents the common characteristics of the group. The individual objects of the group are the members of the class or category. For example, a serial card opens a link to a device (peripheral) through a communication port in order to send or receive data to that device at a particular speed (bps—*bits per second*). The serial card sends or receives the data by a direct connection or through some type of modem device. The data is represented as binary numbers, a series of bits. Serial cards can only send or receive data one bit at a time. A parallel card can also open a link to a device through a port in order to send or receive data at a particular speed. The difference is a parallel card sends data 8 bits (one byte) at a time. The byte represents a complete character. Therefore, a serial card has to make 8 transmissions before one complete character is sent where a parallel card need only make one transmission to send a complete character. This is one distinctive difference between the two types of cards. The similarities between the serial and parallel cards can be captured in a class called **communication__card**. Figure 2.1 illustrates the concept of the categorization of the communication cards. The **communication__card** class would be the category and the serial and parallel cards would be members of the class.

## Classes as Models

Classes can be used to create software models. Software models are reproductions in software of some real-world task, process, or idea. The purpose of the model is to imitate or duplicate the behavior and characteristics of some real-world entity in a particular domain. The class **communication__card** models the behavior and characteristics of the entity communication card. A class can be a declaration, a definition or a description. Abstract data types, categories, and models are classes used as descriptions.

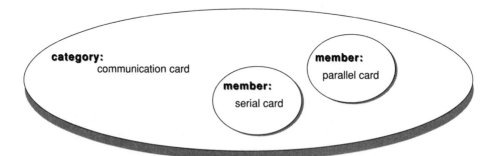

**Figure 2.1**   Communication card is a category and serial and parallel are the members of the category.

# WHAT IS AN OBJECT?

An *object* is the runtime implementation of a class. *Instantiation* is the provision of an instance or the concrete evidence of something. A class is said to be instantiated at runtime. The instantiation of a class is an *object*. The object provides the concrete evidence of the class. Where the class is an abstraction describing the structure and behavior of the object, the object qualifies those behaviors as a particular instance of the class. The object has a *state* and an *identity*. The state of the object expresses the current values of the properties. For example, in Figure 2.2 the class **serial_communication_card** can represent a class of serial communication cards that has the same abilities as the class **communication_card** but receives and sends data one bit at a time. A particular serial card transfers data to a computer at 9600 bps. This particular serial card is an instance of the class **serial_communication_card**. Once a particular card defines the com port and the speed the data (9600 bps) is transferred, the state of the object is instantiated. Once the class **serial_communication_card** is instantiated, it is no longer a concept but a real entity. A serial card can open a link to another computer and transmit data at 9600 bps and another serial card can open a link to a modem and transmit data at 28800 bps. Both instances of the serial communications cards share common attributes but are distinct in the com port they are linked to and the speed at which data is transferred.

# WHAT IS ENCAPSULATION?

*Encapsulation* is the binding together of data and operation into a single well-defined unit or one point of reference. Figure 2.3 illustrates the binding of data and operations into one unit or class. Encapsulation can be enhanced with *information hiding*. The implementation of the operations is not accessible to anything outside the object. The internal

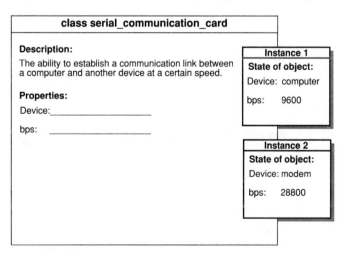

**Figure 2.2** The **serial_communication_card** class can be instantiated by specifying a device and a speed. These are called instances of the class. Instance 1 instantiates the state of the object differently from Instance 2.

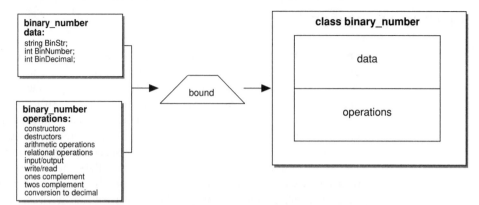

**Figure 2.3** Encapsulation occurs when data and operations are bound together into one single unit. This diagram illustrates the encapsulation of the **binary_number** class.

structure is hidden. In order to use the object, it is not necessary to know how the object is implemented. Permission to access information or use certain services can only be granted by the object itself. Only specific operations determined by the object can be used outside the object. Figure 2.4 illustrates this concept. The periphery or boundaries of the object represent the operations that are accessible outside the object. At the center of the object is the implementation of the operations that are hidden from the outside. Encapsulation with information hiding prevents accidental alterations to the object by the user.

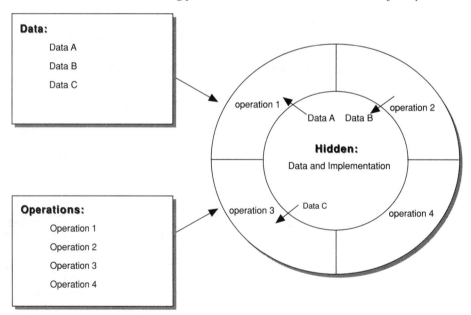

**Figure 2.4** Encapsulation can be enhanced with information hiding. The implementation of the object is hidden from the outside as illustrated in this diagram. The implementation of the object is at the center. The only access permitted is by the public services, which surrounds it.

# HOW CLASSES ARE REPRESENTED IN C++

C++ supports the class construct by using three keywords: **class, struct**, and **union**. To declare a class, the keywords class, struct, or union are placed before the class name followed by curly braces ({}). Within the curly braces is the entire class declaration. For example, Listing 2.1 is the class declaration of the class **binary_number** using the class keyword.

### Listing 2.1

```
// This is the class declaration for the class binary_number

class binary_number{
private:
   void binToDec(void);
protected:
// data members of the class
   string BinStr;
   int BinDecimal;
public:
// member functions of the class
   binary_number(void);
   binary_number(string Str);
   ~binary_number(void);
   string binaryNumber(void);
   void binaryNumber(string Str);
   int BinDecimal(void);
   binary_number &operator=(binary_number &Numb);
   binary_number &operator+(binary_number Numb);
   binary_number &operator*(binary_number Numb);
   binary_number &operator-(binary_number Numb);
   friend ostream &operator<<(ostream &Out,binary_number &Numb);
   int operator>(binary_number Numb);
   int operator<(binary_number Numb);
   int operator>=(binary_number Numb);
   int operator<=(binary_number Numb);
   int operator!=(binary_number Numb);
   int operator= =(binary_number Numb);
   string twosComplement(string Numb);
   string onesComplement(string Numb);
};
```

A class declaration specifies all the data members (variables declared within a class) and operations (member functions) of the class. A class declared using the keyword class can take advantage of all the object-oriented concepts: encapsulation, inheritance, and polymorphism. It allows information to be hidden and only accessed through operations defined by the class. Virtual functions can be used as a way to support polymorphism.

Classes declared by using the union keyword can only hold one data member at a time. Storage space is allocated at the size of the largest data member. Listing 2.2 is the declaration of the class **binary_number** using the **union** keyword.

**Listing 2.2**

```
// This is the declaration of the class binary_number declared as a union.
union binary_number{
private:
    void binToDec(void);
protected:
    string BinStr;
    int BinDecimal;
public:
    binary_number(void);
    binary_number(string Str);
    ~binary_number(void);
    ...
};
```

The data member **BinStr** is declared as a **string** and **BinDecimal** is declared as an **int**. The **int** and the **string** would share storage. The allocation of memory of the largest data member is implementation dependent. Either an **int** or a **string** would occupy that space at a time. Once a value is assigned to that space, the previous value is replaced. Unions support encapsulation. The data members and member functions of the union are accessible by a class name. unions do not support polymorphism involving virtual functions. They cannot be used as a base class and cannot have base classes.

By default, all data members and member functions when using the class keyword are private. When using the union or struct keyword all data members and member functions are by default public. The default access is one of the significant differences among class declarations using the class, struct and union keywords.

## Member Functions

Classes encapsulate data (data members) and operations into one unit. The operations or services are implemented by procedures or functions called *member functions*. Member functions are sometimes called *methods*. Both procedures and functions are programming units representing a set of instructions referred to by a single name. A function is a mathematical construct that produces a single output value. A procedure may perform some task and not return any value. In C++, both procedures and the mathematical concept of a function are called functions.

Member functions are declared as members of the class. The member functions are linked to the class along with the data members to create a single unit. The member functions are the implementations of the behavior of the class. Member functions are declared in the class declaration. In the declaration of the class **binary_number**, the member functions are declared in the public part and the data members are declared in the protected part.

### DEFINING MEMBER FUNCTIONS

When defining the implementation of member functions, the class name is specified. This is necessary because the name of a member function may be used by many different classes.

The compiler must be able to determine which class the member function is associated with. A scope resolution operator (::) is placed between the name of the class and the member function name. The scope resolution operator allows member functions of different types of classes to share the same name. The member function that is invoked will depend upon the class type. Listing 2.3 is an example of a definition of a member function for the class **binary _number**.

### Listing 2.3

```
string binary_number:: binaryNumber(void){
   return(BinStr);
}
```

This member function returns the **string BinStr** and is called **binaryNumber**. It is associated with the class **binary_number**. Member functions can directly access the data members and other member functions of its class.

### PUBLIC, PROTECTED, AND PRIVATE MEMBER ACCESS

Member access is the means by which a class grants permission to access members of its class. The members of a class include the data and member functions. There are three types of access: **public, protected**, and **private** access. Private access means that the member can only be used by the member functions and friend functions of the class in which it is declared. Protected access means that the members can only be accessed by the member functions, friend functions of its class, and by any derived classes. Public access means that the member can be accessed by any function. Figure 2.5 shows the

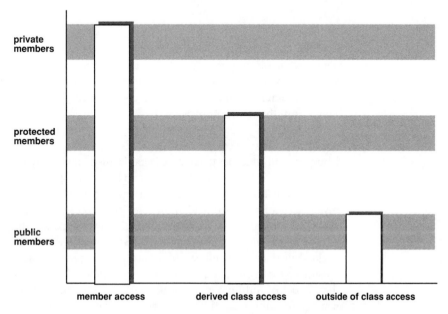

**Figure 2.5** The access policies of private, protected and public members.

access permission of the members and friends of a class, derived classes and outside functions. The keyword private, protected, or public is used to identify the private, protected, or public members of the class, respectively. The keywords are followed by a colon and are placed at the beginning of a list of members. The keyword and the members that follow form an access section of the class declaration. The keyword or access specifier delimits each section until the end of the class or another access specifier is encountered. For example, the class **access** in Listing 2.4 has three access sections: private, protected, and public.

### Listing 2.4

```
// This is an example of private, protected, and public access
// sections of a class declaration.

class access{
private:
   int PrivMem1;
   int PrivMem2;
   int privMem3(void);
protected:
   int ProMem1;
   void proMem2(void);
public:
   access(void);
   ~access(void);
   int pubMem1(void);
   void pubMem2(int);
}
```

When the access specifier is not explicitly used then members have a default access. Classes declared using the class keyword have a default access of private. This means that members that are not preceded by an access specifier will be private members of the class. Classes declared using the union or struct keywords have a default access of public. The class **binary_number** has two access sections: protected and public. The class **binary_number** has no private access section.

Encapsulation with information hiding is an important aspect of C++. Information hiding prevents accidental modification of the behavior of the class and its data. It allows debugging and code maintenance to be performed more easily since access to certain parts of the class are restricted. Declaring certain members of the class as private is a means by which information can be hidden. Data can be placed in the private section of the class. Private access prevents outside functions from accessing its private members. Another level of information hiding is achieved by placing members in the protected section of the class. For example, the data member **BinStr** is a protected data member. It can only be accessed directly by member and friend functions of its class and any derived classes. Outside access to protected data members is achieved by using public member functions. These types of **public** member functions are *write-* and *read-only* functions. The write member function assigns its argument to a data member. The read member function returns the value of a data member. In the class **binary_number**, there are three of this type of public member functions. Listing 2.5 shows the write- and read-only member functions of class **binary＿number**.

**Listing 2.5**

```
void binary＿number::binaryNumber(string Str)
{
    BinStr=Str;
}
string binary＿number::binaryNumber(void)
{
    return(BinStr)
}
int binary＿number::BinDecimal(void)
{
    return(BinDecimal)
}
```

The first member function is the write member function. Its argument is a string that represents a binary number. Its value is assigned to the data member **BinStr**. The second member function is a read-only function. It returns the data member **BinStr**. The third member function is a read-only function that returns the decimal equivalent of the binary number. These three member functions provide access to the protected data members **BinStr** and **BinDecimal**.

## Types of Data Members

Data members of a class can be static or non-static. A static data member produces only one instance of the variable that is shared by all the instances of the object. The static data member is not associated with any particular object; therefore each object has access to this one copy of data. Because there is only one copy of the data and it is not associated with any particular object, it does not take up space in any object. When a data member is non-static, each object of the class has a duplicate of the non-static data element. When the data member is static the objects share one copy. Figure 2.6 illustrates the concept of static and non-static data members. If there are no objects of a class declared, the static data member still exists. The static data member acts similarly to a global variable except that its scope is still local to the class. When a static data member is defined, it should be separate from its declaration. Look at Listing 2.6.

**Listing 2.6**

```
#include<string.h>

class binary＿number{
private:
    void binToDec(void);
protected:
    static string BinStr;
```

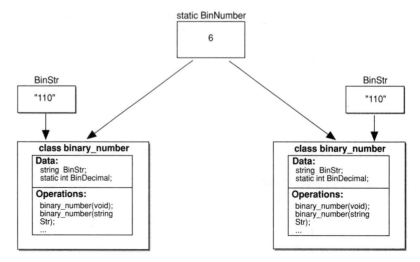

**Figure 2.6** When a data member is static, objects share one copy of the data member. When a data member is nonstatic, each object has its own copy of the data member.

```
    int binDecimal;
public:
    binary_number(void);
    binary_number(string Str);
    ~binary_number(void);
    ...
};
    int binary_number::BinStr="1010";
```

In Listing 2.6, a static and non-static data member is declared. To declare a data member static, the keyword static is placed before the data type. The definition is separate from the declaration of the static data member. Listing 2.7 would create a compile error:

**Listing 2.7**

```
// This class declaration will create a compile error because the static
// data member is not defined separately from it declaration.
class binary_number{
    void binToDec(void);
protected:
    string BinStr="1010";//compile error
    int BinDecimal;
public:
    binary_number(void);
    binary_number(string Str);
    ~binary_number(void);
    ...
};
```

The definition of the static data member utilizes the class name and the scope resolution operator. The definition is outside any member function body. The static data members have private, protected, or public access.

## Types of Member Functions

There are a number of different types of member functions. Table 2.1 lists the types of member functions and some of their defining characteristics.

### CONSTRUCTORS

A *constructor* member function has the same name as the class in which it is declared. The purpose of the constructor is to initialize an object of its class. The initialization may include setting values to data members, opening files, initializing devices, or calling the **new()** function to allocate memory for the object. A constructor may call other member functions. The constructor is called as soon as an object of its class is declared. Constructors do not have return types, not even void. Listing 2.8 is an example of a constructor for the class **binary_number**:

**Listing 2.8**

```
binary_number::binary_number(void)
{
   BinStr=" ";
   BinDecimal=0;
}
```

This constructor initializes the values of the data members of class **binary_number**. The name of the constructor is the same as the name of the class. The scope resolution operator is placed between the name of the class and the name of the constructor.

Constructors can be overloaded. This means that there can be more than one constructor for an object. Listing 2.9 shows the two constructors for the class **binary-_number**:

**Listing 2.9**

```
binary_number::binary_number(void)
{
   BinStr=" ";
   BinDecimal=0;
}
binary_number::binary_number(string Str)
{
   BinStr=Str;
   binToDec();
}
```

**Table 2.1   Types of member functions and some of their defining characteristics.**

| *Types of Member Functions* | *Characteristics* |
|---|---|
| **Static** | * Is not associated with a particular object but associated with an entire class.<br>* Is not passed a pointer to an object.<br>* Can only access static data and static member functions.<br>* Can be referenced without an object variable by using the scope resolution operator.<br>* Cannot be a virtual function.<br>* Nonstatic functions with the same argument types cannot have the same names. |
| **Const** | * Cannot alter the data of an object of its class within the body of the function.<br>* Can be called by both const or non-const objects of its class.<br>* Non-const objects can only call non-const member functions of its class.<br>* A member function can be both const and volatile.<br>* Constructors and destructors cannot be declared const.<br>* In the declaration of the const member function, the keyword const appears after the argument list.<br>* In the definition of the member function, the keyword const appears between the argument list and the body of the function.<br>* The keyword const has to appear in both the declaration and the definition. |
| **Friend** | * Is not a member of a class but can access private and protected members of a class.<br>* Can be a member function of another class thus permitting the class access to the private and protected members of the originating class.<br>* Can be a function that is not associated with any class but is shared by classes.<br>* A class can be a friend of another class.<br>* Cannot be inherited.<br>* In the declaration of a friend function, the keyword friend appears before the return type of the function.<br>* In the definition of a friend function, the keyword friend does not appear. |
| **Constructor** | * initializes an object of its class, allocates memory for an object.<br>* Has the same name as the class name.<br>* Can be called as soon as an object of its class is declared.<br>* Can be overloaded; there can be more than one constructor. |

| Types of Member Functions | Characteristics |
| --- | --- |
| | * Can have a parameter list. |
| | * Does not have return types. |
| | * Member functions can be called within a constructor |
| | * Can be called by a const or volatile object. |
| | * Cannot be static or virtual. |
| | * If a constructor is not defined for a class, the compiler will generate a default constructor with no arguments. |
| | * Generated constructors are public. |
| | * Base class constructors are called before derived class constructors. |
| | * Constructors defined for a class with no arguments are also called default constructors. |
| **Copy Constructor** | * Copies an object by value when the object is an argument of a function or is returned by the function. |
| | * Initializes a new object from an old object. |
| | * The argument of a copy constructor is a reference to an object of its type. |
| **Destructor** | * Destroys the values of an object when the object goes out of scope. |
| | * Has the same name as the class name with a tilde ($\sim$) in front. |
| | * There can be only one destructor for a class. |
| | * Calls the delete operator. |
| | * Takes no argument and has no return type. |
| | * Can be called by const or volatile objects. |
| | * Cannot be static. |
| | * Is not inherited. |
| | * If a base class or a member has a destructor but no destructor is declared for the derived classes, a default destructor is generated. |
| | * Generated destructors are public. |
| | * Destructors for nonstatic member objects are executed before the destructors for base classes. |
| | * Destructors for nonvirtual base classes are executed before destructors for virtual base classes; they are executed in reverse order of their declaration in the derived classes. |
| | * Can be virtual. |
| | * Member functions can be called within a destructor. |
| **Virtual** | * Uses the keyword **virtual** placed before the return type. |
| | * Used to support dynamic polymorphism. |
| | * The function to be executed is not determined until runtime. |
| | * Virtual function in the base class can be overridden in the derived class. |

**Table 2.1   Types of member functions and some of their defining characteristics.** (*continued*)

| Types of Member Functions | Characteristics |
|---|---|
| **Virtual** | * If the derived class does not redefine the virtual function of the base class, the base class version of the function is executed. <br> * Must be a member of the class that defines it. <br> * Can be friends of other classes. <br> * Stays virtual through the lineage of derived classes. |
| **Pure Virtual Functions** | * The virtual function in the base has no meaning; assigned a value of 0. <br> * The derived class has to define the function. <br> * A class with pure virtual functions is called a pure abstract base class. <br> * Pure abstract base classes cannot have any objects of that class. <br> * If the derived class does not define the pure virtual function, it is also a pure abstract base class. |

Constructors can have argument lists. The second constructor accepts a string and assigns it to the data member **BinStr**. The constructor calls the member function **binToDec()**, which converts the data member **BinStr** to a decimal number and assigns that value to the data member **BinDecimal**. At compile time, the parameters passed to the constructors determine which constructor will be called.

If the class does not define a constructor, then the compiler will generate a constructor for the class. A default constructor is a constructor with no arguments. Therefore, the first constructor for the class **binary_number** is also a default constructor. Generated constructors are public. Base class constructors are called before derived class constructors. Constructors can be called by const objects. Constructors cannot be static or virtual functions.

### Copy Constructors

Another type of constructor is a *copy constructor*. A copy constructor copies an object. The argument of a copy constructor is a reference to an object of its class. A copy constructor can be used to copy the object passed by value into a function or the object being returned from a function. It also can be used for object initialization.

### An Object as an Argument or Return Value of a Function

When an object is passed to a function by value, the compiler makes a copy of the object and pushes it onto the stack. The copy constructor instructs the compiler how the object is to be copied. If a copy constructor is not defined, then the compiler will generate a copy constructor. The generated copy constructor will simply copy the data values member by member. This method of copying is called *shallow copy*. If the object is a simple class, comprised of built-in types and no pointers, this would be acceptable. The function would use the values and the object and its behavior would not be altered. With a shallow copy, only the addresses of pointers that are members are copied and not the value the address is pointing to. The data values of the object could then be inadvertently altered by the function. When the function goes out of scope, the copy of the object with all its data is popped off the stack. If the object has any pointers, a deep copy needs to be executed. With a *deep copy* of an object, memory is allocated for the object in free store and the elements pointed to are copied. Figure 2.7 illustrates the difference between the shallow and deep copy.

A deep copy would also be used for objects that are returned from a function. When an object is declared within a function, the data values of that object or data members are copied to an object of its class outside the function. The copy constructor is used to copy the object within the function to an object outside the function.

### Initialization of Objects

The copy constructor can also initialize a new object with the values from an already existing object. This may sound similar to an assignment operation. The difference is the copy constructor copies objects that are not yet initialized. The assignment operation copies or assigns one already initialized object to another already initialized object.

### DESTRUCTORS

*Destructors* are member functions that perform an object shutdown. An object shutdown can be shutting down com ports, releasing memory, calling other functions, closing files, destroying values of an object when the object goes out of scope, and so on. It is called by the compiler and cannot be called explicitly. Destructors have the same name as the class name with a tilde (~) in front. Where there can be more than one constructor, there can only be one destructor for a class. Destructors take no arguments and have no return type. If a destructor is not defined for a class, the compiler will generate a destructor. Like the generated constructor, it is also public. A default destructor is generated for derived classes with no destructor when its base class has defined a destructor.

Destructors for base classes are executed after the destructors for non-static member objects. Destructors for virtual base classes are executed after the destructors for non-virtual base classes. Non-virtual base class destructors are executed in the opposite order of how they appear in their declaration. Destructors can be called by const objects but cannot be declared as const. They cannot be static. They can be virtual. Other member functions can be called within the body of the destructor.

### STATIC MEMBER FUNCTIONS

A member function can also be static. Like static data members, the static member function is not associated with any particular object of its class but is associated with the entire class. Non-static member functions have a *this* pointer that is the address of the object calling the member function. The pointer serves as a reference to the data members of the object in order for them to be accessible. A static member function is not

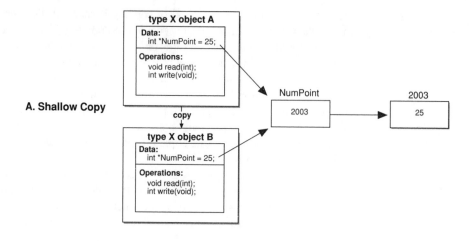

A. Shallow Copy

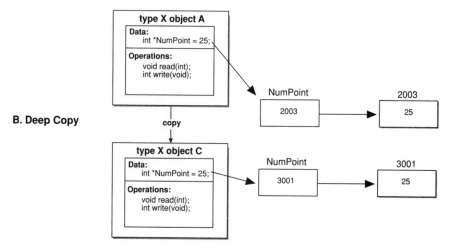

B. Deep Copy

**Figure 2.7**   With a shallow copy of an object, both objects access the same address when dealing with data members that are pointers. With a deep copy of an object, each object accesses the data value by a different address.

passed a pointer to the object, therefore it can only access the static data members and static member functions. For example, look at Listing 2.10:

**Listing 2.10**

```
// This class declartion declares both static and non-static
// data emembers. The defining of the static member function
// is not legal.
class binary_number{
    void binToDec(void);
```

```
protected:
   static string BinStr;
   int BinDecimal;
public:
   binary_number(void);
   binary_number(string Str);
   ~binary_number(void);
   static void setBinaryNumber(string Str) {BinStr=Str};//not legal
   ...
};
```

In Listing 2.10, the class **binary_number** has two data members, **BinStr**, a static **string**, and **BinDecimal**, a non-static **int**. Both are protected data members. The static member function **setBinaryNumber()** accepts a **string** and attempts to assigns it to the static data member **BinStr**. The static member function cannot access the non-static data member **BinStr**.

A static member function can be referenced without declaring a variable of its class by using the scope resolution operator. For example, the static member function **set-BinaryNumber()** can be referenced outside the class in this way:

```
binary_class::setBinaryNumber(Str);
```

Static member functions cannot be virtual. There cannot be two member functions, one static and the other non-static, with the same function name and the same argument types.

## Const Member Functions

When a member function is declared a const member function, the data members of the object of its class cannot be changed within the body of the function. The **const** member function is restricted from altering any of the data members of the object. It can perform such services as reading data, or comparing values. It can perform any type of service that does not change the data values of the object. When declaring a const member function, the const keyword is placed after the argument list. When defining the const member function, the keyword const is placed between the argument list and before the body of the function. The keyword is used in both the declaration and the definition of the member function. Consider the member function in Listing 2.11 for the class **binary_number**:

### Listing 2.11

// This listing declares and defines a const member function.

```
class binary_number{
private:
   void binToDec(void);
protected:
   string BinStr;
   int BinDecimal;
```

```
public:
  binary_number(void);
  binary_number(string Str);
  ~binary_number(void);
  int operator>(binary_number Binary) const;
  ...
};

int binary_number::operator>(binary_number Binary) const
{
  if(BinDecimal > Binary.BinDecimal){
    return(1);
  {
  else {
    return(0);
  }
}
```

This member function compares the decimal equivalent of the binary number objects and returns a 1 if the statement is true and a 0 otherwise. This const member function does not alter the decimal numbers in any way; it just compares them.

The const member function can be called by a const or non-const objects of its class. A non-const member function can only be called by non-const objects of its class. For example, Listing 2.12 is the declaration and definition of the class **binary _number**:

### Listing 2.12

```
// This listing demonstrates the declaring and defining of
// a const member function.

class binary_number{
private:
  void binToDec(void);
protected:
  string BinStr;
  int BinDecimal;
public:
  binary_number(void);
  binary_number(string Str);
  ~binary_number(void);
  int operator >(binary_number Binary) const;
  void setBinaryNumber(string Str) { BinNumb=Str};
  ...
};

int binary_number:: operator >(binary_number Binary) const
{
  if(BinDecimal > Binary.BinDecimal){
    return(1);
  {
  else {
```

```
      return(0);
    }
}
```

The **setBinaryNumber()** member function is not const. Look at Listing 2.13:

### Listing 2.13

```
// This listing shows how const and non-const member functions
// can and cannot be called.
void constantTest(binary_number C1, const binary_number C2)
{
    string Str= "1100";

    C1.setBinaryNumber(Str);
    C2.setBinaryNumber(Str); // error
    if(C1 > C2) {
        cout << 1;
    }
}
```

In Listing 2.13, there are two objects of type **binary_number. C1** is a non-**const** object and **C2** is a const object. A comparison can be performed on both of these objects. The **const** object **C2** cannot call the non-const member function **setBinaryNumber()**. This will cause a compile error.

## FRIEND FUNCTIONS

Friend functions are functions that are not members of a class but have access to the private and protected members of the class. The friend function can access private and protected members as if it was a member of the class. The class **binary_number** has an output friend function. The keyword friend is placed before the return type of the function in the declaration. In the definition of the function, the keyword friend is not displayed. Listing 2.14 is the declaration and the definition of the output friend function for the class **binary_number**.

### Listing 2.14

```
// This listing shows how the friend function declaration appears
// in the class declaration of binary_number.

friend ostream &operator<<(ostream &Out, binary_number &Binary);

// the definition of the output friend function
ostream &operator<<(ostream &Out, binary_number &Binary)
{
    Out << Binary.BinStr;
}
```

Member functions from other classes can be declared as a friend function of a class. Friend functions can also be functions that are not member functions of any class but are shared among classes. For example, see Listing 2.15:

**Listing 2.15**

```
// This listing demonstrates how the friend function can be used
class K{
  int Number1;
  friend int friendTest(K NumK, P NumP );
};
class P{
  int Number2;
  friend int friendTest(K NumK, P NumP);
};
int friendTest(K NumK, P NumP)
{
  if(NumK.Number1==NumP. Number2){
    return(1);
  }
  else{
    return(0);
  }
}
```

In Listing 2.15, the friend function **friendTest()** compares for equality the private data of the classes **K** and **P**. The function **friendTest()** is not a member of either class but has access to the private data of both classes because it was declared as a friend function to both classes.

## VIRTUAL AND PURE VIRTUAL MEMBER FUNCTIONS

Virtual member functions are used to implement polymorphism. *Dynamic polymorphism or runtime polymorphism is accomplished at runtime.* Virtual functions are the mechanism that supports runtime polymorphism. Virtual member functions allow a base class and a derived class to have functions with the same interface. The derived class can redefine the function. In that case, the derived class version of the function will be executed by an object of its type. This is called *overriding*. The function in the base class is overriden by the redefinition of the function in the derived class. In order for this to be accomplished, the member function in the base class must be declared as a virtual member function. The keyword **virtual** is placed before the return type of the function in the class declaration but not in the definition of the function. At runtime, the compiler determines which version of the function is to be executed. If the derived class does not override the virtual function of the base class, the base class version of the function will be executed. When overriding the function in the derived class, the keyword virtual is not necessary.

Consider the example class **communication—card** and the class **serial—communication—card**. Both are classes. The class **serial— communication—card** is derived from the class **communication—card**. class **communication—card** is the base class for the class **serial—communication—card**. Listing 2.16 is the class declaration for both classes:

### Listing 2.16

```
// This is the class declaration for the class serial_communication_card
// and class communication_card. class communication_card is
// the base class for class serial_communication_card.

class communication_card{
protected:
   int BitsPerSecond;
   int PacketSize;
   string ComPort;
public:
   communication_card(void);
   communication_card(int Baud, int PSize, string CPort);
   ~communication_card(void);
   int setDevice(string CPort, int PSize, string CPort);
   int openStream(void);
   virtual int sendData(void);
   virtual int receiveData(void);
}

class serial_communication_card:public communication_card{
public:
   serial_communication_card(void);
   serial_communication_card(int Baud, int PSize, string CPort);
   ~serial_communication_card(void);
   int sendData(void);
   int receiveData(void);
}
```

The class **communication—card** defines a class that opens a link to a com port and transfer data at a particular speed. **sendData()** and **receiveData()** member functions are declared as virtual. The class **serial—communication—card** is derived from this class thus inheriting the abilities of its base. The class **serial—communication—card** has overridden the **sendData()** and **receiveData()** functions. The implementation of these two member functions will be customized specifically for serial transfer. Once an object of the derived class **serial—communication—card** is instantiated, any calls to the virtual functions **sendData()** and **receiveData()** will be executed by the derived class implementations of these functions.

Once a virtual function is declared virtual, it stays virtual. If the derived class is inherited by a class and that class is inherited and so on, the virtual member function is still actively virtual through each class inheritance and can be redefined by any of the derived classes. Virtual functions cannot be global or nonmembers. They cannot be static. They can be declared as friend functions in some other class.

Sometimes when creating a base class, a function has no real meaning and no implementation. For example, in our class **communication_card**, the two functions that transfer data, **sendData()** and **receiveData()** functions, would not have an implementation. When implementing these functions, the method of data transmission has to be defined. Is the transmission serial or parallel? Because the class is an abstraction of all communication cards, this cannot be resolved in the base class. The class **serial_communication_card** defines the data transmission as serial. A class **parallel_communication_card** defines the data transmission as parallel, a byte at a time. The virtual member functions in the base class, **sendData()** and **receiveData()**, are *pure virtual* functions. Pure virtual functions are virtual functions in which the body of the function is assigned to 0:

```
virtual sendData()=0;
virtual receiveData()=0;
```

This is how the functions would be defined in the base class **communication_card**. A function assigned to 0 means that the function has no body. Pure virtual functions serve as placeholders. With pure virtual functions, any derived classes would be forced to override the function. Any class that contains even one pure virtual function is an *abstract base* class. Abstract base classes are only used for defining an interface or minimal implementation policy for the derived classes. The derived classes are to use this interface as a guideline in its own design. The derived classes are to supply the implementation of the pure virtual functions. Abstract base classes cannot create objects of its type. If a derived class does not override the pure virtual functions of its base, it becomes an abstract class as well and no objects can be created of its type.

### Calling Member Functions and Accessing Data Members

Member functions are executed when they receive a message expression. A message expression is a request to an object to perform some service or give access to a data member. A message can be sent from outside the class, from within the class, from a derived class, or from another class.

When a message is sent from outside the class, the expression must specify the object and tell what service is to be performed or what data member is to be accessed by specifying the service or data member by name. An object of the member's class type is declared. Objects declared outside a class only have access to the public members of the class. Only public members can receive messages from outside the class. In the message expression, a (.) is placed between the object name and the member name. For example, the function in Listing 2.17 declares an object of class **binary_number**, sends a message to the public member function **binaryNumber()**, and then outputs the object.

#### Listing 2.17

```
// This listing declares a binary_number object. It calls the
// binaryNumber() member function and then the object
// is inserted.
```

```
void testBinaryNumber(void)
{
    string Test = "1010";
    binary_number One;

    One.binaryNumber(Test);
    cout << One;
}
```

As you recall, the member function **binaryNumber()** accepts a string and assigns it to the private data member **BinStr**.

When calling a member function or accessing a data member from other member functions within a class, an object specifier is not needed. Member functions have access to all members of its class. The name of the member is used directly with no specifiers or operators needed.

Derived classes have access to the public and protected members of its base class. Therefore, when the derived class member functions make calls to the protected and public member functions or access data members of its base class, the derived class uses the member names directly. The derived class does not have access to the private members of the base class. In that regard, its access privilege is on the same level as outside the class. In order for the derived class to access the private members of the base class, a message will have to be sent to the public member functions of the class. On the other hand, if class *A* is declared a friend of class *B*, class *B* will have the same access privilege to class *A* as its members. That is, class *B* will have access to the private, protected, and public members of class *A*.

## Interfaces

The class declaration supplies the view and the method of interaction between the users and implementers of the class and the class. The class declaration is comprised of, at most, three interfaces: private, protected, and public. The interface includes member function names, naming conventions, the argument and the argument types, data members, and the access policies.

The private interface is utilized by the members and friends of the class. The protected interface of the class is utilized by the members, friends, and the derived classes. Both the private and the protected interfaces serve the implementers of the class. They are the hidden aspect of the class that has to do with how the class is implemented. The public interface serves the users of the class. The public interface reveals the services available to the users of the class. The public interface should be descriptive of the purpose and nature of the class.

An interface should be designed to be ideal. An ideal interface, as a whole, should present the concepts of the class in a complete and consistent manner. A consistent interface could be across classes within in a library. Consistent interfaces across classes deal with the concept of *fat interfaces*. A fat interface is a generic interface that is used for many different classes. A consistent interface could also be within a single class. That consistency could be manifested in something as simple as naming conventions. We use the technique of data member names being capitalized and class and member function names starting in lowercase. Class names consisting of more than one word are separated by an underscore. For function names consisting of more than one word, the first word is in lowercase and subsequent words are capitalized. For example:

BinaryNumber; // data member
binary_number; // class name
binaryNumber; // member function

This method allows easy distinction between them. Consistent interfaces are easier to remember and learn.

Besides being consistent, an ideal interface should request any data needed by the class in an unambiguous way. Arguments should be descriptive. Class interfaces should define concisely and restrict its dependencies to other interfaces. The public interface should not reveal any implementation details to functions outside the class. Data members should always be considered a part of the private interface. If necessary, any access to private data members outside the class should be granted by the public interface.

It can be argued that all ideal interfaces should provide certain services. These services may include: input and output services, relational operations, logical operations, assignment operations, constructors and destructors, and the returning of some data members. This concept is called a *minimal standard interface*. In some cases, a member function for a specific class may have no meaning or the service may be difficult or impossible to implement. For example, equality for a polygon object would be difficult if not impossible to implement. Also, the minimal standard interface philosophy may differ as far as what function should be considered as minimal. Default and copy constructors, destructors, assignment, and equality operators are considered by Margaret Ellis as members of a *nice class*. She argues that any class that does not at least provide these functions will severely restrict how the class can be used (Carroll, Ellis 1995, 16).

## INHERITANCE AND CONTAINMENT

Inheritance and containment are methods of organizing, building, and reusing classes in the creation of a new class. Classes are not entities that are to be used once and discarded with the notion that new classes for new structures will be created from scratch. Classes have inherent relationships with other classes already created and classes yet to be created. The relationship between two classes can be no relationship, an inheritance relationship, or a containment relationship. There are other relationships that can exist between classes.

### Inheritance

When creating new classes, already existing classes can be used to build and organize the new class. If the new class is to have the same features as an already existing class, the new class can inherit those features. The new class has a "is a . . ." relationship with the already existing class. The new class is called the *derived* class and the already existing class is called the *base* class. The new class is said to *derive* from the already existing class and the already existing class supplies the *base* features for the derived class. The compiler will consider the members of the base class as members of the derived class. The derived class can alter the characteristics of its base and add some characteristics of its own. The derived class can inherit an abstract base class. In that case, features aren't necessarily inherited for the purpose of evolving the base class or the interface, but for the purpose of implementing it.

In order to achieve inheritance, the base class name is placed after the derived class name separated by a colon (:) in the class declaration of the derived class. Before the base class name is the access specifier. The access specifier defines the access relationship the derived class will have with the base class. The access, like members, can be public, protected, and private. If the derived class inherits a public base class then the protected members of the base class will be considered protected members of the derived class and the public members of the base class will be considered public members of the derived class. If the derived class inherits a protected base class then the protected and public members of the base class will be considered protected members of the derived class. If the derived class inherits a private base class then the protected and public members of the base class will be considered private members of the derived class. If the access specifier is not used then the base class will be assumed public if the derived class was declared using the struct keyword and private if the derived class was declared using the class keyword.

For example, lets consider the class **serial_communication_card** and the class **communication_card** in Listing 2.16. The class **serial_communication_card** has inherited the class **communication_card**. The class **serial_communication_card** is the derived class and the class **communication_card** is the base class. The public and protected members of the base class **communication_card** will be public and protected members in the derived class respectively, therefore the base class is public. Figure 2.8 is the class relationship diagram for the class **serial_communica-tion_card**.

The similarity between the derived class and the base class is contained in the base class. The difference between the derived class and the base class is contained in the derived class. The difference between them could be member functions and/or data members or there could be no difference, meaning that the derived class has added no abilities of its own to its structure. The derived class may be the implementation of an abstract base class. The *class relationship diagram* in Figure 2.8 represents the difference between the class **serial_communication_card** and the class **communication_card** and a *protoclass*. The class relationship diagram will be discussed in detail later in this chapter. The protoclass cannot stand alone as a complete class. As Figure 2.8 illustrates, the protoclass and the base class together comprise the derived class. The derived class depends upon the base class for its structure and cannot be referenced apart from its base.

Any class can be a base class creating a lineage of inheriting classes. Changes made in the base class or *ancestor* will affect all of its derived classes or *descendants*. Those changes will only have to be made in one central place, in the base class definition. Any modifications made to the descendants will not affect the ancestors. When a class is derived from only one base class, this is called single inheritance.

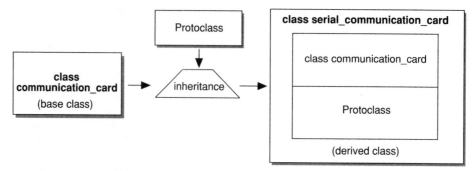

**Figure 2.8**   The **communication_card** class is inherited by the **serial communication- _card** class. The **communication_card** class is the base class. The **serial_communica- tion_card** class is the derived class.

## Multiple Inheritance

A derived class can inherit more than one base class. This is called *multiple inheritance.* Each base class has its own access specifier. The base classes are separated by a comma. For example, a class **network_adapter_card** can be created. The class **network- _adapter_card** simulates a network card's ability to send and receive data to or from a node on a network. The class **network_adapter_card** can move data in serial and parallel form, inherits both class **serial_communication_card** and class **parallel- _communication_card** and can transmit and receive data in 8-bit chunks called *bytes.* Listing 2.18 is the class declaration for the derived class **network_adapter_card**.

### Listing 2.18

```
// Listing 2.18 shows the class declaration for
// network_adapter_card which inherits both
// serial_communication_card and parallel_com-
// munication_card classes.

class network_adapter_card: public serial_communication_card, public
        parallel_communication_card{
public:
  network_adapter_card(void);
  network_adapter_card(int Baud, int PSize, string Str);
  ~network_adapter_card(void);
  int sendData(void);
  int receiveData(void);
}
```

Both the **serial_communication_card** class and the **parallel_communication_card** class are public base classes. The public and protected members of both classes will be public and protected members respectively of the derived class **network_adapter- _card**. The **sendData()** and **receiveData()** member functions of both bases can be called by the derived class versions of these member functions by using the scope resolution operator.

## Containment: Member Classes

A class can be a member of another class. Given a class *A* and *B* where class *B* has a *containment* relationship with class *A*, class *B* is said to be a class member of *A*, *contained* in class *A* or class *A* has a *B*. With inheritance, if class *B* was derived from class *A*, it is said that class *B* *is a kind of* class *A*. The class **network_adapter_card** is a kind of class **serial _communication_card** and a kind of class **parallel_communication_card**. The class **network_adapter_card** can be altered to contain a *frame buffer*. While data is being processed by the network adapter card, the data is held in a buffer. The data is broken down into chunks called *frames* that can be easily managed by the network adapter card. The frame buffer allows the adapter card to have access to an entire frame at once in order for the card to manage the data rate of the network and the rate in which the computers can process the data. A class **frame_buffer** is created that simulates this behavior. The class **network_adapter_card** is not a kind of class **frame_buffer**. The class **frame_buffer** is contained in the class **network_adapter_card** as Listing 2.19 demonstrates.

### Listing 2.19

```
// The class network_adapter_card contains class frame_buffer.
// The containment is private to the class.
class network_adapter_card: public serial_communication_card, public
        parallel_communication_card{
   frame_buffer Buffer;
   ...
}
```

The class member, **Buffer**, is declared like any other type. The class name is used and a variable of that type is declared. When calling the class members of **Buffer**, the (.) operator is placed between the variable name and the member name.

Class members can be pointers to objects as well. Look at Listing 2.20.

### Listing 2.20

```
// In this Listing, Buffer is a pointer to a class
// frame_buffer.
class network_adapter_card: public serial_communication_card, public
        parallel_communication_card{
   frame_buffer* Buffer;
public:
   ...
}
```

Listing 2.20 demonstrates a pointer to an object. Pointers to class objects should be used when the object is to be passed to a member function as an argument or during the life of the contained object the pointer will be changed.

Because the class is a member, the public and protected members of class members are not considered part of the public, protected, and private interfaces as they are inheritance. Access to the class member is the same as an outside function. The class only has access to public members of class members.

## Class Relationship Diagrams

The *class relationship diagram* is used as a design and documentation technique to describe the relationships between classes in a software system. The class relationship diagram can be used to show whether classes are related through inheritance, containment, as in Figure 2.9, or some other method. It can show whether the class is a product of single inheritance, multiple inheritance, or aggregation as illustrated in Figure 2.10. The CRD (class relationship diagram) can show any level of relational detail in a class from a high-level overview to low-level relationship telescoped to the source code level.

The CRD consists of four basic components:

1. A relation operator symbol
2. Flow lines
3. Vertical and horizontal specification
4. Class grouping symbol

Figure 2.11 shows the CRD diagramming symbols and their meanings. The diagramming technique introduces the *protoclass* abstraction to the object-oriented paradigm. As mentioned earlier, the protoclass is the set difference between *n* classes. For example, given two classes, A and B, the protoclass is the set difference between the

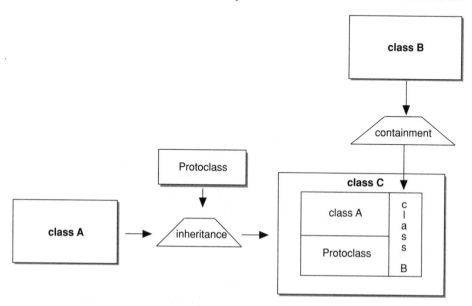

**Figure 2.9**   This diagram shows how an inherited and contained class is represented in the class relationship diagram.

**A. Single Inheritance**

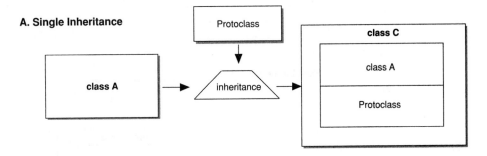

**B. Multiple Inheritance**

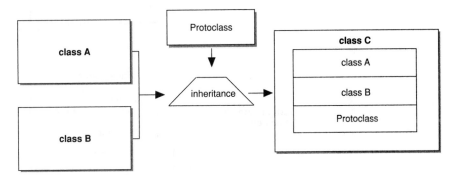

**Figure 2.10** The representation of single and multiple inheritance in the class relationship diagram.

classes *A* and *B*. For example, if class *A* contains the members {1,2,3,4}, and the class *B* contains the members {1,2,3,4,5}, the protoclass for classes *A* and *B* is {5}. The protoclass would belong to class *B*.

In describing the relationship between a class and itself, we show the existence of the protoclass. Given a base class *A* with the members {1,2,3,4}, the protoclass for *A* could be determined by performing the set difference between class *A* and the NULL class{}. Hence, {1,2,3,4}/{} is {1,2,3,4}. The protoclass for the base class *A* is exactly its members. The implication of this is that every class has a protoclass and a NULL class.

The *relationship symbol* shows how classes are related. Whatever relationship exists between the classes is expressed within in a *relationship symbol*. The flow lines connect the two classes in which the relationship exists. There are no assumptions about the types of relationships that can be contained in the relationship symbol. The only rule to follow is if there is more than one relation that is to be represented, one relationship is represented horizontally and the other relationship is represented vertically. Figure 2.12 shows the relationships that are used in this book, inheritance and containment. The flow lines have the semantic interpretation "*A* is related to *B*" by the relationship contained in the relationship symbols.

The *grouping symbol* is used to show the collection of classes under consideration in

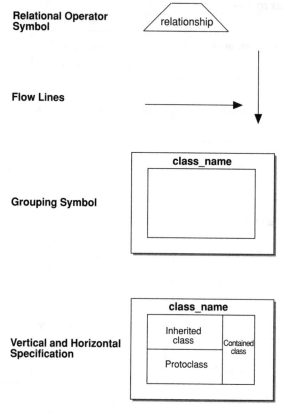

**Relational Operator Symbol**

relationship

**Flow Lines**

**Grouping Symbol**

class_name

**Vertical and Horizontal Specification**

class_name

| Inherited class | Contained class |
| Protoclass | |

**Figure 2.11** The CRD symbols.

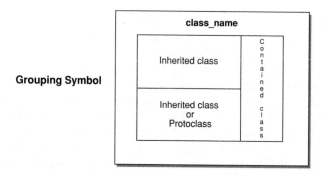

**Grouping Symbol**

class_name

| Inherited class | Contained class |
| Inherited class or Protoclass | |

**Figure 2.12** The grouping symbol for a class in the class relationship diagram. The symbol shows both inheritance and containment.

the relational analysis. The class grouping symbol may show the highest representation of a class (i.e., class name) or the lowest representation of a class (i.e., source code specifying data members and member functions). Figure 2.13 shows the grouping of the class **network_adapter_card** at its highest level and the class **binary_number** at a lower level.

# POLYMORPHISM

Polymorphism is the ability to have many forms. A user utilizes one name or interface that can implement different variations of a task. This is why polymorphism is sometimes described as "one interface, multiple implementations." As mentioned earlier, a message is sent to an object as a request to perform a task. Polymorphism changes the responsibility from the user in determining the correct implementation, to the receiver of the message or the object. The resolution of a function call may be outside the source file in a library or other file, for instance. The function is resolved when the function call is replaced with the address of the function definition. This resolution can be made at compile time or runtime and is called static or *early binding* and dynamic or *late binding*, respectively.

Polymorphism can also be achieved by parameterized types. This type of polymorphism is called *parametric polymorphism*. Parametric polymorphism is the mechanism by which the same code is used on different types passed as parameters. This is accomplished in C++ by using templates. Templates are discussed later in this chapter in the section called "Templates." Table 2.2 lists the types of polymorphism and gives a brief description of each.

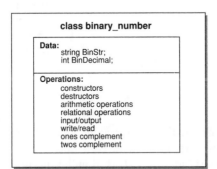
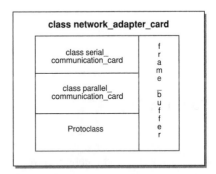

**Figure 2.13**   The group symbol can represent a class at a low level, showing the data and operations. The **binary_number** class is depicted in this way. The grouping symbol can represent a class at a high level, showing the relationships the class has with other classes. The **network_adapter_card** class is depicted in this way.

**Table 2.2**   Static and runtime polymorphism, the mechanism in which they work, and a brief description of each mechanism.

| Types of Polymorphism | Mechanism | Description |
|---|---|---|
| **Static (Early Binding)**<br>* When the specific function to be executed is determined at compile time. | Function/Operator Overloading | * Functions names are the same but return type and the argument list does not match.<br>* Operator overloading allows an operator to take a specific meaning relative to a user-defined class. |
| **Runtime (Late Binding)**<br>* The specific function that is to be executed is determined at runtime. | Overriding | * The use of virtual functions declared in base class that can be redefined in the derived class. |
| | Pure Virtual Functions | * The virtual function in the base has no meaning; the derived class has to define the function or it will also be considered a pure abstract base class. |
| | Pointers to Derived Type | * A pointer to a base class can also point to a derived class; all members of the derived class inherited from the base class are accessible but members specific to the derived class are not accessible to the base class. |

## Early Binding

Binding is the process in which modules or functions are incorporated to make executable code. Memory addresses are assigned to each one, and external references are patched with correct memory addresses. Early binding occurs at compile time. At compile time the object is bound to the correct implementation of the function call. This means that all information needed to determine which function is to be executed is known at compile time. Standard function calls, overloaded function calls, and overloaded operator calls are examples of early binding.

## OVERLOADING FUNCTIONS

The *function overloading* is achieved when the same name of a function is used for different implementations of a task. The difference between overloaded functions besides the implementation of the task is the *argument list*. The argument list can have different arguments or the same arguments but in a different order. The constructors for the class **binary_number** are examples of function overloading discussed earlier in the section called "Constructors" in this chapter.

## OVERLOADING OPERATORS

Operators can also be overloaded. Operators are already defined for built-in data types and are therefore already overloaded. Two integers can be compared like this:

```
int Int1= 24, Int2 = 45;
Int2 < Int1;
```

Essentially, this is a call to a function that compares two integers. The function will return a 1 if the statement is true and a number other than 1 if the statement is not true. This function is called with the (<) operator and is passed two integers. The function call could look like this:

```
<(Int2, Int1);
```

This calls a function that compares two integers. That function is overloaded when passed a different built-in data type like floats:

```
float Float1= 65.9, Float2 = 78.9;
Float1 < Float2;
```

This is a call to a function that compares two floating points. The call to that function could look like this:

```
<(Float1, Float2);
```

The overloading of an operator does not cause the loss of the original meaning. When the less than operation is defined for the **float** data type, the less than operation for integers is still viable.

The < operator, or any operator, can again be overloaded for user-defined objects by defining a function the compiler can call when user-defined objects are parameters. The function defines what the operation will mean relative to the user-defined type it was created for. Whenever the user-defined type is used with the operator, that function will be called. Multiple implementations can be defined as along as the function accepts different arguments.

When defining the function that overloads an operator, the keyword **operator** and the operator succeeds the return type. This is followed by the argument list and the body of the function. The function will have this general form:

```
return_type operator@(argument_list)
{
   //body of function
}
```

The @ represents the overloaded operator. The return type is the type of value that will be returned by the operation. The operator function must be a function that accepts at least one argument of a class or reference to a class or a member function. Operator functions can be friend functions of a class. An operator function that is a member function of a class will have this general form:

```
return_type class_name::operator@(argument_list)
{
   //body of function
}
```

This form will include the class name and the scope resolution operator.

In the class **binary_number**, the < operator is overloaded. The < operation will compare two binary numbers. If $A$ and $B$ are binary numbers, the < operation will determine the truthfulness of the statement B<A.

Listing 2.21 is the definition of the member function that overloads the < operator for the class **binary_number**.

**Listing 2.21**

```
// Listing 2.21 defines the < operation for the
// class binary_number.
int binary_number::operator<(binary_number Binary)
{
   if(BinDecimal < Binary.BinDecimal){
      return(1);
   }
else{
      return(0);
   }
```

The < member function compares two binary numbers by comparing their decimal equivalent stored in the data member **BinDecimal**. The **BinDecimal** data member is supplied by the two **binary_number** objects represented as the left and right operands in the calling function. The right operand is passed to the member function in the argument **Binary**. The left operand value is a data member of the class **binary_number** of which this member function is a member. As you recall, a member function has direct access to all the members of its class. The member function compares the data members and returns a 1 if the statement is true and a 0 otherwise.

It is the object of the left operand that will be invoked. The right operand is passed to that operator function. The right operand can be of any type, user-defined or built in.

The object must define a different operator function for each data type that is passed.

In this example of operator overloading, the return type was an **int**. The return type could be the same type as the class. The operator function returning the same type as the class is used to facilitate complex expression, for example, stringing along a number of operations as follows:

$$A<B<C$$

Binary operations usually return a value of the same type as the operands. For example:

$$C = A + B$$

If *A* and *B* are integers, then *C* will also be an integer or a type that has conversion capabilities with an integer. If *A* and *B* are binary numbers, then *C* will be a binary number. In this case, the operator function's return type should be of the same type as the class. Listing 2.21 demonstrates how a binary operation can be overloaded with an **int** return type.

Unary operators can also be overloaded. When unary operators are overloaded, the operator function will accept no arguments if it is a member function and one argument if it is a nonmember function. Table 2.3 lists all the unary and binary operators that can and cannot be overloaded.

It is important to remember that in overloading operators there are restrictions that must be adhered to. These restrictions have to do with the original definition of the operator symbol. For example, a binary operator cannot be overloaded to create a unary operator. The reciprocal is also true. The general form of the operator syntax must be

**Table 2.3   The operators and functions that can be overloaded. The operators are divided into categories: unary operators, binary operators, and operators that are both unary and binary.**

| Type of Operator | Operator | | | | | |
|---|---|---|---|---|---|---|
| **Binary** | / | % | *= | /= | += | -= |
| | \| | ∧ | \|\| | && | < | <= |
| | > | >= | << | >> | \|= | ∧= |
| | &= | <<= | >>= | == | != | + |
| | - | | | | | |
| **Unary** | * | & | + | - | ! | ~ |
| **Both** | * | - | + | & | | |
| **Function** | new | delete | 0 | | | |
| **Subscripting** | [ ] | | | | | |

maintained. Operator overloading does not change the syntax of the operation; it defines how that operation will perform relative to a user-defined type. Operators that can perform both unary and binary operations can be used in either context.

The precedence of the operations is also to be maintained. The precedence of operations has to do with the order that operations are performed when two or more operators are used in an expression. The definition of the operator can be changed but the precedence of the operator cannot be altered. Table 2.4 lists the precedence of operators.

### Overloading Operators with Friend Functions

When overloading binary operators with friend functions, both the left and right operands are passed to the function and one operand is passed to the function when overloading unary operators. As you recall, the friend function is not passed the

**Table 2.4**  Precedence of operators (from highest to lowest) and their meaning. (The operators in the same box have the same precedence.)

| Precedence | Operator | Meaning |
|---|---|---|
| 1 | :: | scope resolution/global |
| 2 | . | member selection |
| | -> | member selection |
| | [] | subscripting |
| | () | function call/value construction |
| | sizeof | size of object/type |
| 3 | ++ | post-/preincrement |
| | -- | post-/predecrement |
| | ~ | complement |
| | ! | not |
| | - | unary minus |
| | + | unary plus |
| | & | address of |
| | * | dereference |
| | new | create (allocate) memory |
| | delete | destroy (deallocate) memory |
| | delete□ | destroy array |
| | () | cast (type conversion) |
| 4 | .* | member section |
| | -> | member section |
| 5 | * | multiply |
| | / | divide |
| | % | modulo |
| 6 | + | add |

| Precedence | Operator | Meaning |
|---|---|---|
| | − | subtract |
| 7 | << | shift left |
| | >> | shift right |
| 8 | < | less than |
| | <= | less than or equal to |
| | > | greater than |
| | >= | greater than or equal to |
| 9 | == | equal |
| | != | not equal |
| 10 | & | bitwise AND |
| 11 | ^ | bitwise exclusive OR |
| 12 | \| | bitwise inclusive OR |
| 14 | \|\| | logical inclusive OR |
| 15 | ?: | conditional expression |
| 16 | = | simple assignment |
| | *= | multiply and assign |
| | /= | divide and assign |
| | %= | modulo and assign |
| | += | add and assign |
| | −= | subtract and assign |
| | <<= | shift left and assign |
| | >>= | shift right and assign |
| | &= | AND and assign |
| | \|= | inclusive OR and assign |
| | ∧= | exclusive OR and assign |
| 17 | , | comma (sequencing) |

**this** pointer of the calling object, therefore it must explicitly be passed both operands. Not all operators can be overloaded by friend functions. As listed in Table 2.3, pointer (−>), subscript ([]), parentheses (()), and assignment (=) operators cannot be overloaded by friend functions. Listing 2.22 is the < operation overloaded using a friend function.

**Listing 2.22**

```
// Listing 2.22 defines the < operation as a friend
// function of class binary_number.

int binary_number::operator<(binary_number BinLeftOp, binary_number Bin
    RightOp)
{
  if(BinLeftOP.BinDecimal < BinRightOp.BinDecimal){
    return(1);
```

```
    }
    else{
        return(0);
    }
```

A friend operator function is used when a built-in data type is the left operand. A member function expects the left operand to be an object of the class that invoked the operation. If the left operand is not an object of the class that invoked the operation, then a friend function will have to be used to define the operator function.

## Late Binding

*Late binding* occurs at runtime. At runtime the object is bound to the correct implementation of the function call. This means that all information needed to determine which function is to be executed is not known until runtime. Late binding supports common interfaces among classes allowing the derived classes to define their own implementations. Late binding is achieved in C++ by using virtual functions that are discussed earlier in this chapter.

# TYPES OF CLASSES

There are a number of different types of classes. They are different in respect to design notions but have nothing to do with constructs in the C++ language. Classes can be derived from these various design notions to serve different purposes within an application or library. The different types of classes are listed in Table 2.5 along with a brief description of each. The different types of classes follow.

## Concrete Class

A *concrete class* is a complete class whose implementation is defined and instances of the class can be declared. The concrete class is not intended to be a base class and no attempt to create operations of commonality are made. If a change to its interface is needed, this is done directly to its interface. Concrete classes attempt to minimize dependency on other classes in the implementation or behavior of the class.

The concrete class works in a way similar to built-in data types. They are used to supply fundamental types to an application. These types are not supplied by the C++ compiler. Date, complex number, binary number, and clock class may be examples of concrete types. Concrete classes are in contrast to abstract classes.

**Table 2.5  Different types of classes and a brief description.**

| Type of Class | Description |
| --- | --- |
| **Concrete Class** | * A complete class whose implementation is defined and instances of the class can be declared; not intended to be a base class and no attempt to create operations of commonality. |
| **Abstract Class** | * A class that supplies the interface for derived classes; used as the form or layout for the construction of other classes; can only be used as the base class. |
| **Interface Class** | * A class that is used to adjust the interface of another class. |
| **Node Class** | * A class that has added new services or functionality beyond the services inherited from its base class. |
| **Domain Class** | * A class created to simulate some entity within a specific domain; the meaning of the class is relative to that domain. |
| **Support/Utility Class** | * Classes that are constructed regardless of a domain; a *utility class* is a class that is useful within different applications. |
| **Aggregate Class** | * A class that contains other classes; another class is "a part" of the aggregate class. |
| **Virtual Base Class** | * A base class where during multiple inheritance the class is the indirect and/or direct base of a derived class; only one copy of the class is shared by all the derived classes. |
| **Container Class** | * A class that is used to hold objects in memory or external storage. |
| **Templates** | * A parameterized type containing generic code that can use or manipulate any type; an actual type is the parameter for the code body. |

## Abstract Class

An *abstract class* is a class that supplies the interface for derived classes. An abstract class is used as the form or layout for the construction of other classes. It can only be used as the base class. A class is an abstract class if it has at least one pure virtual function. The derived class inherits the abstract class and implements the pure virtual functions of the abstract class. If a class is abstract no objects of its type can be declared.

## Interface Class

An *interface class* is used to adjust the interface of a class. An interface class adjusts or fine tunes the interface to make it more useful or more efficient. Some examples of interface adjustments are: changing a function or a data member name, or changing a data type, return type, argument list, and so on. Interface classes are lean classes sometimes utilizing inline functions. The interface class inherits the class then defines the adjustments that are to be made.

## Node Class

A *node class* is a class that has added new services or functionality beyond the services inherited from its base class. This may include some virtual functions as public member functions that can be redefined by its derived classes. A node class can be a base class. Node classes are designed to permit derivation.

## Domain Class

A *domain class* is a class created to simulate some entity within a specific domain. The meaning of the class is relative to that domain. It is not a programming support class but a construct that is needed to implement an application. For example, in creating an application that will be used to calculate the taxes of an individual, classes relative to that domain will have to be constructed like a **1040_tax_form** class, a **W-2_form** class, and so on. The **1040_tax_form** class may inherit a base class called **tax_form** and contain a class called **deduction** class.

## Support/Utility Class

*Support/Utility classes* are classes that are constructed regardless of a domain. They are used across domains. A *utility class* is a class that is very useful in different applications. For example, a utility class can be a date class, a time/clock class, or a meter class that determines how long it takes for an operation or task to perform. This type of functionality is used during the installation of software, the downloading or uploading of files, and so on. Another type of support/utility class can be a user interface class, for example, a **list_box** class, or a **scroll_bar** class.

## Aggregate Class

An *aggregate class* is a class that contains other classes. As mentioned earlier in this chapter, classes can have relationships with other classes. Some of those relationships are inheritance or containment. (This is not to say there only two types of relationships between classes.) With inheritance, the class "is a type" of another class and with the containment relationship, the class "has or contains" another class. An aggregate class has a whole/part relationship with another class. The relationship is not a dependent relationship. The aggregate class exists separately from its parts and the parts exist independently from the aggregate class.

## Virtual Base Class

When a derived class has more than one base class, this is called multiple inheritance. The base classes are explicitly named along with the access specifier. They are the *direct base* classes of the derived class. The derived class can inherit a base class that it has not explicitly named in its base-class list. This is called an *indirect base* class. This occurs when direct base classes have a base class in common. This will cause an ambiguity error to be reported by the compiler when the derived class accesses **public** or **protected** members of the in-common base class. The compiler will not be able to determine which subobject member to access and will report an ambiguity error. For example, the class **network_adaptor_card** has two base classes, class **serial_communication_card** and class **parallel_communication_card**. Both classes have the base class **communication_card**. **Communication_card** class is the indirect base for the class **network_adaptor_card**. This concept is illustrated in Figure 2.14, which also illustrates the ambiguity error that will occur when the derived class **network_adaptor_card** accesses the **protected** data member **BitsPerSecond** declared in class **communication_card**.

This type of error can be eliminated by making the subobject a *virtual base class*. The virtual base class would be shared among all its derived classes. No duplication will occur during multiple inheritance. For example, the class **network_adapter_card** has duplicate class **communication_card**. To prevent this duplication, the class **serial_communication_card** and the class **parallel_communication_card** inherit class **communication_card** as a virtual base class. The keyword virtual is placed before the access specifier, for example:

```
class serial_communication_card: virtual public communication_card{...};
class parallel_communication_card: virtual public communication_card{...};
```

## Collection and Container Classes

A *container class* is a class that is used to hold objects in memory or external storage. A container class acts as a *generic holder*. All the objects in the container class can be different kinds of objects or objects that are the same type. When a container class contains a group of mixed objects, the container is called a *heterogenous* container. When the container is holding a group of objects that are all the same, the container is called a *homogenous* container.

In this book, the terms *collection* and *container* classes are used. There is a difference between a collection class and a container class. A collection class has a predefined behavior and a well-known interface. An example of a collection class is a stack. A stack has a predefined behavior and interface. Objects are pushed onto the stack and popped off the stack. A container class is more generic than a collection class. Examples of containers classes are lists, vectors, and flat files. The container class does not have to exhibit any other behavior except the ability to contain objects. The container class can be designed to hold many types of objects because of the mechanism supplied by C++ called a *template*.

## Templates

One of the most important features of C++ is its support of code reuse. The goal of code reuse is to implement the code for a class, structure, function, and so forth once and allow that code to be used over and over in different ways. In order for code to be

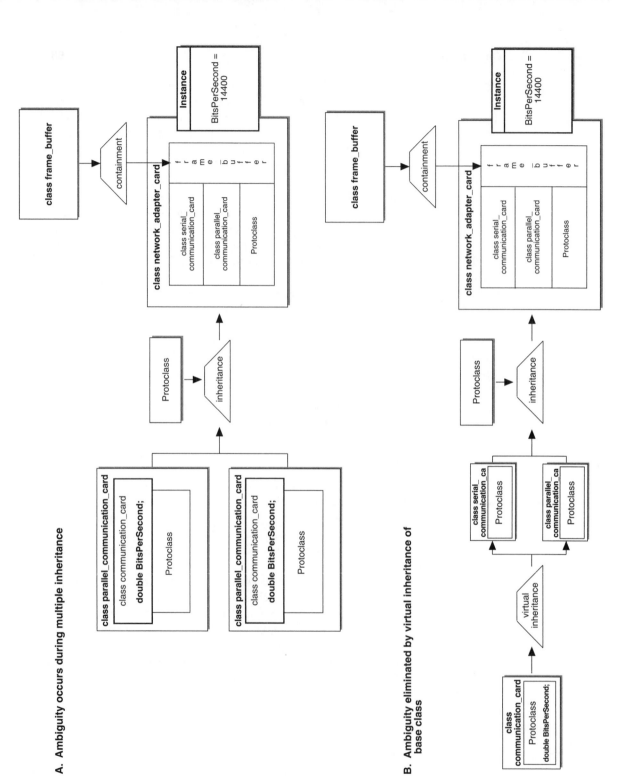

**A. Ambiguity occurs during multiple inheritance**

**B. Ambiguity eliminated by virtual inheritance of base class**

**Figure 2.14** Ambiguity occurs during multiple inheritance when an instance of the **network_ adapter_ card** class accesses the data member **BitsPerSecond**. Ambiguity is eliminated by the virtual inheritance of **communication_ card** class.

66

reusable, the code should be *generic*. The implementation of generic code should be unaffected by the type the construct uses or manipulates. It has the same form regardless of the type. This makes generic code very reusable. In most cases, the more generic the code is, the more reusable it is. This type of programming is called *parameterized programming*. In parameterized programming, new software modules can be constructed by using a parameterized type called a *template*.

A *template* is a parameterized construct containing generic code that can use or manipulate any type. It is called parameterized because an actual type is the parameter for the code body. The template is a specification of how a group of related classes or functions can be constructed. Templates are used to achieve parametric polymorphism. This type of polymorphism can also be called *horizontal genericity*. It is called *horizontal* because the genericity is across different types of classes in a horizontal fashion. This is in contrast to polymorphism achieved by the use of virtual methods called *vertical genericity*. It is called *vertical* because the genericity is within one lineage of classes. Figure 2.15 contrasts the type of polymorphism that occurs with virtual methods and templates. Templates can be used to construct a family of classes called *class templates* and a family of functions called *function templates*.

To create a template, the keyword template is followed by the argument that will be used in the declaration of the template class or template function. The argument is bracketed as follows:

```
template<class Type>
```

What follows is the class or function declaration. The argument **Type** represents any type that is passed to the template. **Type** can represent a built-in data type or a user-defined class. In the declaration and definition of the template **Type** is used like other data or user-defined type. Once the template has been declared, objects of the template class or function can be instantiated. The instantiation of the template is the passing of a specific type to the template and the declaration of a variable.

A vector is a container that can hold types that are assessed directly by using an index. A vector can hold any built-in data types such as integers, floats, char, and so on. They can also hold user-defined objects. How the array is implemented is independent from any specific type. Listing 2.23 is a class template declaration for a vector that can hold any type.

### Listing 2.23

```
// Listing 2.23 is a template declaration for a vector.
template<class T> class vector{
protected:
   T *Data;
   unsigned int Size;
public:
   vector(int Size);
   ~vector();
   T& operator[](int Index);
   // other required member functions
}
```

**A. Polymorphism using virtual methods.**

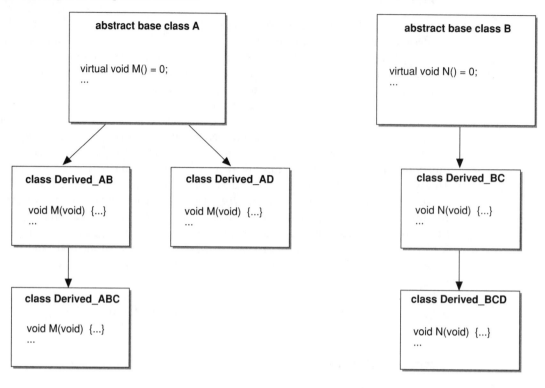

**B. Polymorphism using templates.**

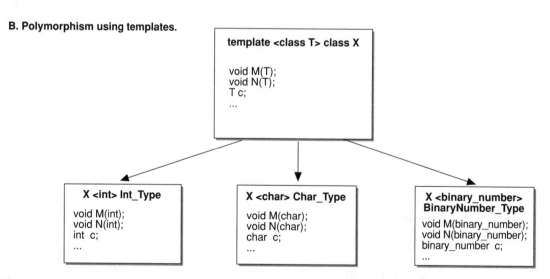

**Figure 2.15** Contrasts polymorphism using virtual methods and templates. Polymorphism using virtual methods accomplishes vertical genericity, only within a single class and its descendants. Polymorphism using templates accomplishes horizontal genericity, across groups of classes.

**template<class T>** is placed before a rather usual class declaration. **Type T** represents the type passed to the template. **T** will be used in the declaration and the definition whenever the reference to the type is needed. For example, the protected data member **Data** is of type **T**. **Data** of type **T** is a vector element. The subscript operator is overloaded. It will return an element of type **T** in position **Index** of the vector. The class template name must be a unique name. It cannot be the name of some other class, template, function, object, value, or type within the scope of the template. Other than the prefix and the use of type **T**, the class template declaration is the same as a non-template class declaration.

## FUNCTION TEMPLATE

A *function template* is a template that specifies the form of a family of functions. The individual function that is constructed from a function template is called a *template function*. The function template is generic so that the implementation of the function is not dependent on a specific type. The template function that is generated can manipulate or use the type passed to the template's parameters. The template function is referred to by a variable name.

A selection sort function can be declared as a function template. A selection sort sorts values in descending order. Listing 2.24 is a function template for a selection sort of any type.

### Listing 2.24

```
// Listing 2.24 is a function template for a selection sort.

template<class T> void selection_sort(T A[], int Size)
{
    int i,j,index;
    T large;
    for(i = Size − 1; i > 0; 1−−){
        large = A[0];
        index = 0;
        for(j = 1;j <= i;j++){
            if(A[j] > large){
                large = A[j];
                index = j;
            }
            A[index] = A[i];
            A[i] = large;
        }
    }
}
```

**template<class T>** is placed before the implementation of a selection sort function. **Type T** represents the type passed to the function that will be sorted. The selection sort will sort in descending order any type passed to the template's parameters. In order for the sort to work with user-defined types, the class must define the member functions for comparison, and an assignment operator.

The function template is used with a function call. The formal parameters will pass the type and all other information that is needed to the function template. Listing 2.25 shows an example of a function call to the function template **selection__sort**.

**Listing 2.25**

```
// Listing 2.25 demonstrates a function call to the
// selection__sort function template. It is used to
// sort a vector of binary__number objects.
void Test(binary__number ABinNum[20], int Size = 20)
{
    selection__sort(ABinNum, Size);
}
```

In Listing 2.25, a function call was made to the **selection__sort** function template. A vector of **binary__number** objects and the size of the vector is passed to the function. The **selection__sort** function will sort the vector of **binary__number** objects in descending order. As you recall, the class **binary__number** has defined comparison and assignment operations. These operations have to be defined by the class in order for the selection sort to perform.

## MEMBER FUNCTIONS OF THE CLASS TEMPLATE

Member functions of a class template are function templates. The definitions of the member functions must handle arbitrary types. Data members that represent elements of the class have to be of type **T**. The prototypes of the member functions are structured in the same way as the prototypes for nontemplate classes. The member function name is preceded by the name of the class and a colon. This will include the **template<class T>** prefix. For example, Listing 2.26 is the member function definition of the subscript operator of the class template **vector**.

**Listing 2.26**

```
// Listing 2.26 is the member function for the subscript
// operator for the class template vector.

template<class T> T& vector<T>::operator[](int Index)
{
    return(Data[Index]);
}
```

In Listing 2.26 following the **template<class T>**, the prototype has the same structure as any class member prototype. The return type is succeeded by the class name, the scope resolution operator, then the member function name and its argument list.

## CREATING AN OBJECT FROM A CLASS TEMPLATE

When creating an object from a class template, the name of the template class is followed by the type bracketed and the variable name of the instantiated class. For example:

```
vector <binary_number>ABin(6);
```

declares a template class **vector** of six **binary_number** objects. The variable name for this class template is **ABin**. The variable name can be used like any other class name object.

A type definition can be used to create a synonym for a template of a specific parameterized type. For example:

```
typedef vector<binary_number>ABin;
typedef vector<network_adapter_card>ANetCard;
ABin(10);
ANetCard(3);
```

are two type definitions. The first type definition defines a template class **vector** of **binary_number** objects using the identifier **ABin**. The second type definition defines a template class **vector** of **network_adapter_card** objects using the identifier **ANet-Card**. The identifiers **ABin** and **ANetCard** are synonyms of the template class declarations **vector<binary_number>** and **vector<network_adapter_card>**, respectively.

## TEMPLATE ARGUMENTS

Template arguments do not have to be user-defined classes. They can be built-in types, an identifier or an argument declaration. There can also be multiple arguments. All the arguments are within the angle brackets.

In order to instantiate objects of a template, the supplied arguments have to match the required objects. For example, if a template was declared as follows:

```
template<class T, int M> class X{..}
```

and a template class was declared:

```
X<binary_number, char > TestClass; // this is not correct
```

this would create a compile error because a type mismatch has occured. The class template accepts an arbitrary type and an **int**, not a **char**. This would be the legal declaration:

```
X<binary_number, int M> TestClass;
```

If the class template requires two different arbitrary types, two of the same types will cause a compile error. For example, if a template was declared as follows:

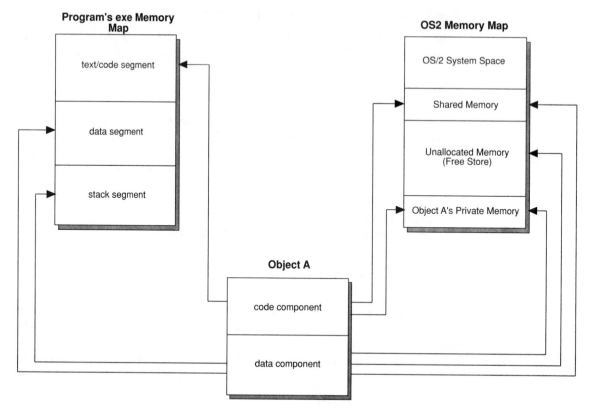

**Figure 2.16** The storage of an object's data and code components.

**Table 2.6** The data and code components of an object is stored in memory under the conditions specified in this table.

| | | Conditions for Storage | | | |
| | defined locally | defined outside of function | new( ) malloc( ) | always code | DLL, Pipe, semaphores |
|---|---|---|---|---|---|
| | stack segment | data segment | free store | text/code segment | shared memory |
| Object's Data Component | √ | √ | √ | √ | √ |
| Object's Code Component | | | | √ | √ |

```
template<class T, class P> class X{..}
```

and a template class was declared:

```
X<binary_number, binary_number> TestClass; //this is not correct
```

a compile error would occur because a type mismatch has occurred. The class template accepts two different arbitrary types. The types of the actual parameters of a function call and the types passed to a class template have to conform.

## WHERE DO OBJECTS LIVE?

Objects are the runtime versions of a class. Whereas the class only lives in source code, the object can live in internal memory, virtual memory, or disk. Objects are two-part structures. Since objects encapsulate both data and operations, objects have a *data component* and a *code component*. Figure 2.16 illustrates the storage of the code and data components of an object. The code component of an object can usually be found in one of two places: It can be found in the text segment of a process that has been loaded by the operating system, or in shared memory (i.e., as a dynamic link library—DLL) controlled by the operating system. It is stored in shared memory when the object accesses code that is defined externally.

The data component of an object can be stored in the stack, data segment, free store, or in shared memory. Data is stored in the stack when it is locally declared within a function. Data is stored in the data segment when data is declared outside a function. The stack and the data segments are controlled by the program. This memory is set aside by the program.

Data is stored in free store when a request for memory is made by the **new()** or **malloc()** family of functions. This request is made to the operating system and the memory is allocated in the free store of the operating system. The data component is stored in shared memory when the object utilizes data members from an outside source like a dynalink module or a dynamic link library component. The data member will occupy the shared memory of the operating system. Table 2.6 shows the possible conditions of storage for the data and code component of an object.

CHAPTER 3

# COLLECTIONS AND CONTAINERS

## WHAT ARE COLLECTIONS AND CONTAINERS?

Collections and containers are objects that are designed to hold or *contain* groups or collections of objects. In the same fashion that a box can contain a set of books or a bag can hold a collection of pencils, a C++ collection or container can contain an object or collection of objects. Containers act as *generic holders*. Containers in C++ may be mixed. This means they may contain collections of different kinds of objects or may contain objects that are all the same type. When a container contains a group of mixed objects, it is called a *heterogenous* container. When the container is holding a group of objects that are all the same, it is called a *homogenous* container. Collections and containers get their name from their function. They are used to hold things. Although many times in this book we use the terms *collection* and *container* interchangeably, there is a distinction. A collection in its strictest sense has a predefined behavior and a well-known interface. For instance, a *set* is an example of a collection. We all remember sets from grade school as being an unordered group or collection. We also encountered the interface for the set in grade school, namely, that a set has several operations: union, intersection, subset evaluation, and membership testing. Many collections are mathematical notions. A container, on the other hand, is more generic than a collection. The container has less personality. With containers we are only concerned with putting objects in, accessing the objects, and getting objects out. The container itself does not have to meet any other requirements except the ability to contain.

Because collections and containers are objects they support inheritance and polymorphism. This means that collection and container classes can be inherited, and then specialized or tailored to hold any kind of object the programmer has designed. One of the best features of containers is that they can be designed to hold many types of objects.

A C++ collection or container can be designed to hold multiple types of objects in the same way that a box can hold a collection of balls, or blocks, or hats, or tools, or chocolates. This is in contrast to languages like C or Pascal. For example, in C or Pascal one type of container that may be used is a list. The list must be designed from scratch because there is no built-in support for a *list type*. The list is built to hold a specific data type. If the programmer wishes to hold groups of more than one type of data, more than one list container must be designed, one for each data type that is to be stored. The collection and container classes in C++ allow the programmer to design one container that can contain many types of objects.

# TYPES OF COLLECTIONS AND CONTAINERS

Because collections and containers can be designed by the programmer, the types of collections and containers are only limited by the time, imagination, and effort required to design them. However, most of the collection and container classes that we talk about are based on data structures that are used in languages such as Pascal, Ada, C, FOR-TRAN, and Lisp. When the techniques of object orientation are applied to some of these data structures, the data structures are transformed and become containers! We will discuss the relationship between data structures as they are found in non–object-oriented languages and collections and containers as they are implemented in the C++ language later in this chapter. Table 3.1 shows some of the most common types of collections and containers and their defining characteristics.

## The List

Lists are containers that can hold an arbitrary number of objects. A list is a dynamic container. We use the term *dynamic* because the list can change size during the execution of the program. It is not a fixed-size container. Some containers, like the standard array in C++, are of a fixed length or fixed size. Once the space has been allocated for a fixed-size container, it maintains that size throughout the execution of the program. A list can either grow or shrink. The objects in a list are stored in a sequential fashion. This means they are stored one after the other. Figures 3.1 a, b, and c show the logical structure of a list.

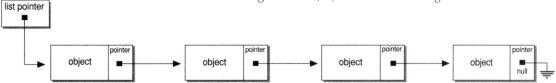

**Figure 3.1A**  A logical representation of a linked list.

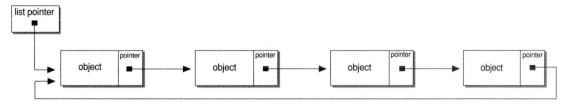

**Figure 3.1B**  A logical representation of circular list.

**Table 3.1   Some common collections and containers, their various types, and some of their defining characteristics.**

| Collections/ Containers | Characteristics |
| --- | --- |
| **List** | * A container that holds an arbitrary number of objects of the same type.<br>* A dynamic container; can change size during the execution of the program.<br>* Objects are stored and retrieved sequentially.<br>* Sequential access through the list is called *traversing* the list.<br>* Time needed to access an element in the list will depend upon the position the element has in the list. |
| *Types of Lists* | |
| **Linked** | * Elements in the list contain a pointer; the pointer points to the next element or a null value.<br>* The head of the list is the node that has no predecessor and the tail of the list is a node that has no successor.<br>* Traversal through the list is in one direction. |
| **Doubly Linked** | * Has two pointers in each object; one that points to the head and one that points to the tail.<br>* Traversal through the list is bidirectional. |
| **Circular** | * The tail of the list refers back to the head.<br>* Traversal starting at the head will eventually process the tail and return to the head of the list. |
| **Queue** | * Objects stored in FIFO (first-in-first-out) order meaning the first object placed in the stack will be the first object removed from the queue.<br>* Objects are inserted into the rear and deleted from the front of the queue; the oldest object is removed first and the youngest object is removed last.<br>* Uses a sequential access method.<br>* Dynamic container; can change size during execution of the program.<br>* The process of removing an object is called *dequeuing* and the process of adding an object is called *enqueuing*. |
| *Types of Queues* | |
| **Ascending Priority** | * Objects are placed into the queue from smallest to largest; only able to dequeue from the front and enqueue from the rear. |

| Collections/ Containers | Characteristics |
| --- | --- |
| **Descending Priority** | * Objects are placed into the queue from largest to smallest; only able to dequeue from the front and enqueue from the rear. |
| **Deques** | * Objects are enqueued or dequeued from the front or rear of the queue.<br>* No inherent sort order. |
| **Circular** | * Shifts a pointer continuously from the front as objects are dequeued from the front. |
| **Stacks** | * Objects are stored in LIFO (last-in-first-out) order meaning the last object placed in the stack will be the first object that can be removed from the stack.<br>* Restricted-access container—objects can only be removed from the top of the stack one at a time.<br>* Dynamic container—can change size during execution of the program.<br>* First object inserted in the stack will be the last object removed; removing an object from the stack is called *popping* and inserting an object is called *pushing*.<br>* Sequential access only.<br>* *Upwardly unbounded* meaning there is no conceptual limit to how large a stack can grow; *no lower bound* meaning once the last object has been popped no more items are available.<br>* Physical limit of the stack is determined by how much computer memory is available for the stack. |
| **Vector** | * Supplies direct access to the objects it contains; objects are directly accessed by an index that specifies the relative position of the object.<br>* *Constant time access*, meaning it take no longer to access the last item than it takes to access the first item. |
| **Sets** | * A collection of objects where no object appears more than once.<br>* Containment for an object is achieved if the object is compatible with the other objects in the set and the object meets a set of membership conditions for the set. |

**Table 3.1**   Some common collections and containers, their various types, and some of their defining characteristics. (*continued*)

| Collections/ Containers | Characteristics |
| --- | --- |
| | * Objects in the set are called *members* and are unordered.<br>* Dynamic or fixed-size container.<br>* Operations for a set: membership, union, subset, compliment, difference. |
| **Graphs** | * Polylithic container, meaning a graph needs other structures to complete its definition.<br>* Consists of two sets: vertices and edges; the vertices are the set of objects and the edges are the set of relationships between the vertices. |
| **General Trees** | * A connected graph that contains no circuits; connected means that from any two objects, there is a path connecting them; a circuit is a traversal through a graph that returns to the starting vertex without traversing any edge or any vertex more than once.<br>* Introduces the ideas of: leaf, forest, father, son, brother, ancestor descendant, level, depth, and degree. |
| *Types of Graphs* | |
| **Binary Tree** | * A type of tree in which each node cannot have more than two children. |
| **B Tree** | * Ordered, optimally balanced tree. |

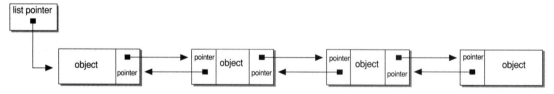

**Figure 3.1C**   A logical representation of double-linked list.

In a list container the objects that have been stored can only be retrieved in a sequential order. This means that to access the third object in the list, the programmer must get past the first object, then the second object, and then the third object is available for processing. Access to the objects in a list is referred to as *sequential access*. The process of moving through a list container object by object from the beginning of the list to the end of the list is referred to as *traversing* the list. Here are three common types of lists: *linked lists, doubly linked lists,* and *circular lists.*

### LINKED LISTS

Lists are called linked because each object in a list refers or points to the next object in the list. The programmer only has to know how to get to the first object in the list, and the first object in the list will know the location of the next object in the list, and so on. The *link* is the reference to the *next* object in the list. Also, linked lists are only traversed in one direction. The beginning of the list is called the *head* of the list, and the end of the list is called the *tail* of the list. The links point from the head of the list toward the tail of the list, or from the tail of the list toward the head of the list. Linked lists are *one-way sequential structures*.

### DOUBLY LINKED LISTS

Doubly linked lists, like linked lists, are connected by each object referring to the next object in the list. Whereas the linked list can only be traversed from either head to tail or tail to head, the doubly linked list has two references in each object. It has one reference pointing toward the head, and the other reference pointing toward the tail. In this way a list can be traversed in *both* directions. The doubly linked list is called *bidirectional*.

### CIRCULAR LIST

A circular list is a linked list where the tail refers to the head. Sometimes circular lists are called *rings*. This is because if the traversal of the list is started at the head of the list and each member of the list is visited, the traversal will eventually come full circle after it processes the tail and end up back at the head of the list.

Because the list is so generic in nature we classify the list as more of a container than a collection. The basic operations on a list involve insertion into the list, deletion from the list, and access to the current object in the list. The objects in a list container are sometimes called *nodes* and each node is said to be connected to either the next node or the previous node or both.

## The Queue

We are all familiar with the notion of front-to-back ordering. For instance, a line in a grocery store or the line in front of a teller at a bank is a front-to-back ordering. The people in the line are serviced starting with the first person in the line and ending with the last person in the line. Well, a queue is a front-to-back ordering whose logical structure looks like a line. Figure 3.2 shows the logical view of a queue. We use the phrase *logical view* or *logical representation* throughout this book in contrast to *physical representation*. The logical view or representation is conceptually how the programmer accesses or manipulates a structure or container. The physical representation is how and where the container or structure is actually stored in internal or external memory. In most cases the logical representation of a container or structure is different from its physical representation.

In a queue the items are deleted from the front and inserted into the rear of the queue. The queue is known as a *FIFO* (first-in-first-out) structure. This means that the first item that has been inserted will be the first item to be removed. The queue can naturally represent aging relationships, because in a queue the oldest object is removed first and the youngest object is removed last. Queues like lists are sequential structures and any method accessing a queue is a sequential access method. Queues are also *dynamic* structures. That is, they can grow or shrink during program execution. When objects are inserted into a queue the queue grows; when objects are deleted from the queue it shrinks. The process of removing an object from a queue is known as *dequeuing*. The process of adding and object to a queue is called *enqueuing*. Here are three of the commonly used queues: *priority queues, deques,* and *circular queues.*

## PRIORITY QUEUES

A priority queue is an ordered queue. This means that the objects that are placed into a priority queue are sorted into some kind of order. However, this does not change the restriction of only being able to dequeue from the front of the queue and enqueue into the rear of the queue. There are two types of priority queues, *descending* priority queues and *ascending* priority queues. In a descending priority queue the objects are sorted from largest to smallest. The largest object is dequeued from the queue, and then the next largest object is dequeued, and so on. In this way the queue is said to be descending, because as the values are dequeued they get smaller. The ascending priority queue is just the opposite. In an ascending queue the objects are stored in

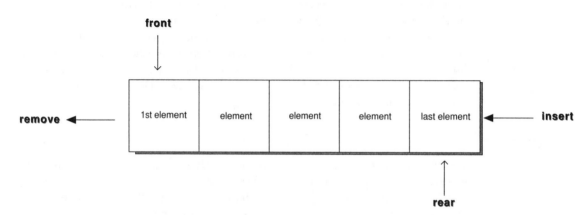

**Figure 3.2**   A logical representation of a queue.

sequence from smallest to largest. As the objects are dequeued they begin with the smallest and proceed to the largest. Although the priority queue maintains a sort order it can still be used for aging relationships, or as the names ascending and descending relationships suggest. If the importance of an object can be associated with its position in the queue then the queue can be used as a sort of emergency room, where the most critical objects can get attention first.

## DEQUES

Deques (pronounced *decks*) are queues with the restricted access relieved a little. A queue is said to have restricted access. If there is a group of objects stored in a queue they may only be dequeued one at a time from the front of the queue, and may only be enqueued one at a time into the rear of the queue. The deque relaxes this constraint somewhat. In a deque objects may be enqueued into either the rear of the queue or the front of the queue. Likewise, objects may be dequeued from either the front or the rear of the queue. Unlike the priority queues the deques have no inherent sort order.

## CIRCULAR QUEUES

Circular queues are sometimes called *ring buffers*. Circular queues are queues that wrap around. Circular queues usually involve a moving pointer that continues to shift to the front as objects are dequeued from the front. Circular queues are good for cyclic modeling.

# Stacks

Stacks are containers that can hold an arbitrary number of objects. Stacks are dynamic containers. When objects are inserted into a stack the stack's size grows. The stack shrinks as objects are removed from the stack. The stack is a restricted-access container. Just as with lists and queues, objects may only be removed from a stack one at a time. The stack is known as a *LIFO* (last-in-first-out) structure. The first item inserted into a stack is the last item removed, and the last item inserted is the first item removed. Figure 3.3 shows a logical view of a stack container. The process of inserting objects into a stack is called *pushing* the stack. The process of removing or deleting objects from a stack is referred to as *popping* the stack. Objects are pushed onto the top of the stack, and objects are popped from the top of the stack.

Stacks have a wide variety of applications. They are used in everything from graphical user interface windowing processing to mathematical expression and computer language parsing. They can be used to process aging relationships also. Whereas the queue is used to process the oldest element first, the stack is used to process the youngest element first. Stacks like lists permit only sequential access. If a stack contains a collection of objects, there is no way to jump into the middle of a stack to access an object. The stack must be popped the appropriate number of times before an object in the middle of the stack can be removed.

The basic operations of stacks include popping the stack, pushing the stack, looking at the top member of the stack, and checking the stack for *underflow* conditions. A stack is

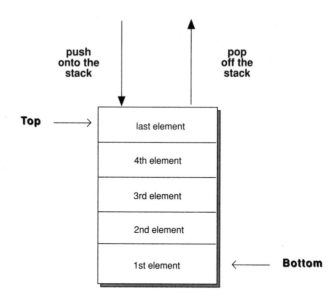

**Figure 3.3**  A logical representation of a stack.

theoretically upwardly unbounded. This means that there is no conceptual limit to how large a stack may grow. While there is no theoretical limit, there is a physical limit. The physical limit is dictated by how much computer memory is available to a stack. When a stack operation would exceed the physical limit of the memory available, the operation is said to cause a *stack overflow*. On the other hand, stacks do have a lower bound. Once the last item has been popped from a stack no more items are available. When an operation attempts to pop an item from an empty stack, the operation is said to have caused a *stack underflow*.

## Vectors and Arrays

A vector is a container that provides direct access to the objects it contains. This is in contrast to lists, queues, and stacks. Lists, queues, and stacks only provide sequential access. This means that the objects that are stored in lists, queues, and stacks can only be accessed in a serial fashion. Objects can only be processed at the beginning, end, top, bottom, front, or back. To access an object in the middle of a container all the objects that precede that object must first be processed. When objects are stored in a vector they may be directly accessed by an index. The index specifies the relative location of the object in the list. For example, an index of 5 would specify the fifth object in the vector. If we had a vector called Myvector, the operation Myvector[5] would return the fifth object in the vector. There is no need to first access objects 1 through 4. The fifth object may be accessed directly, hence the term *direct access*. The vector is an indexed structure. The vector container may be either a fixed-size container or a dynamic container. The number of objects that a vector is to hold can be specified in advance, or the vector may be allowed to grow or shrink during program execution.

Vectors are said to provide *constant time* access. Constant time refers to the amount of time that it takes to locate an object in the vector container. When a container has constant time access, then it should take no longer to access the last item in the container than it takes to access the first item in the container. Although the vector is a sequential structure like a list, the access methods of the vector allow direct access as well as sequential access. Figure 3.4 shows the logical structure of a vector container. The vector container does not impose any specific ordering on the member. However, each of the members is assigned a *position* within the container. This position is called the *index*. By specifying the object's position, direct access can be achieved.

### Is It a Vector? Or Is It an Array?

The term *array* is sometimes used instead of *vector*. The distinction, however, is normally discipline specific and is a matter of aesthetics. Folks with scientific or mathematical backgrounds tend to use the term vector, while folks with business backgrounds tend to use the term array. In most cases they are referring to the same type of structure. A vector is a one-dimensional array and vice versa. A two-dimensional array is called a matrix and vice versa.

### The Flexibility of Vectors

As we shall find out in Chapter 6, the vector can be used to implement queues, stacks, and lists. The vector or array can be used to implement virtually any other container. The only other container that has this distinction is the list. The list also can be used to implement most other containers. In languages such as C, Pascal, FORTRAN, and COBOL, the array or vector is the only built-in container that is provided. It is assumed that all other containers can be simulated using this one container. We shall have much to say about this in our discussions on adaptors in Chapter 4 and on object-oriented vectors in Chapter 6. Most sorting and searching algorithms requires that the objects to be sorted and searched be stored in a vector. In fact, one of the most often used searches in computer science, the *binary search*, requires that the objects be stored in a vector.

## Sets

A set is a collection of objects where no object is contained more than once, and where membership in the set is determined by whether the object meets some list of criteria. The set container is unlike any of the other containers we have discussed. For lists, queues, stacks, and vectors there are no membership rules. The only condition of containment is that the object be compatible in type with the kinds of things the

| element[0] | element[1] | element[2] | element[3] | ⋯ element[n-1] |
|---|---|---|---|---|

container is allowed to hold. The set container is in a class by itself. Every member that is under consideration for membership in a set must meet the conditions of membership for the set. For example, if we have a set, let's call it *A*, that contains only men over 35 who are *Star Trek* fans, then any other human that cannot be described as a male *Star Trek* fan over 35 cannot belong to set *A*. Sets are said to include some things while excluding others. This is part of the definition for sets. In order for a set to be considered a set, it must specifically include some class or classes of things while implicitly or explicitly excluding other classes. A set that is composed of only even numbers would not allow the number 5 to get a membership card.

The other defining characteristic of the set besides its membership conditions is the uniqueness of all of its members. For instance, if we had a set containing only even numbers, then that set could only contain the number 2 once. Although −2 would also be allowed in the set it is considered a different number from 2. This means that there is no duplication in a set.

The objects that are placed in a set are called *members* or *elements* of the set. Sets are unordered collections. This means that the position a member has within a set is unimportant and is not a defining feature. Sets are not considered sequences, and are therefore not serial structures. Sets can be either dynamic or fixed-size containers. If the maximum number of elements the set can hold is predefined then the set is said to have a fixed size. The size of a dynamic set can grow or shrink during the execution of the program. As members are inserted into the set it grows, and when members are removed from the set it shrinks.

Another interesting characteristic of the set is that it doesn't formally have an access mechanism. Whereas lists, queues, and stacks have sequential access specifications and the objects in a vector may be accessed sequentially or directly, the formal notion of a set does not specify how it is to be accessed. This presents challenges for implementers of set collections, because they must pick some access mechanism without destroying the concept of the set. While the set concept does not present any specific access mechanism, it does present several operations:

Set membership
Set intersection
Set union
Subset
Complement
Set difference

Figure 3.5 shows a logical representation of a set. Some objects are included while other objects are excluded. The objects that are included only appear once. Sets are very powerful notions. In fact, practically the entire area of databases and database management systems is based on variations on set theory. The set concept is a mathematical notion, and provides the foundation for entire fields within mathematics. Because of the set's power of representation and the operations that are defined on sets this container provides the programmer with an exceptionally expressive collection. We present a detailed discussion of the set container, the STL implementation of the set, and set theory in Chapter 5.

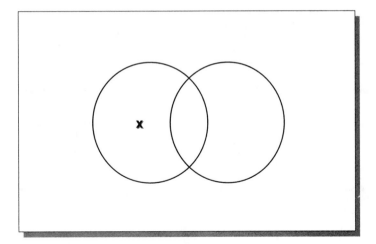

**Figure 3.5** A logical representation of a set.

# Graphs

A graph is a *polylithic* container. That is, a graph is a structure that requires other structures to complete its definition. A graph is a collection that consists of two sets: a set of vertices and a set of edges. The graph structure is not to be confused with the notion of a *pictorial graph*. Pictorial graphs are visual representations of data that has been plotted to show some information or relationship. This is not to say that graphs cannot be represented visually. Figure 3.6 shows an example of how a graph could be depicted. The graph, like the set, is an extremely expressive collection. Note that sets and graphs represent good examples of collections, because they have personality that goes above and beyond the objects they contain. This is in contrast to containers, which simply provide holding areas and whose characteristics and behavior provide only base insertion, deletion, and access. Collections have powerful characteristics and behaviors apart from the objects they contain.

### A FORMAL DEFINITION

A graph $G$ is a structure $G=\{V,E\}$ that consists of a nonempty set $V$ of points (called *vertices*) and a set $E$ of segments (called *edges*) such that each edge $e$ contains exactly two vertices, one vertex at each endpoint of the segment.

### BUT WHAT DOES THE FORMAL DEFINITION MEAN?

Simply put, a graph contains two collections. One collection is a set of objects (vertices), and the other collection is the set of relationships (edges) between those objects. Note how general this description of graphs is. We do not specify what kinds of objects are in the first set, and we do not specify what the relationships between the objects are that are contained in the second set. This is what makes the graph such a powerful collection. We can represent any objects and their relationships with the graph structure. In general,

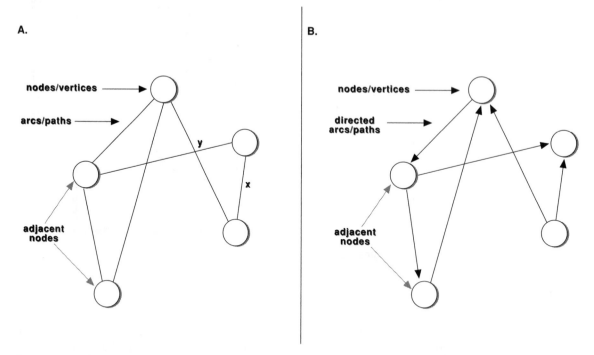

**Figure 3.6**  A logical representation of a graph. This diagram also shows the parts of a graph. A directed graph is depicted in B.

there is no limit to the complexity of the relationships that can be represented. For example, Figure 3.7 shows a collection of modems whose baud rate ranges from 300 to 28800. It also shows the relationship that we are concerned with between each of those modems. The relationship that we are concerned with is *greater than*. Each object is connected to another object based on a baud rate evaluation. We have a connection if the relationship can be described as greater than or less than.

## WHAT ARE GRAPHS USED FOR?

Graphs are used to store objects that are related or connected in some way and to represent *search spaces*. Graphs are nonsequential structures. This is in contrast to lists, stacks, queues, and vectors. Objects contained in a graph can only be reached by their relationships to other objects in the graph. Objects in a graph are not accessible by position, sequence, or index. For instance, let's say we have an e-mail friend and family circle, where you are allowed to send e-mail only to people you know. We can demonstrate the use of a graph container by allowing an e-mailer to get an emergency message to someone that the e-mailer doesn't know. Let's say that Bobby, Sally, Sue, Dick, and Greg are the only people in the e-mail friends and family circle. Furthermore, Bobby knows Dick, Dick knows Sue, Sue knows Greg, Greg knows Sally, and Sally knows Bobby. Let's say that Sue needs to get an emergency e-mail message to Bobby; however, Sue only knows Greg. Therefore, technically she can only send an e-mail message to

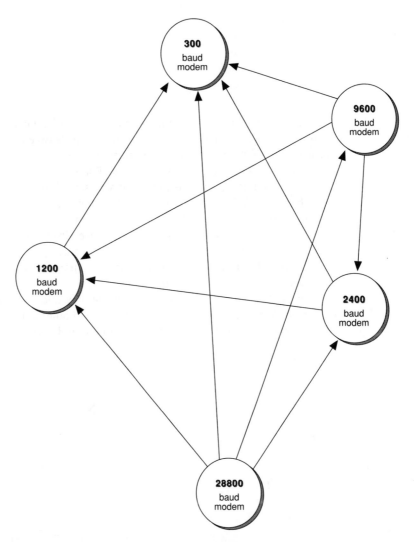

**Figure 3.7** A collection of modems in a graph whose baud rate ranges from 300–28800. The edges represent the > relationship between the nodes in the graph. They illustrate a <or> evaluation.

Greg. Figure 3.8 shows how we might use a graph to get the e-mail message to Bobby. In the example in Figure 3.8, Bobby, Sally, Sue, Dick, and Greg represent the list of vertices that a graph contains. The sender permission represents the relationships between each of the objects. In this example each object has a sender permission with only one object. The process of moving from one object in a graph to another object in a graph is called *traversal*. The relationship between each object or set of objects in graph theory is known as a *path*, or edge. Hence the set of paths in this example is:

Bobby knows Dick
Dick knows Sue
Sue knows Greg
Greg knows Sally
Sally knows Bobby

Graphs do not have beginnings, endings, or middles. Graphs only have a collection of objects (vertices) and a collection of relationships between those objects called paths or edges. The solution to our problem in this example is also a path. The path went from Sue to Greg, Greg to Sally, and Sally to Bobby. Although this path is not explicitly represented in the graph it is implicitly represented in the graph.

The set of relationships in this example represents the sender permission of the e-mail family and friend's circle. The sender permission is based on whom you know. So in our example Sue could not send an e-mail message directly to Bobby because she does not know Bobby. However, if she needs to get a message to him she can get it to him indirectly. This brings up another important use for graphs. They allow us to ask questions about objects that are indirectly related. Graphs are used in problem solving (how can Sue get a message to Bobby if she only knows Greg?), searching for objects based on their direct or indirect relationships to other objects, and simulation. Almost any scenario can be described as a set of objects and a set of relationships between those

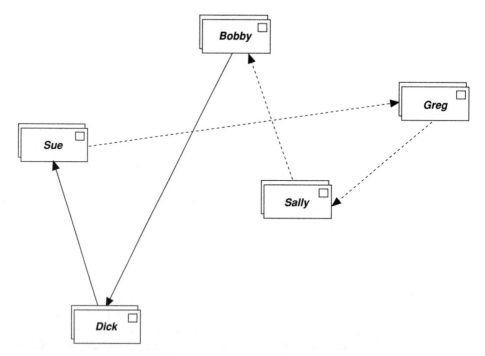

**Figure 3.8**   The graph shows how to get an e-mail message from Sue to Bobby. The nodes represent these relationships: Bobby to Dick, Dick to Sue, Sue to Greg, Greg to Sally, and Sally to Bobby.

objects. Also any problem can be represented as a pathfinding problem. (See Kowalski 1979, 75.) This means that graphs can be used to simulate reasoning, which is why they are so prevalent in the field of artificial intelligence.

Many uses of the computer involve simply the retrieval and storage of data. This is because computers can be used to store vast amounts of data and retrieve that data relatively quick. For this reason the main focus of many programs is simple, efficient data storage and retrieval. However, when programs need to do more than just retrieve data, or perform fast lookups, or simply write data to some form of storage, the graph structure may be useful. The graph's ability to represent virtually unlimited relationships between objects and the very powerful methods that have been invented to traverse graphs provide the programmer with a means of pushing the computer beyond simple storage and retrieval to advanced forms of information processing. In Chapter 8 we present a discussion of graph theory, the various types of graphs, the application of the graph collection to problem solving and search spaces, and how the graph collection can be implemented in C++ using components from the STL.

## TREES

A tree is a special case of a graph. While all graphs are not trees, all trees are graphs. (See Finkbeiner, Lindstrom 1987, 267.) So everything that was said in the discussion above about graphs can be said about trees. The tree is a collection as opposed to a container because the tree structure is more than just a generic holder providing only storage, insertion, removal, and access interfaces. The tree has a well-defined rich definition, set of interfaces, structure, and vocabulary. The tree structure introduces the notions of leaf, forest, father, son, brother, ancestor, descendant, level, depth, and degree. (See Tennebaum, Langsam, and Augenstein 1990, 289.) These notions are in addition to the notions of vertices and edges, which are a part of all graphs.

### Formal Definition

*A tree is a connected graph that contains no circuit.* This definition hinges on the meanings of three words: *graph, connected,* and *circuit.* From the discussion above on graphs we know that a graph is a structure that has two sets in it. Let's call those sets *V* and *E.* Set *V* is a set of objects called *vertices.* Set *E* is a set of relationships between those objects, called *edges.* A graph is said to be connected if there is a relationship between any pair of distinct objects in set *V.* That means that any two of the objects can be chosen at random, and there must be a path or relationship between those objects in order for the graph to be considered connected. A *circuit* is a traversal through the graph that returns to its starting vertex without traversing any edge more than once and without passing through any intermediate vertex more than once. Simply stated, a circuit is a trip around a graph that ends where it started without visiting any vertex more than once. There are three commonly used types of trees: *binary trees, B trees,* and *general trees.*

### What Are Trees Used For?

The formal definition of trees may seem a bit much, but trees are some of the most important and widely used structures in computer science and software engineering.

They provide the basis for most commercial databases. There is a form of binary search that is implemented using a binary search tree that is faster and more efficient than the binary search that is implemented using vectors. The tree, like the graph, provides an effective structure to represent *search spaces*. Since all problems have some sort of search space, problem-solving techniques can be implemented in software using the tree structure. For an introductory discussion of C++ and trees, see Budd (1994).

# CLASSIFICATION OF COLLECTIONS AND CONTAINERS

First, we shall make the distinction between collections and containers. In some of the earlier implementation of container classes in C++ the term *collection* was used to designate a class that was one of the primary base classes for all container classes. This meant that classes like set, queue, stack, and list would all be descendants of type collection. According to this scheme all containers could be called collections. This inheritance scheme was true for the NIH (National Institute of Health) container library, and the Smalltalk container library. These provided the model for many of the current container libraries available. Different library implementers started to use the terms collections and containers in different ways and in time they came to be used interchangeably. In some of the current implementations of container classes such as the Standard Template Library (STL) there is no inheritance hierarchy and so these two terms will become even more ambiguous as time goes on.

In this book we make a distinction between collections and containers. We do not consider collections as a base class for all containers. Instead we use quality of interface and behavior to differentiate between the two. When we use the word *container* in its strictest since, we are referring to a generic object that can hold a group of other objects, where the generic object provides only the basic form of insertion, deletion, and access. We classify lists, arrays, unordered vectors, and matrices as containers. The list provides the simplest form of sequential access, and the arrays, unordered vectors, and matrices provide the simplest form of direct access. When we use the word *collection* in its strictest since we are referring to an object that can hold a group of other objects, and that provides more than the base container behavior, and whose operations provide more than just the simple notion of insertion, deletion, and access. In this category we place stacks, queues, sets, graphs, trees, and maps. We chose this distinction for collections because it is more mathematically correct, and is consistent with the mathematical notion of a collection. Table 3.2 lists the classifications of the common object-oriented structures.

## Understanding the Collection and Container Classes

When working with the discrete structures of computer science and software engineering there will be many ways to organize, approach, view, and represent the structures. Collection and container classes are no exception to this. There are several ways the collections and container classes can be approached and understood from a (OOD) Object-Oriented Design or (OOP) Object-Oriented Programming perspective:

Table 3.2  Common object-oriented structures listed as a collection or a container.

| Collection | Container |
|------------|-----------|
| Queue | List |
| Stacks | Vector |
| Sets | Matrix |
| Multisets | File |
| Maps | |
| Multimaps | |
| Graph | |
| Trees | |

Logical views
Geometrical views
Access methods
Mathematical descriptions
Implementation representations
Physical representations

## LOGICAL VIEWS

The logical view of a collection or container is a perspective that the programmer uses to understand, access, and manage a programming construct. The logical view helps to organize and make sense of the components of the structures and their operations. The logical view is how we conceptually look at something. In many cases, the logical view consists of an analogy between the programming construct under consideration and some other well-known real-world concept. For instance, the logical view of a queue could be a waiting line of people where individuals at the front of the line are serviced before individuals at the back of the line. Another logical view would be to consider a queue, a front-to-back sequence of blocks. Another logical view would be to compare a queue with a set of contiguous memory locations where the smallest memory location is processed first and the largest location is processed last (as in a priority queue). Note that the logical view of a collection or container may not be how the actual collection or container is implemented or physically stored. In the logical view we use terms like linear, sequential, hierarchical, recursive, nonlinear, FIFO, LIFO, and multidimensional to describe the nature of the collection or container.

### Linear and Sequential Analogies

Lists, queues, stacks, and vectors can all be logically viewed as linear or sequential. That is, they can be viewed as consisting of sequences of objects in a straight line, where each object is distinguished by its position or index in the line. In the linear or sequential view of a collection we can think of the collection as having a beginning, or end, top, or bottom, front, or back. We think of the objects in the collection or container as moving from left to right or right to left. The objects in linear collections or containers are understood as being in an increasing, decreasing, or sequentially adjacent order.

### Hierarchical Views

Some collections and containers are conceptualized as trees. The tree will have a root, which in turn will have branches, which in turn will have leaves. Using the view of a collection and container as a tree, the notion of *hierarchy* is introduced. The notions of top and bottom, left branch and right branch become techniques to help organize the processing. The structure is perceived as either growing from the root up or from the root down. This helps the programmer to devise tree traversal algorithms. The programmer manages the relationships between the objects because the notion of hierarchy and span of control are familiar.

### Recursive Collections

Trees and graphs can be considered to be recursive structures. When one is familiar with the concept of recursion, then the ability to conceptualize a collection or a container as a recursive structure has a very elegant appeal. Because a tree can be loosely defined as a structure that contains nodes, which are also trees, the tree has a kind of *recursive feel*. For this reason recursive techniques that greatly simplify the structure of an algorithm can be applied to many trees and graphs.

### Nonlinear Collections

Sets, multisets, maps, multimaps, trees, and graphs are all nonlinear structures. This means they cannot be thought of as consisting of a sequence of objects. They require other than sequential access methods. By using the logical view *nonlinear*, the programmer is able to "rule out" certain types of access methods and "rule in" other types of techniques. The concepts of front, back, head, tail, or consecutive do not in general apply to nonlinear containers.

### Multidimensional Collections and Containers

Some containers, like matrices or maps, can be viewed as multidimensional. It helps to think of a matrix as consisting of rows and columns. Many algorithms and access techniques have been devised that work nicely on structures with rows and columns. Maps can be viewed as associations where the key is one dimension and the value is another. In the case of matrices multidimensional simply means a two-way linear structure that simultaneously has a sequence that goes up and down and a sequence that goes left and right. Multidimensional can be used to refer to multigraphs and trees, where there are multiple paths leading in different directions to other objects.

### Geometrical Views

The geometrical view helps the program picture what the relationships in the collection or container class look like. For instance, it sometimes helps to imagine a list whose tail points to its head as a circle. Actually drawing or depicting the list as a circle helps to devise algorithms and access methods to process the list. In fact, a list that has a tail that points to its head is called a circular list. Viewing a structure *G* that consists of two sets *V* and *E* as a tree helps the programmer to organize approaches to objects that are stored in this manner. The programmer is actually able to see the root, the branches, the leaves, and so forth. Geometrical views help the programmer construct visual models of what the collection or container looks like.

## ACCESS METHODS

The manner in which a collection or container is accessed is also instrumental in helping the programmer to approach, classify, and manage those collections and containers. There are three broad categories for access methods: *sequential access methods, direct access methods*, and *relational access methods*.

### Sequential Access Methods

When a collection can only be processed from front to back or back to front, and when there is no way to get to the $N+1$ element without processing the Nth element, then the access method is called a sequential access method. Lists, queues, and stacks are examples of collections and containers with sequential access methods. Sequential access methods are fairly straightforward and simple to implement.

### Direct Access Methods

When any particular object can be retrieved from any position within a container without the need to process other objects first, this is called direct access. Vectors, and maps are examples of containers that have direct access methods. The Nth element can be accessed in a vector without the need to process the $N-1$ or $N+1$ element. The association in a map can be provided and the data value can be directly returned without having to process any other objects.

### Relational Access Methods

When a collection or container has a relational access method, this means that storage, retrieval, and access of one object are dependent upon its relationship to another object. Trees, graphs, maps, and sorted collections have relational access methods. For example, when integers are put into a binary tree, the value of the integer determines where in the tree it is inserted. Likewise when an integer is being searched for in a tree its relationship to the other integers in the tree must first be considered to determine whether it is in the tree. In the graph structure I may access vertex *C* only if *C* happens to be the starting place in the graph or if there is some other vertex that is related to *C* that I have access to. Of all the access methods the relational access method is the most powerful.

Mathematical descriptions provide the designer and the programmer with precise ways to describe collections and containers. By describing a graph as a structure $G = \{V,E\}$ it is exactly clear what we mean. Most of the collection and container classes are based on mathematical notions. When we say that $A$ is a proper subset of $B$ there can be no confusion about the relationship between $A$ and $B$. Mathematical descriptions provide a universal method and language to communicate what is meant, and what a class represents. When a map is described as $a\,R\,b$ if and only if $a$ is the square of $b$ then we can be confident about validation and verification testing, because we know exactly what we are looking for. The collection and container categorization matrix in Table 3.3 shows some of the mathematical descriptions of commonly used collections and containers.

# COLLECTION AND CONTAINER CLASS FUNDAMENTALS

Every kind of collection or container regardless of type must provide a certain basic functionality. The foremost feature that a collection or container must have is the ability to hold an object or group of objects. The collection or container must also provide the user with the ability to insert objects or pointers to objects. The collection must also provide the user with the ability to remove objects or pointers to objects. Finally, the collection or container must provide the user with the ability to access each object that has been inserted. If the object does not provide *containment functionality, insertion operations, removal operations*, and *basic object access operations*, then that object is not a collection or container.

## Containment Functionality

One of the main functions of the collection and container object is to provide the programmer with the ability to manage a group of objects. Suppose we had a group of communication port objects. Lets call them COM1, COM2, COM3, and COM4. Also suppose the communication objects had the specific set of characteristics that are shown in Table 3.4. Although it is certainly possible to refer to each object individually by a separate variable name, the programmer may wish to group the objects and refer to them collectively by a single variable name. In the case of container objects, the programmer would still have access to each of the characteristics of each of the objects that are stored in the container. Storing the communication port objects that are shown in Table 3.4 in a container or collection may seem only a simple convenience; however, if we had, say, several hundred communication port objects, not only would it be desirable to be able to refer to them collectively by one variable name, it would be necessary for sanity's sake! Collection and container objects can be used to group objects under a single name. When a group of objects is bound under a singly named object, the singly named object is said to contain or hold the group of objects. The notion of one object being able to contain other objects has powerful implications. Because collections and containers are themselves objects, they can be passed as parameters. Most collection or container objects can be used in assignment. For instance, we may have a group of objects stored in

**Table 3.3 Classification of collections matrix showing the geometrical, logical, mathematical representations of a collection or container. Also showing the access method as sequential, direct, and/or relational for each type of collection or container.**

| Container/ Collection | Geometrical View | Logical View | Mathematical View | Access Methods | | |
|---|---|---|---|---|---|---|
| | | | | Sequential | Direct | Relational |
| Stack | | Linear Sequential LIFO Dynamic | $a_1\ a_2\ a_3\ a_4\ a_5\ a_6...a_n$ | √ | | |
| Queue | | Linear Sequential LIFO Dynamic | $a_1\ a_2\ a_3\ a_4\ a_5\ a_6...a_n$ | √ | | |
| Tree | | No unique entry point Hierarchical Recursive Nonlinear Multidimensional Dynamic | $G = <V, E>$ $V$ = set of vertices $E$ = set of edges | | | √ |
| Set | | Unordered Collection Dynamic | $A = \{x: x\ in\ R\}$ | | | √ |
| Graph | | No unique entry point Unordered Collection Polylithic Superstructure | $G = <V, E>$ $V$ = set of vertices $E$ = set of edges | | | √ |
| List | | Linear Sequential Dynamic | $a_1\ a_2\ a_3\ a_4\ a_5\ a_6...a_n$ | √ | | |
| Vector | | Linear Dynamic or Fixed | $a_1\ a_2\ a_3\ a_4\ a_5\ a_6...a_n$ | √ | √ | |
| Map | | Associative Matrix Dynamic or Fixed | $f:A->B$ $xRy$ $xRyuAxA$ | | √ | √ |

**Table 3.4   Communication port objects (COM1, COM2, COM3, COM4) and some possible settings.**

| Com Post | Baud | Parity | Databits | Stopbits | P |
|---|---|---|---|---|---|
| **Com1** | 3600 | N(none) | 8 | 2 | 30 sec. |
| **Com2** | 1200 | E (even) | 7 | 1 | 30 sec. |
| **Com3** | 14400 | M(mark) | 5 | 1 | 30 sec. |
| **Com4** | 3600 | N(none) | 6 | 1 | 30 sec. |

a set $A$, and an empty set $B$. If the container or collection provides the basic insertion operations we may assign $A$ to $B$ by $B=A$.

At this point $B$ now contains either a copy of the objects that were stored in $A$, or pointers to objects that are stored in $A$. Because collections and containers are objects we may have collections of containers. There is no reason why we cannot have a vector of sets, or a stack of maps. This containment functionality allows the programmer to build exotic combinations of collections and containers and refer to them as a single structure or under a single variable name. For instance, all the communication port objects from Table 3.4 may be placed into a queue container and referred to simply as *Com Ports*.

## The Insertion Operations

Collection and container classes may provide several methods of allowing the user to insert objects. Most collection and container objects provide an insert, or add *type* member function. This is a member function that can be called to add elements to the container or collection. For instance:

MySet.add('A')

adds the character 'A' to a collection object called **MySet**. These member functions can be called as part of a loop to add as many objects as required to the collection or container object. Another way that objects can be inserted into collection or container classes is through constructors. For example:

set SetB(MySet)

would construct **SetB** as an object of type **set** that contains all the elements of **MySet**. In this way the constructor acts as an insertion operation. Another method that would accomplish insertion into a container object is through the container object's assignment member function. If the container provides assignment, then we may insert an object into the container through it. The statement:

SetB = MySet

inserts all the members from **MySet** into **SetB**.

Every collection or container class must provide at least one of these methods for adding or inserting objects. Most of the common collection and container classes provide all of these methods.

## The Object Removal Operation

All collection and container objects must provide some method of removing or deleting objects. Objects need to be removed if:

The container needs to be used more than once during the execution of the program.
The objects in the container are no longer needed.
The objects in the container need to be replaced.
The collection or container object has gone out of scope.
The objects need to be taken from one collection or container and placed in another.
It is necessary to regain memory that is currently being occupied by the objects.

Without the ability to remove objects, the container object is incomplete and does not meet its base functionality requirements. Object removal is normally accomplished by one of three methods:

1. A member function that has the responsibility for removing an object or specified range of objects
2. A destructor member function that removes all of the objects when it is called
3. Manual destruction of the objects by deleting them from outside of the collection or container

## Object Visitation

There must be some mechanism that allows the user to access each object in a collection or container. Some collections have this mechanism specified as a part of their definitions. For instance, with the **pop** operation of a stack object the user can access every object that has been stored in the stack, or with the [] subscript operation a user can access every object that has been stored in a vector or matrix. However, some collection definitions don't explicitly specify anything about object access. For example, the notion of a set specifies things about set membership, set intersection, set union, subset, set complements, and so forth, but there is no mention about visiting each member in the set. For the set class the designer must specify some sort of access mechanism that allows total object visitation. In order for an object to be called a collection or container it must also meet the base functionality for these types of objects. The base functionality includes object access or *object visitation*.

Object visitation in collections and containers is accomplished by two methods: *member functions*, and *Special-purpose data members* (called *iterators*).

### OBJECT VISITATION USING COLLECTION OR CONTAINER MEMBER FUNCTIONS

As stated above, one example of a collection that uses a member function for object visitation is the stack. The stack object uses a member function to allow the user to visit all the elements it contains. The operation is normally called **pop** or **remove**, and is part of the stack definition. The stack is a LIFO collection. Therefore, any other method of visiting the objects in a stack would be abusive. Using the remove or pop operation on a queue until it is empty also accomplishes total object visitation through a member function. Because the queue is a FIFO object, moving through the queue in any other method would constitute structure abuse. Using other than LIFO access for a stack or FIFO access for a queue is a strong indicator that the wrong type of container has been chosen. Also, program testing and program enhancements are made more difficult by policies that are structure abusive.

Many collections and containers specify member functions that are defined to perform some user-defined operation on all the objects that are contained. These types of member functions are parameterized, because they don't know exactly what operation they are supposed to do until runtime. The parameterized member function gets its specific operation when a user passes the member function either a pointer to a function, or a function object. The member function then uses that operation to process each object in the container. This type of member function is called an *iterator function*. The operations that iterator functions perform can be divided into four basic groups:

Read-only visitors
Write-only visitors
Read/write visitors
Remove or replace visitors

### Read-Only Visitors

Iterator functions that access each object in a container without changing or destroying any data members contained in those objects are called *read-only* or *nonmutating* functions. An example of a read-only iterator function would be a function that was designed to count all of the objects in the container that met some specific criteria. This **count()** function would only need to examine each object in its container. There would be no need to change any of the objects in any way.

### Write-Only Visitors

Iterator functions that only write to each object in a container are called *write-only* functions. An example of a write-only function would be a function that was designed to initialize each object in a container with some value or set of values. This function does not read each object; instead it writes values to each object in a collection or container. This type of iterator function is also a *mutator*, because it changes values in the objects.

### Read/Write Visitors

Iterator functions that can both read and write values of objects that are held in a collection or a container are called read/write iterator functions. An example of a read/write function would be a database update function that is used to read each object in a collection or container and depending on the values that are found in the object update that object with new values.

### Remove or Replace Visitors

Most collections and containers provide member functions that allow the user to remove one, a range, or all the objects that are in the container. Likewise, some collections allow the user to replace one, a range, or all the objects in a container with other objects. These types of iterator functions are called removal iterator functions or replacing iterator functions. They are read-only iterator functions because they don't change data members within an object. These functions either remove the object or replace the object in its entirety with another object.

## SPECIAL-PURPOSE DATA MEMBERS CALLED ITERATORS

An iterator is best described as an *object-oriented, polymorphic, generalized pointer*. The iterator can be a data member of the collection or container. The iterator can be implemented with friend member functions and other similar techniques, but usually the iterator is implemented as a separate but cooperating class with the collection or container it is designed for. The iterator provides a method to perform sequential total object visitation. The iterator acts as a kind of *cursor* into the collection or container class pointing to a specific object. In fact, sometimes iterators are called cursors. Once the iterator has reached the required object, the iterator can be used to access that object. Some iterators provide the * dereferencing operation and can be dereferenced just like traditional C++ pointers. Other iterators provide member functions like **current()**, which return either pointers or references to the objects that the iterator is referring to. The iterator, like a pointer, can be moved sequentially through the container by calling member functions like **next()**, or **previous()**. Many iterators allow the ++, or −−, or += , or *= notation to be used to navigate through a group of objects. Because iterators are usually implemented as separate classes, more than one iterator can be associated with a collection or container object simultaneously. This means that several types of iteration may be applied to the collection and container at once, providing the programmer with extremely flexible object visitation. Iterator processing can be divided into two fundamental types: *sequential iterators*, and *direct access* (or *random access*) *iterators*.

### Sequential Iterators

Sequential Iterators are iterators that move through a collection or container one object at a time. Using a sequential iterator the user cannot just jump into the middle of the container. If the user wants to get to the third object in the container, then the user must iterate through the first and second objects. Sequential iterators can move in forward or backward in a collection or container. Sequential iterators normally use the ++, −−, **next()**, or **previous()** notations. For instance, an iterator called MySet iterator using forward sequential iteration might look something like this:

```
MySet++,
   or
MySet.next()
```

or using reverse or backward iteration might look something like this:

MySet$--$
  or
MySet.previous

These iterators, whether forward or backward, would return either the location, a pointer, or a reference to the object that they were referring to.

### *Direct Access (or Random Access) Iterators*

Direct access iterators do not need to process the top half of the container before accessing an object in the middle of the container. A good example of a direct access iterator is the [] subscript operator for vectors and arrays. By using the [] subscript operator and specifying and index value, the user can directly access any object in the container. For instance, to access the fifth object in a vector container, the user could specify:

MyVector[5]

This would return either a pointer or reference to the fifth object in the vector container. The designation direct access is more accurate than random access. Random access insinuates a blind or unspecified choice. While it is possible to use the [] subscript operator to achieve randomness, direct access is usually what's meant. Direct access can be implemented with the [] subscript operator, or the $+=$ or $*=$ notations. For instance:

MyVector $+= 5$

would move the **MyVector** iterator five objects away from where it currently is.

## TWO APPROACHES TO IMPLEMENTING COLLECTIONS AND CONTAINERS

There are two important approaches to structuring collection and container classes: *object-based structuring*, and *template-based structuring*. While the result of both approaches is a collection or container class that will support containment functionality, insertion operations, removal operations, and total object visitation, the approaches offer radically different design and development philosophies. Each approach has its own memory management policies, code management policies, efficiency tradeoffs, and class component structuring. Object-based structuring relies heavily upon polymorphism and inheritance, and produces highly vertical structures of collections and containers. Template-based structuring relies heavily upon the genericity capabilities of the template construct in C++, and produces horizontal structures of collections and containers. The object-based approach tends to require deep knowledge of class relationships and class hierarchies, and requires the programmer to specialize the collection or container through virtual member functions. The template-based approach tends to require that the programmer understand fat interfaces (see Stroustrup 1991, 452) and requires the programmer to develop one-size-fits-all interfaces for the collections and containers.

Object-based structuring starts with the general and moves to the specific through inheritance. Template-based structuring starts with the specific and moves to the general through fat interfaces. The structuring technique used is often a compromise between design philosophy and efficiency. Using the specification of certain object-oriented philosophies, object-based structuring is the most appropriate approach. This is especially the case for projects that use classes to model and simulate real-world concepts. For these projects it is critical that the class interfaces model or simulate the real-world concepts as closely as possible. Vertical class hierarchies can carry a lot of information. Object-based hierarchies act as *taxonomy maps* that can be used as knowledge representation mechanisms capturing domain and concept knowledge in the hierarchical structure of the collection. Under other conditions and requirements template-based structuring is the most appropriate. There is no single best way to structure a collection or container class. The implementation will be dictated by the environment in which and for which it is developed.

## Object-Based Structuring

Many of the object-oriented techniques and concepts that are used in C++ programming have been borrowed from other object-oriented languages. Several of the well-known concepts such as methods, class attributes, and object-based collection and container classes were borrowed either directly or indirectly from the Smalltalk-80 language. Smalltalk is an object-oriented language that was produced by the Concepts Group at the Xerox Palo Alto Research Center. Where C++ is a general-purpose language that supports object-oriented programming, Smalltalk is a purely object-oriented language that only supports object-oriented programming. In the Smalltalk language everything is an *object*. One of the powerful components of the Smalltalk environment is the collection class library. The collection class library in Smalltalk-80 is an object-based library. When we use the phrase *object-based* we are referring to a type of class hierarchy where every class must be derived from some common ancestor. For instance, Figure 3.9 shows a class relationship diagram for some of the Smalltalk collection classes. All container classes in the Smalltalk library are descended from the *Collection* class.

### THE NIH (NATIONAL INSTITUTE OF HEALTH) CLASS LIBRARY

The structure of the Smalltalk container class library became the model for early C++ container class libraries. One such container library was the NIH container library. The NIH container library was developed by Keith Gorlen, Sandy Orlow, and Perry Plexico of the National Institutes of Health, and is well documented in their (1990) book *Data Abstraction and Object-Oriented Programming in C++*. Figure 3.10 shows the class relationship diagram for the NIH container class library. Notice the similarity between the Smalltalk collection hierarchy in Figure 3.9 and the NIH container class hierarchy in Figure 3.10. The NIH Class library consists of over 60 C++ classes. In the NIH containers, as in the Smalltalk containers, all container classes are descended from the collection class, and the collection class is descended from the object class. The *Collection* or *Object* class in this type of hierarchy we refer to as *object based*, since every container class has an ancestor.

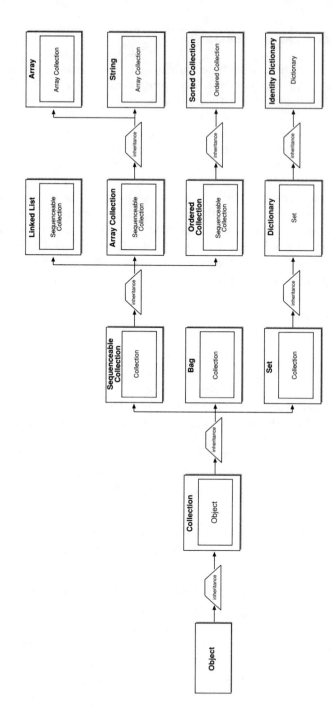

**Figure 3.9** The class relationship diagram for the Smalltalk collection classes.

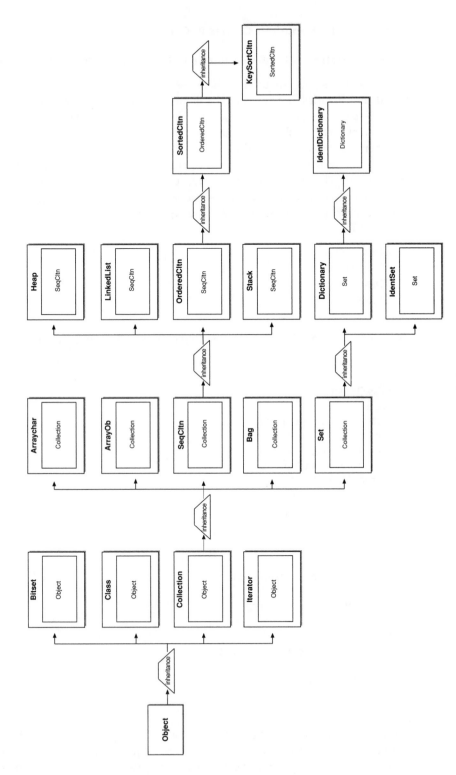

**Figure 3.10** The class relationship diagram for NIH container class library.

## THE FUNDAMENTALS OF AN OBJECT-BASED COLLECTION OR CONTAINER

Throughout this book we use the NIH class library structure when we refer to object-based class libraries, because the NIH library is a solid, robust implementation that is publicly available, and it is a good representative of all the libraries that were later modeled after the Smalltalk-80 collection.

When implementing an object-based collection or container, a generic *object* class must first be designated and a generic base class for that collection or container must first be designed. The class *object* will represent the base class for all objects that will be inserted into the containers. The class *collection* will usually act as the generic base class for all containers. The class *object* will usually provide virtual functions that supply:

Object identification
Object copying
Object comparing
Object printing

A simplified version of the generic class **Object** could be specified with the class keyword in C++.

```
class Object{
protected:
  string Class Description;
public:
  Object(void);
  string description(void);
  void description(string S);
};
Object::Object(void)
{
  ClassDescription = " ";
}
string Object::description(void)
{
  return(ClassDescription);

}
void Object:::description(string S)
{
  ClassDescription = S;
}
```

Once we have this generic **Object** class, then we can declare any class that will need to be placed in a container to be a descendent of type 'Object'. For instance, if we were going to store an object of type **binary_number** from Chapter 2 in a vector class we would have to make **binary_number** a descendent of **Object**:

```
class binary_number : public Object{
};
```

The class collection will usually provide virtual member functions that apply to all container classes (see Gorlen, Orlow, and Plexico 1991, 152). For instance, the collection class would provide virtual member functions to:

Insert or add an object into a container
Remove an object from a container
Return the number of objects in a container
Return the capacity of the container
Test for an empty container
Test for a particular object within the container

We could declare a simplified version of the collection class as follows:

```
class collection{
protected:
   int Size;
public:
   collection(int Sz) {Size = Sz};
   virtual void insert(Object & X) = 0;
   virtual int size(void)= 0;
   virtual int empy(void) = 0;
};
```

This simplified version of the collection class has pure virtual functions in it. This means that we could not declare an object to be of type **collection**, because any class that has a pure virtual function in it is called an *abstract base* class. Abstract base classes cannot have direct instances. Instead the abstract base class acts as a minimum implementation policy for all classes that are descendants. Any class that inherits an abstract base class and fails to define member functions for the pure virtuals that are in the base class is itself an abstract base class. See Chapter 2 for a discussion of pure virtuals, and abstract base classes. Once a derived class has definitions for all the pure virtuals then that derived class can have a runtime instance.

Let's say we wanted to make a vector container that could hold our **binary_number** class. The declaration would look something like the code in Listing 3.1:

### Listing 3.1

// Object-Based Vector Example

```
class vector : public collection:
protected:
   Object *V;
   int Pos;
public:
   vector(int Sz);
```

```
        ~vector(void);
        void insert(Object *X);
        int size(void);
        int empty(void);
        Object operator[](int N);
};

vector::vector(int Sz) : collection(Sz)
{
    Pos = 0;
    V = new Object[Sz];
}

vector::~vector(void)
{
    delete [] V;
}

void vector::invert(Object &X)
{
    V[Pos] = X;
    Pos++;
}

Object vector::operator[](int N)
{
    return(V[N]);
}
int vector::size(void)
{
    return(Size);
}

int vector::empty(void)
{
    if(Size == 0){
        return(1);
    }
    else{
        return(0);
    }
}

void main(void)
{
    vector MyVector;
    binary_number Number('10010001');
    MyVector.insert(Number);
}
```

### How Do Object-Based Collections Work?

The object-based collection and container depends heavily upon runtime polymorphism and inheritance. In order for this simplified **vector** in code Listing 3.1 to work, many of the key concepts in object-oriented programming are put into play, such as *generic object inheritance, generic collection inheritance*, and *runtime polymorphism*.

### Generic Object Inheritance

The **binary_number** class in code Listing 3.1 has to be derived from the **Object** class. This is because the *collection* class only deals with objects that are derived from the **Object** class, or descendants from the **Object** class. This is one of the techniques that gives a container the ability to hold heterogeneous groups of objects. Since every type of object that can be placed in the container will be descended from type **Object**, the container can hold mixed types. For instance, if I derive a rational class from type **Object** and my **binary_number** class has been derived from type **Object** then I may place instances of the rational class, as well as instances of the **binary_number** class into the container because both classes are descended from type **Object**.

### Generic Collection Inheritance

When using an *object-based* scheme the *collection* class or any other class that provides the minimum implementation pattern for derived classes is an abstract base class. This class will provide the minimum protocol for all derived classes in the form of pure virtual member functions. By providing a container-relative definition for the pure virtual functions in the base class, the derived class will implement the fundamental container requirements. This implies that there is a cooperative relationship between the designer of the container class and the user of the container class. Object-based containers and collections require the user to *finish* the functionality of the collection or container that will be used. The ultimate ancestors in object-based collections are usually incomplete and must be finished by the user of the class. In the case of the abstract base class 'collection,' the user of the collection class must supply definitions for the pure virtuals. After a fully functional derived class has been implemented, further classes may be derived from the fully functional derived class. Bjarne Stroustrup refers to these types of classes as *node classes*. (See Stroustrup 1991, 439.)

The programmer can specialize the collections and containers through defining the pure virtual functions and overriding the regular virtual functions when working with object-based collections and containers. This technique is at the heart of object-oriented programming. The technique of overriding virtual functions provides the programmer with the ability to customize class libraries. With this technique the programmer can adapt a class or class library to his or her specific needs.

### Object-Based Polymorphism

Polymorphism allows a single interface with multiple implementations. If we have a class called **Number** with two descendants, **complex_number**, and **rational_number**, we can illustrate how polymorphism works. The base class **Number** may provide a virtual **add()** member function, and a virtual + operation. The class **complex_number** inherits the class **Number** and overrides the **add()** member function and + operation. The class

**rational_number** also inherits the class **Number** and overrides the **add()** member function and the + operation. All three classes have an **add()** member function and a + operation. Although they all look the same (single interface), each class implements the **add()** and + operation differently (multiple implementations).

Let's look back at the declaration for the abstract base class **collection**. This class provides the services of insertions through the

```
void insert(Object &X);
```

member function. However, in code Listing 3.1 we called the **insert()** member function with an object of type **binary_number**, not an object of type **Object**. Why did the insert call accept an object of type **binary_number**? Well, the call resolution that happens here is at the core of runtime polymorphism. The C++ language specification allows a reference or pointer to a base class to accept references or pointers to any derived class. This mechanism is what permits the object-based containers to work. By ensuring that all objects that will be placed in the containers are derived from a common base class the programmer is opening the way for the use of runtime polymorphism. Once code has been written to insert either a reference to or a pointer to an object of type **Object** into a container, then any runtime object of type **Object** or any descendent of type **Object** may be placed into that container. This is the reason for requiring a common base class. The common base class can then be used as a placeholder in the abstract class **collection**. So, every time the abstract base class needs to refer to the type of object that will be contained, the abstract base class can use the common base class **Object**. In this way both the common base classes **Object** and the common base class **collection** serve as placeholders for future derived classes. The abstract base class **collection** will represent all future collections and containers, and the abstract base class **Object** will represent all future objects. This allows the programmer to generalize the code relationships between future objects and collections. Although this is an oversimplified description of the process and components, it does describe the basic mechanics of all *object-based* collections and containers.

### *Memory Management Policies of Object-Based Collections and Containers*

The destructor for an object determines how the memory that the object uses is released. When a local object goes out of scope, the destructor for that object is automatically called. When the delete operation is used on an object, then the object's destructor is called. What happens to a group of pointers to objects that have global scope and that have been placed into a container that has local scope, when the container leaves the local scope? Containers and collections are objects and they have to have destructors. Should the container's destructor delete all the objects that are in the container, or should the container destructor only release the memory that the container is responsible for? What happens when the container has global scope, and the objects that have been placed in the container only have local scope? If the flow of control leaves the scope of the locally declared objects, will the container still contain those objects? Another interesting problem that presents itself in collection and container memory management is what happens to a group of objects that have global scope and have been *removed* from a container that also has global scope?

Should the removal operation call the destructors of those objects, or should the destructors of those objects be called as they go out of scope? Who is responsible to call the destructors for the objects with global scope?

### Pointers to Objects and Memory Problems

Collections and containers can be designed to hold either objects or pointers to objects. When collections and containers hold pointers to objects, the scope and lifetime of the pointers must be carefully considered. If a group of pointers that were placed into a container is deleted manually, and the container still exists, then the container will contain *invalid pointers* that no longer point to objects. The converse of these invalid or dangling pointers is to delete a container that has active pointers in it. There is no way to get to those objects or the memory they occupy unless there are outside references to those pointers. As program execution continues objects will be allocated, but never deleted. This leads to something called *memory leakage*. Memory leakage is exactly what it sounds like. The program continues to use memory, but because of memory mismanagement the program is unable to account for all the memory that it started with. When deleting a container that has pointers to objects, without leaving a way to later delete those objects or without deleting the objects before deleting the container, memory leakage will occur. If memory leakage or dangling pointers are allowed to run rampant in a program, system failure is assured. Table 3.5 contains some container and collection memory management guidelines.

## Template-Based Structuring

*Template-based structuring* is a technique for implementing collection and container classes. In template-based structuring collections and containers are implemented using C++'s template construct. In fact, templates are used more to implement containers and

**Table 3.5   Collection and container memory management guidelines.**

*Collection and Container Memory Management Guidelines*

Optimally, collections, containers, and the objects they will hold should have the same scope and life span. Avoid scenarios that place containers with shorter life spans than the objects they hold.

If the container has a longer life span than the objects it contains, make sure that the container removes the objects before those objects go out of scope.

If the objects must have a longer life span than the container, make sure that there is some other way to access the objects after the container has been destroyed.

Before deleting pointers to objects that have been placed in a container, make sure the objects have been removed from the container; then the pointers to the objects can be deleted.

Provide consistent practices for the responsibility of deleting objects. A good policy is to let the user delete objects that he or she has created and let the container or collection delete objects that it has created. It is usually awkward to have a container delete objects that it does not own.

collections than to implement any other kind of structure. Whereas the *object-based* containers required that every object that was going to be stored had to be derived from a common ancestor, template-based collections and containers normally do not use this type of structuring. However, to have collections and containers that support heterogeneous mixtures a common base class can be used in conjunction with template-based structuring. Because all containers ultimately descend from the same type in the object-based scheme of implementing containers, the container hierarchy is largely vertical. This is in contrast to template-based containers, where most implementations of collections and containers have horizontal structures where each container has no relation to the next.

### TEMPLATE CONTAINERS ARE GENERIC

Because template classes are parameterized, the developer can design one collection or container that can be used to hold any group of objects. (See Chapter 2 for a review of templates.) An example of a container implemented with a template is shown in Listing 3.2, which declares a class named **vector**. The **vector** class is a simple template container.

### Listing 3.2

// This is a declaration for a simple vector template class

```
template<class T> class vector{
protected:
   T *V;
   int Size;
   int Pos;
public:
   vector(int Sz);
   ~vector(void);
   void add(T X);
   T operator[](int N);
};
```

This simple vector container is generic because it is not designed to hold any specific *kind* of object. Since **vector** was implemented with a template, then whatever parameter the template receives is the kind of object that the **vector** will hold. In Listing 3.2 the letter **T** is a placeholder for the type or kind of object that the vector container will hold. Everywhere in the declaration where the class needs to refer to the type of object that will be contained, the letter **T** is used. We use the letter **T** here only as a convention. Any legal variable name could be used in its place. When the user of this class declares an object of type **vector**, a type must be supplied as part of the declaration. For instance:

```
vector<int> MyVector(10);
vector<char> MyVector(10);
vector<float> MyVector(10);
vector<long double> MyVector(10);
```

all declare a **vector** object that holds 10 elements. The first declaration specifies a vector of 10 integers. The second declaration specifies a vector of 10 chars and so on. Although we use **int, char, float** and **long double**, which are all built-in types, we could have made a declaration using a user-defined class. For example, to declare a vector of 10 **binary-_number** objects that we defined in Chapter 2, we would use the following declaration:

```
vector<binary_number> MyVector(10);
```

A close examination of the declaration in Listing 3.2 and the declarations of **MyVector** highlights one of the important features of template classes, namely, the notion of genericity. Because although we used vectors of type **int, char, float, long double**, and **binary_number**, we only had *one* definition for the **vector** class. With the object-based approach to container implementation we would have two choices. Either we could have **int, char, float, long double** and **binary_number** all descend from some common ancestor like **Object**, or we would have to implement a different container for each family of classes. With the template notion we only have to implement one container, and this container is capable of holding any class, user-defined class, or built-in type in C++. The code in Listing 3.3 shows the definitions of the member functions for the simple vector container. In a production version of a vector container there are many more member functions and exception handling in place. The member functions that are shown in Listing 3.3 are presented to illustrate how parameterized types and template-based containers are structured.

### Listing 3.3

```
// These are the member functions for the vector class shown in Listing 3.2
template<class T> vector<T>::vector(int Sz)
{
  Size = Sz;
  V = new T[Size];
  Pos = 0;
}

template<class T> vector<T>::~vector(void)
{
  delete[] V;
}
template<class T> void vector<T>::add(T X)
{
  if(Pos < Size){
    V[Pos] = X;
    Pos++;
  }
}

template<class T> T vector<T>::operator[](int N)
{
  return(V[N]);
}
```

Notice that **V** is a pointer to type **T** in Listing 3.2. The **T** represents the type of object the vector will be used to hold. Now look at the constructor for **vector** in Listing 3.3. The constructor is building a vector of type **T** with (Size * **sizeof(T)**) number of memory locations. Although we do not yet know what type of object we will be allocating space for, we are able to write the constructor using **T** as a placeholder for the object type. This mechanism is at the heart of the template-based containers. We can specify the behavior that the container is to have without specifying the type that the container is to hold. For this reason template containers are said to be *generic* structures.

The simple vector in Listing 3.3 illustrates one of the primary techniques that containers use to hold objects. Notice that **V** is a pointer to an object of type **T**. **V** will be used to point to the beginning memory location or block of memory, called the *storage component*, where the objects are to be stored. In the constructor for **vector** in Listing 3.3 the statement

```
V = new T[Size];
```

dynamically allocates enough space to hold **Size** number of objects of type **T**. The objects that will be placed in this container will be stored in the block of memory that is pointed to by **V**. This introduces one of the primary characteristics of collections and containers. That is, collection and container objects will have a storage component that is *reserved* and used only to store other groups of objects. In the declaration in Listing 3.3, **V** points to the block of memory that the vector object reserves.

This reserved block of memory or storage component can be organized in many ways. In the vector example in Listing 3.3 the block of memory is organized as a set of contiguous memory locations that can be accessed by an index or position. The statement

```
return(V[N]);
```

in Listing 3.3 returns the object that is located at the Nth position or index relative to **V**, which is the beginning of the memory block. This form of organization allows the user of the container to have *direct access* to the objects that are stored. The major requirement for this kind of memory usage is that the size of the memory block must be specified when the container is constructed.

Note: There is a difference between dynamic structures and static structures that have been dynamically allocated. A dynamic structure can change in size during the execution of a program. The memory for that structure can grow or shrink. A static structure is a structure that does not change in size once it has been allocated. A static structure can be allocated at compile time or at runtime. When it is allocated at runtime it is said to be *dynamically allocated*. However, it is not a dynamic structure.

Although the block of memory pointed to by **V** in Listing 3.3 is dynamically allocated, it is a static structure. The reserved block of memory could also be organized as a *linked list*. In the case of a linked list the memory block would be a dynamic structure. Containers or collections that implement reserved memory as dynamic structures are called dynamic containers or dynamic collections. The number of objects that will be placed in dynamic collections and containers does not need to be known in advance. As the program executes, objects can be placed into the container, and the size of the memory block will be increased. As objects are removed from the container, the size of the memory block will decrease. Whereas the simple **vector** class in Listing 3.3 provides direct access to the objects, dynamic collection and containers traditionally supply either sequential or relational access to the objects they hold. However, direct access containers can be implemented using dynamic structures. If the memory that the collection or container uses to store objects in is located on some external storage medium, then that collection or container is called *persistent*. We discuss possibilities for persistent collections in Chapter 9.

## THE CLASS INTERFACE DETERMINES THE TYPE OF COLLECTION OR CONTAINER

The collection or container's *implementation* refers to how the reserved block of memory is accessed. How the container is used by the programmer is referred to as the container's *logical representation*. The set of member functions or services that the collection or container provides the programmer with determines the *logical representation*. A container could provide **push()**, **pop()**, **top()**, and **empty()** services to the outside world presenting the view of a stack, while managing the reserved block of memory as a vector. The vector would be the implementation of the container, while the stack would be the logical representation of the container. Thus collections and containers have at least a *dual* nature: They have an implementation and a representation. Sometimes these two are the same, and sometimes not. This opens the door to many combinations. For instance, a queue could be implemented by a vector, a vector could be implemented by a list, a list could be implemented by a vector, a set could be implemented by a list, and so on. It is the class interface that determines how we classify a collection or container, not its implementation. If the class interface presents a graph, and the container uses sets as the implementation structures, the container is called a graph, not a collection of sets.

## TEMPLATE CONTAINERS AND COOPERATIVE USE

The template container specifies its operations in the most general of terms. The goal is to refer to parameters for object types and to use operations that all objects that could be placed in the container are expected to have. In Listing 3.3 the vector class implements an add member function:

```
template<class T> void vector<T>::add(T X)
{
  if(Pos < Size){
  if(Pos < Size){
    V[Pos] = X;
    Pos++;
  }
 }
 }
```

Looking at this function we cannot tell what specific type of object will be added. We can only say that an object of type **T** will be added. Also, in order for this function to work, that object must provide the assignment operator in order to accommodate the

V[Pos] = X;

statement. Since **V** is of type **T**, and **X** is of type **T**, the compiler must have access to a method that can perform assignments of objects of type **T**. Notice that the vector class does not specify any assignment operation definitions. These definitions must come from the designer of type **T**. In this way using collection and container objects means cooperation between the collection and container designer and the programmer. Most collections and containers will require a minimum set of operations to be defined by the client of the container. These operations normally include:

Assignment
Constructor(s)
Destructor(s)
Copy construction
Some subset of the relation operators (<, >, >=, <=, !=. ==)

Although it is not absolutely necessary to have these operations as a part of every class, in general it is a good rule of thumb to provide them. These operations are traditionally referred to as the *minimal standard interface*. There are good arguments for and arguments against the absolute inclusion in every class of the minimal standard interface (see Carroll, Ellis 1995, 18). However, to use most popular collection and container objects, most if not all of these operations will be required. This is referred to as *client responsibility*. Because the designer of the collection or container class provides part of the functionality, and the client or user of the collection or container class supplies part of the functionality, collections and containers are said to be client-server structures.

## ALGORITHMS, MEMBER FUNCTIONS, AND COLLECTION BEHAVIOR

The behavior of a collection or container is determined by its member functions. How the programmer or a client sees a collection or container is determined by its interface. We want to distinguish between the class interface (logical view of the structure) and the class behavior. The class interface is the list of services and the access policies that are presented to the user of a class. The access polices and services available depend on whether the user of a class is a class member, descendent, or the outside world. Descendants can access at most the protected and public services and data in a class. The outside world can access at most the public services and data in a class. The private data and member functions are off limits to all except the native members of the class. Available services and access policies are only a subset of class behavior. To understand the complete behavior of a class we must have access to all member functions: public, protected, and private.

### What Is an Algorithm?

An algorithm is a finite list of unambiguous steps that specify the solution to a problem or execution of a task. The word *algorithm* has mathematical origins and is associated with the name of a famous Persian mathematician, Abu Ja'far Mohammed Ibn Musa Al-Khowarizmi (A.D. 825). The word is used heavily in the disciplines of computer science and mathematics. There are many famous sorting, searching, parsing, traversing, and computation algorithms that are used in conjunction with collection and container classes. While it is not necessary to master the concept of algorithms, it is necessary to have a basic understanding of how they are used to implement member functions, and how they affect the behavior of a collection or container class. An understanding of the algorithms that have been used to implement member functions of container and collection classes can help to determine which collection or container object is appropriate for the problem at hand. Table 3.6 lists the six types of algorithms and their basic uses.

Algorithms are independent of any computer language. Algorithms can be represented in plain English. For instance, an algorithm for printing a list of files that are stored on a computer could be stated in English as follows:

Step 1. Change to the directory containing the files to printed.
Step 2. Pick the next file alphabetically that has not already been printed if there is one.
Step 3. If a file was chosen in step 2, then print it, otherwise STOP.
Step 4. Do Step 2.

Algorithms can be represented mathematically. For instance:

$$SUM(X)=\sum_{I=1}^{N} (X-1)+1$$

Algorithms can be represented in pseudocode. Pseudocode is a mix of English (or some other natural language) and some set of computer constructs. The set of constructs usually include looping constructs, decision constructs, assignment constructs, and some file constructs. The advantage of using pseudocode is that the programmer can specify the logic for a routine or computer program without having to worry about syntax, or other language-specific features, and requirements. Pseudocode captures the list of steps and the logic. Pseudocode is used as a design tool as well as a means of informal communication of routines or algorithms. An algorithm expressed in pseudocode could be written as follows:

```
Start
Set N = 10
Set X = 6
Set I = 1
Set SUM = 0
While I <= N
    SUM = (X − 1) + 1
    I = I + 1
End While
Stop
```

**Table 3.6　Six types of algorithms and some of their basic uses.**

| Types of Algorithms | Description |
|---|---|
| **Mathematical Algorithms** | These include the fundamental methods from arithmetic to numerical analysis. These methods include algorithms for: addition and multiplication of integers; polynomials, matrices, and algorithms for solving problems which arise in contexts of random number generation; solution of simultaneous equations; data fitting; and integration. These are only examples of types of mathematical algorithms. |
| **Sorting** | These methods are concerned with the rearranging of files or objects into some type of order. These algorithms include priority queues, selection, merging, linear, bubble, shell, and quick sorts. |
| **Searching** | These methods are concerned with finding things in files or containers. They include binary search trees, balanced trees, hashing, digital search trees, and methods appropriate for very large files. |
| **String Processing** | These algorithms include a range of methods for dealing with long sequences of characters. String searching leads to pattern matching, which leds to parsing. File compression techniques and cryptology are also included. |
| **Geometric Algorithms** | These algorithms include a collection of methods for solving problems involving points and lines and other simple geometric objects. |
| **Graph Algorithms** | These methods are concerned with fundamental connectivity problems, which include shortest-path, minimal spanning tree, network flow, and matching. |

Flowcharts can also be used to express algorithms. A *flowchart* is a tool used for visualizing a sequence of steps or the logic of a computer program, procedure, or function. Although flowcharts had taken a backseat to other design tools, the introduction of graphic editors and flowcharting software have revitalized them as a useful design tool. A summary of the common flowcharting symbols can be found in Appendix B. The flowchart in Figure 3.11 expresses a binary search algorithm.

## The Five Basic Requirements for All Algorithms

In order for a set of steps or list of instructions to be considered an algorithm, it must meet at least five criteria: *finiteness, unambiguity and detail, effectiveness, correctness,* and *measurability.*

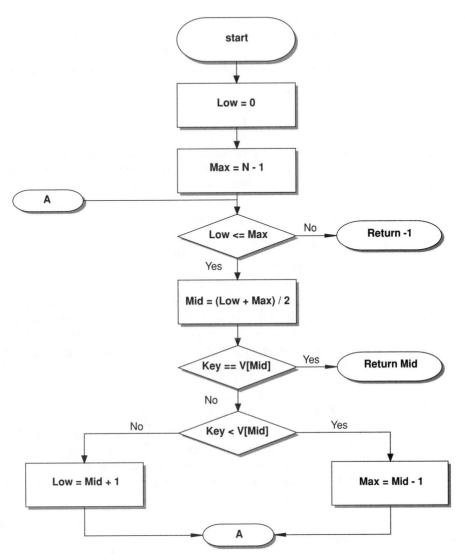

**Figure 3.11**  A flowchart of the binary search algorithm.

## FINITENESS

The set of steps or list of instructions must specify actions that have a definite stopping point. If the steps are not finite then the solution will never be reached or the task will never be accomplished. Since it is the main purpose of an algorithm to specify the solution to a problem or sequence of steps for a task, a list of instructions that does not specify a halting step or *stopping case* is not an algorithm. For instance, the sequence of steps

N = 1
While N < ∞ Do

```
    N = N + 1
EndDo
```

is not an algorithm because $N$ will never reach $\infty$; therefore this process will never stop.

## No Ambiguity

Every action specified at any step of an algorithm must be precisely defined. This means that every action must be clear and not subject to different interpretations. For example, the following procedure is only a potential algorithm.

Step 1. Get a list of 10 numbers.
Step 2. Sort the list of numbers.
Step 3. Print all very large numbers.
Step 4. Stop.

It fails in step 2 and step 3. In step 2 the order the numbers are to be sorted in is not specified. When we get to step 2 we don't know whether to sort the numbers into descending order or ascending order. Step 2 is not detailed enough. In step 3 how does one determine which are the *very large* numbers? This sequence of steps does not constitute an algorithm because step 2 needs more detail and step 3 is ambiguous.

## Effectiveness

Every algorithm must consist of effective steps. This means that each step that an algorithm specifies must be executable. If a list of instructions specifies a step that cannot be done, then we do not have an algorithm. This requirement is closely related to the finite stipulation, because a step that cannot be completed because it cannot be done would not allow the algorithm to halt.

## Correctness

The algorithm must produce the appropriate results based on the conditions and input given. The algorithm must produce the same results every time the same conditions or input is given. A sequence of steps that does not solve the problem it is designed to solve, or that only sometimes solves the problem it is designed to solve, is not an algorithm. The study of algorithm correctness occupies much of the computer scientist's time, and entire books have been dedicated to the topic of algorithm correctness.

## Measurability

If there is no way to measure the steps in an algorithm, then we cannot know whether it is finite or whether it is correct. The consequences of each action in an algorithm must be observable or verifiable in some fashion. A sequence of steps must meet at least the five criteria (see page 116) to be considered an algorithm. If we know that we are dealing with bona fide algorithms, then the behaviors of collections or containers that depend on algorithms can be predicted. Predictability impacts the design, testing, and usefulness of a collection or container class. If we can predict the behavior of an algorithm or member function, then we can measure its performance. If we can measure the performance of the algorithms and member functions for a container, then we can determine which collections or containers best meet our needs.

## Relationships between Algorithms and Class Member functions

Class member functions, sometimes called *methods*, are either functions or procedures. While all algorithms can be considered either procedures or functions, not all procedures and functions are algorithms. Table 3.7 shows the five relationships that normally exist between class member functions and algorithms. They are as follows:

1. Multiple member functions implement a single algorithm
2. A single member function consisting of multiple algorithms
3. A single member function implemented by a single algorithm

**Table 3.7   A matrix showing the four relationships that normally exist between class member functions and algorithms. The fifth relationship is no relationship between the member function and the algorithm. This relationship is not shown on the matrix.**

|  | Single Algorithm | Multiple Algorithms |
|---|---|---|
| **Single Member Function** | 1 | 2 |
| **Multiple Member Functions** | 3 | 4 |

1. Single member function, single algorithm.
2. Single member function, multiple algorithms.
3. Multiple member functions, single algorithm.
4. Multiple member functions, multiple algorithms.
5. Member function, no algorithm.

    4. A single member function as only part of an algorithm

    5. Member functions not related to algorithms

A class member function may be as simple as one statement that returns a single value. On the other hand, a class member function may be very complex, consisting of an algorithm or collection of algorithms that work to contribute to part of the behavior of the class. Algorithms play major roles in the behavior of collection and container classes. This is because the normal use of collections and containers involve iteration mechanisms, storage mechanisms, removal mechanisms, sorting mechanisms, and searching mechanisms.

## A Classic Algorithm

We are all familiar with the notion of a *factorial*. Mathematically, $n$ factorial is represented as $n!$. Recall that $n$ factorial is computed as follows:

$$n! = n(n-1)(n-2)\ldots(2)(1)$$

This is a mathematical representation of the algorithm for $n!$. We could also represent the algorithm for $n!$ in plain English:

    Step 1. Initialize the variable for which the factorial will be computed.

    Step 2. Multiply the variable successively by all the positive integers less than the variable.

This algorithm could also be represented by a flowchart so that we could pictorially see the logic that computes the factorial. Figure 3.12 is a flowchart of the steps used to calculate the factorial.

After we are sure that the algorithm works, the final step is to convert the algorithm into a form suitable for execution by a computer. In our case we will convert all the algorithms into the C++ language. Care must be taken during the conversion of the algorithm from one form to another. It is easy to change a working, correct algorithm into a computer program, procedure, or function that does not work. Each step in the algorithm must be converted, while retaining its meaning and relationship with the rest of the algorithm. The program in Listing 3.4 shows a C++ program that represents the mathematical notion of a factorial. The program was converted from the flowchart shown in Figure 3.12.

### Listing 3.4

```
// This program is a conversion of the algorithm shown in the flowchart in Figure
3.12

#include <iostream.h>

int factorial(int N)
{
    int X = N;
```

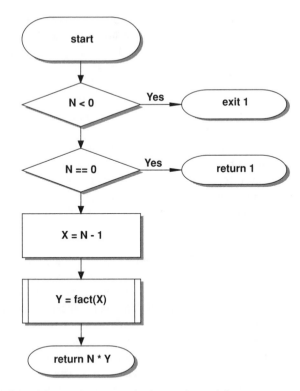

**Figure 3.12** A flowchart on how to calculate a factorial.

```
if(N == 0){
   return(1);
}
X--;
return(N * factorial(X));
}
void main(int Argc, char *Argv[])
{
  if(Argc == 2){
     cout << factorial(abs(atoi(Argv[1])));
}
else{
      cout << "Synatax: fact Num";
}
}
```

The factorial function in Listing 3.4 is an example of a recursive algorithm. A recursive algorithm is an algorithm that calls itself to solve a problem or execute a task (see Sedgewick 1983, 11 for a detailed discussion of recursion). The use of recursion in this example illustrates the *stopping case*, one of the important requirements for all algorithms. In order for a recursive procedure or function to terminate and not call itself forever, there must be some stopping case. All algorithms have this requirement. In the factorial function in Listing 3.4 the stopping case is when $N$ is equal to 0. Given that this function is passed an integer, and the program is not interrupted in the middle of processing, $N$ will necessarily reach 0, because of the line '$X--$'. Because we take the [$N$] prior to it being passed to the function, the proper result is guaranteed.

Notice the line that has $X--$ in Listing 3.4. This statement is one of the keys to the algorithm. This statement insures that we will be multiplying the original value by all the integers less than the original value. This brings us to a fundamental characteristic of all algorithms. Namely, algorithms build paths from some *input state* to some *output state*. Given some input or input state, the algorithm moves from the initial state performing transformations until those transformations meet the conditions of the stopping case. In the factorial program in Listing 3.4 the transformation was the decrementing of the variable $X$ in the statement '$X--$'. This transformation ultimately caused factorial to call itself with a value of 0 causing the recursion to cease. We see that the factorial function meets the five basic requirements of all algorithms. The factorial function is finite. The stopping case is '$N==0$'. It is unambiguous, and it is effective because we have implemented it in the C++ language, and it has passed the compiler. Therefore the level of detail is sufficient, and all operations are capable of being executed. The program is correct. However, algorithm proving is beyond the scope of this book. The reader is referred to Sedgewick's *Algorithms* for an introduction to the topic, and the many mathematical texts that address the topic of proofs, or proof by induction. The factorial algorithm is measurable because it returns values that we can examine. We can conclude that we have a C++ representation for the factorial algorithm because all five criteria have been met. The factorial function is useful and can easily be made a member function for a container object. In this case the member function would have a one-to-one relationship with the algorithm. In other words, the algorithm would directly implement the member function. See Table 3.7 for the relationships between member functions and algorithms.

## Algorithm Analysis and O Notation

There is usually more than one algorithm that solves any particular problem or that executes any particular task. Therefore techniques have been developed that help us to measure algorithm performance. The ability to measure algorithm performance provides us with criteria whereby we can make intelligent choices about which algorithm best suits the problem at hand. Because the analysis of algorithms is a field of study within itself, we have occasion only to introduce the most rudimentary topics and techniques within the field. For an introductory treatment of algorithm analysis the reader is referred to *Algorithms in C++* by Robert Sedgewick.

### COMPONENTS OF ALGORITHMS

Table 3.8 shows the three basic components of all algorithms. The input state can be the original condition of a variable or set of variables. The input state serves as the *precondition* for the algorithm execution. The preconditions for the algorithm are the facts about the algorithm's operands and operators that are assumed to be true before the algorithm

**Table 3.8 An algorithm's three basic components are: an input state, a transformation, and an output state.**

| Input State | Transformation | Output State |
|---|---|---|
| 1. Input Values | 1. Operators | 1. Output Values |
| 2. Conditions | 2. Calculations | 2. Conditions |
| 3. Assertions | 3. Formulas | |
| 4. Rules | 4. Transitions | |

begins execution. Every algorithm must perform some kind of operation or transformation. If the algorithm doesn't perform a transformation or operations, then the algorithm cannot move toward its stopping case. If it does not eventually reach a stopping case then it is not an algorithm. The transformations can include assignment, exchange, comparison, calculation, counting, evaluation, iteration, recursion, reading, or writing. Once the transformations reach the stopping case then the algorithm has an output state. The output state will include any conditions that are true or values that are available at the time the stopping case has been reached. The output state must be measurable or verifiable in some manner. Therefore, the basic pattern of all algorithms is Input→Processing→Output.

One of the first places to start when analyzing algorithms is to evaluate their input state and problem space. Questions like how much input does the algorithm handle? Or how large is the search domain for the algorithm? Other questions include: How many simultaneous inputs does the algorithm take? How large or how small are the values? Once there is a basic understanding of the input state and algorithm preconditions then we can ask how the algorithm processes its input conditions or variables. How many times does it access each input value? How many steps does the algorithm have? How many times are the steps in an algorithm executed? How far does the algorithm search the problem space for a solution? How many times does it iterate over a set of values? As the number of values that an algorithm can process gets larger, how does the algorithm's behavior change? After questions of this type have been answered then we can start to compare algorithms to see which one is preferable. One of the primary ways of describing algorithm performance is by *O notation*.

## O Notation

Because a given algorithm may perform one way on one kind of computer and another way on another kind of computer, there is a problem with using speed as a measurement for algorithms. Also, some algorithms are data dependent and perform differently depending on the type of input they are processing. Further, some operating systems control when and where an algorithm will execute and for how long it will execute. For these reasons among others we use other methods for algorithm measurement or comparison. We ask: How does the algorithm perform relative to the size of the input? Or given an input state, what is the ratio or proportion of algorithm performance to an input size increase or input size decrease? So we use a notation that describes the relative or proportionate running time of an algorithm as it is compared with the size of the input. For instance, if $N$ is the number of data values that an algorithm processes, and if we say the algorithm has a performance of $N^2$, then we mean that if $N$ doubles, the algorithm will take four times as long to execute. If we say that the algorithm has a performance of $N^3$, then when $N$ doubles the algorithm will take 8 times as long to execute. We say that $N$ is *on the order of $N^2$*, or that $N$ is $O(N^2)$. So then big O is short for *on the order of*. Using this type of notation is just a means to talk about algorithms being measured either relative to each other or relative to the data set to be processed by the algorithm. All the measurements of the algorithm's performance are proportionate to the size of the input the algorithm's processes. Formally this type of measurement states how the algorithm is asymptotically bounded by a value, that is, $N^2$ (see Tenenbaum, Langsam, and Augenstein 1992, 318). Note that using big O notation we make no mention of how fast the computer is, or how many processors the computer has. These types of questions are beyond the control of someone who is performing algorithm analysis in a computer-independent manner. Now, if the particular processor is known and is available, then the algorithms may be compared directly and actual results can be used to determine which is best. This type of comparison, however, falls under the category of *benchmarking*. Table 3.9 contains some of the common measurements for algorithm performance. Note that algorithms that have constant running times have the best performance that can be achieved.

## METASTRUCTURES

Many of the commonly used collection and container classes have been taken from traditional computer science data structures. In particular, stacks, queues, arrays, trees, graphs, and lists are all traditional computer science data structures. These structures in their traditional forms can be accessed using non–object-oriented languages such as C, Pascal, Ada, and so on. However, when these structures are implemented using the object-oriented constructs they have more functionality and flexibility. Once a data structure is implemented as an object it then becomes practical and easier to have more than one such object. In C++ we can declare an array of objects, even if these objects happen to be queues or trees. Whereas in languages such as Modula2 or C the data structures are usually bound to a particular type. In C++ the collection and container objects can hold any other type of object, and some collections and containers can hold multiple types of objects simultaneously. The object-oriented constructs in C++ make it possible to pass collections of containers of objects as single parameters to functions. While this type of functionality is achievable in non–object-oriented languages, it is extremely difficult and programs that attempt this type of structuring push the non–object-oriented language beyond its intended use. This normally creates programs that are hard to understand and impossible to maintain.

We have found that object-oriented data structures go beyond the traditional use of data structures. Object-oriented data structure (collections and containers) can be used not only to hold data types both built in and user defined, but can be used to hold models, taxonomy hierarchies, and simulations. Object-oriented data structures are structures that can be designed to hold other complex structures. Because collection and container classes are object oriented they have the obvious benefits of inheritance and

**Table 3.9  Common running time performance measurements for algorithms.**

| Algorithm Function | Description |
| --- | --- |
| 1 | Most instructions of most programs are executed once or at most only a few times. If this is true, almost all the instructions of a program have a constant running time. |
| log N | When the running time of a program is logarithmic, the program gets slightly slower as N grows. This type of running time happens often when programs have to solve a big problem by converting it into a smaller problems. The size of the problem is cut by some constant fraction. The running time can be considered to be less than a "large" constant. The base of the logarithm changes the constant. |
| N | When the running time of a program is linear, it is generally the case that a small amount of processing is done on each input element. |
| N log N | This running time arises in algorithms that solve a problem by breaking it up into smaller subproblems and solving each subproblem independently. The subproblems are combined together for one solution. |
| $N^2$ | When the running time of an algorithm is quadratic, it is practical for use only on relatively small problems. Typically, quadratic running times arise in algorithms that process all pairs of data items (perhaps a double nested loop). |
| $N^3$ | An algorithm that processes triples of data items (perhaps a triple nested loop) has a cubic running time and is practical for use only on small problems. |
| $2^N$ | Very few algorithms with exponential running time are likely to be appropriate for practical use. These types of algorithms arise as "brute-force" solutions to problems. |

polymorphism. Iteration and structure access can have single interfaces and multiple implementations. This is simply not practical in non–object-oriented languages and therefore data structures that are implemented in these languages provide at best a subset of the functionality that collection and container classes provide. Because the collection and container classes can be inherited and specialized through virtual member functions, and because the collection and container classes can take advantage of encapsulation and polymorphism, and because the collection and container classes can be combined in almost endless ways to produce extremely rich object-oriented structures, we do not refer to it as simple data structures. In this book we refer to the collection and container classes as a *metastructure*. The prefix *meta* is taken from the Greek, meaning "beyond." Metastructures are superstructures. They provide more expressive structuring and access possibilities than traditional data structures. The object-oriented constructs available in C++ transform simple data structures into metastructures. Throughout this book we use the term metastructure when we are referring to the formal definition of collection and container classes.

## Two Categories of Metastructures

Metastructures can be divided into two basic categories: They are either *monolithic*, or *polylithic*. Monolithic metastructures are implemented using a single structure, and cannot be understood as containing more than one structure. Polylithic metastructures are implemented using more than one collection or container class. Polylithic structures can be understood as being constructed of multiple structures. A vector container is a good example of a monolithic metastructure. A vector cannot be divided into other structures. A graph is a good example of a polylithic metastructure. A graph consists of two sets. The sets have their own independent interfaces. The graph has an interface that is supported by the interfaces and functionality of the two sets. The graph can be broken down and understood as a collection of structures. All collections and containers can be considered either monolithic or polylithic.

CHAPTER 4

# THE STANDARD TEMPLATE LIBRARY

THE STANDARD Template Library (commonly referred to as the STL) is one of the latest additions to the C++ language. It was accepted by the ANSI committee in July 1994 to be added to the C++ language standard. The STL was originally developed at Hewlett-Packard Laboratories. The STL adds to the C++ language a set of standard collection and container classes, as well as a collection of general-purpose generic algorithms. The STL consists of five basic components: *containers, iterators, adaptors, function objects,* and *algorithms.*

The STL is a flat template-based library. This is in contrast to the traditional *object-based* collection and container libraries. There are very few class hierarchies in the STL. Whereas traditional collection and container class libraries have been vertical and driven by inheritance and polymorphism, the STL is horizontal and is driven by genericity and templates. The STL containers have fat interfaces (see Stroustrup 1991, 452). This is in contrast to the object-based collection and container classes that have interfaces that are based on taxonomy hierarchies. Because the STL is based on templates, it can be used with user-defined objects as well as built-in types. The STL emphasizes the genericity constructs in C++ and favors heavy uses of templates and pointers. Encapsulation of the container functionality is relaxed in the STL. Instead of each container class being a self-contained bundle of data and functions, the STL containers only implement a minimum of the behavior required for the class. The majority of the container's behavior is implemented by the STL's generic algorithms. In this way, the containers and the algorithms form *cooperative patterns* as opposed to encapsulated objects. (For a discussion of software building using pattern classes see Soukup 1994, 48.) The STL provides a balance between the goals of object-oriented programming and the goals of genericity.

In this chapter we discuss the five basic components of the STL. Although all C++ compilers don't currently include the STL library, most current C++ compilers can compile STL code. We have included the public domain version of the STL on the disk accompanying this book. The library can be adapted to any compiler that has good template support. Also compiler-specific memory management will have to be dealt with. The collection and container classes and all examples in the remainder of this book will be implemented using the STL.

## STL CONTAINERS

The STL has seven fundamental containers: vector, deque, list, set, multiset, map, and multimap. Although through the use of adaptors more containers can be derived, these seven represent the native STL containers. Table 4.1 shows each container and its basic characteristics. The STL divides these seven containers into two broad categories, sequence, and associative. Table 4.2 shows the division of the STL containers into sequence and associative. Sequence and associative refer to how the containers are logically ordered and how they are accessed. Recall Table 3.2 from Chapter 3, where we classified collection and container classes.

**Table 4.1   STL containers and some of their basic characteristics.**

| Containers | Description |
|---|---|
| **Vector** | * A type of sequence that supports random access iterators.<br>* Supports a constant time insert and erase operations at the end and linear time in the middle of the sequence.<br>* Storage management is handled automatically. |
| **List** | * A kind of sequence that supports bidirectional iterators.<br>* Supports a constant time insert and erase operation anywhere in the sequence.<br>* Storage management is handled automatically.<br>* Fast random access to the list elements is not supported. |
| **Deque** | * A kind of sequence that supports random access iterators.<br>* Supports a constant time insert and erase operation at the beginning or the end of the sequence and linear time in the middle of the sequence.<br>* Storage management is handled automatically. |
| **Set** | * A kind of associative container that supports unique objects.<br>* Contains at the most one of each object. |
| **Multiset** | * A kind of associative container that supports duplicate objects. |
| **Map** | * A kind of associative container that supports unique keys associated with a value.<br>* Contains at the most one of each key.<br>* Provides fast retrieval of values of type T based on the keys. |
| **Multimap** | * A kind of associative container that supports duplicate keys.<br>* Provides fast retrieval of values of type T based on the keys. |

**Table 4.2   STL containers divided into two categories: associative containers and sequence containers.**

| Sequence | Associative |
|----------|-------------|
| Vector | Set |
| List | Multiset |
| Deque | Map |
| Queue | Multimap |
| Priority Queue | |
| Stack | |

# Sequences

The logical representations of certain containers are linear or sequential. The objects in these types of containers are understood as being logically stored in contiguous memory. The objects in sequence containers have logical positions within the container relative to start, end, top, bottom, front, or back of the container. Access to the sequence containers can be classified as either sequential or direct (sometimes called random). When a container has sequential access the programmer must access the first and second object in order to get to the third object. There is no way to jump to the middle of a container that supports only sequential access. When a container has direct access, the programmer can move directly to any object in the container, without having to process other objects. The STL vector and deque provide direct access, and the list provides sequential access. Do not confuse the terms *sequence* and *sequential* here. Sequence refers to how the objects are logically stored in memory. Sequential refers to how the objects are accessed. Although the vector is a sequence container it has a direct access method.

## USING STL SEQUENCE CONTAINERS

There are three fundamental sequence containers: list, *vector*, and *deque*. Each of the sequence containers is declared in its own header files. So in order to use the container you will have to include the header files. For instance, to use the vector container you must include *vector.h* and then a vector class can be declared. It should also be noted that if user-defined classes are going to be used with the sequence containers, then in general the == operator and the < operator will have to be defined for the user-defined class. These operators are the primary minimum defined interface that the STL collections and containers assume will be supplied for each object. Listing 4.1 shows one way a vector container would be declared.

### Listing 4.1

```
//Declaration of vector containers
#include <vector.h>

void main(void)
{
  vector<int> MyVector1;
```

```
    vector<char> MyVector2;
    vector<float> MyVector3;
    vector<char *> MyVector4;
}
```

After *vector.h* is included, objects of type **vector** can be declared. Notice that **vector** is a template class. Templates are reviewed in Chapter 2. Because **vector** is a template class, when an object of type **vector** is declared the user must provide a type to the class declaration. In the declarations in Listing 4.1 we have declared four vector containers. Each container stores a different type. We have containers that can store **ints, chars, floats,** and pointers to **char**. This emphasizes an important point about template classes. Since they are parameterized, the **vector** class need only be defined once; then a vector container is capable of holding objects of any type. Another thing this simple declaration tells us is that we don't have to declare in advance how many objects the vector will hold. The sequence containers are dynamic. This means that they can grow or shrink during runtime. This is in contrast to static structures like the traditional array in C++. When a traditional array is declared in C++ the size of the array remains fixed until the entire array is deallocated. Although a static structure can be dynamically allocated at runtime, it is not a dynamic structure. Dynamic structures are structures whose size can change during the execution of a program. For instance, the program in Listing 4.2 uses six of the **vector**'s member functions to demonstrate the notion of a dynamic container. The six member functions that are used are **push_back(), size(), capacity(), erase(), begin(),** and **end()**.

### Listing 4.2

```
// This program demonstrates that the sequence container vector
// is a dynamic structure.
#include <vector.h>
#include <iostream.h>

void main(void)
{
  vector<int> MyVector;
  cout << "Size Of MyVector: " << MyVector.size() << endl;
  cout << "Cap. of MyVector: " << MyVector.capacity() << endl << endl;
  MyVector.push_back(4);
  cout << "Size Of MyVector: " << MyVector.size() << endl;
  cout << "Cap. of MyVector: " << MyVector.capacity() << endl << endl;
  int N = 0;
  for(N = 1;N < 10000;N++) // Loop 1
  {
    MyVector.push_back(N);
  }
  cout << "Size Of MyVector Loop 1: " << MyVector.size() << endl;
  cout << "Cap. of MyVector: " << MyVector.capacity() << endl << endl;
  for(N = 10001;N < 20000;N++) // Loop 2
  {
    MyVector.push_back(N);
```

```
    }
    cout << "Size Of MyVector Loop 2: " << MyVector.size() << endl;
    cout << "Cap. of MyVector: " << MyVector.capacity() << endl << endl;
    MyVector.erase(MyVector.begin(),MyVector.end());
    cout << "Size Of MyVector: " << MyVector.size() << endl;
    cout << "Cap. after erase " << MyVector.capacity() << endl;

}
```

A container of type **vector<int>** is declared. As designated by the **int** parameter, this container will hold integers. The container is called **MyVector**. Notice the statement

```
cout << "Size Of MyVector: " << MyVector.size() << endl;
```

in Listing 4.2. This statement sends the number of objects that are stored in **MyVector** to the output. This is done by calling the **size()** member function, of **MyVector**. The **size()** returns the number of elements that are stored in the vector. Table 4.3 shows the output when this program has been executed. The first two member functions that are explicitly called are **size()**, and **capacity()**. The **capacity()** member function of the vector container returns the largest number of objects that can be stored in the vector without reallocating space for the vector. The first call to **size()** and to **capacity()** shows that **MyVector** has 0 objects and has a capacity to store 0 objects.

Notice the statement

```
MyVector.push_back(4);
```

in Listing 4.2. The member function **push_back()** is called with an argument of 4. The **push_back()** member function adds an object to the end of the vector. Table 4.3

**Table 4.3   Output from Program Listing 4.2 demonstrates that the sequence classes are dynamic structures that can be reallocated during program execution.**

*Output from Program Listing 4.2*

Size Of Myvector: 0
Cap. of Myvector: 0

Size Of Myvector: 1
Cap. of Myvector: 1024

Size Of Myvector Loop 1: 10000
Cap. of Myvector: 163484

Size Of Myvector Loop 2: 19999
Cap. of Myvector: 32768

Size of Myvectror: 0
Cap. after erase 32768

shows the results of calling **size()** and **capacity()** after the **push_back()** member functions have been called. Notice that the container has a size of 1 object, and now has the capacity to store 1024 objects. Although only 1 object was added to the container, enough storage for 1024 objects has been allocated. This brings us to another important point about all containers in the Standard Template Library. They all have automatic memory management. The user is not responsible for allocating the space for the objects to be stored in the container, and the user is not responsible for deleting the space that the container has allocated for the objects.

## Containers and Automatic Memory Management

Notice that in the program in Listing 4.2 we did not have to allocate space for the objects that we placed into **MyVector**. All the container classes are dynamic structures and all the container classes have a default memory management allocator class. The allocator class is a data member of the container class. The type of this data member is a parameter to the container. This implies that the user can supply a user-defined allocator. The allocator class is responsible for allocating memory for the objects that will be placed in the container. The allocator class has two member functions **allocate()** and **deallocate()** that request and return memory for the container. Each container's allocator class is responsible for the automatic memory management for that container.

Notice the capacity of **MyVector** in Table 4.3 immediately after we used the **push_back()** member function to insert the number 4 into the container. The **capacity()** member function returned a value of 1024. This means **MyVector** can now hold as many as 1024 **ints** without having to reallocate. If only one **int** was placed into the container, where does the 1024 come from? The answer to this question lies in the fact that the operating system is ultimately responsible for supplying the program with memory. Figure 4.1 shows the basic translation of a request for memory. This process is somewhat transparent to the user. If the container does not have enough memory to hold the object being inserted, the container automatically allocates more memory. This request is initially handled by the allocator data member of the container. The allocator's request is translated into a call to functions like **new()** or **malloc()**, and memory is ultimately returned by operating system functions like **DosAllocMem**, the OS2 memory allocation function. The operating systems that the programs and examples in this book were executed on are virtual paging systems. A virtual paging operating system like UNIX, OS2, or Windows NT manages memory in blocks called *pages*. The smallest *page size* for these operating systems is 4096 bytes. When we added an **int** to the container, the container's automatic memory facility ultimately requested memory from the operating system. The smallest block of memory the operating system could supply was one page. So although we only asked for a block the size of an **int** we got 4096 bytes. The 1024 that the **capacity()** function reports in Table 4.3 can be calculated by dividing the size of the block of memory returned by the size of an **int**. For our compiler an **int** is 4 bytes. Hence 4096/4=1024. For a 16-bit environment like Windows or MSDOS, the capacity would report 2048 because the size of an **int** is 2 bytes as opposed to 4 bytes.

After adding the number 4 to the container **MyVector** in Listing 4.2 the **capacity()** was 1024. The addition of objects to the container is done with a for loop:

```
int N = 0;
for(N = 1;N < 10000;N++) // Loop 1
{
    MyVector.push_back(N);
}
```

Although the current capacity is only 1024, the container is forced to make room for 10,000 more **ints**. Once the container makes room, the new capacity as shown in Table 4.3 is 16384 **ints**. The container has grown in size. This is what we mean by dynamic structure. As long as no more than 16384 **int** objects are added to the container, the container will not have to be reallocated. However, as is shown in Listing 4.2 we add a few thousand more **ints** and more room is allocated for the container and final container capacity is 32768. We next want to erase the objects that are in the container. We call the **erase()** member function. Notice what is passed to **erase()**: **MyVector.begin()** and **MyVector.end()**. These are some of the container's basic iterators. We shall have much to say about iterators later in this chapter, but for now it's important to know that the iterators returned from **begin()** and **end()** point to first and last objects in the containers. Therefore we are passing a range of objects to the **erase()** member function. By using the **begin()** and **end()** member functions we are requesting that the container remove all the objects that it holds.

It is noteworthy that even after we have called the **erase()** member function in the program in Listing 4.2 the capacity as shown in Table 4.3 is still 32768. Although the objects have been removed from the container, the space that the objects occupied is still allocated, and will remain allocated until the container goes out of scope. Once the container goes out of scope the container's destructor ultimately calls the allocator's **deallocate()** member function to release the memory that the objects occupied. At the

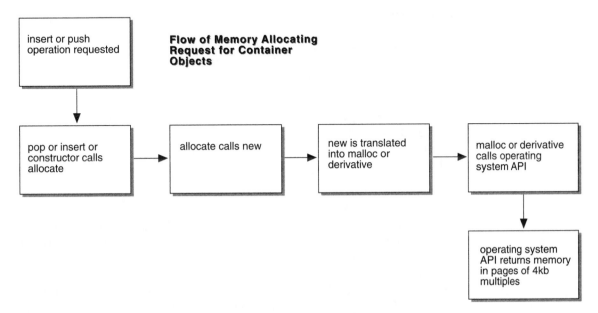

**Figure 4.1** A basic translation for a request for memory.

point that the **deallocate()** member function is being called, it is assumed that the destructors for the objects that were stored have already been called.

## SEQUENCE CONTAINER COMMONALITY

Similar to the vector, the other sequence containers, list and deque, provide basic container functionality. The sequences and the associative classes provide methods to *construct and destruct containers, insert objects, remove objects,* and *access objects.*

### Sequence Constructors and Destructors

The sequence containers provide several ways to construct a container. All sequence containers provide either a constructor that requires no arguments or constructors that have default arguments. These constructors are often referred to in the literature as the *default constructors.* When the constructor that takes no arguments is used the container is constructed with a size of zero. The sequence containers also provide a constructor that allows the user to specify the number of objects the container is to initially hold, and what those objects should be initialized to. For instance, the program in Listing 4.3 declares an object of type **list<double>** called **MyList**.

**Listing 4.3**

```
// Listing 4.3 demonstrates how a constructor can be used to initialize a container
// with a certain number of objects initialized to a specific value.

#include <list.h>
#include <iostream.h>

void main(void)
{
  list<double> MyList(10,1812);
  list<double>::const_iterator N = MyList.begin();
  int Count = MyList.size();
  while(Count)
  {
    cout << "List Element " << Count << " : " << *N << endl;
    Count--;
    N++;
  }
}
```

The declaration for **MyList** specifies that the container should be constructed to initially hold 10 objects of type **double**. Furthermore the declaration specifies that all the **doubles** should be initialized with the value 1812. Table 4.4 shows what **MyList** contains. Notice that **MyList** contains 10 objects, all whose value is 1812. The allocation for the objects in the program in Listing 4.3 is different from the allocation for the objects in Listing 4.2. In Listing 4.2 we constructed the container **MyVector** initially with a size of 0 using the default constructor. The program in Listing 4.3 has been constructed using the second type of constructor that the sequence containers provide.

---

**Table 4.4   Output from Program Listing 4.3 demon-strates how a constructor can be used to initialize the objects within a container. The output shows that the ten objects all contain the value 1812.**

---

*Output from Program Listing 4.3*

---

List Element 10 : 1812
List Element 9 : 1812
List Element 8 : 1812
List Element 7 : 1812
List Element 6 : 1812
List Element 5 : 1812
List Element 4 : 1812
List Element 3 : 1812
List Element 2 : 1812
List Element 1 : 1812

---

All sequence containers provide the *copy constructor*. (For a review of copy constructors see Chapter 2.) This constructor is used for certain types of object initialization and when objects are passed by value to and from functions. The next type of constructor that all the sequences provide is a constructor that constructs the container to contain a group of objects from another container. This constructor basically copies the elements from the provided container into the new container. For example, **MyList2** in Program Listing 4.4 is constructed with the contents of **MyList**.

### Listing 4.4

```
//This Program demonstrates that one container can be
// used to construct another container
#define __MINMAX__DEFINED
#include <list.h>
#include <iostream.h>

void main(void)
{
  list<double> MyList;
  double Count = 1;
  while(Count < 6)
  {
    MyList.push_front(Count / 3);
    Count++;
  }
  list<double> MyList2(MyList);
  list<double>::const_iterator O = MyList2.begin();
  list<double>::const_iterator N = MyList.begin();
  Count = MyList2.size();
  while(Count)
  {
    cout << "MyList1: " << Count << " : " << *N << "\t" << "\t";
```

```
        cout << "MyList2: "<< Count << " : " << *O << endl;
        N++;
        O++;
        Count--;
    }

}
```

The program in Listing 4.4 then inserts the values that are contained in **MyList2** into **cout**. Table 4.5 illustrates the results of using the constructor that accepts another container as its argument. Notice in Table 4.5 that **MyList1** and **MyList2** contain the same elements. All sequence containers provide destructors. The basic operation of the destructor is to:

> Remove all elements from the container, effectively calling the destructors for all contained objects.
> Deallocate in memory for the container, effectively returning all requested memory back to the operating system or memory pool.

### Sequence Object Insertion

All containers must provide some method to add objects to the container. This can be done with constructors, as was done in the case of **MyList2** in program Listing 4.4, or it can be done with an insertion member function. All the sequence containers provide three basic types of insertion member functions. First there are the **push_front()**, or **push_back()** member functions. These member functions add an element to the front of the container or to the back of container. Next there are the **insert()** member functions. Each of the sequence classes has several versions of the **insert()** member function. These member functions can insert an element or group of elements at a specific position or range of positions within a container, whereas the **push_front()** or **push_back()** member function either adds a single element to the front or a single element to the back of a container. The **insert()** member functions can insert a single

---

**Table 4.5    Output from Program Listing 4.4 demonstrates that MyList2 has been constructed containing the members of MyList1. This output shows the results of using the constructor that excepts another container as its argument. MyList1 and MyList2 contains the same elements.**

*Output from Program Listing 4.4*

| | |
|---|---|
| MyList1: 5 : 1.66667 | MyList2: 5 : 1.66667 |
| MyList1: 4 : 1.33333 | MyList2: 4 : 1.33333 |
| MyList1: 3 : 1 | MyList2: 3 : 1 |
| MyList1: 2 : 0.666667 | MyList2: 2 : 0.666667 |
| MyList1: 1 : 0.333333 | MyList2: 1 : 0.333333 |

element or a group of elements into any position or positions within the container. The **insert()** member function can be used to insert *n* copies of an element starting at any specific position in the container that the user specifies. The third method that can be used to add objects to a container is through use of the assignment operator. For example, the program in Listing 4.5 adds objects to **MyList2** by using the assignment operator.

### Listing 4.5

```
// This program demonstrates that elements can be added
// to a container using the assignment operator

#define __MINMAX_DEFINED
#include <list.h>
#include <iostream.h>

void main(void)
{
  list<double> MyList1;
  double Count = 0.56;
  while(Count < 6)
  {
    MyList1.push_front(Count / 5);
    Count++;
  }
  list<double> MyList2;
  MyList2 = MyList1;
  list<double>::const_iterator O = MyList2.begin();
  list<double>::const_iterator N = MyList1.begin();
  Count = MyList2.size();
  while(Count)
  {
    cout << "MyList1 " << Count << " : " << *N << "\t" << "\t";
    cout << "MyList2 " << Count << " : " << *O << endl;
    N++;
    O++;
    Count--;
  }
  cout << endl;
  cout << "Count For MyList1 : " << MyList1.size() << endl << endl;
  cout << "Count For MyList2 : " << MyList2.size() << endl << endl;
}
```

Table 4.6 is the output for the program in Listing 4.5. Notice that **MyList1** and **MyList2** are identical. An important point to note about the program in Listing 4.5 is that **MyList2** is constructed as an empty list. When the program is executed 6 numbers are added to **MyList1**, and then the program assigns **MyList1** to **MyList2**. Because the containers support automatic memory management, **MyList2** automatically allocates memory for the 6 objects that are added. Note the call to the **size()** member function for **MyList1** and **MyList2**. Table 4.6 shows that these lists do contain the same elements, and the same number of elements.

Table 4.6   Output for Program Listing 4.5 shows that MyList1 and MyList2 contain the same elements and have the same count. The output also shows how bi-directional iterators can be used to move forward and backward in a container.

*Output from Program Listing 4.5*

| | |
|---|---|
| MyList1 6 : 1.112 | MyList2 6 : 1.112 |
| MyList1 5 : 0.912 | MyList2 5 : 0.912 |
| MyList1 4 : 0.712 | MyList2 4 : 0.712 |
| MyList1 3 : 0.512 | MyList2 3 : 0.512 |
| MyList1 2 : 0.312 | MyList2 2 : 0.312 |
| MyList1 1 : 0.112 | MyList2 1 : 0.112 |

Count For MyList1 : 6
Count For MyList2 : 6

Using calls to the **push_back()**, **push_front()**, **insert()**, and **operator=()** member functions along with the constructors that accept arguments are the methods that allow the user to add objects to a container.

### Sequence Object Removal

All the sequences provide methods to remove objects from the containers. An important point to remember is that removing objects from a container is not the same as deallocating the space that those objects take up. This point was demonstrated in the program in Listing 4.2. If an object has a constructor that allocates space for that object that constructor is called when the object is created. The container's allocator data member creates space upon construction of the container, or when there is not enough memory allocated during an insertion request. When the object is removed from the container, the object's destructor is called, not the destructor for the container. The container returns the memory it has allocated for an object once the container has left scope, or when the container has been deleted.

Each sequence container has three basic kinds of removal: a pop member function or functions, a collection of **erase()** member functions, and the container's destructor. There are two kinds of pop member functions, the **pop_front()** member function and the **pop_back()** member function. The **pop_front()** member function removes an object from the front of a container, and the **pop_back()** member function removes an object from the back of a container. Like the **insert()** member functions, the **erase()** member functions are *position* functions. They can erase either an element or group of elements from a specified position or positions.

### Access to the Objects in a Sequence Container

Table 4.7 shows the three basic ways to access objects in a sequence container. The **front()** and **back()** member functions are used to access single objects in a container. The **front()** member function can be used to access the front or first element in a

**Table 4.7  Three basic ways to access objects in the STL sequence containers vector, list, and deque.**

| Container | Iterator | front()<br>back() | subscript<br>operator[] |
|-----------|----------|-------------------|-------------------------|
| Vector | √ | √ | √ |
| List | √ | √ | √ |
| Deque | √ | √ | √ |

container. The **back()** member function can be used to access the back or last element in a container. The subscript[] operator is only available for the vector container and the deque container. The subscript operator provides direct access, often referred to as random access, to an object in a container. For instance, if we have a deque named *A* that consists of 15 elements, then we can retrieve any element in *A* by specifying its relative position to the beginning of the container. For instance, *A*[7] returns the seventh element in *A*, or *A*[*N*] returns the *N*th element in *A*. As with the **front()** and **back()** member functions, the subscript[] operator is a method for accessing objects within the container.

### The STL Iterators

The third method of accessing objects in a container is with *iterators*. Iterators are object-oriented generic pointers. The *dereferencing* of an iterator using the * operator returns the object that the iterator points to. Just as a pointer contains an address, or *points to where* an object is in memory, an iterator contains a position, or points to where an object is within the given container. When a pointer is dereferenced the object that the pointer is pointing to is returned, as opposed to the address that the pointer contains. When an iterator is dereferenced the object that the iterator is pointing to is returned, as opposed to the position that the iterator contains. Whereas a pointer is a built-in type in C++, the iterator is a class that is defined in the STL or by the user. This means that iterators can engage in encapsulation, polymorphism, and inheritance. Just as arithmetic can be performed on pointers in C++, arithmetic can be performed on the STL iterators. The iterators in the STL are distinguished by the services they provide. Each iterator has member functions that implement a certain minimum set of services. Whereas there is only one type of pointer in C++, there are five kinds of iterators in the STL.

Table 4.8 shows the five types of iterators and their basic descriptions. The iterators form a hierarchy moving from the least powerful to the most powerful. The least powerful iterators are the input and output iterators. Following the input and output iterators is the forward iterator, following the forward iterator is the bidirectional iterator, and the most powerful and flexible of the iterators is the random access iterator. Table 4.9 shows the fundamental services provided by each class of iterator. Notice as we move from left to right in Table 4.9 the iterator offers more services and more flexibility. Notice that the random access iterator class in Table 4.9 offers the full range of *iterator arithmetic*, by defining operator++, operator−−, operator+, operator−, and all the relational operators.

**Table 4.8**  This table shows the five basic kinds of iterators provided by the STL with a brief description. Every type of container will have at least one of these iterators as a data member.

| Iterator | Description |
|---|---|
| **Input Iterator** | * One direction, read-only iterator. |
| **Output Iterator** | * One direction, write-only iterator. |
| **Forward Iterator** | * One direction, read and write iterator. |
| **Bidirectional Iterator** | * Forward and reverse read and write iterator. |
| **Random Access Iterator** | * Forward and reverse read and write direct access allowing iterator arithmetic. |

The program in Listing 4.6 demonstrates how bidirectional iterators can be used to move forward and backward in a container.

**Listing 4.6**

```
// This program demonstrates the usage of
// the bidirectional iterator for the list container

#define __MINMAX_DEFINED
#include <list.h>
#include <iostream.h>

void main(void)
{
  list<double> MyList;
  int N = 0;
  while(N < 6)
  {
    MyList.push_back(N + 3.14);
    N++;
  }
  list<double>::iterator M = MyList.begin();
  while(N)
  {
    cout << "MyList : " << *M << endl;
    M++;
    N--;
  }
  N = MyList.size();
  M = MyList.end();
  M--;
  cout << " Reverse Direction-----------" << endl;
  while(N)
  {
```

Table 4.9 Fundamental services provided by each type of iterator.

| Interator Interface | Return Type | Input | Output | Forward | Bidirectional | Random Access |
|---|---|:---:|:---:|:---:|:---:|:---:|
| X(a) | | • | • | • | • | • |
| X u(a) | | • | • | • | • | • |
| X() | | | | • | • | • |
| X u=a | | • | | • | • | • |
| a == b | convertible to bool | | | • | • | • |
| a != b | convertible to bool | • | • | • | • | • |
| *a | convertible to T | • | | • | • | • |
| ++r | X& | • | | • | • | • |
| r++ | X | • | • | • | • | • |
| *a = t | | • | • | • | • | • |
| X u | | | • | | | |
| r = a | X& | | | • | • | • |
| --r | X& | | | | • | • |
| r-- | X | | | | • | • |
| r += n | X& | | | | | • |
| r -= n | X& | | | | | • |
| a + n | X | | | | | • |
| n + a | X | | | | | • |
| a - n | X | | | | | • |
| b - a | Distance | | | | | • |
| a[n] | convertible to T | | | | | • |
| a < b | convertible to bool | | | | | • |
| a > b | convertible to bool | | | | | • |
| a >= b | convertible to bool | | | | | • |
| a <= b | convertible to bool | | | | | • |

```
        cout << "MyList : " << *M << endl;
        M−−;
        N−−;
    }
}
```

The iterator for the list container is a *bidirectional* iterator. Along with the ability to be dereferenced, and written to, a bidirectional iterator allows forward movement as well as backward movement in a container by providing definitions for the ++ operator, and −− operator. The program in Listing 4.6 inserts six numbers into **MyList** and then the program does a forward iteration or forward traversal through the list container inserting each element of the list into **cout**. Notice the statement in Listing 4.6:

```
list<double>::iteratorM = MyList.begin();
```

This statement declares **M** to be of type iterator, and initializes it with the location of the first element in the container. Since the iterator for the list class is bidirectional the **M** object will provide forward and backward iteration through the container. **M** is an object and provides at least the services that are shown in Table 4.9 in the column under bidirectional iterators. The ++ operator causes **M** to traverse from the beginning of the **MyList** container to its end. Notice the statement in Listing 4.6:

```
M = MyList.end();
```

This statement assigns one position beyond the last element in the container to **M**. This is a beyond-the-end position; it should not be dereferenced. It is a housekeeping construct. Once we have this position we can traverse backward through the **MyList** container using the −− operator. In each case the * operator is used to return the object that the iterator is pointing to. The statement

```
cout << "MyList : " << *M << endl;
```

in Listing 4.6 uses the * operator. This operator dereferences the **M** iterator and returns the object that **M** is pointing to. Therefore, instead of a location being inserted into **cout**, the object that **M** is pointing to is inserted into **cout**. Table 4.10 shows the output for the program in Listing 4.6.

The program in Listing 4.7 demonstrates the how random access iterators can be used with containers that support direct access.

### Listing 4.7

```
// This program demonstrates some of the uses
// of the random access iterators, the subscript[]
// operator, and iterator arithmetic

#define __MINMAX_DEFINED
#include <deque.h>
#include <iostream.h>
```

---

**Table 4.10** Output from Program Listing 4.6 showing how the bidirectional iterator can be used to move forward and backward in a container. Six numbers are inserted into *MyList*. The program does a forward then a backward iteration through the list container inserting each element of the list into *cout*.

---

*Output from Program Listing 4.6*

List : 3.14
MyList : 4.14
MyList : 5.14
MyList : 6.14
MyList : 7.14
MyList : 8.14

Reverse Direction----------

MyList : 8.14
MyList : 7.14
MyList : 6.14
MyList : 5.14
MyList : 4.14
MyList : 3.14

---

```
void main(void)
{
  deque<double> MyDeque(10,5);
  deque<double>::iterator P = MyDeque.begin();
  P = P + 5;
  *P = 25;
  P = P - 3;
  *P = 15;
  P++;
  *P = 30;
  P += 5;
  *P = 125;
  MyDeque[0] = 0.005;
  MyDeque[9] = 500.05;
  int N = MyDeque.size();
  P = MyDeque.end();
  P--;
  while(N)
  {
    cout << "MyDeque : " << N << " " << *P << endl;
    P--;
    N--;
  }
}
```

The deque container supports direct access, and has a random access iterator. The random access iterator is the most flexible of the iterators, providing read dereferencing, write dereferencing, forward iteration, backward iteration, all the relational operations, as well as iterator arithmetic capability. The statement

deque<double> MyDeque(10,5);

in Listing 4.7 declares **MyDeque** to be a deque collection containing doubles. The container is constructed to hold 10 doubles. Each of those doubles has a value of 5. The statement

deque<double>::iterator P = MyDeque.begin();

in Listing 4.7 declares **P** to be an iterator. Since deque containers have random access iterators, the **P** object will provide the full set of iterator services on **MyDeque**. Figure 4.2 shows how the object **P** is used to iterate through **MyDeque**. Notice in Listing 4.7 that the iterator **P** can be used in arithmetic expressions, such as the statement:

P = P + 5;

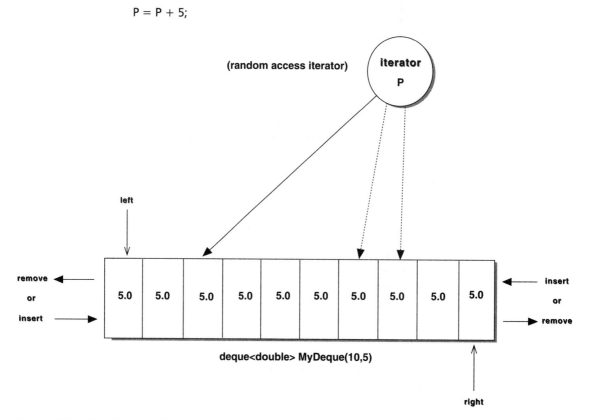

**Figure 4.2**  This diagram illustrates how object **P** (the iterator) is used to iterate through **MyDeque** container.

This type of statement uses *pointer* or *iterator* arithmetic because we are performing addition and assignment on the iterator. This statement adds 5 to the current location of **P**. The 5 is used as a multiplier. In general, this kind of operations uses the numerical constant * the size of the object to determine what value to place in the iterator. In this statement 5 is the numerical constant, and the object has a size of double. So in simple terms 5 * the sizeof(double) is added to **P**. Although this is not exactly what occurs in the STL, it does describe the general logic of iterator or pointer arithmetic. Another important point to note about the processing in Listing 4.7 is that the first position in **MyDeque** is **MyDeque[0]**, and the last position is **MyDeque[9]**. This corresponds to the traditional C++ array where the array index starts at position 0. Also note that the * operator in the program in Listing 4.7 is being used both as a read and write operator. The statement

```
*P = 25;
```

demonstrates how the * operator can provide *write dereferencing* because the number 25 is being assigned to the object that the iterator **P** is pointing at. Note that **P** itself contains the location of the object, and the location is not being set to 25, but the object at the location is set to 25. The object **P** is used to move to any position within the container that is required, allowing read dereferencing and write dereferencing. Table 4.11 shows what the output looks like when the program in Listing 4.7 is executed. The output is generated by using the **P** object to iterate backward through the container using the statement:

```
P--;
```

After each insertion into **cout** the **P** iterator is decremented. Notice the statements

```
P = MyDeque.end();
P--;
```

---

**Table 4.11 Output from Program Listing 4.7 shows how random access iterators can be used to insert, access, dereference, and assign objects to a container that supports random access iterators. The container MyDeque is constructed to hold 10 doubles.**

MyDeque : 10 500.05
MyDeque : 9 125
MyDeque : 8 5
MyDeque : 7 5
MyDeque : 6 25
MyDeque : 5 5
MyDeque : 4 30
MyDeque : 3 15
MyDeque : 2 5
MyDeque : 1 0.0005

in Listing 4.7. The first statement assigns a beyond-the-end position to the **P** iterator. The next statement ensures that **P** is referring to a *valid* position before the while loop is entered.

### *The Necessary and Sufficient Requirement*

These iterators operate with the necessary and sufficient conditions. Each container has a minimum iterator requirement. Some containers require bidirectional while other containers require random access. Still others can be satisfied with input or output iterators. We use the terms *necessary* and *sufficient* to describe whether the iterator meets the container's *traversal interface*. The traversal interface is the logical view that the container presents of its storage and retrieval access capabilities. An iterator can be specified for a class that has a necessary but not sufficient relationship with that class. This means that while the iterator does meet *some* of the necessary conditions for the container's traversal, it does not meet *all* the conditions that are necessary for the container's traversal. For instance, if an input iterator is specified for a container or algorithm that requires a bidirectional iterator, the input iterator is said to be necessary, but not sufficient for the container or algorithm. This is because, while the container does need to have read access iteration, it requires more than read access iteration. In this way, the input iterator is said only to be necessary but not sufficient. On the other hand, if a random access iterator is supplied for a container that only needs a bidirectional iterator, then the random access iterator is sufficient, because it meets *all the necessary conditions* of the bidirectional iterator.

The iterator classes and the STL algorithms form cooperative patterns of use. The algorithms in the STL are dependent on the iterators and their five rankings. Each algorithm in the STL accepts an iterator, or iterators, as arguments. While some algorithms can work with only input and output iterators, some algorithms require forward, bidirectional, or random access iterators. The logic of the algorithm dictates what level of iterator is required. Because the STL algorithms implement large chunks of the STL container's functionality, then the containers are also dependent upon how the algorithms interact with the iterators. With this in mind we see that there is a *cooperative pattern* between the STL containers, the STL iterators, and the STL algorithms.

## STL Associative Collection

The STL provides four basic kinds of associative collections: set, multiset, map, and multimap. The term *associative* here is used to denote the logical way in which objects are stored and held in these collections. Unlike the sequence containers the associative collections are not thought of as containing objects in a sequential fashion. A sequential traversal from the beginning of an associative collection to the end of the associative collection has no special meaning in terms of position, as it does with the sequential containers. We understand the definition of a set more by the group of operations that are performed on the set than by any other factor. The operations of set intersection, set union, set membership, and subsetting dictate the familiar notion that we have of a set.

There are no operations in the definition of a set that specify how to access the set, or that specify the order that members in the set are to be stored in.

Maps and multimaps are mathematical notions that implement the concept of relations. A map associates the elements in one set with the elements in another set. Let's say we have two sets, $A=\{a, b, c, d, e, f\}$ and $B=\{$fish, fred, flea, flower, fox$\}$. A map is a structure that associates pairs of elements, one from each set; $(b, $flower$)$, $(d, $fox$)$, $(a, $fish$)$ and so on. Figure 4.3 shows a complete mapping between set $A$ and set $B$. Multisets, sometimes called *bags*, allow more than one copy of a particular element to be stored. Multimaps, sometimes called *dictionaries*, allow more than one copy of a particular element to be stored. Because sets, multisets, maps, and multimaps have no specified order in their descriptions, the implementer is at liberty to designate an order. The designers of the STL have decided to let the user of the associative collection determine what the order is. One of the differences that the user will notice immediately between the sequence containers and the associative collections is the extra parameters in their declarations.

## USING THE ASSOCIATIVE COLLECTIONS

The associative collections are declared in four header files: *set.h*, *multiset.h*, *map.h*, and *multimap.h*. In order to declare objects of these collections the user must include the appropriate header file. It should also be noted that if these containers are to be used with user-defined classes, the operator $==$, operator $<$ will have to be defined for the user-defined class. The associative collections make use of these operators in many ways; the primary use, though, is in inserting and finding elements in the collection. Whereas the sequence containers only required one argument in the declaration of a container, sets and multisets require two, and maps and multimaps require three. For example, the program in Listing 4.8 declares **MySet** to be a set of **ints**.

### Listing 4.8

```
// This program demonstrates the declaration
// of a set collection and how no duplicate
// members are allowed.

#define __MINMAX_DEFINED
#include <set.h>
#include <iostream.h>
void main(void)
{
    set<int, less<int> >MySet;
    MySet.insert(1960);
    MySet.insert(1952);
    MySet.insert(1771);
    MySet.insert(1812);
    MySet.insert(1960);
    MySet.insert(1996);
    set<int, less<int> >::iterator M = MySet.begin();
```

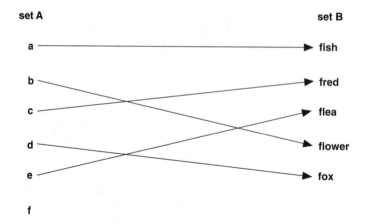

**Figure 4.3**   A complete mapping between set A and set B.

```
cout << "Number Of Elements " << MySet.size() << endl;
while(M != MySet.end())
{
   cout << *M << endl;
   M++;
}
}
```

Notice the declaration:

set<int, less<int> > MySet;

The first argument to the set template is **int**. This argument designates **MySet** to be a collection of **ints**. The next argument, **less<int>**, is new to our discussion of the STL components. The **less<int>** parameter determines the sort order of the objects that will be placed into the set collection. Table 4.12 shows the output of the program in Listing

| Table 4.12   Output from Program Listing 4.8 demonstrates the automatic sort ordering that the set collection performs on its members. The less function object sorts the members from smallest to largest. |
| --- |
| *Output from Program Listing 4.8* |
| Number of Elements 5 |
| 1771 |
| 1812 |
| 1952 |
| 1960 |
| 1996 |

4.8. Notice in Listing 4.8 that the integer values were inserted into **MySet** with no specific ordering; however, Table 4.12 shows the integer values to be in the set from smallest to largest. This is because the **less<int>** argument imposes an order from smallest to largest. The **less<int>** argument is a function object. The function object is another major component of the STL. The function object **less<T>** is just one of the 15 function objects provided by the STL. Table 4.13 shows the STL function objects and their basic descriptions. All associative collections require a function object in their declarations.

### Function Objects

A function object is a class that overloads the () operator. Function objects can be used in the same places that pointers to functions can be used. The difference is a function object can engage in the benefits of object-oriented programming, that is, encapsulation, polymorphism, and inheritance. Let's define a function class to see how function objects work. The declaration

```
template <class T> class less{
public:
    bool operator()(const T& x, const T& y) const { return x < y; }
};
```

declares a template class called **less**. This class has only one member function, although we could have added more. The class has no data members, although, if necessary,

**Table 4.13   STL function objects and their basic descriptions.**

| Type | Description | Function Objects |
|------|-------------|------------------|
| **Base** | * Simplifies the **typedefs** of the argument and result types. | unary_function binary_function |
| **Arithmetic Operations** | * Provides arithmetic operations. | plus minus times divides modulus negate |
| **Comparisons** | * Provides comparison operators. | equal_to not_equal_to greater less greater_equal less_equal |
| **Logical Operations** | * Provides logical operations. | logical_and logical_or logical_not |

data member can be added. We keep the class simple so our discussion of function objects won't be clouded by other object-oriented mechanisms. We can declare an object of type **less** using:

    less < double > MyObject.

Notice that the **less** class defines the () operator to have two arguments of type **T**.

    bool operator()(const T& x, const T& y) const { return x < y; }

This means that **MyObject** can be used accordingly:

    Result = MyObject(5.14,7.4);

In this case Result will be "TRUE" because 5.14 is < 7.4. When the user overloads the () operator for a class this allows objects of this class to be used like a function, as in the statement:

    result = MyObject(5.14,7.4);

Any class can define the () operator. Objects that are instantiated from classes that define the () operator are called *function objects*. The less object is one of the function objects that is defined by the STL. Notice that it is used in the declaration of **MySet** in Listing 4.8 with the declaration:

    set<int, less<int> > MySet;

The set class uses this argument to provide the sort order for the set. So then the set and multiset templates require two arguments:

    set<class T, class FunctionObject>
        or
    set<class T, class T>

the first argument representing the type that the set collection will store, and the second argument providing a () operator that will determine the sort order of the set collection. Note that the second argument can be the same as the first as long as the () operator is defined. The requirement of the second argument does impose some restrictions on how the () operator is defined. First, the () operator must be defined to take arguments of the same type. Second, the () operator must return some type that is convertible to bool. Third, the () operator provides an absolute > or absolute < ordering; no <= or >= relationships should be defined. This last requirement is a policy because the STL uses the second argument to test the equivalence of objects. If the operator () was defined for **MyObject** then the STL says two arguments are equal if and only if:

```
MyObject(X,Y) = = FALSE
   and
MyObject(Y,X) = = FALSE
```

In other words, given two objects $X$ and $Y$, the operator () function must be able to determine whether $X$ is $<Y$ or $X$ is $>Y$. For function objects that are to be used as the ordering argument for sets, multisets, maps, and multimaps, the operator () should not define $X==Y$, or $X<=Y$, or $X>=Y$. If a user-defined function object does this then the containers and algorithms that depend on those function objects will not behave properly.

The **less** function object in the STL provides a $<$ relationship between $X$, $Y$. When the **less<int>** parameter was passed in the declaration of **MySet** in Listing 4.8, we were requesting that the set be ordered from smallest to largest. As the insert member function is adding members to **MySet** the **less<int>** function object is being called to determine where the object should be placed in the set based on its value being less than some other value in the set. Table 4.12 show the members in **MySet** from smallest to largest. This is a result of the **less<int>** function object that was passed as the second argument in the declaration of **MySet**. We could have used the STL's greater function object as the sort order. This would have placed the objects in the set from the largest to the smallest.

The program in Listing 4.8 also demonstrates that only one copy of each member is allowed in the set. Note that we attempted to add the value 1960 twice to **MySet**. This request was ignored. Looking at Table 4.12 we can see that the number of elements in **MySet** is only 5 and not 6. This was determined by using a call to the **size()** member function of **MySet**. The **less<T>** function object was also useful in determining whether an object is already in the set. Since object equality or *key* equality is determined by the function object, then if an object is equal to an object already in the set it is not added.

Note: Object equivalence for the associative collections is not determined by the $==$ operator that is defined for the class. Object equivalence is determined by two calls to the function object, for example, **MyObject(X,Y)** $==$ False, **MyObject(Y,X)** $==$ FALSE.

## CONSTRUCTORS AND DESTRUCTORS FOR STL'S ASSOCIATIVE COLLECTIONS

Each associative collection has three constructors. Each collection provides a default constructor. The default constructor takes one argument. However, the function object that was used to provide the sort order for the collection is used as the default for this argument so the user does not have to specify an argument for the default constructor. It will build an empty collection. The second constructor that the associative collections provide constructs a collection with copies of another collection. For instance, if we declare two sets $A$ and $B$:

```
set<int, less<int> A
A.insert(5);
A.insert(6);
set<int,less<int> B(A);
```

then *B* will contain a copy of the members in set *A*. The third type of constructor that the association containers provide is the range constructor. The containers are supplied with two argument iterators that meet the requirements of input iterators. The first argument represents the beginning of the range, and the second argument represents the end of a range. The program in Listing 4.9 declares three sets: **MySet**, **MySet2**, and **MySet3**. **MySet** is constructed using the first type of constructor. Technically this constructor requires one argument. However, since the sort order function object is the default for this, the user does not have to supply an argument. The collection **MySet2** is constructed with a copy of **MySet** with the statement:

set <int,less<int > > MySet2(MySet);

Table 4.14 shows that **MySet2** contains the same elements that **MySet** contains. It should be noted that the elements that are in **MySet2** are copies of the elements in **MySet**. The collection **MySet3** has been constructed using a range. The range that **MySet3** accepts as an argument comes from the array of **ints** named *A*. Since traditional pointers in C++ meet the requirements of input iterators, we are able to specify the starting address of the array and the ending address of the array as arguments to the constructor of **MySet3**.

### Listing 4.9

```
// This program demonstrates the declaration
// of a set collection and the usage of the
// three types of constructors for a set
#define __MINMAX_DEFINED
#include <function.h>
#include <set.h>
#include <iostream.h>

void main(void)
{
   int A[5];
   A[0] = 1960;
   A[1] = 1952;
   A[2] = 1771;
   A[3] = 1812;
   A[4] = 1996;
   set<int, less<int> > MySet;
   MySet.insert(1960);
   MySet.insert(1952);
   MySet.insert(1771);
   MySet.insert(1812);
   MySet.insert(1960);
   MySet.insert(1996);
   set<int, less<int> >::iterator M = MySet.begin();
   cout << "Number Of Elements " << MySet.size() << endl;
   set <int,less<int > > MySet2(MySet);
```

| Table 4.14 Output from Program Listing 4.9 shows three sets that were constructed differently and ended up holding the same data. |
| --- |
| *Output from Program Listing 4.9* |
| Number of Elements 5<br>MySet 1771 : MySet 2 1771 : MySet 3 1771<br>MySet 1812 : MySet 2 1812 : MySet 3 1812<br>MySet 1952 : MySet 2 1952 : MySet 3 1952<br>MySet 1960 : MySet 2 1960 : MySet 3 1960<br>MySet 1996 : MySet 2 1996 : MySet 3 1996 |

```
set <int,less<int > >::iterator N = MySet2.begin();
set<int,less<int> > MySet3(A,A+5);
set <int, less<int > >::iterator P = MySet3.begin();

while(M != MySet.end())
{
cout << "MySet " << *M << " : MySet2 " << *N;
cout << " : MySet3 " << *P << endl;
M++;
N++;
P++;
}
}
```

Table 4.14 shows the output of the program in Listing 4.9 after it has been executed. Note that **MySet** and **MySet2** have the same elements because of the manner in which **MySet2** was constructed. The while loop in the program in Listing 4.9 demonstrates how iterators can be used for loop control. Since **M** originally points to the beginning of **MySet** we can traverse the set by using the ++ operator. Eventually **M** will be equal to **MySet.end**() causing the loop to exit.

The maps and multimaps are constructed the same as the sets and multisets are constructed. The program in Listing 4.10 uses arrays, sets, and maps to demonstrate how maps can be constructed, and how elements can be inserted and accessed in map collections. One of the STL objects, **pair**, is used to build objects that will be inserted into a map collection. Like the function objects, the object **pair** is one of the *pattern* objects that the STL uses to complete the functionality of the collections and containers. The definition for the pair object can be found in *pair.h*.

### Listing 4.10

```
// This program demonstrates the usage of the three
// constructors for the map collection. It also
// demonstrates how map elements can be accessed
// using associations. The last loop demonstrates
// how a set iterator can be used as an association
// element for a map.
```

```
#include <cstring.h>
#include <map.h>
#include <set.h>
#include <iostream.h>

void main(void)
{

  map<string,string,less<string> > MapA;
  pair<string,string> Group[4];
  Group[0].first = "orange";
  Group[0].second = "clock work";
  Group[1].first = "red";
  Group[1].second = "Herring";
  Group[2].first = "white";
  Group[2].second = "Knight";
  Group[3].first = "silver";
  Group[3].second = "bullet";
  MapA["blue"] = "bird";
  MapA["brown"] = "bear";
  MapA["green"] = "goblin";
  map<string,string,less<string> > MapB(MapA);
  cout << MapB["green"] << endl;
  cout << MapB["blue"] << endl;
  cout << MapB["brown"] << endl;
  map<string,string,less<string > > MapC(Group,Group+4);
  set<string,less<string> > SetA;
  SetA.insert("white");
  SetA.insert("silver");
  SetA.insert("orange");
  SetA.insert("red");
  set<string,less<string> >::iterator P = SetA.begin();
  while(P != SetA.end())
  {
    cout << *P << " " << MapC[*P] << endl;
    P++;
  }
}
```

The program in Listing 4.10 declares three map collections: **MapA**, **MapB**, and **MapC**. **MapA** is constructed with the constructor that acts as the default constructor for the association collection. This means that **MapA** is constructed as an empty collection that has a sort order based on the function object that was passed as part of the collection declaration. Three objects are placed into **MapA**: "bird," "bear," and "goblin." Elements that are placed into map collections are retrieved by specifying the keys they are associated with. This is similar to how elements of an array are retrieved. When accessing elements in an array the user specifies the index of the element and the element is returned. For example, by specifying **A[5]**, we are asking for the fifth element from the array called **A**. Maps provide a similar functionality. Instead of associating each element with an integer value, maps allow any kind of object to be associated. This association is called a relation. In the program in Listing 4.11 we associated "blue" with "bird," "brown" with "bear," and "green" with "goblin." This was done by using the [] subscript operator of the map class. When the container receives the request to assign an element, as in

MapA["blue"] = "bird";

it checks to see whether there is already an element called "bird" that is associated with "blue." If there is no such pairing the pair is added to the container. From then on whenever we select "blue" as the key we get "bird" as the element. After the three elements and keys have been placed into **MapA**, **MapB** is constructed with a copy of the elements in **MapA** by the statement:

map<string,string,less<string> > MapB(MapA);

Table 4.15 shows the output of the program from Listing 4.10. Notice that **MapB** contains the same elements that **MapA** contains. Copying elements from one container to another can be done in a number of ways. One of the simplest is through the use of this constructor. **MapB** could also receive a copy of the elements in **MapA** by using the assignment statement:

MapB = MapA

The collection **MapC** has been constructed using a range of input iterators. The range of iterators in this example belong to an array named **Group. Group** is an array of four pairs of objects. The **pair** class has two data members: **first** and **second**. Each element in the **Group** array is initialized to a pair of strings. The first string will be used for a key. The second string will be used for an element. The **MapC** collection receives the starting address of **Group** and the ending address of **Group**. These two addresses serve as the beginning and ending range for the constructor. The constructor initially constructs the collection as empty. Then it inserts the elements one by one from the range or interval **[first, last)** where first represents the starting input iterator and last represents the ending input iterator.

Note: The STL uses interval notation to express a range of iterators or a range of values.

---

**Table 4.15   Output from Program Listing 4.10 demonstrates which map elements are displayed after the program has been executed.**

*Output from Program Listing 4.10*

goblin
bird
bear
orange clock work
red Herring
silver bullet
white Knight

The [] brackets and the () parentheses are used. The symbol [*a*, *b*] is an interval where *a* and *b* are called endpoints. In the interval [*a*, *b*], *a* is included in the interval and *b* is also included in the interval. This is called a closed interval. The interval (*a*, *b*) includes all the elements between *a* and *b*. However, *a* and *b* are not included in the interval. This is called an open interval. The intervals [*a*, *b*), and (*a*, *b*] are called half-open intervals. Whichever endpoint has a parenthesis, that endpoint is not included in the interval or range.

Table 4.15 shows the elements of **MapC**. Notice the statement:

```
while(P != SetA.end())
{
   cout << *P << " " << MapC[*P] << endl;
   P++;
}
```

in Listing 4.10. A set iterator **P** is used to traverse through **SetA**. **SetA** contains elements that are used as associations, or keys for **MapC**. When **P** is dereferenced it returns a string. This string is used as a key to retrieve an element from **MapC**. Table 4.15 shows the output of this statement. All sequence containers provide destructors. The basic operation of the destructor is to:

Remove all elements from the container, effectively calling the destructors for all contained objects.

Deallocate in memory for the container, effectively returning all requested memory back to the operating system or memory pool.

### ADDING OBJECTS TO ASSOCIATIVE COLLECTIONS

The set and multiset collections provide *three* basic ways to add objects. The map and multimap collections provide *four* basic ways to add objects. Objects can be added to sets and multisets through constructors, the **insert()** member functions, and through assignment. Objects can be added to maps and multimaps through constructors, the **insert()** member functions, assignment, and the [] subscript operator. The program in Listing 4.10 shows how the insert member function is used for sets, and the [] subscript operator is used for maps. There are four versions of the **insert()** member function. Table 4.16 shows the four versions of the **insert()** member function and their definitions.

### REMOVING OBJECTS FROM ASSOCIATIVE COLLECTIONS

Objects are removed from the associative collection in two ways: when the collection leaves scope and when an **erase()** member function is used. When an associative collection leaves scope, any objects that remain in the collection are removed and the destructors for those objects are called. After the objects have been removed, any space that the collection has allocated for those objects is released and the collection object is deleted. The **erase** member function can be used to remove an interval of objects as in [*a*, *b*], (*a*, *b*), [*a*, *b*), or (*a*, *b*]. The **erase** member function can be used to delete all the elements in a collection that have a particular value, or it can be used to erase an element at a specific position. Table 4.17 shows the various versions of the **erase()** member function and its uses.

### ITERATORS FOR THE ASSOCIATIVE COLLECTIONS

The associative collections provide iteration that is fundamentally the same as iteration for the sequence containers. The iterators for associative collections are bidirectional iterators. The **insert()** member function does not affect the validity of the iterators and references to the collection. The **erase()** member function invalidates only the iterators and references to the erased elements (see "STL Iterators").

**Table 4.16   Four versions of the insert() member function and their descriptions.**

| insert() version | Return Type | Description |
|---|---|---|
| **a_uniq.insert(t)** | pair<iterator, bool> | * a_uniq is a value of the associative container class when the associative container class supports unique keys.<br>* t is inserted into the container if and only if there is no element in the container with key equal to the key of t.<br>* bool component of the return type indicates whether the insertion takes place.<br>* Iterator component of the return type points to the element with key equal to the key of t. |
| **a_eq.insert(t)** | iterator | * a_eq is a value of the associative container class when the associative container supports multiple keys.<br>* t is inserted into the container.<br>* Iterator returned points to the newly inserted element. |
| **a.insert(p, t)** | iterator | * a is a value of the associative container class.<br>* p is a valid iterator to where the **insert()** should start to search.<br>* t is inserted into the container if and only if there is no element with key equal to the key of t in a container with unique keys; always inserts t in containers with equal keys.<br>* Iterator returned points to the element with key equal to the key of t. |
| **a.insert(i, j)** | result is not used | * a is a value of the associative container class.<br>* i and j is a range of elements that is inserted into the container. |

**Table 4.17   Three versions of the erase() member function and their descriptions.**

| erase() version | Return Type | Description |
| --- | --- | --- |
| **a.erase(k)** | size_type | * a is a value of the associative container class.<br>* k is the key in which all elements in the container are erased with a key equal to k.<br>* size_type is returned; it is the number of erased elements. |
| **a.erase(q)** | result is not used | * a is a value of the associative container class.<br>* q is a pointer to an element that is erased. |
| **a.erase(q1, q2)** | result is not used | * a is a value of the associative container class.<br>* q1 and q2 is a range of elements erased from the container. |

# THE STL ADAPTORS

The STL supports seven basic containers: vector, list, deque, set, multiset, map, and multimap. These containers and collections provide the fundamental capability to store, retrieve, and access objects. The containers and collections are augmented by a set of algorithms that the STL provides. However, missing from the STL's list of basic containers is the stack, queue, and priority queue. These are standard data structures and are requirements in many important applications. The STL provides three template classes called *adaptors* that can be used in conjunction with the sequence containers to provide the functionality of stacks, queues, and priority queues.

## What Are Adaptors?

Adaptors are classes that modify or adjust the interface of other classes in order to simplify, restrict, make safe, disguise, or change the view of the set of services that the modified class is providing. When a class is used for the sole purpose of changing the interface of another class, it is called a adaptor, or interface class (see Stroustrup 1991, 457). The STL provides three types of adaptors: *container adaptors*, *iterator adaptors*, and *function adaptors*.

### CONTAINER ADAPTORS

The container adaptors are used to extend the seven basic containers to include stack, queue, and priority queue containers. While the container adaptors do provide new containers, they require virtually no new code. This is because the container adaptors largely reuse code from existing containers. For instance, the stack adaptor can be used to change or map the interface of the vector, list, or deque containers. The queue can be used to change or map the interface of the list and deque containers. The priority queue can be used to change the interface of the vector and deque containers. Table 4.18 shows which adaptors can be used with containers. In Chapter 3 we stated that there are several ways the collection and container classes can be approached and understood from a OOD or OOP perspective:

Logical views
Geometrical views
Access methods
Mathematical descriptions
Implementation representations
Physical representations

The common collection and container classes are shown in Table 3.2. The adapter classes present one logical view of a class while providing a different implementation of the class. When we look at the stack adaptor class that has been instantiated with a vector, we say that the class has the logical look of a stack but the implementation of a vector, or it is a stack implemented as a vector. We could have a stack that is instantiated by a list. In this case we would say that we have a stack implemented as a list. Figure 4.4 shows how the services of a stack can be mapped onto some of the services of a vector.

The STL adaptor classes really don't provide any new services; they simply change the names, order of execution, or syntax of services that are already provided in the STL. For example, Listing 4.11 shows a declaration of the STL's stack adaptor.

### Listing 4.11

// This is a declaration of the stack adaptor class

```
template <class Container>
class stack {
friend bool operator==(const stack<Container>& x, const stack<Container>& y);
friend bool operator<(const stack<Container>& x, const stack<Container>& y);
public:
   typedef Container::value_type value_type;
   typedef Container::size_type size_type;
```

**Table 4.18   Shows the adaptors that can be used with the containers.**

| Containers | Operations | Adaptors |
|---|---|---|
| **Stack** | back, push_back, pop_back | List, Vector, Deque |
| **Queue** | front, back, push_back, pop_front | List, Deque |
| **Priority Queue** | front, push_back, pop_back | List, Deque |

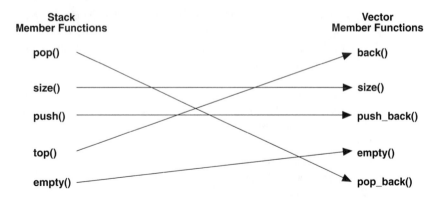

**Figure 4.4** The services of a stack can be mapped to some of the services of a vector.

```
protected:
  Container c;
public:
  bool empty() const { return c.empty(); }
  size_type size() const { return c.size(); }
  value_type& top() { return c.back(); }
  const value_type& top() const { return c.back(); }
  void push(const value_type& x) { c.push_back(x); }
  void pop() { c.pop_back(); }
};
```

Notice that the familiar stack **push**() and **pop**() operations are not implemented by new functions. Instead they are implemented by a call to **Container's push_back**() and **pop_back**() member functions. Since the stack is a parameterized class, any class that provides the member functions that stack is mapping can be used. Notice in the stack adaptor in Listing 4.12 that the **Container c** is *protected*. This prevents nonderived classes or users from directly accessing the **Container's** member functions. In this way the implementer of the stack adaptor can restrict how **Container's** member functions are used, and how they are named. The stack adaptor class demonstrates one of the primary uses for interface classes. By restricting the use of some member functions and masking the use of other member functions with new names, the implementer of the stack adaptor can provide the user with new functionality while reusing code.

The declaration in Listing 4.11 illustrates another important point about adaptors, namely, that they don't use inheritance. Adaptors are flat classes just like the seven basic containers that the STL provides.

## DECLARING CONTAINER ADAPTORS

Since adaptors are templates they must be passed arguments during declaration. The arguments for the container adaptors are chosen from the list of sequence containers. For instance, to declare a stack of characters that is implemented as a vector, we would use the declaration:

stack < vector <char > > MyStack

Once a adaptor container is declared it can be used in the same manner as a sequence or associative container. For instance, to add objects to or remove objects from **MyStack**, we could call the **push()** and **pop()** member functions:

```
MyStack.push('a');
MyStack.pop()
```

To use the adaptor classes their header files must be included. The stack, queue, and priority queue adaptors are declared in *stack.h*. This header file must be included if the adaptor classes are to be used. Since the adaptors are primarily interfaces to existing sequence containers, adaptor construction and destruction are handled by the constructors and destructors of the particular sequence container that is being mapped. The container adaptors all have as protected data members a Container type. Figure 4.5 shows the basic class relationship diagram for the container adaptors.

## ITERATOR ADAPTORS

The STL has adaptors for some of the iterators as well as the sequence containers. For instance, there is a *reverse iterator* that is implemented by a *bidirectional iterator* or *random access iterator*. The reverse iterator can iterate through the container in the opposite direction. For reverse iterators the interface is the same as the interface for the bidirectional or random access iterator, except the container traversal is done in reverse. There are two types of reverse iterators:

- mutable **reverse_iterator**
- **const_reverse_iterator**

The *mutable* **reverse_iterator** allows the contents of the container or collection to be changed when it is used. The **const_reverse_iterator**, while providing for reverse traversal, does not allow the container or collection to be changed through the iterator; in effect, the **const_reverse_iterator** is a *read-only* iterator. Whereas the container adaptors have to be declared by the user, the reverse iterators are already declared and are a part of every container. For example, to use the reverse iterator for a list we could declare an object **P** to be of type:

```
list<double>::reverse_iterator P
```

We could now initialize **P** with one of **MyList's** member functions. For instance:

```
list<double> MyList;
P = MyList.begin();
```

Any traversing through the list, for example, **P++**, would actually be moving in the reverse direction. Using a mutable **reverse_iterator**, statements such as

```
*P = 3.14
```

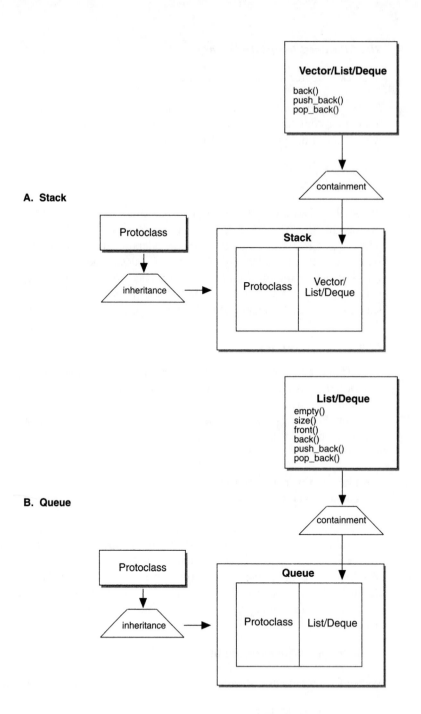

A. Stack

B. Queue

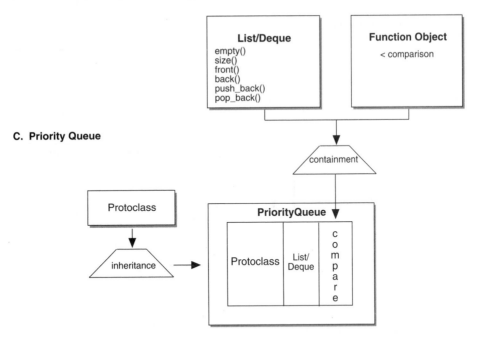

**Figure 4.5**  Basic class relationship diagram for container adaptor's stack, queue, and priority queue.

are legal. Whereas if we are using **const_reverse_iterators**, statements such as

    *P = 3.14

are not allowed. This is because we are attempting to change the value that the **P** iterator is pointing at, and this is not allowed with **const_iterators**, or **const_reverse_iterators**. The **reverse_iterators** can also be used with the STL generic algorithms. The algorithms will function as they do with regular iterators, except the algorithms will work with the container in reverse.

The second type of iterator adaptor is the *inserter adaptor*. Although this adaptor's primary function is to modify an iterator's behavior, it does so by modifying the container's interface. The iterator adaptors are some of the few classes that utilize inheritance. Figure 4.6 shows the class relationship diagrams for the **inserter, front-_inserter,** and **back_inserter** adaptors. Notice that each of the inserter adaptors inherits the class **output_iterator**. This provides each inserter with the necessary write functionality. The inserter adaptor changes an iterator's function by causing it to insert items into a collection or container as opposed to overwriting elements in a collection or container. The inserter adaptor effectively puts the container into *insert mode*, rather than overwrite. The inserter adaptor allows the user to insert an object at any point in the container. The **front_inserter_iterator** inserts objects at the beginning of a container and the **back_insert_iterator** inserts objects at the back or end of a container. In order to use the iterators, include the *iterator.h* header file.

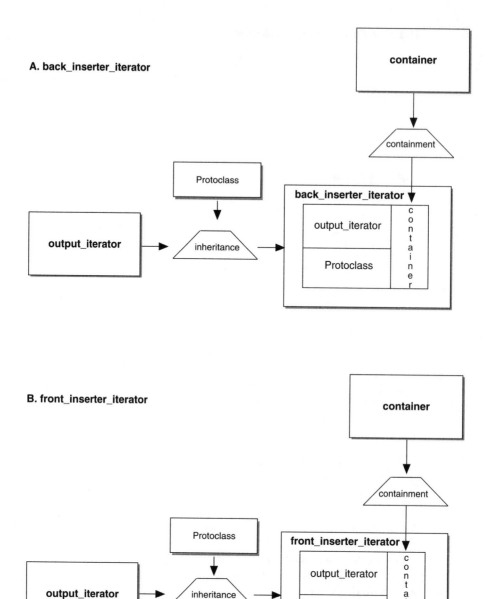

**Figure 4.6** The class relationship diagrams for the **back_inserter_iterator** and **front_inserter_iterator** adaptors.

### FUNCTION ADAPTORS

The third type of adaptor is one that modifies the interface or behavior of functions. These adaptors are called *function adaptors*. Function adaptors work on the STL's function objects or user-defined function objects that meet the basic requirement of the STL's function objects.

## CORE CONTAINER FUNCTIONALITY

There is a certain set of data members and member functions that both the sequence and associative containers provide. All containers will have a set of iterators. These iterators will include:

```
X::iterator
X::const_iterator
X::reverse_iterator
X::const_reverse_iterator
```

All the containers provide data members that document the type of object that they will be storing. These data members include:

```
X::value_type
X::size_type
X::difference_type
```

All the containers provide data members that can hold pointers and references to the objects that they will be storing. These data members include:

```
X::reference
X::const_reference
X::pointer
```

Along with the core set of data members each container provides a set of constructors, including copy constructors. All copy constructors only provide shallow copying. Every container provides a destructor. All containers provide automatic storage management, relational comparison ($<,>,=<,>=,!=,==$), assignment (shallow copy), begin-end iterators, **size()**, **max_size()**, **empty()**, and **swap()** member functions. Table 4.19 shows the core container functionality and general descriptions for each data member and member function. If user-defined template containers are designed, they should include the core container functionality with its operational semantics.

## STL ALGORITHMS

A major component of the Standard Template Library is the algorithm. One of the features that distinguishes the STL from traditional collection and container class libraries is that the STL's containers only implement a part of their functionality. Large chunks of container functionality have been captured in a set of separate algorithms.

Table 4.19   This table lists the core container functionality and a general description for each data member and member function.

| Data Members | Type | Description |
|---|---|---|
| **X :: value_type** | T | * X is a container class containing objects of Type T.<br>* A type that the container holds. |
| **X :: reference** | | * X is a container.<br>* A type that can be used to store X::value_type objects. This type is usually X::value_type&. |
| **X :: const_reference** | | * X is a container<br>* A constant reference type identical to X::reference. |
| **X :: pointer** | a pointer type pointing to X::reference | * X is a container<br>* A pointer to T in the memory model used by the container. |
| **X :: Iterator** | iterator type pointing to X::reference | * X is a container.<br>* An iterator of any category except output iterator. |
| **X :: const_iterator** | iterator type pointing to X::reference | * X is a container.<br>* A constant iterator of any iterator category except output iterator. |
| **X :: difference_type** | signed integral type | * X is a container.<br>* Is identical to the distance type of X::iterator and X::const_iterator. |
| **X :: size_type** | unsigned itegral type | * X is a container.<br>* size_type can represent any non-negative value of difference_type. |
| **X u** | | * X is a container.<br>* u.size() == 0. |
| **a == b** | convertible to bool | * a and b are values of X.<br>* == is an equivalence relation.<br>* Equal is defined as an algorithm. |
| **a != b** | convertible to bool | * a and b are values of X.<br>* Defines not equal relation. |
| **r = a** | X& | * a is a value of X.<br>* r is a value of X&. |

| Data Members | Type | Description |
|---|---|---|
| **a < b** | convertible to bool | * a and b are values of X.<br>* < is defined for value of T (precondition).<br>* < is a total ordering relation.<br>* lexicographical_compare is an algorithm. |
| **a > b** | convertible to bool | * a and b are values of X.<br>* > is defined for value of T (precondition). |
| **a <= b** | convertible to bool | * a and b are values of X.<br>* <= is defined for value of T (precondition). |
| **a >= b** | convertible to bool | * a and b are values of X.<br>* >= is defined for value of T (precondition). |
| **X u=a** | | * X is a container.<br>* u == a (postcondition). |
| **X ()** | | * X is a container.<br>* X().size() == 0. |
| **X(a)** | | * X is a container and a is a value of X.<br>* a == X(a). |
| **X u(a)** | | * X is a container.<br>* a is a value of X and u is an identifier.<br>* u == a (postcondition). |
| **(&a)−>~X()** | result is not used | * X is a container and a is a value of X.<br>* a.size() == 0 (postcondition).<br>* The destructor is applied to every element of a and all the memory is returned. |
| **a.begin()** | iterator; const_iterator for constant a | * a is a value of X.<br>* Returns the iterator that points to the beginning element of the container that can be used to traverse all locations in the container. |

**Table 4.19**   This table lists the core container functionality and a general description for each data member and member function. (*continued*)

| Data Members | Type | Description |
|---|---|---|
| a.end() | iterator; const_iterator for constant a | * Element of the container that can be used in a comparison for ending the traversal through a container. |
| a.size() | size_type | * a is a value of X. <br> * Returns the number of elements in a container. |
| a.max_size() | size_type | * a is a value of X. <br> * size() of the largest possible container. |
| a.empty() | convertible to bool | * a is a value of X. <br> * Returns true if the container is empty. |
| a.swap(b) | void | * a and b are values of X. <br> * Swaps two containers of the same type in constant time. |

These algorithms are free floating and do not belong to any particular class. The object-oriented approach to collections and containers dictates that the functionality and all the services that the container should provide must be encapsulated within the container or collection class declaration. The STL moves away from the object-oriented specification of collection and containers, and moves to a *genericity driven* approach. The STL collection and container functionality is divided between a set of container classes, generic algorithms, and iterator classes. There are more algorithms in the STL than there are containers. So a basic understanding of the STL's algorithms and the way they are used is necessary to get the full use of the STL's containers. For instance, if the user wants to use the **set** container in order to take advantage of the notions of *set intersection* and *set union*, the user must use both the STL's set container and the STL's set intersection and set union algorithms. The set container is a good example of how functionality that is normally encapsulated within the class declaration is separated into various algorithms.

Genericity is accomplished in the STL's algorithms because the algorithms are parameterized. The STL algorithms can take object types and iterators as parameters. Because the algorithms take the type of object as a parameter, they can work with any object that meets certain basic assumptions. Because the algorithms accept iterators as parameters, they are no longer dependent on container structure. This design allows the algorithms that access the container to be separate from the container's design and implementation. Note that this is one of the primary goals of genericity and is in contrast to the main tenet of object-oriented design, namely, "encapsulating algorithms and data in a *single unit*." The techniques of genericity fall under the category of parameterized programming. "The basic idea of parameterized programing is to maximize software reuse by creating and storing software in as general form as possible. One can then construct new software modules from old ones by just instantiating parameters" (Matsumoto, Ohno 1989, 78). Although the goal of software reuse is a primary goal of object-oriented programming and parameterized programming, both techniques go about it in different ways. The C++ language supports both object-oriented programming and parameterized programming; therefore the C++ programmer can take advantage of both techniques. The STL mixes object-oriented programming with parameterized programming to achieve power and flexible programming structures.

The STL provides over 30 algorithms that can be used to access containers. These algorithms include a wide range of functionality, from searching, sorting, and counting objects in containers to partitioning and permutating objects in the collections and containers. The STL algorithms can be divided into two major categories: *nonmutating algorithms* and *mutating algorithms*.

The *nonmutating algorithms* are those algorithms that access the objects in the container but do not change any of the values of the objects in the container. The *mutating algorithms* are those algorithms that can access objects as well as change the values of the objects in a container. The majority of the STL algorithms have known performance measurements. For instance, some algorithms are said to take linear time, or constant time. O notation is also used to describe algorithm performance; for instance, the **binary_search** algorithm takes **Olog(n) + 2** steps.

## Algorithm Parameter Requirements

The STL algorithms take iterators as parameters. Since the iterators provide generic access to the sequence and associative containers, the algorithms do not need to know the structures of the containers. The algorithms rely upon assumptions about the iterators in order to process the containers. Certain algorithms require random access iterators, while other algorithms require only input iterators, while others require forward iterators, and so on. The information that is carried by the type of iterator supplied is enough for the algorithm to work. As long as the iterators are *sufficient* for the algorithm's requirements, the structure and type of the container are needed.

Let's look at a traditional implementation of a binary search to see how the algorithm depends on the data structure and data type to work. The function **binarySearch** in Listing 4.12 is a recursive implementation of the classic binary search algorithm.

### Listing 4.12

// Example of a traditional binary search algorithm

```
#include <iostream.h>

int binarySearch(int Data[],int X,int Begin, int End)
{
  int Middle = 0;
  if(Begin > End){
    return( - 1);
  }
  Middle =(Begin + End) /2;
  if(X == Data[Middle]){
```

```
      return(Middle);
    }
    else
      if(X < Data[Middle]){
        return(binarySearch(Data,X,Begin,(Middle − 1)));
      }
      else
        return(binarySearch(Data,X,(Middle + 1),End)));
  }
  void main(void)
  {
    int R[5];
    R[0] = 1111;
    R[1] = 1343;
    R[2] = 4321;
    R[3] = 8889;
    R[4] = 9134;
    int Position = binarySearch(R,9134,0,4);
    cout << Position;
  }
```

Notice the parameters that the **binarySearch** algorithm accepts:

```
int Data[]
int X
int Begin
int End
```

The first parameter tells the **binarySearch** algorithm that the container that it is going to be working with is an array. The first parameter also tells the **binarySearch** algorithm that the array will be an array of **ints**. This means that if the user passes an array of **chars**, or **doubles**, or **strings** either the program won't compile or the algorithm will not work properly. The second parameter tells the algorithm what objects to search for, as well as the objects' type. Again, since this algorithm is expecting an **int** as the item to be searched for, if the user passes a **struct** or some other data type, then the algorithm will not perform properly. Also the beginning of the container and the end of the container is passed to this algorithm.

This implementation of the binary search is data type dependent, and data structure dependent. It will only work with **int** data types, and will only work on arrays of **ints**. Also the beginning and ending locations in the array container must be of type **int**. If we wanted to search a list of doubles we would have to write a **binarySearch** for **doubles**, and if we wanted to search a list of **chars** we would have to write a **binarySearch** for **chars**, and so on. Although there are some workarounds like implementing the algorithms to accept void pointers, these complicate the logic and elegance of the algorithms and make them more difficult to understand and maintain. The STL algorithm removes the data type dependence and the data structure dependence by relying on generic container iterators. The program in Listing 4.13 demonstrates how the **binary_search** algorithm is used in conjunction with an STL container.

**Listing 4.13**

```
// This program demonstrates the usage of the binary_search
// algorithm
#define __MINMAX_DEFINED
#include <algo.h>
#include <set.h>
#include <iostream.h>

void main(void)
{
    set <int ,less<int> > SetA;
    SetA.insert(8192);
    SetA.insert(4096);
    SetA.insert(2048);
    SetA.insert(1024);
    int Value = 4096;
    set <int, less<int> >::iterator P = SetA.begin();
    set <int, less<int> >::iterator Q = SetA.end();
    cout << (binary_search(P,Q,Value) ? "found" : "not found");
}
```

Notice that the **binary_search** algorithm is looking for the number 4096 in a set called **SetA**. In the call to the **binary_search** algorithm there are references to any particular container, or container type. Only iterators and a value to search for are passed to the **binary_search** algorithm. This is in contrast to the information necessary for the **binarySearch** function that was used in Listing 4.12. The STL's **binary_search** algorithm can work with any type of collection or container given that the container supports iterators that meet the *sufficient* conditions of the **ForwardIterator**.

It is important to determine whether an algorithm can be used with a specific container. Not all algorithms can be used with all containers. For instance, the sort algorithm requires two **RandomAccessIterators**, and the list container only supports **BidirectionalIterators**. While **BidirectionalIterator** capability is *necessary* in random iteration, it is not *sufficient*, therefore the list container cannot be used around this problem. Table 4.20 shows a list of the STL algorithms and their iterator requirements. When using these algorithms with any of the STL containers, the user must make sure that the iterator capabilities of the container are sufficient for the iterator requirements of the algorithm.

## Nonmutating Algorithms

The STL has seven nonmutating sequence algorithms: find, **adjacent_find**, **for_each**, **count**, **mismatch**, **equal**, and **search**. Table 4.21 shows the nonmutating algorithm, the iterator requirement, and performance.

**Table 4.20    A list of the STL generic algorithms and their iterator requirements.**

| Algorithms | | Input | Output | Forward | Bidirectional | Random Access | Function Object |
|---|---|---|---|---|---|---|---|
| Nonmutating Sequence Operations | for_each | • | | | | | |
| | find | • | | | | | |
| | find_if | • | | | | | • |
| | adjacent_find* | • | | | | | • |
| | count | • | | | | | |
| | count_if | • | | | | | • |
| | mismatch* | • | | | | | • |
| | equal* | • | | | | | • |
| | search* | | | • | | | • |
| Mutating Sequence Operations | copy | • | • | | | | |
| | copy_backward | | | | • | | |
| | swap | | | | | | |
| | iter_swap | | | • | | | |
| | swap_ranges | | | • | | | |
| | transform | • | • | | | | • |
| | replace | | | • | | | |
| | replace_if | | | • | | | • |
| | replace_copy | • | • | | | | |
| | replace_copy_if | | • | | | | • |
| | fill | | | • | | | |
| | fill_n | | • | | | | |
| | generate | | | • | | | • |
| | generate_n | | • | | | | • |
| | remove | | | • | | | |
| | remove_if | | | • | | | • |
| | remove_copy | • | • | | | | • |
| | remove_copy_if | • | • | | | | • |
| | unique* | | | • | | | • |
| | unique_copy* | • | • | | | | • |
| | reverse | | | | • | | |
| | reverse_copy | | • | | • | | |

| | | Iterators | | | | | |
|---|---|---|---|---|---|---|---|
| Algorithms | | Input | Output | Forward | Bidirectional | Random Access | Function Object |
| Mutating Sequence Operations | rotate<br>rotate_copy | | • | •<br>• | | | |
| | random_shuffle | | | | | • | • |
| | partition<br>stable_partition | | | | •<br>• | | •<br>• |
| Sorting & Related Operations | sort*<br>stable_sort*<br>partial_sort*<br>partial_sort_copy* | • | | | | •<br>•<br>•<br>• | •<br>•<br>•<br>• |
| | nth_element* | | | | | • | • |
| | lower_bound*<br>upper_bound*<br>equal_range*<br>binary_search* | | | •<br>•<br>•<br>• | | | •<br>•<br>•<br>• |
| | merge* | • | • | | | | • |
| | inplace_merge* | | | | • | | • |
| Set Operations on Sorted Structures | includes*<br>set_union*<br>set_intersection*<br>set_difference*<br>set_symmetric_<br>difference* | •<br>•<br>•<br>•<br>• | •<br>•<br>•<br>•<br>• | | | | •<br>•<br>•<br>•<br>•<br>• |
| Heap Operations | push_heap*<br>pop_heap*<br>make_heap*<br>sort_heap* | | | | | •<br>•<br>•<br>• | •<br>•<br>•<br>• |
| Minimum and Maximum Operations | min<br>min<br>max<br>max<br>max_element*<br>min_element* | •<br>• | | | | | •<br>•<br>• |
| Lexicographical Comparison | lexicographical_<br>compare* | • | | | | | • |

**Table 4.20    A list of the STL generic algorithms and their iterator requirements. (*continued*)**

| | | Iterators | | | | | |
|---|---|---|---|---|---|---|---|
| *Algorithms* | | *Input* | *Output* | *Forward* | *Bidirectional* | *Random Access* | *Function Object* |
| Permutation Generators | next_permutation* | | | | • | | • |
| | prev_permutation* | | | | • | | • |
| Generalized Numeric Operations | accumulate* | • | | | | | • |
| | inner_product* | • | | | | | • |
| | partial_sum* | • | • | | | | • |
| | adjacent_ difference* | • | • | | | | • |

* This algorithm has a version that does not require a function object.

## Mutating Algorithms

The STL has 12 mutating-sequence algorithms: **copy**, **swap**, **replace**, **fill**, **transform**, **generate**, **reverse**, **rotate**, **random_shuffle**, **partition**, **remove**, and **unique**.

Table 4.22 shows the mutating algorithms, the iterator requirements, and performance.

## Sorting and Related Algorithms

The STL offers another group of algorithms that include sorts, merging, permutation, set operations on sorted containers, binary searches, and lexicographical comparison. Table 4.23 shows the sort-related algorithms, the iterator requirements, and performance. All of these algorithms have two versions; one that takes a function object of type **Compare**, and one that uses the < operator.

**Table 4.21   A list of the nonmutating algorithms, their runtime performance, and their iterator requirements for each algorithm.**

| Non-mutating Algorithms | Performance | Input | Output | Forward | Bidirectional | Random Access | Function Object |
|---|---|---|---|---|---|---|---|
| for_each | f is applied exactly last - first times. | ● | | | | | |
| find<br>find_if | find(first, last, value) - first applications of the corresponding predicate are done. | ●<br>● | | | | | ● |
| adjacent_find* | at most max((last - first)-1, 0) applications of the corresponding predicate are done. | ● | | | | | ● |
| count<br>count_if | exactly last - first applications of the corresponding predicate are done. | ●<br>● | | | | | ● |
| mismatch* | at most last1 - first1 applications of the corresponding predicate are done. | ● | | | | | ● |
| equal* | at most last1 - first1 applications of the corresponding predicate are done. | ● | | | | | ● |
| search* | at most (last1 - first1)*(last2 - first2) applications of the corresponding predicate are done. | | | ● | | | ● |

\* This algorithm has a version that does not require a function object.

**Table 4.22   A list of mutating algorithms, their runtime performance, and their iterator requirements for each algorithm.**

| Mutating Algorithms | Performance | Input | Output | Forward | Bidirectional | Random Access | Function Object |
|---|---|:---:|:---:|:---:|:---:|:---:|:---:|
| copy<br>copy_backward<br>swap<br>iter_swap<br>swap_ranges | exactly last - first assignments or swaps are performed. | • | • | •<br>• | • | | |
| transform | exactly last1 - first1 operations are done. | • | • | | | | • |
| replace<br>replace_if<br>replace_copy<br>replace_copy_if | exactly last - first applications of corresponding predicate are done. | • | •<br>• | •<br>• | | | •<br>• |
| fill<br>fill_n | exactly last - first (or n) assignments are done. | | • | • | | | |
| generate<br>generate_n | exactly last - first (or n) invocations of function object are done. | | • | • | | | •<br>• |
| remove<br>remove_if<br>remove_copy<br>remove_copy_if | exactly last - first applications of the corresponding predicate are done. | •<br>• | •<br>• | •<br>• | | | •<br>• |
| unique*<br>unique_copy* | exactly (last - first) -1 or last - first applications of function object are done. | • | • | • | | | •<br>• |
| reverse<br>reverse_copy | exactly (last - first)/2 swaps or last - first assignments are done. | | • | | •<br>• | | |
| rotate<br>rotate_copy | last - first swaps or assignments are done. | | • | •<br>• | | | |
| random_shuffle | exactly (last - first)-1 swaps are done. | | | | | • | • |
| partition<br>stable_partition | exactly last - first applications of function object are done. | | | | •<br>• | | •<br>• |

* This algorithm has a version that does not require a function object.

**Table 4.23   A list of sort-related algorithms, their runtime performance, and their iterator requirements.**

| Sort Algorithms | Performance | Input | Output | Forward | Bidirectional | Random Access | Function Object |
|---|---|---|---|---|---|---|---|
| sort* <br> stable_sort* <br> partial_sort* <br> partial_sort_copy* | various performance levels. | ● | | | | ● ● ● ● | ● ● ● ● |
| nth_element* | linear on average. | | | | | ● | ● |
| lower_bound* <br> upper_bound* <br> equal_range* <br> binary_search* | log(last - first) + 1 <br> 2*log(last - first) + 1 <br> log(last - first) + 2 <br> comparisons are done at most. | | | ● ● ● ● | | | ● ● ● ● |
| merge* <br> inplace_merge* | (last1 - first1) + (last2 - first2) - 1 or (last - first) - 1 comparisons at most are done. | ● | ● | | | | ● |

\* This algorithm has a version that does not require a function object.

CHAPTER 5

# THE OBJECT-ORIENTED SET

A SET IS a collection of objects. Sets are more than just containers because they specify a rich interface and restriction on the objects that can be a part of the set. We are all familiar with the notion of a set of things: a set of red balls, a set of blue blocks, a set of even numbers, and so on. Membership in a set is determined by whether an object meets a condition or set of conditions. For instance, if we have a set of even numbers, then any number that is divisible by 2 with no remainder can be an element of that set. This excludes odd numbers. That a set of even numbers *excludes* all numbers that are not even emphasizes an important point about the notion of a set. Not only does set membership specify the conditions for inclusion, set membership inclusion implies what objects are excluded from the set. This is an important characteristic of sets. Sometimes it is as important to know if an object is not in a set as it is to know if an object is a member of the set. Another important characteristic of sets is that they only allow an object to be included once. Along with the characteristics of set membership, inclusion and exclusion, the set operations provide powerful means for grouping and counting collections of objects. Set intersection, set union, set difference, set complement, set subset operations give the user the ability to identify a group of objects based on very complex set membership rules. Because the set membership conditions are virtually infinite, we can specify sets that are highly particular that contain few or no members, like the set of all U.S. presidents who were elected under the age of 18, or we can specify broad categories of objects, like the set of blue products sold before the year 1960. Set membership inclusion and exclusion conditions can be very intricate and complex, or simple with very few exclusions. Sets form the basis for many of the areas in mathematics and computer science. In fact, the entire field of database theory is based on the notion of the set and set operations.

Traditional languages such as Pascal provide elementary set data structures. Usually the set operations for these types of languages are limited to testing set membership. Typically there has been no native data type called *set*. Using C++ object-oriented constructs or template facilities we can build set classes. Because C++ has support for object-oriented programming, we can extend the techniques of object orientation to the notion of sets. We can design set classes, and specialize the classes with inheritance and virtual member functions. We can instantiate the set classes to get set objects. Once we have set objects we can store those set objects into vectors, or queues, or stacks, or lists, or even other set objects. We can use multiple inheritance to create hybrid sets. Because the sets can take advantage of object orientation we can store all kinds of diverse objects into sets, like bitmaps, sound files, built-in types, images, function objects, and so on. Once we have objects stored in our object-oriented sets we can use the set operations to build new sets, with new membership conditions. The set is one of the most versatile and expressive structures available to the C++ programmer.

Here are nine major types of sets: empty set, infinite set, ordered set, cartesian product, partition set, multiset, singleton set, universal set, and Power Set. In this chapter we shall explore how to use the set collection in the C++ language. We will use the STL's set and the STL's generic set operations as the basis for all of our set classes. We will specialize the STL's set class to add operations that have not been defined. We will explore the various types of sets and how the STL's set can be extended to implement them where possible.

# DISCUSSION

## AN INTRODUCTION TO SETS

A *set* is a collection of people, places, things, or ideas. For example, we may speak of the set of all men over the age of 35 who are married and own pink cars, or the set of all of fish that grow to a length of 100 feet, or the set of all C++ compilers that require less than 1 MB to execute, and so on. We call the people, places, things, or ideas in a given set its members or elements. If $x$ represents something or someone that is a member or element of a set that we call $A$, we use the notation:

$$x \in A$$

to mean that $x$ is a member of $A$, or $x$ is an element of $A$. If $x$ is not an element of $A$ we use the notation:

$$x \notin A$$

to mean that $x$ is not an element of $A$. This means that $x$ does not satisfy the membership rules for inclusion into set $A$. When we want to list elements of a set explicitly, we use { } notation. For example, if we have a set named $B$ that consists of all the odd whole numbers between 0 and 6 we write:

$$B = \{ 1,3,5 \}$$
$$\text{or}$$
$$\{ 1,3,5 \}$$

This notation works fine for sets that only have a few elements. However, if we wanted to use set notation to denote a large set, for instance, the set of all telephone numbers in Los Angeles, then this type of notation is not appropriate. It is not practical to list every phone number in Los Angeles explicitly, so we use another form of notation. To talk about large, compound, or complex sets, we use *set-builder notation*. Set-builder notation is a form of set shorthand. For instance, if the set $A$ is to contain all telephone numbers in Los Angeles we would write:

$$A = \{x : x \text{ is a Los Angeles telephone number}\}$$

We read this as "$A$ is the set of all values of $x$ such that $x$ is a Los Angeles telephone number." By using set-builder notation we are able to take a shortcut, and get around enumerating all the members of a particular set. In general, set-builder notation takes the form:

$$M = \{ x : P(x)\}$$

where $P(x)$ is a predicate describing the membership rules or membership conditions for the set $M$. Note that the : is used to represent the phrase *such that*. Any element meeting the conditions or rules stated in $P(x)$ are members of the set $M$.

## SET RELATIONSHIPS

The set that contains all of the elements or members that are under consideration is called the *universal set*. Two sets $A$ and $B$ are equal if every member in set $A$ is in set $B$, and every member in set $B$ is in set $A$. Set $A$ is a subset of set $B$ if every member in set $A$ is also a member in set $B$. We denote this relationship with the $\subset$ sign, such as:

$$A \subset B$$

This statement expresses that $A$ is a subset of $B$. For example, if set $M$ is the set of all people who use computers, and set $N$ is the set of all teenagers that use computers, then we could denote the sets and their relationship as follows:

$$M = \{ x : x \text{ is a person who uses computers}\}$$
$$N = \{ x : x \text{ is a teenager who uses computers}\}$$

$$N \subset M$$

Figure 5.1 shows how the subset relationship between $N$ and $M$ is depicted using *Venn diagrams*. Venn diagrams are used to pictorially show relationships between sets. When we have two sets such as $N$ and $M$, where $N \subset M$ but $N \neq M$, then we say that $N$ is a proper subset of $M$. However, if $N = M$ then we can say that $N$ is a subset of $M$, or $M$ is a subset of $N$. In this case we write:

$$N \subseteq M$$

to denote that although $N$ is not a *proper* subset of $M$, it is a subset of $M$.

If we have a set $A$, then $A'$ is the set of all elements that are not members of set $A$. The set $A'$ is called the *complement* of $A$. If

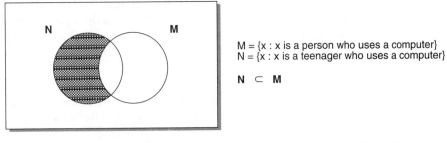

**Figure 5.1**   The Venn diagram for a subset relationship between N and M.

$$A = \{x : x \text{ is a Los Angeles phone number}\}$$

then

$$A' = \{x : x \text{ is not a Los Angeles phone number}\}$$

Figure 5.2 shows the Venn diagram of the relationships between $A$ and its complement $A'$. The empty set is the set that has no elements, and the empty set is denoted by $\varnothing$, or $\{\ \}$.

# SET OPERATIONS

There are three basic set operations: *set intersection, set union*, and *set difference*. Let's say we have two sets $A$ and $B$, then the intersection of set $A$ and $B$ is written as:

$$A \cap B$$

If set $M$ is the intersection of set $A$ and set $B$, then set $M$ contains all of those elements that are common to both $A$ and $B$. Set $M$ is denoted:

$$M = A \cap B$$

Let's say that set $A$ is the set of all people who use the Internet, and set $B$ is the set of all people who use computers; then the intersection $A \cap B$ is the set of all people who use

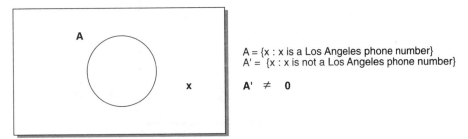

**Figure 5.2**   The Venn diagram for the relationship between A and its complement.

their computers and who also use the Internet. Figure 5.3 shows a Venn diagram that depicts the intersection of set $A$ and $B$. If set $C$ is the set of all people who use modems, then the intersection $A \cap B \cap C$ is the set of all people who use computers, modems, and the Internet. Figure 5.4 shows the intersection $A \cap B \cap C$. Where

$$A = \{x : x \text{ is a person who uses the Internet}\}$$
$$B = \{x : x \text{ is a person who uses a computer}\}$$
$$C = \{x : x \text{ is a person who uses a modem}\}$$

then the complement $(A \cap B \cap C)'$ is the set of all people who do not use computers, modems, or the Internet.

If we have two sets $B$ and $C$:

$$B = \{x : x \text{ is a person who uses a computer}\}$$
$$C = \{x : x \text{ is a person who uses a modem}\}$$

then the *union* of $B$ and $C$ is denoted as

$$B \cup C$$

If set $M = B\ C$, then $M$ contains all of the members that are in set $B$, and all of the members that are in set $C$. So that in this case $M$ is the set of all people who use computers and modems. Figure 5.5 shows the union $B \cup C$.

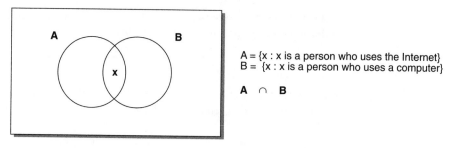

**Figure 5.3**   The Venn diagram for the intersection of A and B.

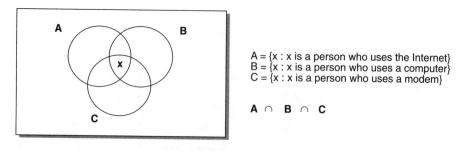

**Figure 5.4**   The Venn diagram for the intersection A, B, and C.

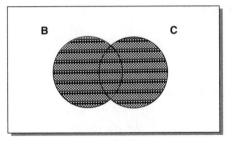

B = {x : x is a person who uses a computer}
C = {x : x is a person who uses a modem}

B ∪ C

**Figure 5.5**   The Venn diagram for the union of B and C.

Let's say set $U$ is the universal set, and that

$$U = \{ x : x \text{ is a person who uses a computer}\}$$

Also we have two others sets $M$, and $N$, and that

$$M = \{ x : x \text{ is a person who uses spreadsheets}\}$$
$$N = \{ x : x \text{ is a person who uses databases}\}$$

Then the set difference $M/N$ denotes the set of all people who use their computers and who use spreadsheets but *do not* use databases. Note that the set difference between $M$ and $N$ could have also been expressed

$$M \cap N'$$

Figure 5.6 shows a Venn diagram of the difference between set $M$ and set $N$. Set difference operations usually imply the existence of some universal set.

It is important to note that the operations on sets, intersection, union, and difference can be combined in all sorts of ways. For instance, if we have 5 sets:

$$A = \{x : x \text{ is a person who uses the internet}\}$$
$$B = \{x : x \text{ is a person who uses a computer}\}$$
$$C = \{x : x \text{ is a person who uses a modem}\}$$
$$M = \{ x : x \text{ is a person who uses spreadsheets}\}$$
$$N = \{ x : x \text{ is a person who uses databases}\}$$

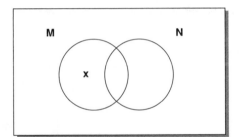

M = {x : x is a person who uses spreadsheets}
N = {x : x is a person who uses databases}

M \ N

**Figure 5.6**   The Venn diagram for the difference between set M and N.

then we may have expressions like:

$$P = ((M \cap N') \cap B) \cup (C \cap A)$$

where $P$ is the set of all people who use computers and modems. We can evaluate the expression in the innermost parenthesis first:

$$(M \cap N')$$

This represents the set of all people who use computers. We then can intersect this set with $B$. This again leaves us only with the set of people who use computers. Next we evaluate the expression:

$$(C \cap A)$$

This gives us the set of people who use modems. Finally, we union these two sets and get a set containing all the people who use modems and computers.

## CARDINALITY OF SETS

We call the number of members in a finite set $M$ the cardinality of $M$. We denote the cardinality of a set by the notation:

$$N = | M |$$
$$\text{or}$$
$$N = \text{Card } (M)$$

These statements mean that the number of elements in set $M$ is $N$. To determine $| M | = N$ we count the elements of $M$. In other words, we establish a one-to-one correspondence between the elements of $M$ and the elements of the set $\{1,2,3 \ldots N\}$.

## TYPES OF SETS

There are several types of sets that are commonly encountered:

Empty sets
Singleton sets
Power sets
Universal sets
Cartisian products
Infinite sets
Partition sets
Multisets

The *empty set* is the set that contains no members. It is sometimes called the *null* set and is denoted by ø { }. A set with exactly one element is called a *singleton set*.

For any set A, the *power set* of A, denoted by P(A), is the set of all subsets of A, and is written:

$$P(A) = \{\, X \mid X \subseteq A\}$$

Lets say that set $M = \{x \mid x$ is a common modem baud rate $<9600\}$, then

$$M = \{300, 1200, 2400\}$$

The power set of M is

$$P(M) = \{\varnothing, \{300\}, \{1200\}, \{2400\}, \{300,1200\}, \{300,2400\}, \{1200,2400\}, M\}$$

Note that ø set is a part of every set, including the power set.

The *universal set* is the set of all members under consideration. The universal set is only a subset of itself.

The *Cartesian product* is a set that has pairs of elements that come from two sets. Let A and B be sets. The Cartesian product of A and B, denoted by

$$A \times B$$

is the set of all ordered pairs $(x,y)$ where $x$ is an element of A, and $y$ is an element of B. If

$$A = \{\, 1,2,\}$$

and

$$B = \{a,b,c\}$$

and if C is the Cartesian product of A and B, denoted by

$$C = A \times B$$

then

$$C = \{\, (1,a), (2,a), (1,b), (2,b), (1,c), (2,c)\}$$

An *infinite set* is a set without bounds. For instance, the set of all even numbers, or the set of all fractions between the 1 and 2, are infinite sets. Infinite sets can be denoted by:

$$A = \{\, 2,4,6,8...\}$$
$$B = \{1\ 1/2,\ 1,1/4,1\ 1\ 1/16,\ 1\ 1/32\ ...\}$$

Or infinite sets can be stated using set-builder notation, for instance:

$$M = \{ \, x : x \text{ is a negative number } \}$$

Let $M$ and $N$ be two sets. If $M$ and $N$ have no members in common, then $M$ and $N$ are said to be *disjoint sets*. A separation of a nonempty set $A$ into mutually disjoint nonempty subsets is called a *partition* of the set $A$. For example, if

$$M = \{300,1200,2400,9600,14400,28800\}$$

then one partition of $M$ is

$$M_1 = \{300,2400\}, M_2 = \{14400,1200\}, M_3 = \{28800,9600\}$$

since $M = M_1 \; M_2 \; M_3$

Another partition is

$$M_1 = \{300\}, M_2 = \{14400,1200,2400,9600,28800\}$$

since $M = M_1 \; M_2$

Note that the partition uses every member of the universal set.

A multiset is a set that can contain duplicates of members. A set is an unordered collection of unique elements. A multiset is an unordered collection of not necessarily unique elements.

## WHAT IS AN OBJECT-ORIENTED SET?

An object-oriented set is a class that models our notion of a set. The class encapsulates the attributes and characteristics of the set. The member functions of the class provide the traditional set operations. Once we have a set class then we can use polymorphism and inheritance to generate specializations of the set class. The set class can be instantiated to create set objects. An object-oriented set will take advantage of the object-oriented constructs. An object-oriented set should allow the inclusion of built-in types or user-defined types. Although the set would normally be treated as a collection of data structures and algorithms, an object-oriented set is treated as a self-contained single object within a program. We are able to declare a vector of set objects, or pass set objects as parameters. We are able to store set objects into other set objects.

## THE SET'S LOGICAL REPRESENTATION VERSUS THE SET'S IMPLEMENTATION

The logical representation of the set is what provides the programmer with the familiar set operations and the set notion. Set intersection, union, complement, and set subsets are a part of the logical representation of the set. The fact that a set is an unordered collection of unique elements is a part of the logical representation of a set. The logical representation represents how the programmer or user of the structure accesses it. In the case of a set, the logical representation is totally different from the actual implementation.

A set may be implemented by many high-level collections or containers, as well as by low-level data structures. A set could be implemented by a list, a vector, a tree, a graph, and so on. This is true of any container or collection. Once we have a block of internal or external memory that can hold objects we can begin to build a container or collection around that block of memory. The block of memory serves as the generic holder for the objects, and by providing member functions to access that block of memory in certain ways we provide the programmer with logical representations of various collections and containers. Figure 5.7 illustrates the layers of abstraction between internal or external memory and an object-oriented set class. Once we have some data structure that provides a block of memory or *storage component* to store objects in, we can encapsulate the data structure within a class, and provide set operations against that data structure.

The implementation of the collection and container class dictates the efficiency and flexibility of the class. If the set class is implemented with a fixed structure, then the set's allocation is efficient. However, the fixed size poses an undesirable restriction in some cases. If the set is implemented by a list, then we have a dynamic structure that can grow or shrink during program execution. However, accessing the elements in the set will have a linear performance. If we want to test for set inclusion we could conceivably have to access every element in the list. The intersection operation would also suffer, because we might have to access $N * M$ elements where $N$ is the number of objects in each set and $M$ is the number of sets to be intersected. We could improve on the efficiency of the set's

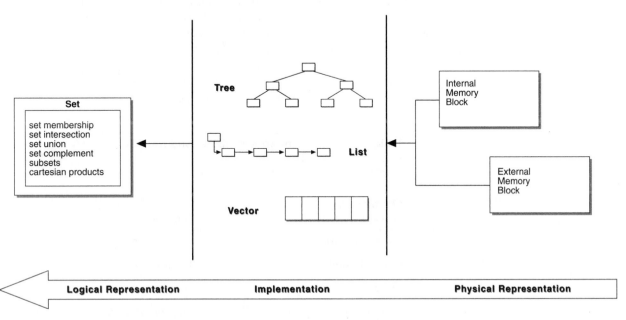

**Figure 5.7**   The layers of abstraction showing the physical representation, implementation, and logical representation of an object-oriented set.

operations by implementing the set with a tree structure. Although the complexity of the set's implementation increases, the performance of the set's member functions dramatically improves. The tradeoffs must be evaluated when deciding how to implement a collection or container class. Obviously the best-case scenario is to provide a number of implementations, and then use the implementation appropriate for the job at hand.

Whatever the implementation, the logical representation of a set should provide at least the core functionality of a set. Table 5.1 lists the core attributes and core services a set class should provide. We use the set class from the STL. Currently the set class is implemented by a red black tree. This provides very efficient implementations for the set's member functions.

# THE STL SET CLASS

The STL's set is an *ordered collection*. This is in contrast to the formal notion of a set. The formal notion of a set is an *unordered collection*. When a collection or container is unordered, then the interface to that collection or container does not depend on the members being in a specific order. When a collection or container is ordered, the services and member functions for that container depend on and take advantage of the fact that the container is ordered. Because the traditional notion of the set is that of an unordered collection and does not specify any particular manner in which to access the elements in the set, set iteration is undefined. The STL implementors have decided to impose an *artificial order* on the set class for efficiency purposes. There are many operations that are more efficient if they are performed on ordered data. For instance, if we wanted to make sure an object that is about to be inserted into a list was unique, then we would have to examine every member of the list in an unordered list. In an ordered list we could move to the position in the list where the object would be inserted and only examine surrounding objects. In the STL's set collection, object insertion, removal, and certain object access take advantage of the fact that the set has been put into a specific order. The

**Table 5.1    A list of the core attributes and core services the STL set class provides.**
MINIMUM CORE FUNCTIONALITY OF A SET CLASS

| Characteristics and Attributes | Services |
|---|---|
| unique members | set intersection |
| cardinal number | set union |
| finite or infinite | set complement |
| ordered | set membership |
| unordered | set difference subset operator |

user of a set collection must specify a function object that designates the *sort* order that the set should be put in. See Chapter 4, "Function Objects," for a discussion of what a function object is, and how they are used with the STL.

The set class is declared in *set.h*. Since the set class is a template class the user must supply the template with certain arguments in order to declare a set class. The user must supply the type of object that will be stored in the set, and the user must supply a function object that specifies the *sort order* for the objects that will be placed into the set. **Any** class that is to be used with the **set** is required to have the operator = = and the operator < defined for that class. So then the user or *client* of a set collection is only responsible for supplying four things:

1. A type for the set to store
2. A function object for set's sort order
3. A definition for the < operator
4. A definition for the = = operator

## Client Responsibilities for Built-In Types

Since the < operator and the = = operator are already defined for all of the built-in data types in C++, the user or client of the set collection can provide any of the built-in types without worrying about the < operator and the = = operator requirement. These operators already have meaning for the built-in data types. The STL provides two function objects that can be used with any of the built-in data types: **less** and **greater**.

These function objects are templates, and therefore take arguments, for example:

```
less<double>
greater<int>
```

The declarations for the **greater** and the **less** function template look like this:

```
template <class T>
struct greater : binary_function<T, T, bool> {
    bool operator()(const T& x, const T& y) const { return x > y; }
};
template <class T>
struct less : binary_function<T, T, bool> {
    bool operator()(const T& x, const T&y) const { return x < y; }
};
```

Notice the **operator()** that is defined in both classes. The **operator()** for **greater** function template returns the result of the operator > applied to its two arguments *x* and *y*. The **operator ()** for **less** returns the result of the operator < applied to its two arguments *x* and *y*. For built-in types the < and > operators are already defined. In order for the user to use the **greater** and **less** function objects with user-defined classes, the user must define operator > for use with the **greater** function object and operator < for use with the **less** function object.

If a set collection is declared using the **less** function object then the members in the set would be sorted from the smallest element to the largest element. Likewise, if a set collection is declared with the **greater** function object then the set would be sorted from the largest element to the smallest element. To declare a set *A* of **doubles** that will be sorted from the largest to the smallest the code would look like this:

```
#include <set.h>
.

.
set < double, greater<double> > A
```

So then after the user has supplied the set template with the type the set is to hold, the only other action the user must take is to decide whether the set should be sorted in ascending order (using the **less** function object) or be sorted in descending order (using the greater function object).

## Client Responsibilities for User-Defined Objects

When using user-defined objects with the set collection the user must provide definitions for the < operator and the = = operator. Also the user must provide the set collection declaration with a function object that will be used to designate the sort order for the set. The class **walk** in Listing 5.1 is a declaration of a class that we will be using throughout this book.

### Listing 5.1

```
// Declaration of the walk class

#include "clktime.h"
#include <cstring.h>
#include <iostream.h>

class walk{
protected:
   string Origin;
   string Destination;
   double Duration;
   clock_time StartTime;
   clock_time EndTime;
public:
   walk(void);
   walk(string X,string Y, double Dur, clock_time ST, clock_time ET);
   walk(const walk &X);
   int operator<(const walk &X) const;
   int operator>(const walk &X) const;
   int operator==(const walk &X) const;
   walk operator=(walk &X);
   int operator()(walk X, walk Y);
   void origin(string X);
```

```
    void destination(string X);
    void duration(double X);
    void startTime(clock_time X);
    void endTime(clock_time X);
    string origin(void);
    string destination(void);
    double duration(void);
    clock_time startTime(void);
    clock_time endTime(void);
    friend ostream &operator<<(ostream &Out, walk X);

};
```

The **walk** class models a trip between two points. To declare two sets of **walks** called **SetA** and **Set B** that will be sorted in descending order based on a user-defined function object and ascending order based on the **less** function object, the code would look like this:

```
#include <set.h>
#include<walk.h>
..
..
..
set<walk, walk > SetA;
set<walk, less<walk> > SetB;
```

Notice in the declaration of **Set A** that walk serves as the declaration for the *type* of objects that **SetA** will hold, as well as providing a function object for **SetA**. Because the **walk** class defines the operator(), it can be used as a function object. Notice that the function object for **SetB** uses the STL's built-in **less** object. We are able to do this because the operator < has been defined for the **walk** class.

Although it is only necessary to define the = = operator and the < operator for the user-defined class, the user should define any operators that make sense for the class. The user should also supply copy constructors, if compiler-supplied copy constructors will not be adequate. If the user supplies a copy constructor, it is important to remember to supply a destructor that deletes any temporary objects. Once a class with the appropriate operators has been supplied and a function object has been supplied, the user can declare a set object. The set object initially is empty, or can be constructed with objects.

# SET CONSTRUCTION

The STL's set class has three constructors:

```
set(const Compare&comp = Compare();

set(const value_type* first,
```

```
        const value_type* last,
        const Compare& comp = Compare())

    set(const set<Key, Compare>& x);
```

The first constructor takes a function object as a parameter and constructs an empty set. The function object will be used to determine the sort order for the set. An interesting note here is that the instantiation of the set template already requires a function object, as in:

```
    set < walk, less<walk> > SetB
```

If the instantiation of the template requires a function object, why is there a constructor that accepts a function object as a parameter? One of the biggest reasons for this is convenience. Another reason depends on the type of instantiator that the user's C++ compiler or linker uses. The **typedef** declaration is often used to simplify numerous, complex, ugly, or long declarations. For instance, we could use a **typedef** to simplify our set instantiation:

```
    typedef set <walk, less<walk> > Set;
```

Because this is a **typedef** the **Set** declaration does not occupy any space, it only acts as a shortcut way of specifying **set <walk, less<walk> >**. Everywhere that we declare a object of type Set, the compiler knows to use **set <walk, less<walk> >**. So we can declare a list of **set <walk, less<walk> >** objects by only using the short-cut **Set**. For example:

```
    Set SetA(greater<walk>)
    Set SetB
    Set SetC
```

These sets all hold walk objects. The sets **SetB** and **SetC** hold **walk** objects and are sorted in ascending order based on the **less<walk>** function object that was provided in the **typedef** of **Set**. Notice, however, that **SetA** provides its own function object and does not rely on the function object that was supplied in the **typedef**. **SetA** will be sorted in descending order based on the **greater<walk>** function object. This is one of the primary uses for providing a constructor that accepts a function object. It allows sets that are being declared from a **typedef** to supply different sort orders. Another implication that **typedef** may have is, depending on the compiler's or linker's template instantiator, the user could save code generation and prevent code bloat. For a nice discussion of template instantiators, see *Designing and Coding Reusable C++* (1995) by Martin D. Carroll and Margaret A. Ellis.

The second constructor takes three arguments. The third argument defaults to the function object that was used to instantiate the template. The first and second arguments are pointers to the types of objects that will be stored in the set and represent a range $[i,j)$ of elements to be copied into the set, where $i$ is the first element that will be stored and $j$ is a past-the-end element for the range. For example:

```
#include <set.h>

int A[4];
A[0] = 1;
A[1] = 100;
A[2] = 300;
A[3] = 500;
set <int, greater<int> > SetA(A,A+4);
```

**SetA** is constructed as a empty set, and then elements from the array *A* in the range *A* to *A*+4 are copied into the set.

The third constructor accepts another set collection as an argument. When this constructor is used the set being constructed will receive copies of another set.

## SET DESTRUCTION

When a set collection leaves scope or when the delete function is called, all the space that was allocated by the set is returned. Before the space is returned, any members that were in the set are erased and the destructors for the members are called.

## COLLECTION OR CONTAINER INFORMATION MEMBER FUNCTIONS

There are four member functions that provide information about the set collection: **size()**, **max_size()**, **empty()**, and **count()**. The **size()** member function returns the number of objects that are currently in the set. This is in contrast to what the name suggests. The **size()** member function does not return the amount of space, or the *size* of the set collection. The actual amount of space of the set collection will be at least **size()** * the *real* size of the objects that are being stored in the set. We use real size to accommodate object elements that are pointing to blocks of memory on the free store. Also the operating system memory calls may allocate more space than the actual size of the objects because of minimum memory page sizes. See the discussion in Chapter 4 on allocators. The **max_size()** member function returns the maximum number of objects that can be stored in the set collection. This number is going to be operating-system specific, or tied to particular hardware memory models. The **empty()** member function returns boolean true if the set is empty and false otherwise. The **count(X)** member function returns the number of objects that are in the set that are equal to X. For the set collection this member function can be used to test for set *inclusion*. If the count function returns a 1, then we know the element is in the set, and if it returns a 0 then we know the element is not in the set.

## ADDING OBJECTS TO THE SET COLLECTION

There are three ways that objects can be added to a set collection: through constructors, assignment, and the **insert()** member functions. There are two set constructors that accept elements. One constructor accepts a range of objects to be inserted into the set. The other constructor accepts a **set** of objects to be inserted. Assignment is defined for the set collection. Therefore we can assign all the elements of a set **SetA** to an empty set **SetB** as follows:

SetB = SetA

This assignment statement will assign copies of all the elements in **SetA** to **SetB**. The assignment statement uses the *shallow copy*. If the objects that are stored in the set do not have data members that are pointers, then the shallow copy poses no problem. However, if the objects that are stored in the set do have data members that are pointers then the shallow copy will only copy the pointers. This means that **SetA** and **SetB** would have objects that are pointing to the same block of memory for the elements that had pointers. It follows that any elements that were changed in **SetB** would also be changed in **SetA**, for those members that had elements that were pointers.

The set class has three **insert()** member functions: (1) There is a *single object* **insert()** member function. This member function only inserts one object into the container. That insertion only takes place if that object is not already a member of the set. (2) There is an **insert()** member function that inserts a range of objects into the set. The range of objects is assumed to be taken from some container that supports a pointer to the type of object that is being stored in the set, that is, **X::value_type**. (3) The third type of **insert()** member function inserts a single object into a particular position. This **insert()** member function takes two arguments. The first argument is the object to be inserted. The second object is a hint to where the collection should place the object. The actual location will be determined by the objects that are already in the set collection along with the *sort* order that is in effect. The time for the range **insert()** member function in general has *linear* complexity. The time taken for the other two types of **insert()** has a logarithmic complexity.

The program in Listing 5.2 demonstrates the usage of set constructors, assignment statements, and the **insert()** member function to add user-defined objects to a set collection. The program also shows how **typedef** can be used to simplify template declarations.

### Listing 5.2

```
1 // Listing 5.2
2 // This program demonstrates the usage of
3 // The set assignment statement, the
4 // set constructors, the size() function
5 // and the max_size() function. It also
6 // demonstrates the usage of typedef
7 // to simplify template declarations
8 // and instantiations.
9
10 #define __MINMAX_DEFINED
11 #include <set.h>
12 #include "walk.h"
```

```
13 #include <iostream.h>
14
15 typedef set<walk,walk> my_set;
16 typedef set<walk,walk>::iterator my_iterator;
17
18
19 void main(void)
20 {
21    walk Trip[2];
22    my_set MyDailyWalk;
23    walk Morning;
24    Morning.origin("home");
25    Morning.destination("golf course");
26    Morning.duration(5.2);
27    MyDailyWalk.insert(Morning);
28    Morning.origin("golf course");
29    Morning.destination("grocery store");
30    Morning.duration(2.7);
31    MyDailyWalk.insert(Morning);
32    my_set FriendsWalk;
33    FriendsWalk = MyDailyWalk;
34    my_set FamilysWalk(FriendsWalk);
35    my_set PetsWalk(Trip,Trip + 2);
36    my_iterator P = FamilysWalk.begin();
37    PetsWalk.insert(*P);
38    P++;
39    PetsWalk.insert(*P);
40    my_iterator M = MyDailyWalk.begin();
41    my_iterator N = FriendsWalk.begin();
42    my_iterator O = PetsWalk.begin();
43    P = FamilysWalk.begin();
44    while(P != FamilysWalk.end()
45    {
46      cout << "My Daily Walk " << *M << endl;
47      cout << "Friends Walk " << *N << endl;
48      cout << "Familys Walk " << *P << endl;
49      cout << "Pets Walk " << *O << endl;
50      P++;
51      M++;
52      N++;
53      O++;
54    }
55    cout << "Number in MyDailyWalk " << MyDailyWalk.size() << endl;
56    cout << "Largest Possible Number for MyDailyWalk ";
57    cout << MyDailyWalk.max_size();
58 }
59
60
```

# REMOVING OBJECTS FROM A SET COLLECTION

The STL's set collection class provides three **erase()** member functions. The set has an **erase(X)** member function that removes the object that is located at position **X**. The set has an **erase(X)** member function that removes the object **X** from the set. The set has an **erase(i,j)** member function that removes all the elements from the ith location through the jth location. If the set collection dynamically allocates memory for the objects and object copies still remain in the set when it leaves scope, then the set will erase the objects and then deallocate any memory that was dynamically allocated.

# OBJECT VISITATION IN A SET COLLECTION

The traditional notion of the set does not specify any particular manner in which the elements of a set are accessed. This is in contrast to other collections, and containers like stacks, queues, or priority queues. For instance, the last element placed into the stack must be the first element removed. Therefore as the user is iterating through a stack using **pop()** functions, the user is moving from the most recent member inserted to the member that has been in the stack the longest. Likewise with a queue, the first object placed into the queue must be the first element out. In other words, a queue is a first come, first serve structure. With structures such as stacks, queues, and priority queues the notion of iteration is provided by definition. However, with the set collection there is no such specification for how to move from one element to the next. Therefore we must invent the notion of iteration for a set.

The STL set is a well-ordered set. The objects in the set have a sort order based on the function object that was passed in the constructor or in the instantiation of the template of the set. The set collection supports *bidirectional iterators* and *reverse iterators*. The bidirectional iterators allow us to move one object at a time forward or backward in the container. The reverse iterators switch the front with the back, and the back with the front. Using the reverse iterator we can also only move one object at a time through the container. We can start at the beginning of a set collection and traverse to the end of it, or we can start at the end and traverse toward the beginning. The iterators are like traditional C++ pointers in that they can be dereferenced. We can compare the iterators for equality or inequality using the == operator and != operator. We can assign iterators to other iterators. We can save the values for iterators through iterator assignment. This allows us to jump into the middle of a set. This cannot be done with all collections and containers. For instance, by definition we should not get to the middle of a stack until we have popped all the objects that precede the middle. The iterators for the set class support the ability to move to the middle of the container through assignment. Keep in mind that iterators are just C++ classes that have the necessary member function and operators defined. Think of iterators as object-oriented pointers. We can assign one of the set's smart pointers to point to the first object in the container, or to the last object in the container, and then we can increment or decrement the pointer accordingly. Once we are at the location in the container that we want, we can dereference the smart pointer to get the object that it is pointing at.

Every set collection knows the value of four iterators.

```
iterator::begin
iterator::end
reverse_iterator::rbegin
reverse_iterator::rend
```

These iterators or smart pointers point to the first object in the container, and one past the last object in the container. The values that these pointers hold are returned by four member functions: **begin()**, **end()**, **rbegin()**, and **rend()**.

The programmer can declare objects of the appropriate iterator type for instance:

```
set<T, Compare>::iterator P
   or
set::<T,Compare>::reverse_iterator P
```

Once an object of the appropriate iterator type has been defined, then the user can initialize that iterator with a call to one of the set's iterator member functions, such as:

```
P = MySet.begin()
```

The iteration through the set collection can begin after the iterator has been initialized with a valid object location in the set. It is important to note that the iterator P in this case must first be initialized with a valid position within the collection before it can be dereferenced. This can be done in a couple of ways: through assignment of one iterator to another, or through calling one of the set's iterator functions. Dereferencing an uninitialized iterator will not return an element from the set. The **begin()** member function returns the iterator that points to the first object in the set. The **end()** member function returns a value that can be used to test the end of the set. The value that the **end()** member function returns should not be dereferenced. The primary purpose of this value is for testing whether the iteration is at the end of the set. The **rbegin()** turns the set collection upside down and starts to iterate from the bottom up. The **rend()** is used to test whether a **reverse_iterator** has reached the end of the set collection. In the case of the **reverse_iterator**, the end of the collection is actually the beginning of the collection. Like the value that the **end()** member function returns, the value that the **rend()** member function returns should not be dereferenced.

Using the objects of type bidirectional iterator, we can visit every object in a set collection in a sequential fashion. The set iteration does not support random or direct access. If direct or random access is required, then containers such as the vector, deque, or map can be used. The set only provides sequential access. However, because the set is ordered, the set algorithms intersection, union, difference, and includes are efficient. An object can also be visited by using the **find**(X) member function. The **find**(X) member function returns an iterator pointing to **X** if it is in the set. If **X** is not in the set, **find**() returns the value stored at **end()**. This iterator can be used to retrieve the object from the set. The member functions **lower_bound()**, **upper_bound()**, and **equal_range()** can also be used to visit specific objects in a set collection. The **lower_bound**(X) member function returns an iterator to the first object in the set collection that is not less than **X**. If **X** is in the set, it will return an iterator. Using the iterator you can go directly to that object. The **upper_bound**(X) member function returns the first object in the set collection that is not greater than **X**. If **X** is not in the set then **lower_bound**() and **upper_bound**() return **end**(). The **equal_range**() member function returns the pair, **lower_bound**() and **upper_bound**().

Note: Any member function or algorithm that returns at least a bidirectional iterator can be used to get an iterator that can visit objects in a set collection.

## SET COLLECTION OR CONTAINER OPERATORS

The set collection supports the relational operators $==$, $!=$, $<$, $>$, $<=$, and $>=$. This means that given two sets A and B, we can do comparisons $A == B$, $A <= B$, $B != A$, and so on. These comparisons will return boolean true, or boolean false. The logical operators and arithmetic operators are not defined for the set collection. However, nothing prevents the user from doing so.

## SET OPERATIONS

One of the most powerful features of the set structure is the operations that are available on sets. These operations include: *set intersection, set union, set difference, set membership*, and *subset membership*. The STL set supports all of these operations. Testing set membership can be done by using the **count**() member function of the set collection. The other set operations are implemented as STL *generic* algorithms and are not a part of the set class. In this sense the STL's set object is not a self-contained object because it depends on procedures and functions that are not members of the class to complete its functionality. The generic set operations work with the set container because the set container has iterators that are compatible with the arguments that the set algorithms expect. So the *generic set algorithms* + the *set collection class = complete set functionality*. Although this departs from the object-oriented implementation of the set class, it is a valid implementation of parameterized set functionality. Since C++ provides the programmer with object-oriented constructs as well as with generic programming constructs we can choose the most flexible methods to implement structures.

The set operations allow the programmer to deal with collections of objects based on how they are related to other collections of objects, or how a collection of objects is related to a condition or set of conditions. Any set of objects has *identifying characteristics* that are based on set membership. The identifying characteristics give information about the objects in the set. For instance, we can conclude many things from the set of integers. We know that each integer is only contained once in the set. We know that there are no real numbers or complex numbers in the set. We know that alphabets are not allowed in the set. We can be sure that the number 1 is in the set. We know that the set is infinite, and so on. We can therefore classify sets based on their membership rules or conditions. Because we can use the set's membership rules or conditions to classify sets, we can classify groups of objects by placing them into sets. This is important because it allows the programmer to organize and manipulate groups of objects based on *category* and *classification.* It is important to note that the categories and classifications that the set structure supports are based on the membership rules or conditions. The membership rules designate which objects are included in a set, and which objects will not be allowed. These membership rules or conditions are totally under the control of the programmer. By specifying what requirements an object must meet, the programmer has full control over each set's membership. In any application, object oriented or otherwise, there will be many groups of items that need to be classified, categorized, organized, compared, and counted based on some set of rules or conditions. This is where the set collection comes in. Two of the primary functions of a set are:

1. Object classification based on rules or conditions
2. Counting objects based on rules or conditions

The rules are specified by the programmer in the form of *if-then-else* sequences, *looping* conditions, template *parameter specifications*, object *hierarchies*, and *pattern matching*. We use the user-defined class **walk** in Listing 5.3 to demonstrate how rules and conditions are used to place objects in a set. We also use the class **walk** to show how sets can be used with user-defined rules, conditions, and objects.

### Listing 5.3

```
1 // Listing 5.3
2 // This program demonstrates the uses of if-then
3 // rules to place user-defined objects in Set
4 // Collections. The program also uses the union
5 // operation and the intersection operation to
6 // combine set collections together
7
8 #define __MINMAX_DEFINED
9 #include <set.h>
10 #include "walk.h"
11 #include <fstream.h>
12 #include <algo.h>
13
14
15
16 set<walk,walk> SuspiciousTrips;
17 set<walk,walk> InnocentTrips;
18 set<walk,walk> Questionable;
19 set<walk,walk>::iterator P;
20 set<walk,walk> Investigated;
21
22 void main(void)
23 {
24    walk Stroll;
25    ifstream In;
26    clock_time SuspiciousTime(10,10);
27    In.open("walk.txt");
```

```
28    while(!In.eof()){
29      In >> Stroll;
30      if(Stroll.destination() == "bank"){
31    SuspiciousTrips.insert(Stroll);
32      }
33      if(Stroll.origin() == "work"){
34    SuspiciousTrips.insert(Stroll);
35      }
36      if((Stroll.duration() > 5.00) && (Stroll.destination() != "home")){
37      SuspiciousTrips.insert(Stroll);
38      }
39      if(Stroll.startTime() < SuspiciousTime){
40    SuspiciousTrips.insert(Stroll);
41      }
42    if(Stroll, destination() == "home"){
43 InnocentTrips.insert(Stroll);
44    }
45    if(Stroll.origin() == "work"){
46 InnocentTrips.insert(Stroll);
47    }
48
49 }
50 In.close();
51 set_intersection(SuspiciousTrips.begin(),SuspiciousTrips.end(),
52        InnocentTrips.begin(),InnocentTrips.end(),
53        inserter(Questionable,Questionable.begin()),Stroll);
54
55 set_union(SuspiciousTrips.begin(),SuspiciousTrips.end(),
56      Questionable.begin(),Questionable.end(),
57      inserter(Investigated,Investigated.begin()),Stroll);
58
59 cout << "Suspicious Trips " << endl;
60 cout << "Cardinality: " << SuspiciousTrips.size() << endl;
61 P = SuspiciousTrips.begin();
62 while(P != SuspiciousTrips.end())
63 {
64 cout << *P << endl;
65 P++;
66    }
67    cout << endl << "Innocent Trips" << endl;
68    cout << "Cardinality: " << innocentTrips.size() << endl;
69    P = InnocentTrips.begin();
70    while(P != InnocentTrips.end())
71    {
72      cout << *P << endl;
73      P++;
74    }
75    cout << endl << "Questionable Trips" << endl;
76    cout << "Cardinality: " <<Questionable.size() << endl;
77    P = Questionable.begin();
```

```
78    while(P != Questionable.end()
79    {
80       cout << *P << endl;
81       P++;
82    }
83    cout << endl << "Investigated Trips" << endl;
84    cout << "Cardinality: " << Investigated.size() << endl;
85    P = Investigated.begin();
86    while(P != Investigated.end())
87    {
88    cout << *P << endl;
89    P++;
90       }
91
92
93
94    }
95
```

The program in Listing 5.3 works with four sets: **SuspiciousTrips**, **InnocentTrips**, **Questionable**, and **Investigated**.

SupiciousTrips = {X |X has a destination = "bank" or
      X has a origin = "work" or
      X has a duration > 5hr and destination != "home" or
      X has a suspicious time}

InnocentTrips = {X |X has a destination of "home" or
      X has a origin of "work"}

Questionable = SuspiciousTrips ∩ InnocentTrips

Investigated = SuspiciousTrips ∪ Questionable

The objects that the program in Listing 5.3 uses are read in from a file called *walk.txt*. This file is stored on the disk that accompanies this book in the "examples" directory. The objects are stored in this file in ASCII format so that they will be easy to see. Table 5.2 shows the input objects that are used in this program. The program reads each object from the *walk.txt* file, and based on the set membership rules for **SuspiciousTrips** and **InnocentTrips**, the objects are included in the appropriate sets. Once all the objects have been read in and evaluated, the **Questionable** and **Investigated** sets are built using the STL's **set_intersection** algorithm and **set_union** algorithm. Figure 5.8 shows a Venn diagram for the **Questionable** set, and a Venn diagram for the **Investigated** set.

As the program in Listing 5.3 reads in the objects, each object is tested with a set of *if-then* rules. The if-then rules match the *set-builder notation* for these sets. These rules or conditions are used to classify and categorize the strolls that were made in the program. In this program strolls are suspicious, innocent, or questionable. Every object that was read in was categorized as either belonging to or not belonging to these sets. The set-builder notation for these sets is:

**Table 5.2** Each line in this table represents the values stored in an object of type walk. The *walk* class has five attributes: *origin, destination, start_time,* and *end_time*.

INPUT FOR PROGRAM LISTING 5.3

| Origin | Destination | Duration | Start_Time | End_Time |
|---|---|---|---|---|
| work | restaurant | 4.00 | 1200 | 1600 |
| bank | home | 1.15 | 1300 | 1415 |
| movies | home | 5.23 | 1500 | 2023 |
| play | bank | 2.15 | 1300 | 1415 |
| park | bar | 9.00 | 1300 | 2200 |
| friends_house | bank | 15.00 | 0000 | 1300 |

SuspiciousTrips = {X |X has a destination = "bank" or
　　　　　　　　　　X has a origin = "work" or
　　　　　　　　　　X has a duration > 5hr and destination ! = "home" or
　　　　　　　　　　X has a suspicious time}

InnocentTrips = {X |X has a destination of "home" or
　　　　　　　　　X has a origin of "work"}

The set-builder notation is implemented in the program in Listing 5.3 by the series of statements on lines 30 through 46. These statements use the if-then construct for member evaluation. The **Questionable** and **Investigated** sets are built by set intersection and set union:

Questionable = SuspiciousTrips ∩ InnocentTrips

Investigated　= SuspiciousTrips ∪ Questionable

**A.**

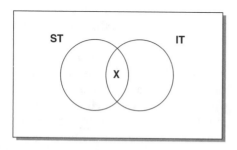

Questionable = Suspicious Trips ∩ Innocent Trips

**B.**

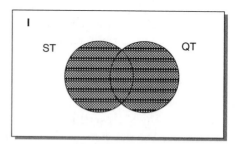

Investigated = Suspicious Trips ∪ Questionable Trips

**Figure 5.8** The Venn diagrams for Questionable set and Investigated set. Questionable set is an intersection between Suspicious Trips and Innocent Trips. Investigated set is a union of Suspicious Trips and Questionable Trips.

These operations are implemented by STL *generic* set operations on lines 51 through 57 in Listing 5.3. The STL has five generic set algorithms:

```
includes
set_union
set_intersection
set_difference
set_symmetric_difference
```

Each of these algorithms takes at least 4 arguments. Let's say that we have two sets, A and B. The first two arguments for any of the set algorithms are *input iterators*, and represent a range of elements from set A or set B. The second two arguments are input iterators, and represent a range of elements from set A or set B. The **set_union**, **set_intersection**, and **set_difference** algorithms have at least 5 arguments. The fifth argument is an *output iterator*, representing the beginning of a collection or container object that will be used to store the results of the **set_union**, **set_intersection**, or **set_difference** operations. Each of these algorithms has a couple of versions. One version takes a user-defined *function object* to designate the sort order. Table 5.3 shows five generic set algorithms, and their iterator and argument requirements. Each of these algorithms assumes that the collections or containers that they are passed are already sorted. If the collection or container is not sorted, the result of the algorithm processing is likely to be incorrect. Given that the collections or containers are sorted, then the results of any of these operations are also sorted. In general these operations are stable operations. This means that given the two sets A and B, if the element is in both sets, then the element from the first set is included in the resulting operation. The operations are nonmutable for the input collections or containers, and mutable for the output collection or container. That means that given three collections or containers A, B, and C, where A and B are input collections and C is an output

**Table 5.3   Five generic set algorithms, their runtime performance, and their iterator and argument requirements.**

| Set Algorithms | Performance | Input | Output | Forward | Bidirectional | Random Access | Function Object |
|---|---|:---:|:---:|:---:|:---:|:---:|:---:|
| includes*<br>set_union*<br>set_intersection*<br>set_difference*<br>set_symmetric_<br>difference* | ((last1 - first1) + (last2 - first2)) * 2 - 1 comparisons are performed. | •<br>•<br>•<br>•<br>•<br>• | •<br>•<br>•<br>•<br>• |  |  |  | •<br>•<br>•<br>•<br>•<br>• |

collection or container, then *A, B* are not changed by the set operations, while *C* can be changed by the set operations. It is not good practice to use one of the input ranges also as an output range. In most cases the results would be undefined.

The program in Listing 5.3 also shows the *cardinality* for each set. The cardinality of a set is the number of elements in that set. The cardinality of *N* of *M* is denoted by

$$N = |M|$$

Our set collections **SuspiciousTrips**, **InnocentTrips**, **Questionable**, and **Investigated** all report their cardinality. Table 5.4 shows the cardinality for each set. The cardinality of a set can be determined by calling the **size()** member function.

So using a set collection class built with the C++ constructs we are able to model the traditional notion of a set. Our set collection supports the core set requirements that are listed in Table 5.1.

---

**Table 5.4   This table shows the result of the set operations and the cardinality of each set. The set operations were set inclusion, set intersection, and set union. The program in Listing 5.3 used if-then rules to place objects into the sets.**

*Output from Program Listing 5.3*

Suspicious Trips
Cardinality: 4
friends_house bank 15 0 0 13 0
park bar 9 13 0 22 0
work restaurant 4 12 0 16 0
play bank 2.15 13 0 14 15

Innocent Trips
Cardinality: 3
movies home 5.23 15 0 20 23
work restaurant 4 12 0 16 0
bank home 1.15 13 0 14 15

Questionable Trips
Cardinality: 1
work restaurant 4 12 0 16 0

Investigated Trips
Cardinality: 4
friends_house bank 15 0 0 13 0
park bar 9 13 0 22 0
work restaurant 4 12 0 16 0
play bank 2.15 13 0 14 15

# TYPES OF SETS

Our set collection can be used to represent the most commonly found types of sets:

Empty sets
Singleton sets
Cartesian products
Power sets
Universal sets
Multisets

The *empty* set is simply a set with no members. Any set that is constructed with a default constructor is an empty set. A *singleton* set is a set with only one member. *Cartesian* products can be implemented with vectors of sets, or vectors of pairs. Cartesian products can also be implemented with lists of sets and maps. See the Introduction to Sets sidebar for a discussion of Cartesian products. The power set is a *set of sets*. If we have a set M then P(M) is the power set. The power set of M is all of the possible subsets of M. For instance, if $M = \{a,b,c\}$, then the P(M) is

$$P(M) = \{\{\ \},\{a\},\{b\},\{c\},\{a,b\},\{a,c\},\{b,c\},\{a,b,d\}\}$$

Notice that each element of the set P is also a set. The empty set is also an element of the power set, since the empty set is an element of every set. If P is a power set of M, and the cardinality of M is N, then the cardinality of P is

$$|P| = 2N$$

In other words, the number of elements in a power set P of set M is equal to $2^N$, where N is the number of elements in set M. We can use the STL set collection to implement a power set. However, it should be noted that because the cardinality of a power set is 2N, memory resources can be easily exhausted. Depending on the real size of the objects that are placed into a power set, power set operations can be extremely expensive.

The *universal* set is the set of all elements under consideration. When we use the STL set collection to declare a set, then the instantiation of that set represents the universal set. For instance:

```
set<int,<less> > SetA
set<walk,walk> >SetB
```

The universal set of **SetA** is all the possible integers that can be represented on the computer that **SetA** is used on. Although the user may not be working with all possible integers, the universal set of **SetA** includes all possible integers. Most likely the user will be using subsets of **SetA**. Likewise the universal set of **SetB** is the set of all possible instantiations of a **walk** class. Although the user will most likely be using and manipulating subsets of these instantiations, the universal set includes all possible instantiations. Another commonly found type of set is the *multiset*, sometimes referred to as a *bag*.

Multisets are exactly the same as the traditional sets, except that they allow member duplication. The user of a multiset can include an object more than once. The STL set class supports all of these types of sets either directly or indirectly.

The program in Listing 5.4 demonstrates how the STL set collection and vector container can be used to implement a Cartesian product collection. The Cartesian product collection then becomes an addition to the programmer's collection and container class library. The program in Listing 5.4 also demonstrates the usage of the **set _difference** algorithm and the **set _union** algorithm.

### Listing 5.4

```
1 // Listing 5.4
2 // This program demonstrates how a collection
3 // can be implemented by a container. It also
4 // demonstrates the uses of the set_difference
5 // and set_union operations. It uses a set collection
6 // and a vector container to implement a Cartesian
7 // product.
8
9
10 #define _MINMAX_DEFINED
11 #include <pair.h>
12 #include <set.h>
13 #include <algo.h>
14 #include <vector.h>
15 #include <iostream.h>
16 #include <iterator.h>
17
18 template<class T,class U> class cartisian_product{
19 protected:
20    vector<set<T,U> >Product;
21    int End;
22    int Begin;
23    int P;
24
25 public:
26    cartisian_product(void);
27    cartisian_product(set<T,U> &X,set<T,U> &Y);
28    vector<set<T,U> > &operator=(set<T,U> &X);
29    vector<set<T,U> > &product(set<T,U> &X,set<T,U> &Y);
30    vector<set<T,U> > &product(void);
31    set<T,U> operator()(void);
32    set <T,U> &operator++(intX);
33    void restart(void);
34    set<T,U> begin(void);
35    set<T,U> end(void);
36    int size(void);
37 };
38
```

```
39
40
41 template<class T,class U> cartisian_product<T,U>::cartisian_product(void)
42 {
43
44   P = 0;
45   Begin = 0;
46   End = 0;
47
48 }
49
50 template<class T,class U> cartisian_product<T,U>::cartisian_product(set<T,
   U> &X,set<T,U> &Y)
51 {
52   set<T,U>::iterator N = X.begin();
53   set<T,U>::iterator M = Y.begin();
54
55   while(N != X.end())
56     {
57   M = Y.begin();
58   while(M != Y.end())
59   {
60     set<T,U> Temp;
61     Temp.insert(*N);
62     Temp.insert(*M);
63     Product.push_back(Temp);
64     M++;
65   }
66   N++;
67     }
68 }
69
70 template<class T,class U> vector<set<T,U> > &cartisian_product<T,U>::
   operator=(set<T,U> &X)
71 {
72
73   Product.erase(Product.begin(),Product.end());
74   Product.push_back(X);
75   return(Product);
76 }
77
78
79 template<class T,classU> set<T,U> cartisian_product<T,U>::begin(void)
80 {
81
82   Begin = 0;
83   return(Product[Begin]);
84 }
85
86 template<class T,class U> void cartisian_product<T,U>::restart(void)
```

```
87 {
88    P = 0;
89 }
90
91 template<class T,class U> set<T,U> cartisian_product<T,U>::end(void)
92 {
93
94    End = Product.size();
95    return(Product[End]);
96 }
97
98
99 template<class T,classU> set<T,U> &cartisian_product<T,U>::operator++
   (int X)
100 {
101    P++;
102    return (Product[P]);
103 }
104
105 template<class T,class U> set<T,U> cartisian_product<T,U>::operator()
   (void)
106 {
107    return(Product[P]);
108 }
109
110
111 template<class T,class U> vector<set<T,U> > &cartisian_product<T,U>::
   product(set<T,U> &X,set<T,U> &Y)
112 {
113
114    set <T,U>::iterator N = X.begin();
115    set <T,U>::iterator M = Y.begin();
116
117    while(N != X.end())
118    {
119 M = Y.begin();
120 while(M != Y.end())
121 {
122    set<T,U> Temp;
123    Temp.insert(*N);
124    Temp.insert(*M);
125    Product.push_back(Temp);
126    M++;
127 }
128 N++;
129    }
130
131    return(Product);
132 }
133
```

```
134 template<class T, class U> vector<set<T,U> > &cartisian_product<T,U>::
    product(void)
135 {
136   return(Product);
137 }
138
139 template<class T, class U> int cartisian_product<T,U>::size(void)
140 {
141   return(Product.size());
142 }
143
144
145 set<char,less<char> > SetA;
146 set<char,less<char> > SetB;
147 set<char,less<char> > Tuple;
148 set<char,less<char> >::iterator P;
149 set<char,less<char> > SetD;
150 set<char,less<char> > SetE;
151
152
153 void main(void)
154 {
155
156   SetA.insert('A');
157   SetA.insert('B');
158   SetA.insert('C');
159   SetB.insert('1');
160   SetB.insert('2');
161
162   set_difference(SetA.begin(),SetA.end(),SetB.begin(),
163     SetB.end(),inserter(SetD,SetD.begin()));
164   cartisian_product<char,less<char> > SetC;
165   SetC.product(SetA,SetB);
166   SetC.restart();
167   int N = 1;
168   cout << "Cartisian Product of SetA X SetB" << endl;
169   while(N <= SetC.size())
170   {
171     Tuple = SetC();
172     P = Tuple.begin();
173     cout << N << " " << "Tuple";
174     while(P!= Tuple.end())
175     {
176   cout << *P << " ";
177   SetE.insert(*P);
178   P++;
179     }
180     cout << endl;
181     SetC++;
182     N++;
```

```
183   }
184   cout << endl;
185   set_union(SetA.begin(),SetA.end(),
186     SetB.begin(),SetB.end(),inserter(SetE,SetE.begin()));
187   P = SetD.begin();
188   cout << "SetD = SetA difference SetB" << endl;
189   cout << "Cardinality : " << SetD.size() << endl;
190   while(P != SetD.end())
191   {
192     cout << *P << " ";
193     P++;
194   }
195   cout << endl << endl;
196   P = SetE.begin();
197   cout << "SetE = SetA Union SetB " << endl;
198   cout << "Cardinality : " << SetE.size() << endl;
199   while(P != SetE.end())
200   {
201     cout << *P << " ";
202     P++;
203   }
204
205 }
```

The output for the program in Listing 5.4 is shown in Table 5.5. Notice that the set difference between **SetA** and **SetB** is exactly those elements that are in **SetA** but are not in **SetB**. Also note the cardinality for each set is returned by the **size()** member function.

---

**Table 5.5   This output shows the results of performing a Cartesian product of *Set A* and *Set B* and the set difference of *Set A* with *Set B* as well as the union of *Set A* with *Set B*.**

---

*Output from Program Listing 5.4*

---

Cartesian Product of SetA × SetB
1 Tuple 1 A
2 Tuple 2 A
3 Tuple 1 B
4 Tuple 2 B
5 Tuple 1 C
6 Tuple 2 C

SetD = SetA difference SetB
Cardinality : 3
A B C

SetE = SetA Union SetB
Cardinality : 5
1 2 A B C

---

The tuples that are shown in Table 5.5 are members of the Cartesian product **SetC**. Because the Cartesian product is a list of ordered pairs we could have used the list or queue containers instead of the vector to implement the Cartesian product collection. Also notice that the Cartesian product collection has a superstructure for its memory block. Every collection or container must have a memory block. The memory block is the internal or external storage used to store the objects that the collection or container will hold. The memory block for the Cartesian product is a superstructure. It was implemented using two STL components:

```
vector<set<T,U> >Product;
```

The **Product** object is a *vector of sets*. In other words, **Product** is implemented by a vector container that consists of a collection of sets, where each element of the vector is a set collection, whereas a metastructure is a collection or container that holds noncollection or container objects. Our formal definition of a superstructure is *a collection or container class that holds other collection or container classes*. The Cartesian product in Listing 5.4 is implemented by a superstructure, and is therefore a superstructure.

Any collection and container that holds other metastructures is a superstructure. The power set is a superstructure by definition because it is a set of sets. The Set Application Sidebar at the end of this chapter demonstrates how superstructures and metastructures can be used in the C++ language.

# THE STL MULTISET

The STL's *multiset*, sometimes called *bag*, is an *ordered collection*. When a collection or container is ordered, the services and member functions for that container depend on and take advantage of the fact that the container is ordered. Because the traditional notion of the set is that of an unordered collection, and does not specify any particular manner in which to access the elements in the multiset, multiset iteration is undefined. The STL implementers have decided to impose an *artificial order* on the multiset class for efficiency purposes. There are many operations that are more efficient if they are performed on ordered data. In the STL's multiset collection object insertion, removal, and certain object access take advantage of the fact that the multiset has been put into a specific order. The multiset has the same functionality as the traditional set except it allows the user to add duplicate objects into the set. The user of a multiset collection must specify a function object that designates the sort order that the set should be put in. See Chapter 4, "Function Objects," for a discussion of what a function object is, and how it is used with the STL.

The multiset class is declared in *multiset.h*. Since the multiset class is a template class the user must supply the template with certain arguments to declare a multiset class. The user must supply the type of object that will be stored in the multiset, and the user must supply a function object that specifies the sort order for the objects that will be placed into the set. *Any* class that is to be used with the multiset is required to have the operator == and the operator < defined for that class. So then the user or *client* of a multiset collection is only responsible for supplying four things:

1. A type for the set to store
2. A function object for set's sort order
3. A definition for the $<$ operator
4. A definition for the $==$ operator

## ADDING OBJECTS TO THE MULTISET COLLECTION

There are three ways that objects can be added to a set collection: through constructors, assignment, and the **insert()** member functions. There are two multiset constructors that accept elements. One constructor accepts a range of objects to be inserted into the multiset. The other constructor accepts a set of objects to be inserted. Assignment is defined for the multiset collection. Therefore we can assign all the elements of a multiset **SetA** to an empty multiset **SetB** as follows:

$$SetB = SetA$$

This assignment statement will assign copies of all the elements in **SetA** to **SetB**. The assignment statement uses the *shallow copy*. If the objects that are stored in the multiset do not have data members that are pointers, then the shallow copy poses no problem. However if the objects that are stored in the multiset do have data members that are pointers then the shallow copy will only copy the pointers. This means that **SetA** and **SetB** would have objects that are pointing to the same block of memory for the elements that had pointers. It follow that any elements that were changed in **SetB** would also be changed in **SetA** for those members that had elements that were pointers.

The multiset class has three **insert()** member functions: (1) There is a single object **insert()** member function. This member function only inserts one object into the container. Unlike the STL set class, when this member function is used the multiset class will allow object duplication. That means even if the object is already a member of the multiset it will be inserted anyway. (2) There is an **insert()** member function that inserts a range of objects into the multiset. The range of objects is assumed to be taken from some container that supports a pointer to the type of object that is being stored in the multiset, that is, **X::value_type**. (3) The third type of **insert()** member function inserts a single object into a particular position. This **insert()** member function takes two arguments. The first argument is the object to be inserted. The second object is a hint to where the collection should place the object. The actual location will be determined by the objects that are already in the multiset collection along with the sort order that is in effect. The time for the range **insert()** member function in general has linear complexity. The time taken for the other two types of **insert()** has a logarithmic complexity.

## REMOVING OBJECTS FROM A MULTISET COLLECTION

The STL's multiset collection class has three **erase()** member functions. The multiset has an **erase(X)** member function that removes the object that is located at position **X**. The multiset has an **erase(X)** member function that removes *every* occurrence of the object **X** from the set. Whereas in the set class this function only removes one object, in the multiset class this function removes every object that is equal to **X**. This member function returns the number of elements or members that were erased. The set has an **erase(i,j)** member function that removes all the elements from the ith location through the jth location. If the set collection dynamically allocates memory for the objects and object copies still remain in the set when it leaves scope, then the set will erase the objects and then deallocate any memory that was dynamically allocated. The first **erase()** member function has a time that is amortized constant. The second and third **erase()** member functions have a size that is logarithmic relative to the number of objects being removed from the multiset.

## OBJECT VISITATION IN A MULTISET COLLECTION

As was the traditional notion of the set, the multiset does not specify any particular manner in which the elements or members are accessed. This is in contrast to other collections, and containers like stacks, queues, or priority queues. For instance the last element placed into the *stack* must be the first element removed. Therefore as the user is iterating through a stack using **pop()** functions, the user is moving from the most recent member inserted to the member that has been in the stack the longest. Likewise with a queue, the first object placed into the queue must be the first element out. In other words, a queue is a first come, first serve structure. With structures such as stacks, queues, and priority queues the notion of iteration is provided by definition. However, with the multiset collection there is no such specification for how to move from one element to the next. Therefore we must invent the notion of iteration for a multiset.

The multiset, like the set, is a well-ordered set. The objects in the multiset have a sort order based on the function object that was passed in the constructor or in the instantiation of the template of the multiset. The multiset collection supports bidirectional iterators, and reverse iterators. The bidirectional iterators allow us to move one object at a time forward or backward in the container. The reverse iterators switch the front with the back, and the back with the front. Using the reverse iterator we can also only move one object at a time through the container. We can start at the beginning of a multiset collection and traverse to the end of it, or we can start at the end and traverse toward the beginning. The iterators are like traditional C++ pointers in that they can be dereferenced. We can compare the iterators for equality or inequality using the $==$ operator and $!=$ operator. We can assign iterators to other iterators. We can save the values for iterators through iterator assignment. This allows us to jump into the middle of a multiset. This cannot be done with all collections and containers. For instance, by definition we should not get to the middle of a stack until we have popped all the objects that precede the middle. The iterators for the multiset class support the ability to move to the middle of the container through assignment.

Every multiset collection has four iterators.

```
iterator::begin
iterator::end
reverse_iterator::rbegin
reverse_iterator::rend
```

These iterators or smart pointers point to the first object in the container and one past the last object in the container. The values that these pointers hold are returned by four member functions: **begin()**, **end()**, **rbegin()**, and **rend()**.

The programmer can declare objects of the appropriate iterator type for instance:

multiset<T, Compare>::iterator P
  or
multiset::<T,Comapre>::reverse_iterator P

Once an object of the appropriate iterator type has been defined, then the user can initialize that iterator with a call to one of the multiset's iterator member functions, such as:

P = MySet.begin()

After the iterator has been initialized with a valid object location in the multiset, then the iteration through the multiset collection can begin. It is important to note that the iterator **P** in this case must first be initialized with a valid position within the collection before it can be dereferenced. This can be done in a couple of ways: through assignment of one iterator to another, or through calling one of the multiset's iterator functions. Dereferencing an uninitialized iterator will not return an element from the multiset. The **begin()** member function returns the iterator that points to the first object in the multiset. The **end()** member function returns a value that can be used to test the end of the multiset. The value that the **end()** member function returns should not be dereferenced. The primary purpose of this value is for testing whether the iteration is at the end of the multiset. The **rbegin()** turns the multiset collection upside down and starts to iterate from the bottom up. The **rend()** is used to test whether a **reverse_iterator** has reached the end of the multiset collection. In the case of the **reverse_iterator**, the end of the collection is actually the beginning of the collection. Like the value that the **end()** member function returns, the value that the **rend()** member function returns should not be dereferenced.

Using the objects of type bidirectional iterator, we can visit every object in a multiset collection in a sequential fashion. The multiset iteration does not support random or direct access. If direct or random access is required, then containers such as the vector, deque, or map can be used. The multiset only provides sequential access. However, because the multiset is ordered, the set algorithms intersection, union, difference, and includes are efficient. An object can also be visited by using the **find(X)** member function. The **find(X)** member function returns an iterator pointing to **X** if it is in the set. Remember that a multiset may include an object more than once; **find(X)** only returns the iterator to one of those objects. If **X** is not in the set, **find()** returns the value stored at **end()**. If **X** is in the set, the iterator that **find()** returns can be used to retrieve the object from the multiset. The member function **lower_bound()**, **upper_bound()**, and **equal_range()** can also be used to visit specific objects in a multiset collection. The **lower_bound(X)** member function returns an iterator to the first object in the multiset collection that is not less than **X**. If **X** is in the multiset it will return an iterator. Using the iterator you can go directly to that object. The **upper_bound(X)** member function returns the first object in the multiset collection that is not greater than **X**. If **X** is not in the multiset then **lower_bound()** and **upper_bound()** return **end()**. The **equal_range()** member function returns the pair, **lower_bound()** and **upper_bound()**.

Note: Any member function or algorithm that returns at least a bidirectional iterator can be used to get an iterator that can visit objects in a multiset collection.

The **count()** member function of the multiset behaves differently than the **count**(X) member function for the set. The **count**(X) member function for the set returns a 1 if **X** is in the set, and returns a 0 if **X** is not in the set. The **count**(X) member function for the multiset returns the number of elements in the set equal to **X**.

## MULTISET OPERATORS

The multiset collection supports the relational operators $==, !=, <, >, <=,$ and $>=$. This means that given two sets *A* and *B*, we can do comparisons $A == B$, $A <= B$, $B != A$, and so on. These comparisons will return boolean true or boolean false. The logical operators and arithmetic operators are not defined for the set collection. However, nothing prevents the user from doing so.

## APPLICATION

## SETS—AN INVESTIGATION SIMULATION

Sets can be used to categorize, classify, enumerate, identify, and pinpoint groups or collections of objects. Whereas many containers are used just to hold objects for further processing, the set collection is used to perform operations on groups of objects at one time. Usually when we apply an operator to an operand, the operand represents a single object or at most two objects. For instance, applying the $+$ operation usually combines two objects in some fashion. The ! operation takes the inverse or reverse of some object. The operations are applied to a collection of objects when performing operations on sets. The set collection is used to perform operations like intersection and union on combinations of objects. We use the STL set class as the basis for an *investigation simulation*. This simulation is an entry-level example of using sets to simulate or model the *process of elimination*. Although we use the STL set class, any set class that supports the *core functionality* of the set collection can be used (see Table 5.1).

## SIMULATION AND MODELING IN PROGRAMMING

Simulation and modeling are central activities in any kind of programming, specially in object-oriented programming. The craft of programming involves reproducing some real-world task, process, or idea in software. This *reproduction in software* is either a model or a simulation. Models and simulations have several important characteristics. The first thing that all models and simulations have in common is that they are only representations of some person, place, thing, or idea. They are only a similitude or stand-in for the real thing. Because models and simulations resemble the real thing without being the real thing we can use the model or simulation as we like with no harm done.

In general, models can be categorized as either physical models or mathematical models. A toy train, a model airplane, or an engineer's blueprint are good examples of physical models. The Big Bang theory, the Nielsen Rating Technique, and computer programs are good examples of mathematical models. Logical models and abstract models are types of mathematical models. A *simulation* is a representation that captures and imitates the changes over time to some person, place, thing, or idea. These changes are normally captured as *events*. The common uses for models and simulations include:

Testing
Exploration
Education
Explanation
Communication
Demonstration
Imitation

In this discussion we are concerned with the use of the model and simulation as a tool for communication. The interesting point here is that the communication is between programmer and computer. To communicate with the computer the programmer must produce a representation of some real-world process or idea that is suitable for execution by the computer. This representation or model is given to the computer in the form of a computer program. We use computer programs to communicate to the machine what work we want done. The computer program is a list of instructions that when executed simulates some real-world task, process, or idea. The list of instructions in a computer program act as a software blueprint of some piece of reality. The execution of that blueprint by the computer produces a resemblance, or simulation, of that piece of reality. The software blueprint + computer's execution = model or simulation.

## THE PROCESS OF ELIMINATION

In our set example we want to create a computer simulation of the process of elimination that humans use in problem solving. Part of the process of elimination involves identification and categorization. This simulation uses the notions of union, difference, and intersection to approximate certain aspects of the process of elimination. It makes sense to use a set class in this simulation because the types of operations that need to be performed are already defined on a set. While we could have used other collections or containers, the operations defined on the set collection can be used to make the simulation of the investigative process easier and more natural. It is important to note that there is no one right way to develop a model or simulation. Models and simulations can be crude and simple, or elaborate and complex. The only requirement is that they capture those attributes and behaviors that they are designed to model or simulate. Modeling is a major goal of object-oriented design and programming. The closer the structures and operations are logically to what they represent, the easier it is for designers and programmers to implement the model in software. In the case of modeling and simulation, it is desirable to pick structures and algorithms that logically match what is being simulated and modeled. If the behavior of something that is to be modeled is readily matched by the behavior of a collection or container, then it makes sense to use that collection or container in the model or simulation.

Although performance is clearly a consideration, power of representation is more important for simulation and modeling. Very efficient structures and fast algorithms that are logically removed from the domain of the model or simulation are difficult to implement, maintain, and understand. This defeats one of the primary purposes of modeling and simulation. Modeling and simulation are often used to investigate the behavior or characteristics of some system, concept, or process. If the model or simulation itself is difficult to understand or does not easily map to what is being imitated, then the goal of the simulation is in jeopardy. The technique of simulation consists of following the changes in a *model* of a system, concept, or process. So to have a simulation we must have at least two things: a model and a set of changes that can occur within the domain of that model. Simulation involves producing a *sequence of events* that are meaningful within the context of the model that has been developed.

## THE INVESTIGATION COMPONENTS

We use classes to model events. We use set operations to produce changes in the model. We use sets to hold or *contain* the objects under consideration. Our simulation includes three user-defined classes: **walk, session,** and **clock_time**.

### User-Defined Objects

Figure 5.9 shows the class relationship diagram for these three classes. These three classes are used to model each of the authorized and unauthorized Internet accesses. The **session** class is a node class and is derived from the **walk** class. These two classes encapsulate the origin, destination, start time, end time, and user id of every recorded session. The class **clock_time** is a simple time stamp class that is used to model *hours* and *minutes*. These three classes form a simple aggregate class. One interesting note about the **walk** class is that it can be used for the basis of any class that needs to encapsulate the notion of *input state, output state*, and the time required for a *transition* between the input state and output state. Many of the computer programming techniques that implement problem-solving strategies use such a class. Along with the collection, container, and user-defined classes, we use **ifstream** objects from the **iostream** classes.

### Set Collections Used in the Simulation

One of the primary functions in any investigation is to sort through available information and determine which information is relevant and which information is not and which information moves the investigator closer to some goal. Investigations pinpoint and zoom in on pertinent objects while ignoring others. We use the set operations

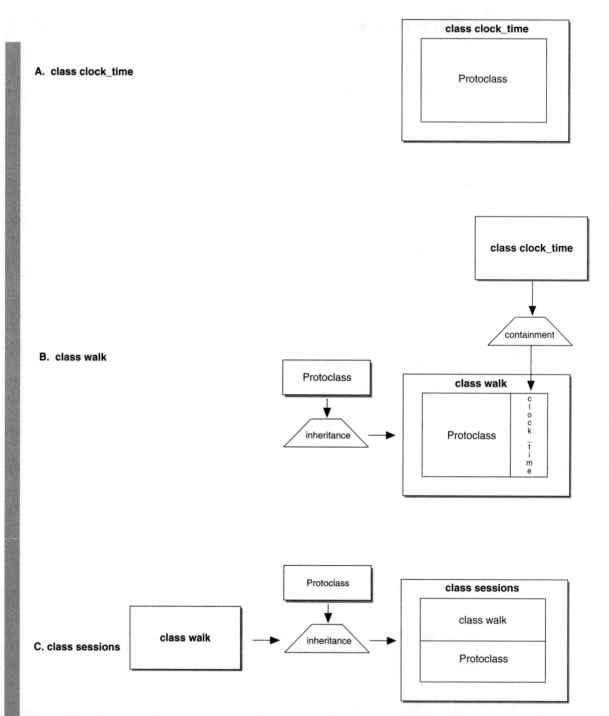

**Figure 5.9** The class relationship diagram for **walk, session,** and **clock_time** classes.

intersection, union, and difference to perform a simple simulation of an investigation. We use universal sets, subsets, and power sets to hold all the objects that are under investigation. The objects that are under investigation in this simulation represent Internet sessions, where a user logs into one computer and uses that computer to gain authorized or unauthorized access to another computer. We are interested in finding any unauthorized access. The universal set in this simulation is called **Sessions. Sessions** is enumerated as:

Sessions = { X : X is a recorded logon to one computer and logout of another computer}

The simulation also includes seven other sets:

LegalSessions
Suspicious
Questionable
Investigated
SuspiciousTimes
SuspiciousPlaces
SuspiciousLengths

Our eight sets and operations performed on them are used to simulate the type of investigation that uses the process of elimination. The set **LegalSessions** consists of those recorded sessions that are authorized. The set **LegalSessions** is enumerated by:

LegalSessions = {SiteR, SiteO,SiteP,SiteQ}

The set **Suspicious** is enumerated by performing a *set difference* between **Sessions** and the **LegalSessions. Suspicious** is enumerated by:

$$Suspicious = Sessions / LegalSessions$$

The sets **SuspiciousLengths**, **SuspiciousTimes**, and **SuspiciousPlaces** are defined by user-defined rules that classify and categorize the recorded sessions. Remember it is the user-defined rules and conditions that allow sets to be used for classification or for categorization. The set **SuspiciousLengths** is enumerated as:

SuspiciousLengths = { X : X > 4 hours}

These **SuspiciousLengths** are taken out of the set **Suspicious**. Any session that is over 4 hours in duration is considered a suspicious length. The set **SuspiciousTimes** is enumerated as:

SuspiciousTimes = { X : X's Start Time < 5.00 am}

If a session started earlier than 5.00 A.M., then the set is added to the set **SuspiciousTimes**. These suspicious times are taken from the set **Suspicious**. The set **SuspiciousPlaces** is built by:

SuspiciousPlaces = {X : X's origin = "SiteM", or "SiteA", or "SiteB"}

The set **Questionable** is enumerated as:

Questionable = SuspiciousLengths ∩ SuspiciousTimes ∪ SuspiciousPlaces

The set **Investigated** is enumerated as:

Investigated = SuspiciousLengths ∩ SuspiciousTimes ∩ SuspiciousPlaces

The simulation uses two ASCII files *session.txt*, and *legal.txt*. The file *session.txt* has all of the recorded logins and logouts. The file *legal.txt* contains the only sites that involve completely safe and authorized logins. Table 5.6 shows what is contained in *session.txt*. Table 5.7 shows what is contained in *legal.txt*.

The investigator's process of elimination is the subject of this simulation. The set operations represent the decisions to pinpoint, categorize, or identify. By changing the order of the set operations, the process of elimination is changed. The user can experiment with the number and order of steps that the investigator goes through in attempting to identify unauthorized access. The two files *session.txt* and *legal.txt* were saved in

**Table 5.6   This table shows what is contained in session.txt.**

*Contents of session.txt*

SiteA SiteE 3.00 15 30 18 30 plato_hack
SiteC SiteG 4.16 12 00 16 16 jazz_surf
SiteD SiteA 1.15 13 00 14 15 jazz_surf
SiteE SiteE 5.23 15 00 20 23 ajax
SiteB SiteG 2.15 13 30 15 45 plato_hack
SiteB SiteC 9.25 13 00 22 25 jazz_surf
SiteA SiteM 15.15 05 15 18 00 plato_hack
SiteE SiteM 5.00 13 00 18 00 ajax
SiteF SiteA 4.30 18 00 22 30 duck_zan
SiteB SiteG 2.30 17 00 19 30 duck_zan
SiteB SiteC 0.45 00 00 00 45 vis-a-vie
SiteM SiteF 15.00 00 00 15 00 plato_hack
SiteC SiteB 3.30 14 30 18 00 duck_zan
SiteA SiteC 12.15 00 00 12 15 ajax
SiteC SiteC 0.30 1 00 1 30 plato_hack
SiteD SiteG 2.30 04 30 07 00 vis-a-vie

**Table 5.7   This table shows what is contained in legal.txt.**

*Contents of legal.txt*

SiteR SiteQ 3.00 15 30 18 30 anonymous
SiteX SiteL 9.25 13 00 22 25 anonymous

an ASCII format so that they could be easily changed. By changing the files and running the program different sessions can be identified. This simulation has several objectives. The first is to see how an investigator might identify particular objects by manipulating groups of larger objects. The second is to see how many steps it takes using the operations of union, intersection, and difference to isolate unauthorized sessions. The third is evaluate how certain objects are classified and categorized into groups in order to help the process of elimination.

## SOURCE EXPLANATIONS

The investigation simulation is written using C++ and STL containers. The code was tested in OS/2, MSDOS environments. The code was compiled using Borland's C++ for OS/2, IBM's CSet++, and Borland's C++ 4.5. Because the code has a console mode interface and only uses standard C++, it should be able to run in any environment that supports C++, templates, and the STL.

## SETAPP.MAK

```
#===============================================
#
#       SETAPP.MAK-Makefile for project SETAPP.PRJ
#
#
#===============================================
AUTODEPEND
#===============================================
#        Translator Definitions
#===============================================
CC = bcc +SETAPP.CFG
TASM = tasm.exe
TLIB = tlib.exe
TLINK = tlink
RC = brcc.exe
RB = rc.exe
LIBPATH = C:\BCOS2\LIB
INCLUDEPATH = C:\BCOS2\INCLUDE;c:\stl
#===============================================
#        Implicit Rules
#===============================================
.c.obj:
$(CC) −c {$< }

.cpp.obj:
$(CC) −c {$< }

.asm.obj:
$(TASM) −Mx $*.asm,$*.obj
```

```
.rc.res:
$(RC) −r $*.rc

#==============================================
#          List Macros
#==============================================

EXE_DEPENDENCIES = \
setapp.obj \
clktime.obj \
walk.obj \
session.obj

#==============================================
#          Explicit Rules
#==============================================
setapp.exe: setapp.cfg $(EXE_DEPENDENCIES)
$(TLINK) /v /c /Toe /ap /L$(LIBPATH) @&&|
C:\BCOS2\LIB\CO2.OBJ+
setapp.obj+
clktime.obj+
walk.obj+
session.obj
setapp,setapp
C:\BCOS2\LIB\C2.LIB+
C:\BCOS2\LIB\OS2.LIB

|

#==============================================
#          Individual File Dependencies
#==============================================
SETAPP.obj: setapp.cfg SETAPP.CPP

CLKTIME.obj: setapp.cfg CLKTIME.CPP

WALK.obj: setapp.cfg WALK.CPP

SESSION.obj: setapp.cfg SESSION.CPP

#==============================================
#          Compiler Configuration File
#==============================================
setapp.cfg: setapp.mak
copy &&|
-R
-L$(LIBPATH)
-I$(INCLUDEPATH)
-vi
-v
-w-inl
| setapp.cfg
```

*walk.h* contains the declaration of the **walk** and **session** classes. *clktime.h* contains the declaration for the **clock_time** class. *walk.cpp*, *session.cpp*, and *clktime.cpp*, contain the definitions for the **walk, session**, and **clock_time** classes. *setapp.cpp* contains the simulation program.

## Header Files

1 **walk.h**

```
2 // Declaration of the walk and session classes
3
4 #include "clktime.h"
5 #include <cstring.h>
6 #include <fstream.h>
7 #define __WALK__H
8
9 class walk{
10 protected:
11    string Origin;
12    string Destination;
13    double Duration;
14    clock_time StartTime;
15    clock_time EndTime;
16 public:
17    walk(void);
18    walk(string X,string Y, double Dur,clock_time ST, clock_time ET);
19    walk(const walk &X);
20    int operator<(const walk &X) const;
21    int operator>(const walk &X) const;
22    int operator==(const walk &X) const;
23    walk operator=(walk &X);
24    virtual int operator()(walk X, walk Y) const;
25    void origin(string X);
26    void destination(string X);
27    void duration(double X);
28    void startTime(clock_time X);
29    void endTime(clock_time X);
30    string origin(void);
31    string destination(void);
32    double duration(void);
33    clock_time startTime(void);
34    clock_time endTime(void);
35    friend ostream &operator<<(ostream &Out, walk &X);
36    friend istream &operator>>(istream &In, walk &X);
37 };
```

38 **session.h**

```
39 class session : public walk{
40 protected:
41    string UserID;
```

```
42 public:
43    session(void);
44    session(string X,string Y, double Dur,clock_time ST, clock_time ET, string Id);
45    session(const session &X);
46    session &operator=(const session &X);
47    int operator<(const session &X) const;
48    friend ostream &operator<<(ostream &Out, session &X);
49    friend istream &operator>>(istream &In, session &X);
50    string userID(void);
51    void userID(string X);
52    };
53 //= = = = = = = = = = = = = = = = = = = = = = = = = = = = = = = = = = = =
```

1 **clktime.h**

```
2 // Declaration of the clock_time class
3
4    #include <iostream.h>
5
6    class clock_time{
7 protected:
8    int Minutes;
9    int Hours;
10 public:
11    clock_time(void);
12    clock_time(int HrsMin);
13    clock_time(int Hrs,int Min);
14    clock_time(const clock_time &Time);
15    clock_time &operator=(clock_time &Time);
16    friend ostream &operator<<(ostream &Out,clock_time &Time);
17    friend istream &operator>>(istream &In,clock_time &Time);
18    clock_time operator+(clock_time Time);
19    clock_time operator-(clock_time Time);
20    clock_time operator*(int X);
21    int operator>(clock_time Time) const;
22    int operator<(clock_time Time) const;
23    int operator>=(clock_time Time) const;
24    int operator<=(clock_time Time) const;
25    int operator!=(clock_time Time) const;
26    int operator==(clock_time Time) const;
27    void time(int Clock);
28    void minutes(int M);
29    void hours(int H);
30    int minutes(void);
31    int hours(void);
32 };
//= = = = = = = = = = = = = = = = = = = = = = = = = = = = = = = = = = = =
```

1 **walk.cpp**

```
2 // Definitions for the walk class
3
4 #include "walk.h"
```

```
 5
 6 walk::walk(void)
 7 {
 8    Origin = "";
 9    Destination = "";
10    Duration = -1;
11    StartTime.hours(0);
12    StartTime.minutes(0);
13    EndTime.hours(0);
14    EndTime.minutes(0);
15 }
16
17 walk::walk(const walk &X)
18 {
19    Origin = X.Origin;
20    Destination = X.Destination;
21    StartTime = X.StartTime;
22    EndTime = X.EndTime;
23    Duration = X.Duration;
24 }
25
26 walk::walk(string X,string Y, double Dur,clock_time ST, clock_time ET)
27 {
28    Origin = X;
29    Destination = Y;
30    Duration = Dur;
31    StartTime = ST;
32    EndTime = ET;
33 }
34
35 walk walk::operator=(walk &X)
36 {
37    Origin = X.Origin;
38    Destination = X.Destination;
39    StartTime = X.StartTime;
40    EndTime = X.EndTime;
41    Duration = X.Duration;
42    return(*this);
43 }
44
45 int walk::operator<(const walk &X) const
46 {
47    if(Duration < X.Duration){
48      return(1);
49    }
50    else{
51    return(0);
52    }
53 }
54
```

```
55
56 int walk::operator>(const walk &X) const
57 {
58   if(Duration > X.Duration){
59   return(1);
60   }
61   else{
62   return(0);
63   }
64 }
65 int walk::operator==(const walk &X) const
66 {
67   if((StartTime == X.StartTime) &&
68     (EndTime == X.EndTime)){
69   return(1);
70   }
71   else{
72   return(0);
73   }
74 }
75
76 int walk::operator()(walk X, walk Y) const
77 {
78   if(X > Y){
79     return(1);
80   }
81   else{
82   return(0);
83   }
84 }
85
86
87 void walk::origin(string X)
88 {
89   Origin = X;
90 }
91
92
93 void walk::destination(string X)
94 {
95   Destination = X;
96 }
97
98
99 void walk::duration(double X)
100 {
101
102   Duration = X;
103
104 }
```

```
105
106 void walk::startTime(clock_time X)
107 {
108    StartTime = X;
109 }
110
111 void walk::endTime(clock_time X)
112 {
113    EndTime = X;
114 }
115
116 string walk::origin(void)
117 {
118    return(Origin);
119 }
120
121 string walk::destination(void)
122 {
123    return(Destination);
124 }
125
126
127 double walk::duration(void)
128 {
129    return(Duration);
130 }
131
132 clock_time walk::startTime(void)
133 {
134    return(StartTime);
135 }
136
137 clock_time walk::endTime(void)
138 {
139
140    return(EndTime);
141 }
142
143
144 ostream &operator<<(ostream &Out, walk &X)
145 {
146    Out << X.Origin << " " << " " << X.Destination <<÷< " ";
147    Out << X.Duration << " " << X.StartTime << " ";
148    Out << X.EndTime;
149    return(Out);
150 }
151
152
153 istream &operator>>(istream &In, walk &X)
154 {
```

```
155   In >> X.Origin >> X.Destination >> X.Duration;
156   In >> X.StartTime >> X.EndTime;
157   return(In);
}
159 //= = = = = = = = = = = = = = = = = = = = = = = = = = = = = = = = = = = = =
  1 session.cpp
  2 // Definition of the session class

      3

  4
  5 #include "session.h"
  6
  7
  8
  9 session::session(void)
 10 {
 11
 12   UserID = "";
 13
 14 }
 15
 16 session::session(string X,string Y, double Dur,clock_time ST, clock_time ET,
    string Id):
 17   walk(X,Y,Dur,ST,ET)
 18 {
 19

 20
 21   UserID = Id;
 22 }
 23
 24
 25
 26 session::session(const session &X)
 27 {
 28   Origin = X.Origin;
 29   Destination = X.Destination;
 30   StartTime = X.StartTime;
 31   EndTime = X.EndTime;
 32   Duration = X.Duration;
 33   UserID = X.UserID;
 34 }
 35
 36
 37 int session::operator<(const session &X) const
 38 {
 39   if(Origin < X.Origin){
 40     return(1);
 41   }
 42   else{
 43   return(0);
```

```
44   }
45 }
46 session &session::operator=(const session &X)
47 {
48
49   Origin = X.Origin;
50   Destination = X.Destination;
51   StartTime = X.StartTime;
52   EndTime = X.EndTime;
53   Duration = X.Duration;
54   UserID = X.UserID;
55   return(*this);}
56
57 ostream &operator<<(ostream &Out, session &X)
58 {
59   Out << X.Origin << " " << " " << X.Destination <<÷< " ";
60   Out << X.Duration << " " << X.StartTime << " ";
61   Out << X.EndTime << " " << X.UserID;
62   return(Out);
63
64
65 }
66
67 istream &operator>>(istream &In, session &X)
68 {
69   In >> X.Origin >> X.Destination >> X.Duration;
70   In >> X.StartTime >> X.EndTime >> X.UserID;
71   return(In);
72 }
73
74
75 string session::userID(void)
76 {
77   return(UserID);
78 }
79
80 void session::userID(string X)
81 {
82   UserID = X;
83 }
//= = = = = = = = = = = = = = = = = = = = = = = = = = = = = = = = = =
 1 clktime.cpp
 2 // Definitions for the clock_time class

 3

 4 #include "clktime.h"
 5 #include <iomanip.h>
 6 #include <stdlib.h>
 7
 8
```

```
 9
10 clock_time::clock_time(const clock_time &Time)
11 {
12    Hours = Time.Hours;
13    Minutes = Time.Minutes;
14 }
15
16 clock_time::clock_time(int HrsMin)
17 {
18    div_t Value;
19    Value = div(HrsMin,100);
20    Hours = Value.quot;
21    Minutes = Value.rem;
22
23
24 }
25
26
27 clock_time &clock_time::operator=(clock_time &Time)
28 {
29    Hours = Time.Hours;
30    Minutes = Time. Minutes;
31    return(*this);
32 }
33
34
35 clock_time::clock_time(int Hrs,int Min)
36 {
37    Hours = Hrs;
38    Minutes = Min;
39 }
40
41 clock_time::clock_time(void)
42 {
43    Hours = 0;
44    Minutes = 0;
45 }
46
47
48 clock_time clock_time::operator+(clock_time Time)
49 {
50    clock_time X;
51    X.Hours = Hours;
52    X.Minutes = Minutes;
53    X.Hours = X.Hours + Time.Hours;
54    X.Minutes = X.Minutes + Time.Minutes;
55    return(X);
56 }
57
58
```

```
59 int clock_time::operator>(clock_time Time) const
60 {
61    if(Hours > Time.Hours){
62       return(1);
63    }
64    else
65       if((Hours == Time.Hours) && (Minutes > Time.Minutes)){
66       return(1);
67       }
68       else{
69       return(0);
70       }
71 }
72
73 int clock_time::operator<(clock_time Time) const
74 {
75    if(Hours < Time.Hours){
76       return(1);
77    }
78    else
79       if((Hours == Time.Hours) && (Minutes < Time.Minutes)){
80       return(1);
81       }
82       else{
83       return(0);
84       }
85
86 }
87
88 int clock_time::operator>=(clock_time Time) const
89 {
90    if((Hours >= Time.Hours) && (Minutes >= Time.Minutes)){
91       return(1);
92    }
93    else
94       if((Hours == Time.Hours) && (Minutes >= Time.Minutes)){
95       return(1);
96       }
97       else
98    if(Hours > Time.Hours){
99       return(1);
100    }
101    else{
102       return(0);
103    }
104
105 }
106
107
108 int clock_time::operator<=(clock_time Time) const
```

```
109 {
110    if((Hours <= Time.Hours) && (Minutes <= Time.Minutes)){
111       return(1);
112    }
113    else
114      if((Hours == Time.Hours) && (Minutes <= Time.Minutes)){
115    return(1);
116      }
117      else
118    if(Hours < Time.Hours){
119       return(1);
120    }
121    else{
122       return(0);
123    }
124
125 }
126
127 int clock_time::operator!=(clock_time Time) const
128 {
129    if((Hours != Time.Hours) || (Minutes != Time.Minutes)){
130       return(1);
131    }
132    else{
133    return(0);
134    }
135
136 }
137
138 void clock_time::time(int Clock)
139 {
140    div_t Value;
141    Value = div(Clock,100);
142    Hours = Value.quot;
143    Minutes = Value.rem;
144
145 }
146 int clock_time::operator==(clock_time Time) const
147 {
148    if((Hours == Time.Hours) && (Minutes == Time.Minutes)){
149       return(1);
150    }
151    return(0);
152 }
153
154
155 clock_time clock_time::operator*(int X)
156 {
157    clock_time T;
158    T.Hours = Hours;
```

```
159    T.Minutes = Minutes;
160    if(X < 1){
161       T.Hours *= -1;
162       T.Minutes *= -1;
163    }
164    return(X);
165
166 }
167 clock_time clock_time::operator-(clock_time Time)
168 {
169    clock_time X;
170    X.Hours = Hours;
171    X.Minutes = Minutes;
172    if(Time.Minutes <= X.Minutes){
173       X.Minutes = (X.Minutes - Time.Minutes);
174       X.Hours = (X.Hours - Time.Hours);
175    }
176    else
177    if((Time.Minutes > X.Minutes) && (X.Hours > 0)){
178       X.Minutes = X.Minutes + 60;
179       X.Minutes = (X.Minutes - Time.Minutes);
180       X.Hours--;
181       X.Hours = (X.Hours - Time.Hours);
182    }
183    else{
184       X.Hours = X.Hours - Time.Hours;
185       X.Minutes = Minutes - Time.Minutes;
186    }
187    return(X);
188 }
189
190
191
192
193 void clock_time::minutes(int M)
194 {
195    Minutes = M;
196 }
197
198 void clock_time::hours(int H)
199 {
200    Hours = H;
201 }
202
203
204
205 int clock_time::minutes(void)
206 {
207    return(Minutes);
208 }
```

```
209
210
211 int clock_time::hours(void)
212 {
213    return(Hours);
214 }
215
216
217
218 ostream &operator<<(ostream &Out,clock_time &Time)
219 {
220
221    Out << Time.Hours << " ";
222    Out << Time.Minutes;
223    return(Out);
224 }
225
226
227 istream &operator>>(istream &In,clock_time &Time)
228 {
229    In >> Time.Hours;
230    In >> Time.Minutes;
231    return(In);
232 }
233
234
//= = = = = = = = = = = = = = = = = = = = = = = = = = = = = = = = =
 1 // setapp.cpp
 2 // This is the investigation simulation program
 3 // it uses the set collection and set operations to simulate
 4 // various aspects of the process of elimination
 5
 6 #define __MINMAX_DEFINED
 7 #include <pair.h>
 8 #include <set.h>
 9 #include <multiset.h>
10 #include <algo.h>
11 #include <vector.h>
12 #include <fstream.h>
13 #include <iterator.h>
14 #include "walk.h"
15 #include "session.h"
16 #include <iomanip.h>
17 #include "spaces.cpp"
18
19
20
21
22 template <class T, class U> class check{
23 public:
```

```
24 int operator()(set<T,U> X, set<T,U> Y) const;
25 };
26
27
28 template<class T, class U> int check<T,U>::operator()(set<T,U> X, set<T,U>
    Y) const
29 {
30     if (X < Y){
31   return(1);
32     }
33     else{
34     return(0);
35     }
36 }
37
38 // Example of a declaration for a built in type of set of sets
39 //= = = = = = = = = = = = = = = = = = = = = = = = = = = = = = = = = =
40 //set<set<char,less<char> >,check<char,less<char> > >::iterator PS;
41 //set<set<char,less<char> >,check<char,less<char> > > PowerSet;
42 //= = = = = = = = = = = = = = = = = = = = = = = = = = = = = = = = = =
43
44 /* set<char,less<char> >::iterator Anchor;
45    set<char,less<char> >::iterator Current;
46    set<char,less<char> >::iterator Element;
47    set<char,less<char> >::iterator Next;
48    set<char,less<char> >::iterator P;
49    set<char,less<char> > SetA;
50 */
51
52 set<set<session,session> ,check<session,session> > PowerSet;
53 set<set<session,session> ,check<session,session> >::iterator PS;
54 set<session,session>::iterator Anchor;
55 set<session,session>::iterator Current;
56 set<session,session>::iterator Element;
57 set<session,session>::iterator Next;
58 set<session,session>::iterator P;
59 set<session,session> SetA;
60 set<session,session> UniversalSet;
61 set<session,session> Null;
62 multiset<session,session> Sessions;
63 set<session,session> LegalSessions;
64 set<session,session> Suspicious;
65 set<session,session> Questionable;
66 set<session,session> Investigated;
67 set<session,session> Culprits;
68 set<session,session> SuspiciousTimes;
69 set<session,session> SuspiciousPlaces;
70 set<session,session> SuspiciousLengths;
71
72
```

```
73 clock_time STime(5,0);
74
75
76. ifstream In;
77
78 session User;
79
80 void powerSet(set<session,session> &Culprits)
81 {
82
83
84    int Limit = 2;
85    int N;
86    int CurrentPos = 0;
87    int AnchorPos = 1;
88    int NextPos = 1;
89    session Stroll;
90    P = Culprits.begin();
91    while(P != Culprits.end())
92    {
93       UniversalSet.insert(*P);
94       P++;
95    }
96    In.close();
97    P = UniversalSet.begin();
98    while(P != UniversalSet.end())
99    {
100       set<session,session> Temp;
101       Temp.insert(*P);
102       P++;
103       PowerSet.insert(Temp);
104    }
105    while(Limit <= UniversalSet.size())
106    {
107    if(Limit > 2){
108       Anchor = UniversalSet.begin();
109       AnchorPos = 1;
110       while(Anchor != UniversalSet.end())
111       {
112         Next = Anchor;
113         Next++;
114         NextPos = NextPos + 1;
115         Current = Next;
116         CurrentPos = AnchorPos + 1;
117         while((Next != UniversalSet.end()) &&
118           ((UniversalSet.size() - NextPos) >= 1))
119         {
120           CurrentPos = NextPos;
121           Current = Next;
122           while((Current != UniversalSet.end()) &&
```

```
123                  ((UniversalSet.size() − CurrentPos) >= 1))
124             {
125               set<session,session> Temp;
126               Temp.insert(*Anchor);
127               Temp.insert(*Next);
128               Element = Current;
129               Element++;
130               for(N = 1;N < (Limit − 1);N++)
131               {
132               if(Element!= UniversalSet.end()){
133                 Temp.insert(*Element);
134                 Element++;
135                 }
136               }
137               PowerSet.insert(Temp);
138               Current++;
139               CurrentPos++;
140             }
141           Next++;
142           NextPos++;
143          }
144        Anchor++;
145        AnchorPos++;
146     }
147   }
148   else{
149       Anchor = UniversalSet.begin();
150       AnchorPos = 1;
151       while(Anchor != UniversalSet.end())
152       {
153         Current = Anchor;
154         Current++;
155         CurrentPos = AnchorPos;
156         while((Current != UniversalSet.end()) &&
157           ((UniversalSet.size() − CurrentPos) >= 1))
158         {
159           set<session,session> Temp;
160           Temp.insert(*Anchor);
161           Element = Current;
162           for(N = 1;N < Limit;N++)
163           {
164             Temp.insert(*Element);
165             Element++;
166           }
167           PowerSet.insert(Temp);
168           Current++;
169           CurrentPos++;
170         }
171         Anchor++;
172         AnchorPos++;
```

```
173          }
174
175     }
176     Limit++;
177     }
178     PowerSet.insert(UniversalSet);
179
180     session Empty;
181     Null.insert(User);
182     PowerSet.insert(Null);
183 }
184
185
186
187 void displayInvestigation(void)
188 {
189     session Temp;
190     P = Questionable.begin();
191     cout << "Questionable " << endl << endl;
192     cout << "Logged In" << spaces(5) << "Logged Out" << endl << endl;
193     while(P != Questionable.end())
194     {
195
196     Temp = *P;
197     cout << Temp.origin() << spaces(9) << Temp.destination() << endl;
198     P++;
199     }
200     cout << "Investigated " << endl << endl;
201     cout << "Logged In" << spaces(5) << "Logged Out" << endl << endl;
202     P = Investigated.begin();
203     while(P != Investigated.end())
204     {
205     Temp= *P;
206     cout << Temp.origin() << spaces(9) << Temp.destination() << endl;
207     P++;
208     }
209     cout << endl << "Suspicious Times " << endl << endl;
210     cout << "IN" << spaces(7) << "OUT" << endl;
211     cout << "HR" << spaces(2) << "MIN" << spaces(2) << "HR" << spaces(2);
212     cout << "MIN" << endl;
213     P = SuspiciousTimes.begin();
214     while(P != SuspiciousTimes.end())
215     {
216     Temp = *P;
217     cout << setw(2) << setiosflags(ios::right) << Temp.startTime() << spaces
        (4);
218     cout << setw(2) << setiosflags(ios::left) << Temp.endTime() << endl;
219     P++;
220     }
221     cout << endl << "Suspicious Places " << endl << endl;
```

```
222    cout << "Logged In" << spaces(5) << "Logged Out" << endl;
223
224    P = SuspiciousPlaces.begin();
225    while(P != SuspiciousPlaces.end())
226    {
227
228    Temp = *P;
229    cout << Temp.origin() << spaces(9) << Temp.destination() << endl;
230    P++;
231    }
232    cout << endl << "Suspicious Lengths " << endl << endl;
233    P = SuspiciousLengths.begin();
234    while(P != SuspiciousLengths.end())
235    {
236
237    Temp = *P;
238
239    cout << setiosflags(ios::showpoint | ios::fixed);
240    cout << setw(3)<< setprecision(3)<< Temp.duration() <<÷< endl;
241    P++;
242    }
243
244    cout << endl << "Power Set " << endl << endl;
245    powerSet(Investigated);
246    PS = PowerSet.begin();
247    while(PS != PowerSet.end())
248    {
249      SetA = *PS;
250      P = SetA.begin();
251      cout << "{";
252      while(P != SetA.end())
253      {
254    Temp = *P;
255    cout << Temp.userID() << spaces(1);
256    P++;
257      }
258      cout << "}" << endl;
259      PS++;
260    }
261
262
263
264
265 }
266
267 ifstream Fin;
268
269 void getTheFacts(void)
270 {
271    Fin.open("session.txt");
```

```
272    while(!Fin.eof() && Fin.good())
273    {
274      {
275      session User;
276      Fin >> User;
277      Sessions.insert(User);
278    }
279    }
280    Fin.close();
281    Fin.open("legal.txt");
282    while(!Fin.eof() & Fin.good())
283    {
284      {
285    session User;
286    Fin >> User;
287    LegalSessions.insert(User);
288      }
289    }
290    Fin.close();
291  }
292
293
294  void main(void)
295  {
296
297    getTheFacts();
298    set_difference(Sessions.begin(),Sessions.end(),
299        LegalSessions.begin(),LegalSessions.end(),
300        inserter(Suspicious,suspicious.begin()));
301    P = Suspicious.begin();
302    while(P != Suspicious.end())
303    {
304      session Suspect;
305      Suspect = *P;
306      if(Suspect.duration() > 4.00){
307    SuspiciousLengths.insert(Suspect);
308      }
309      if(Suspect.startTime() < STime){
310    SuspiciousTimes.insert(Suspect);
311      }
312      if(Suspect.origin() == "SiteB"){
313    SuspiciousPlaces.insert(Suspect);
314      }
315      if((Suspect.origin() == "SiteM") || (Suspect.origin() == "SiteA")){
316    SuspiciousPlaces.insert(Suspect);
317      }
318      P++;
319    }
320    session Suspect;
321    set_union(SuspiciousLengths.begin(),SuspiciousLengths.end(),
```

```
322      SuspiciousTimes.begin(),SuspiciousTimes.end(),
323      inserter(Questionable,Questionable.begin()),Suspect);
324   set_union(SuspiciousPlaces.begin(),SuspiciousPlaces.end(),
325      SuspiciousPlaces.begin(),SuspiciousPlaces.end(),
326      inserter(Questionable,Questionable.begin()),Suspect);
327
328   set_intersection(SuspiciousLengths.begin(),SuspiciousLengths.end(),
329        SuspiciousTimes.begin(),SuspiciousTimes.end(),
330        inserter(SetA,SetA.begin()),Suspect);
331   set_intersection(SuspiciousPlaces.begin(),SuspiciousPlaces.end(),
332        SetA.begin(),SetA.end(),
333        inserter(Investigated,Investigated.begin()),Suspect);
334   displayInvestigation();
335 }
//= = = = = = = = = = = = = = = = = = = = = = = = = = = = = = = = = = = = = =
```

## PROCEDURE AND FUNCTION DESCRIPTIONS

The work in this simulation is divided into three procedures. The **powerSet()** procedure takes the set Investigated and generates a power set. The power set is called **PowerSet**. This set will contain all the possible combinations of teams that the culprits under investigation could have formed. In an investigation a good investigator will be aware of the important combinations and permutations of suspects. The **displayInvestigation()** procedure simply sends the results of our process of elimination to standard **out**. The majority of the work is done in function **main()**. The set **union, set_difference**, and **set-_intersection** are the operations that when properly combined can be used to imitate the process of elimination.

Table 5.8 shows the input files for the simulation program. Table 5.9 shows what the output is when the simulation program is executed.

**Table 5.8   This table shows the input of the SetApp simulation.**

*Input for SetApp Simulation*

*session.txt*
SiteA SiteE 3.00 15 30 18 30 plato_hack
SiteC SiteG 4.16 12 00 16 16 jazz_surf
SiteD SiteA 1.15 13 00 14 15 jazz_surf
SiteE SiteE 5.23 15 00 20 23 ajax
SiteB SiteG 2.15 13 30 15 45 plato_hack
SiteB SiteC 9.25 13 00 22 25 jazz_surf
SiteA SiteM 15.15 05 15 18 00 plato_hack
SiteE SiteM 5.00 13 00 18 00 ajax
SiteF SiteA 4.30 18 00 22 30 duck_zan
SiteB SiteG 2.30 17 00 19 30 duck_zan
SiteB SiteC 0.45 00 00 00 45 vis-a-vie
SiteM SiteF 15.00 00 00 15 00 plato_hack
SiteC SiteB 3.30 14 30 18 00 duck_zan
SiteA SiteC 12.15 00 00 12 15 ajax
SiteC SiteC 0.30 1 00 1 30 plato_hack
SiteD SiteG 2.30 04 30 07 00 vis-a-vie

*legal.txt*
SiteR SiteQ 3.00 15 30 18 30 anonymous
SiteX SiteL 9.25 13 00 22 25 anonymous

**Table 5.9** This table shows the output of the SetApp simulation.

*Output for SetApp Simulation*

| Questionable | | | Investigated | | |
|---|---|---|---|---|---|
| Logged in | Logged out | | Logged in | Logged out | |
| SiteA | SiteM | | SiteM | SiteB | |
| SiteM | SiteF | | SiteA | SiteC | |
| SiteA | SiteC | | | | |
| SiteB | SiteC | | **Suspicious Times** | | |
| SiteE | SiteE | | | | |
| SiteE | SiteM | | In | | Out | |
| SiteF | SiteA | | HR | MIN | HR | Min |
| SiteC | SiteG | | 0 | 0 | 15 | 0 |
| SiteA | SiteE | | 0 | 0 | 12 | 15 |
| SiteB | SiteG | | 0 | 0 | 0 | 45 |
| SiteB | SiteG | | 1 | 0 | 1 | 30 |
| SiteB | SiteC | | 0 | 0 | 0 | 0 |
| SiteC | SiteC | | | | |

**Suspicious Places**

**Suspicious Lengths**

| Logged In | Logged Out | | Suspicious Lengths |
|---|---|---|---|
| | | | 15.150 |
| | | | 15.000 |
| SiteA | SiteM | | 12.150 |
| SiteM | SiteF | | 9.250 |
| SiteA | SiteC | | 5.230 |
| SiteB | SiteC | | 5.000 |
| SiteA | SiteE | | 4.300 |
| SiteB | SiteG | | 4.160 |
| SiteB | SiteG | | |
| SiteB | SiteC | | |

**Power Set**

```
{ }
(ajax }
{plato_hack }
(plato_hack ajax )
```

CHAPTER 6

# OBJECT-BASED SEQUENCES

ANY COLLECTION or container that can be viewed as a linear or sequential structure can be classified as a sequence. Just as files can be looked at as a stream of bytes, linear collections and containers can be looked at as a sequence of objects. Sequence refers to the logical view of how the objects are stored as well as to the access methods that can be used. Vectors, lists, queues, and stacks are all examples of sequences. When a group of objects is stored in a collection or container and is accessed based on an index or a linear position within the container, the group of objects represents a sequence. The STL supports six sequences: *vector, list, deque, stack, queue*, and *priority queue*. Table 6.1 lists the six sequences and their basic characteristics. The six sequences have been implemented using template classes. This means that they are generic structures as well as object-oriented structures. The runtime version of each of these sequences is an object. This means that the sequences can be used in the same way that any other object in the C++ environment can be used. We can use inheritance, polymorphism, and encapsulation with these sequences to derive new collection and container classes. The runtime version of these sequences can be passed as parameters and compared with relational operators. Object-oriented sequences can be used as return values from functions. We may declare arrays of sequences, or structs whose fields consist of sequences. We can have pointers to sequences, linked lists of sequences, and so on. Because these sequences are provided in the STL, we do not have to develop them from scratch. Instead, we can use these collections and containers directly in applications or build new collections or containers upon these existing sequences.

The non–object-oriented form of these sequences represents traditional data structures. Practically everything that is true about the traditional data structure form of these sequences is also true about their object-oriented counterparts. However, the reverse is not true. The object-oriented versions of these traditional data structures are more powerful and flexible than the non–object-oriented versions. In this chapter we discuss the object-oriented sequences that are implemented in the STL, and how they can be used to enhance traditional algorithms to support genericity as well as object orientation.

**Table 6.1   A list of the six sequences and their basic characteristics.**

| Sequence Containers | Basic Characteristics |
|---|---|
| **List** | * A sequence container that holds an arbitrary number of objects of the same type.<br>* Objects are stored and retrieved sequentially.<br>* Time needed to access an object depends upon the position the element has in the list.<br>* Supports bidirectional iterators and allows constant time insert and erase operations anywhere in the sequence.<br>* Automatic storage management. |
| **Vector** | * A sequence container that supplies direct access to the objects that it contains by the use of an index which specifies the relative position of the object.<br>* Supports random access iterators.<br>* Constant time access and constant time insert and erase operations at the end: insert and erase in the middle takes linear time.<br>* Automatic storage management. |
| **Deque** | * A sequence container where objects are enqueued or dequeued from the front or rear of the queue.<br>* Supports random access iterators.<br>* Constant time insert and erase operations at the beginning or end; insert and erase in the middle takes linear time. |
| **Queue** | * A sequence container that stores objects in FIFO order; objects are inserted in the rear and deleted from the front by the use of sequential access methods.<br>* Can be instantiated by any sequence container that supports **front(), back(), push_back()** or **pop_front()** operations. |
| **Priority Queue** | * A sequence container that stores objects in a sorted order (descending or ascending), objects are dequeued or enqueued from either the front or the rear of the queue.<br>* Can be instantiated by any sequence with random access iterators and supporting **front(), push_back(),** and **pop_back()** operations. |
| **Stack** | * A sequence container that stores objects in LIFO order; objects can only be inserted or removed from the top of the stack.<br>* Can be instantiated by any sequence that supports **back(), push_back(),** and **pop_back()** operations. |

# OBJECT-ORIENTED VECTOR

A vector that has been designed using the object-oriented constructs and is encapsulated within a class or struct is an object-oriented vector. The C++ language supports a basic array container. However, this container is not object oriented. It cannot be specialized with polymorphism. The array has no member functions or support for encapsulation. The array container in C++ is a fixed-size container. Although it can be dynamically allocated, it is not a dynamic structure. The amount of space that is allocated for a traditional C++ array does not change throughout the life of that array. This is in contrast to the object-oriented vector. The object-oriented vector is a dynamic structure. This means that its size is not fixed. The size of the object-oriented vector may grow or shrink during program execution. This is one of the primary advantages of using the object-oriented vector over using the traditional C++ array.

Like the traditional C++ array, a vector is a container that provides direct access to the objects it contains. This is in contrast to lists, queues, and stacks. Lists, queues, and stacks only provide sequential access. This means that the objects that are stored in lists, queues, and stacks can only be accessed in a serial fashion. Objects can only be processed at the beginning, end, top, bottom, front, or back. To access an object in the middle of a container, all the objects that precede that object must first be processed. When objects are stored in a vector they may be directly accessed by an index. The index specifies the relative location of the object in the list. The relative position may be relative to either the beginning or the end of a logical block of memory. For example, an index of 5 would specify the fifth object in the vector. If we had a vector called **MyVector**, then the operation **MyVector[5]** would return the fifth object in the vector. There is no need to first access objects 1 through 4. The fifth object may be accessed directly, hence the term *direct access*. The vector is an indexed structure.

Like the traditional C++ array, vectors also provide *constant time* access. Constant time refers to the amount of time that it takes to locate an object in the vector container. When a container has constant time access, it should take no longer to access the last item in the container than it takes to access the first item in the container. Although the vector is a sequential structure like a list, the access methods of the vector allow direct access as well as sequential access. Figure 6.1 shows the logical structure of a vector container. The vector container does not impose any specific ordering on the member. However, each of the members is assigned a *position* or *index* within the container. By specifying the object's position or index, direct access can be achieved.

## Why Are Vectors Useful?

The vector can be used to implement queues, stacks, lists, and other more complex structures. The vector can be used to implement virtually any other container. The only other container that has this distinction is the list. The list also can be used to implement most other containers. In languages such as C, Pascal, FORTRAN, and COBOL, the array or vector is the only built in container that is provided. It is assumed that all other containers can be simulated using this one container. Many important sorting and searching algorithms require that the objects to be sorted and searched be stored in a vector. In fact, one of the most often used searches in computer science, the *binary search*,

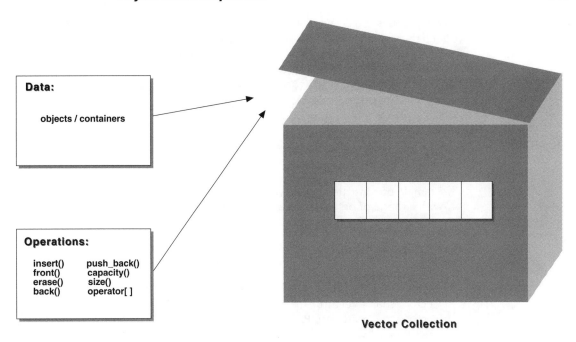

**Figure 6.1** A logical representation of an object-oriented vector container.

requires that the objects be stored in a vector. The fact that the vector is a dynamic, direct access structure means that it can be used in any situation where the programmer needs to store a group of objects and later access those objects in an efficient manner. That the vector has a constant time access makes the vector's performance as a container predictable. We can determine the efficiency of this structure easily. Another major reason vectors are so useful is that they are easy to implement and to use. The user can easily insert, remove, and access objects that are stored in a vector. Vectors do not require advanced knowledge of data structures and algorithms.

The STL provides a vector container. This vector can be used to store built-in data types as well as user-defined data types. If the vector is used to store user-defined data types it is assumed that operator $==$ and operator $<$ are defined for the user-defined type.

## Constructing a Vector

The STL vector has four constructors. One of the constructors takes no arguments. This is the default constructor. This constructor builds a vector with size zero. The **vector** class also has a constructor that accepts the size the vector is to be constructed with as well as the value to initialize the vector with:

```
vector(size_type n, const T& value = T())
```

For this constructor **n** is the number of elements of type **T** that the vector will be able to hold when it is constructed. Notice that this constructor has a default value of **T()**. The constructor uses the default constructor of type **T** to initialize all the elements in the vector if this argument is not passed. The **vector** class also has a constructor that accepts another vector as its argument. This means that a vector can be constructed using a copy of another vector. The final constructor for the **vector** class takes two iterators as arguments. This means that a vector can be constructed from a range of objects from some other collection or container. The program in Listing 6.1 illustrates how a vector can be constructed from a range of objects.

**Listing 6.1**

```
//Listing 6.1.cpp
//Example of constructing one vector
//with a range of objects from another vector

#define __MINMAX_DEFINED

#include <vector.h>

void main(void)
{
   vector<char> VectorB;
   vector<char>::iterator P;
   VectorB.push_back('B');
   VectorB.push_back('@');
   VectorB.push_back('#');
   VectorB.push_back('Z');
   VectorB.push_back('%');
   P = VectorB.begin();
   P += 2;
   vector<char> MyVector(P,VectorB.end());
   int N = 0;
   for(N = 0;N < MyVector.size();N++)
   {
      cout << MyVector[N] << endl;
   }

}
```

## Vector Destruction

As with all the STL's collections and containers the vector has automatic storage management. The programmer does not have to manually allocate or deallocate memory for the objects a vector will store. The vector automatically allocates memory. When a vector object leaves scope the vector's object destructor is called. The destructor first removes any objects that remain in the container. The destructors are called for each of these objects. The vector uses its allocator class to deallocate any memory that it has allocated for objects after the objects have been removed. It important to note that removing objects from a container does not deallocate the memory that the object occupied. Removing the object only causes that object's destructor to be called. Using the **erase()** member function does not deallocate memory, it only removes the object from the container. Allocated memory is not returned to the free store until the container leaves scope or is deleted.

## Information on the Vector Container

The vector container has four member functions that return information about vectors. The **size()**, **max_size()**, **capacity()**, and **empty()** member functions report information about vector objects.

### SIZE() AND MAX_SIZE()

These member functions of the STL's collection and container classes are to some extent misnomers. On the surface they look as if they would report the container's size. This size would presumably be measured in kilobytes, megabytes, gigabytes, and so forth. However, these member functions do not directly report the size of the container. The **size()** member function reports how many objects are currently in the container. The **max_size()** member function returns the largest number of objects that can be placed in the container. The **max_size()** member function's calculation is memory-model dependent. For instance, the **max_size()** member function will return a number of objects that take up no more than 64 K in an MSDOS or 16-bit Windows environment. Likewise the **max_size()** member function will return a much larger number of objects in virtual paging operating system environments like OS/2, UNIX, or VMS. The reason that **max_size()** returns a larger possible number of objects in these environments is due to the virtual memory management capabilities and flat memory models of these operating systems. Since these operating systems do not have 64 K segment limits, all available RAM can be used to store objects. Furthermore, because these operating systems are virtual paging operating systems, the operating system can use disk space as an internal memory supplement.

### CAPACITY()

The **capacity()** member function reports the largest number of objects that can be stored without reallocating more memory. Whereas the **max_size()** member function returns largest possible number of objects that can be stored in the container, the **capacity()** member function only reports how many can be stored before more memory has to be reallocated. Because the vector container has automatic memory management it increases the amount of memory that it needs as necessary. As the user inserts objects into the container, if the container does not have enough memory available it allocates more memory. How much memory does the container allocate? Well, this is dependent upon the operating system environment. This is because the operating system is ultimately responsible for supplying the program with memory. (See Figure 4.1 in Chapter 4.) This diagram shows the basic translation of a request for memory. This process is somewhat transparent to the user. If the container does not have enough memory to hold the object being inserted, the container automatically allocates more memory. This request is initially handled by the allocator data member of the container. The allocator's request is translated into a call to functions like **new()** or **malloc()**, and memory is ultimately returned by operating system functions like **DosAllocMem**, the OS2 memory allocation function. Virtual paging operating systems are pretty much standard issue these days. A virtual paging operating system like UNIX, OS2, VMS, Windows NT, or Windows 95 manage memory in blocks called *pages*. The smallest *page size* for these operating systems is 4096 bytes. When a container needs to allocate more memory for an object, the container makes a request to the operating system for memory. The operating system returns a block of memory that is evenly divisible by the operating system's page size. For example, if an empty container got a request to store 5003 one-byte objects, the container would make a memory request of the operating system. An operating system with a 4096-byte page would return 8192 bytes. This is why the **capacity()** member function may return a different number than the **size()** member function. Although our container would have 5003 one-byte objects, the container has the *capacity* to store 8192 one-byte objects. See the section "Containers and Automatic Memory Management" in Chapter 4 for a discussion of memory management issues and collection and container classes.

### EMPTY()

The **empty()** member function returns a boolean *true* if the vector contains no objects and a boolean *false* if the vector contains objects.

## Placing Objects into a Vector Container

Objects can be placed in a vector in a variety of ways. Objects may be inserted into the vector using vector constructors. Objects can be placed in the vector using one of the **insert()** member functions, the **push_back()** member functions, using assignment with the [] operator as an rvalue, or using assignment from one vector to another. Objects can also be placed into a vector using the **swap()** member function. The **vector** class has three constructors that can be used to insert objects. The **vector** class has three forms of the **insert()** member function. The **insert()** member functions allow the programmer to place either a single object at a particular location, a range of objects starting at a particular location, or *n* copies of a single object starting at any given location. This allows the program to place objects into the middle or at the end of a container. The **push_back()** member function inserts a single object into the rear of the vector. The operator [] and an index position can also be used to insert an object at a particular location within the vector. Because the vector does have automatic memory management, the constructors, the **insert()** member functions, and the **push_back()** member functions will automatically allocate as much memory as is necessary to fulfill the object insertion request. The **swap(X)** member function takes the elements from **X** and stores them in the vector. The objects that are stored in the vector will be placed in the vector called **X**. These member functions can be used with whatever legal *object-type* the vector has been constructed to hold.

The vector container has a member function called **reserve()**. When this member function is called, it lets the vector container know that there is a planned change in the number of objects that the vector will be holding. It is important to note that calling the **reserve()** member function does not actually cause any new memory to be allocated. Calling the **reserve()** member function is only a hint to the container that more memory may be needed. More memory will not be allocated until the amount of memory that the objects are taking up exceeds **capacity()**. After the **reserve()** member function is called, **capacity()** is greater than or equal to the argument of **reserve()** if there is a reallocation. It should be noted that any reallocation of a vector container invalidates all the pointers, iterators, and references that refer to elements in a vector.

## Removing Objects from a Vector

As with the insertion, there are several ways to remove objects from a vector object. The **pop_back()** member function removes the last object in the vector. If the vector has *n* elements, then **pop_back()** removes the object at the **N-1** position. For the **vector** container this is the same as (end() − 1). The **vector** class has two **erase()** member functions. The **erase(X)** member function erases the element that is pointed to by **X**. The **erase(First,Last)** member function erases all the elements in the range [First,Last), where **First** and **Last** are iterators. Using interval notation, this means all the objects including the object pointed to by **First** and up to but not including the object pointed to by **Last**. Remember that **Last** is past the **end()** of the container value. **Last** should not be dereferenced. Its value should only be used to test the end of the container. In the event the **Last** parameter is not the **end()** of some container, the values are removed up to but not including the value that **Last** points at. Recall that using the **erase()** member function to remove objects from the container does not deallocate the space that these objects occupied in that container. It only serves to remove the objects and call destructors for those objects, not the destructor for the container. When the destructor for the container is called, any remaining objects that still remain in the container are removed. At that point the memory that those objects took up is returned.

## Accessing Objects from a Vector

The **front()** member function can be used to return the first element in a vector. If we have a vector *A*, then calling **front()** accesses the **A[0]** element of the vector. Just like the traditional C++ array, the vector's first element is found at index *0*. Calling the **front()** member function returns this object. The **back()** member function can be used to return (end() − 1) element in the vector. The operator **[N]** can be used to access the object located at the *Nth* position relative to the beginning of the vector. The operator **[N]** is one of the operations that give the user direct access to any object that is stored in a vector. Although the user could begin at position 0 and step through the position in the vector for a sequential or linear access, by using the [] operator, the user can jump right into the middle of the container. The vector class also supports random access iterators. The program in Listing 6.2 uses the **front()**, **back()**, **insert()**, **erase()**, **push_back()**, **size()**, **max_size()**, **capacity()**, and operator [] to demonstrate how vectors are accessed, and how some of the vectors member functions work.

### Listing 6.2

```
1 //Listing 6.2.cpp
2 // Example of using vector container's
3 // information, object insertion, object removal,
```

```
 4 // and object iterator member functions
 5
 6 #define __MINMAX_DEFINED
 7
 8 #include <vector.h>
 9
10 void main(void)
11 {
12    vector<double> VectorA;
13    vector<double>::iterator P;
14    VectorA.push_back(1.1414);
15    VectorA.push_back(3.1415);
16    VectorA.push_back(-5.3);
17    VectorA.push_back(7);
18    P = VectorA.begin();
19    P += 2;
20    cout << "The value at 2 + begin() " << *P << endl;
21    VectorA.insert(P,9.99);
22    cout << "The value at 2 + begin() " << *P << endl;
23    VectorA[2] = 0.33333;
24    cout << "The value at VectorA[2] "<< VectorA[2] << endl;
25    cout << "The value at the 0th position in VectorA " << VectorA[0] << endl;
26    cout << "The value returned by the front() member function ";
27    cout << VectorA.front() << endl;
28    P = VectorA.end();
29    P--;
30    cout << "The value at the N - 1 position in VectorA ";
31    cout << VectorA[VectorA.size() - 1] << endl;
32    cout << "The value at the end() - 1 position " << *P << endl;
33    cout << "The value returned by the back() member function ";
34    cout << VectorA.back() << endl;
35    cout << "Vector's size before erase " << VectorA.size() << endl;
36    cout << "Vector's max size before erase " << VectorA.max_size() << endl;
37    cout << "Vector's capacity before erase " << VectorA.capacity() << endl;
38    VectorA.erase(VectorA.begin(), VectorA.end());
39    cout << "Vector's size after erase " << VectorA.size() << endl;
40    cout << "Vector's max size after erase " << VectorA.max_size() << endl;
41    cout << "Vector's capacity after erase " << VectorA.capacity() << endl;
42    VectorA.reserve(2000);
43    cout << "Vector's capacity after a call to reserve ";
44    cout << VectorA.capacity() << endl;
45    cout << "Vector's size after a call to reserve ";
46    cout << VectorA.size() << endl;
47 }
```

Table 6.2 shows what the output looks like when the program in Listing 6.2 is executed. Notice that the call to the **front()** and **back()** member functions are equivalent to calls to **VectorA[0]**, and **VectorA[VectorA.size() − 1]**, respectively. This demonstrates that the vector container is accessed in the same manner as the traditional C++ array. Another important feature of the vector class is demonstrated on line #19 in

**Table 6.2** **This output shows information about VectorA before and after memory allocation. It also illustrates that the *front()* and *back()* commands are equivalent to Vector[0] and Vector[N-1]. This output also shows that although a call has been made to the *reserve()* member function, VectorA's size is still 0 because it contains zero objects.**

*Output from Program Listing 6.2*

```
The value at 2 + begin() −5.3
The value at 2 + begin() 9.99
The value at VectorA[2] 0.33333
The value at the 0th position in VectorA 1.1414
The value returned by the front() member function 1.1414
The value at the N − 1 position in VectorA 7
The value at the end() − 1 position 7
The value returned by the back() member function 7
Vector's size before erase 5
Vector's max size before erase 536870911
Vector's capacity before erase 512
Vector's size after erase 0
Vector's max size after erase 536870911
Vector's capacity after erase 512
Vector's capacity after a call to reserve 2000
Vector's size after a call to reserve 0
```

Listing 6.2. This is an example of iterator arithmetic. Iterator arithmetic is the object oriented version of pointer arithmetic that is available in C++. Only random access iterators support iterator arithmetic. Using iterator arithmetic is another method of gaining direct access to any object within a vector container. Also, many of the generic algorithms require random access iterators. Since the vector class supports random access iterators, vector objects can be used with any of these algorithms. By adding 2 to the iterator in line #19 we effectively moved the iterator to point to the third object in the vector. The reason that this is the third object is that the zeroth position refers to the first object. Another interesting characteristic of the vector object is what happens to allocated memory when all the objects are erased but the destructor for the container has not been called. Notice on line #38 we erased all the objects out of the container **VectorA**; however, the call to **capacity()** on line #41 still shows that the **VectorA** as a capacity of 512. This is because **erase()** only calls destructors for the objects and removes them from the container. The erase member function does not deallocate memory. Another important point the program in Listing 6.2 demonstrates is how the **reserve()** member function affects **capacity()**. Even though **reserve()** has been called, the **size()** of the container is still zero. However, the capacity is now 2000.

The **erase()** member function invalidates all references and iterators after the point of the **erase()** call. So if there are iterators pointing to objects that come after the objects that were erased, these iterators or references will no longer be valid. There is a similar restriction on iterators after an insertion has occurred. If the insertion into the vector does not cause reallocation, then any iterators, pointers, or references are still valid.

However, if the insertion does cause container reallocation, then any iterators, pointers, or references that point to objects should be considered undefined.

## Relational Operations on Type Vector

The operators = = and < are defined for the vector container. The operator = = returns a boolean *true* if the objects in both sets are equal using the = = operator that has been defined for those objects. In other words, the = = operator for the vector will take each object from the two vectors being compared. It will use the = = operator that the user has defined to determine whether those two objects are equal. The first mismatch will cause the = = operator to return a boolean *false*. Likewise, the operator < compares each object one by one from the two vectors **x** and **y**. If an object is found in **x** that is less than **y** the operator returns boolean *true*. If an object is found first in **y** that is less than the corresponding object in **x** then a boolean *false* is returned.

# CLASSIC ALGORITHMS THAT USE VECTORS

Even after the advent of flashy computer graphics, studio-quality sound capabilities, and full-motion video, information storage, information retrieval, and numerical computation remains among the primary uses of computers. Once information is stored it must be retrieved. The retrieval must be accurate as well as efficient. The basic requirements of accurate and efficient information retrieval and storage gave rise to two of the largest areas of concentration in computer programming: sorting and searching. Information is stored only to be retrieved and processed at some later time. Because computer technology makes it possible to store millions, even billions, of pieces of information it is important to be able to sift through the information and find a particular item or items. The process of using the computer to look through or *search* through massive collections of data is constantly being investigated and improved. It was determined early on that *sorting* the information prior to searching it dramatically improves the performance of a search. Hence sorting and searching data usually are done in concert for purposes of effective information storage and retrieval.

## Sorting and Searching

If we are looking for a particular name in a list, how many names do we have to look through until we find the name we are looking for? If the list contained a thousand names, we might have to look through as few as one name or we might have to look through as many as a thousand. If the list is not organized in any fashion, where should we start searching? It is possible that the name that we are looking for is not in the list. In this case if the list is not organized we may have to look through all one thousand names only to find out that the name we are looking for is not in the list. By sorting the list by last name, or first name, and then searching the list, we know once we get to the position in the list where our name should be whether or not it is there. Once we know a list is sorted then we can devise efficient means of searching it.

Two of the most important uses of vectors are: (1) holding information to be searched, and (2) holding information to be sorted. If a vector is used to hold a sorted collection of names then we use various search techniques to determine whether the name we are searching for is in the collection. If the name we are searching for is in the collection we can also use searching techniques to determine where the name is in the collection. Many types of search techniques have been developed that can be used to search a vector. Two of the most commonly used techniques are the sequential search and the binary search.

## THE SEQUENTIAL SEARCH

The vector does not have to be sorted to use a sequential sort. By starting at the beginning of a vector and moving to each succeeding element, the vector can be searched until the item being sought is found. If the item is not found after the entire vector has been searched, then we know that the item is not in the vector. Listing 6.3 shows how a simple sequential search template function can be implemented using the STL's vector container.

**Listing 6.3**

```
1 // Listing 6.3
2 // Example of a simple sequential search
3 // using a vector
4 #define __MINMAX_DEFINED
5 #include <vector.h>
6
7
8 template <class X, class T> int sequentialSearch(vector<T> Vect, X Element)
9 {
10
11   int Found = 0;
12   int N = 0;
13   int Limit = Vect.size();
14   while(!Found && N < Limit)
15   {
16     if(Vect[N] == Element){
17       Found = 1;
18     }
19     else{
20     N++;
21     }
22   }
23   return(N);
24 }
25
26
27 void main(void)
28 {
29   vector<double> MyVect;
30   int Position = 0;
```

```
31   MyVect.push_back(12.2);
32   MyVect.push_back(7.6);
33   MyVect.push_back(9.3);
34   MyVect.push_back(38.2);
35   Position = sequentialSearch(MyVect,9.3);
36   if(Position != MyVect.size()){
37      cout << MyVect[Position] << endl;
38   }
39   else{
40   cout << "element not found";
41   }
42 }
43
```

For vectors that contain only a few objects or for scenarios where speed is not important, the **sequentialSearch()** function is appropriate. The performance of a sequential search on a vector depends on where in the vector the element is. If the element is at the beginning of the vector then the sequential search performs well. However, if the element is at the end of the vector, the sequential search has to process every element prior to the searched element first. The worst-case scenario for the sequential search is if the element that is being sought is at the end of the list. Again if efficiency is not a key concern, the sequential search is adequate. Since implementation of a sequential search is straightforward it is a much-used algorithm. However, for moderate to large collections of objects this basic **sequentialSearch()** is hopelessly inefficient. This algorithm can be improved if it is known that the list is sorted. The **sequentialSearch()** will search for **Element** until it is found or until the end of the vector is reached, whichever comes first. One of the major weaknesses of the sequential search is that in the worst-case scenario it has to search the entire list, only to find out that the element being sought is not in the list. The stopping condition for the search is on line #14. If the vector to be searched is small, or if the element to be found is near the beginning of the vector, this **sequentialSearch()** is fairly effective. However, by sorting the vector before it is searched the algorithm can be improved dramatically. The improvement comes when the element to be located is not in the vector. Instead of searching the entire vector for an element that will not be found, the **sequentialSearch()** can stop after it has reached the position in the vector where **Element** should be. The program in Listing 6.4 makes a few minor changes to the stopping condition in the **sequentialSearch()** algorithm. The stopping condition on line #16 will not cause the sequential search to stop if the **Vect[N]>Element**, in other words, if **Element** is not in **Vect**.

### Listing 6.4

```
1 // Listing 6.4
2 // Example of a simple sequential search
3 // using a sorted vector
4 #define __MINMAX_DEFINED
5 #include <vector.h>
6 #include <algo.h>
7
```

```
 8
 9
10 template <class X, class T> int sequentialSearch(vector<T> Vect, X Element)
11 {
12
13    int Found = 0;
14    int N = 0;
15    int Limit = Vect.size();
16    while((Vect[N] <= Element) && (N < Limit) && (!Found))
17    {
18      if(Vect[N] == Element){
19         Found = 1;
20      }
21      else{
22      N++;
23      }
24    }
25    return((Found ? N : -1));
26 }
27
28
29 void main(void)
30 {
31    vector<double> MyVect;
32    int Position = 0;
33    for(double X = 3.0; X < 100; X = X + 0.5)
34    {
35      MyVect.push_back(X);
36    }
37    sort(MyVect.begin(),MyVect.end());
38    Position = sequentialSearch(MyVect,22.3);
39    if(Position != - 1){
40      cout << MyVect[Position] << endl;
41    }
42    else{
43    cout << "element not found";
44    }
45 }
```

The sequential search algorithm can return the position of the object if it is in the vector, the object if it is in the vector, or both the position and the object. If the object is not in the vector the sequential search should return some illegal value relative to the vector's index or possibly through an exception. Notice on line #37 that one of the STL's sort algorithms was used to sort **MyVect** prior to its being searched. This is a standard processing sequence for many information retrieval operations. First a sort is done, then a search is done. However, if an efficient method is needed to search a moderate to large collection of objects, then a binary search on a vector has a much better performance than a sequential search on a vector.

### THE BINARY SEARCH

On the average, the sequential search takes about $N/2$ for a successful search, where $N$ is the number of elements in the vector. For an unsuccessful search the sequential search can take $N$ time. The worse-case scenario is not as bad for a sequential search on a sorted vector, unless of course the object being sought is at the end of the vector. When a sequential search is not appropriate, another technique that is often employed is the binary search. Figure 6.2 contains a flowchart of one implementation of the famous binary search. The binary search gets its name from the fact that it works by iteratively dividing the vector to be searched into halves until the value to be found is located. To

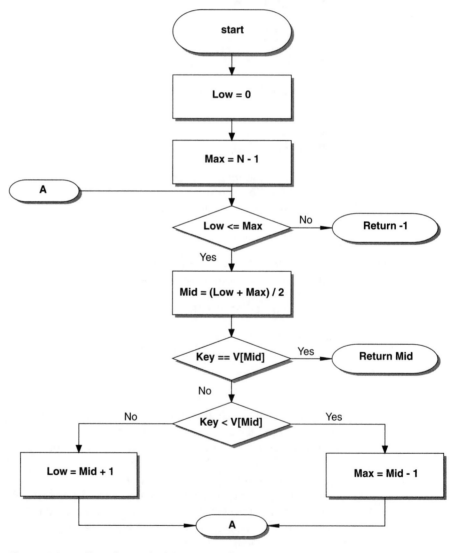

**Figure 6.2**  A flowchart of a binary search.

locate a given element **X** in a vector, first compare it with the element at the middle position of the vector. If **X** is less than the element in the middle position of the vector, then **X** must be in the first half of the vector. If **X** is greater than the element in the middle position of the vector, then **X** must be in the second half of the vector. This comparison is made and the vector is divided in twos recursively until the element is found or the vector is exhausted. In general, the binary search has an o(log N) performance, where N is the number of elements in the vector.

Before a binary search algorithm can be used on a vector, the vector must first be sorted. The binary search algorithm will initially divide the vector in half. The binary search algorithm depends on the middle to divide everything less than the element in the middle into the lower half of the vector, and every element larger than the middle into the upper half of the vector. As the middle moves up or down, the binary search requires that the sort relationship be maintained. The binary search can be designed to return either the position or the element being sought. The binary search can also be defined using recursion. Figure 6.3 is a flowchart depicting a recursive version of the binary search algorithm.

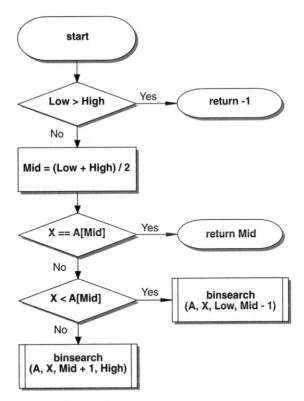

**Figure 6.3**   A flowchart depicting the recursive version of the binary search.

### SORTING THE VECTOR

It is a requirement that the vector be sorted to use a binary search. A sequential search can also be improved by using a sorted vector. There are many ways to sort a vector. Some of the most commonly found are the *bubble sort, insertion sort, selection sort, quick sort*, and the *shell sort.*

There are good reasons that more than one sort technique exists. Some sort techniques are appropriate for large amounts of data; some are more appropriate for small amounts of data. The nature of the data to be sorted is also important in choosing sort techniques. Sometimes a collection of objects only needs to be sorted once. Sometimes a collection of objects must be sorted many times during the execution of a program. There are times when the speed of the sort is critical, and there are times where speed is of no concern but sort stability is. For an introductory discussion of sorting requirements and techniques see *Algorithms in C++* by Robert Sedgewick.

Every sort must have some way to compare one object with another object. This comparison becomes one of the primary features that affects the performance of a sort. The comparison may require a simple relational comparison, or it may require complex calculations and data manipulations. In object-oriented programming where user-defined types are common, the comparison of two such objects may be very complex. In order for objects to be sorted the programmer must define a collating sequence or equivalence semantics for that class of objects. Without equivalence semantics or a collating sequence a collection of objects cannot be sorted. For instance, how should a collection of polygons be sorted? Should they be sorted based on length of sides or area? What of the polygons that don't have sides? Maybe sorting the polygons by color is a better alternative. A sorting technique must be able to compare two objects and put them in an ordered sequence. Along with comparisons most sorts must be able to exchange places between two objects or their aliases. That is, some sorts physically move objects around in a container, while other sorts only move pointers to, or representatives of, objects around. In either case the sort will need to move something. This is the second feature that greatly affects the performance of a sort. The amount of data that the sort has to move to put the objects in proper sequence and complexity of the object-to-object comparisons largely determines how efficient a sorting algorithm is. Of course, hardware performance and operating system responsiveness are also major contributors to performance capability.

### *Operator Requirements for Objects to Be Sorted*

If the vector container is going to be used to sort user-defined objects, then the objects will have to define the minimum number of relational operators that the sort requires as well as proper object copy semantics. The sorts in Listings 6.5, 6.6, and 6.7 are all implemented using the STL's vector container. The sort in Listing 6.5 is a selection sort, which will sort the objects in ascending order. The user will need to define at most two operators for any user-defined object that will be used with this sort.

### Listing 6.5

```
1 // Listing 6.5
2 // A selection sort template using the STL vector
```

```
3
4 template<class T> void selectionSort(vector<T> &X)
5 {
6
7 int Size = X.size();
8 int I = 0;
9 int K = 0;
10 int J = 0;
11 T Extra;
12 for( I = 1;I < Size − 1;I++)
13 {
14    K = I;
15    for(J = I + 1;J <= Size; J++)
16    {
17    if(X[J] < X[K]){
18       K = J;
19    }
20    if(I != K){
21        Extra = X[I];
22        X[I] = X[K];
23        X[K] = Extra;
24      }
25      }
26   }
27 }
```

`//= = = = = = = = = = = = = = = = = = = = = = = = = = = = = = = =`

**Listing 6.6**

```
1 // Listing 6.6
2 // Shell sort template using the STL vector
3
4
5 template <class T> void shellSort(vector<T> &X)
6 {
7
8    int Distance = 0;
9    int I = 0;
10    int J = 0;
11    int Size = X.size();
12    T Extra;
13    Distance = X.size() / 2;
14    while(Distance > 0)
15    {
16      for(I = 1;I <= (Size − Distance);I++)
17      {
18    J = I;
19    while((J > 0) && (X[J] > X[J + Distance]))
20    {
21        Extra = X[J];
```

```
22      X[J] = X[J + Distance];
23      X[J + Distance] = Extra;
24      J = J - Distance;
25   }
26     }
27      Distance = Distance / 2;
28   }
29
30 }
//= = = = = = = = = = = = = = = = = = = = = = = = = = = = = =
```

**Listing 6.7**

```
 1 // Listing 6.7
 2 // Bubble sort template using STL vector
 3
 4
 5 template<class T> void bubbleSort(vector<T>&X)
 6 {
 7
 8      int I = 0;
 9      int J = 0;
10      int Size = X.size();
11      T Extra;
12
13      for(I = 0;I < Size - 1;I++)
14      {
15   J = I;
16   while((J > 0) && (X[J] > X[J+1]))
17   {
18          Extra = X[J];
19          X[J] = X[J+1];
20          X[J+1] = Extra;
21          J--;
22   }
23   }
24
25 }
26
27
```

The user will have to define operator < and operator = for the user-defined class in order for this selection sort to work. Since the < operator is a requirement for any object that will be used with the vector container, it will already have been defined and therefore the user has only to add the operator =. If the user-defined class does not contain any pointers, then the compiler-defined operator = can be used. In this case the user has only to define the < operator for the class.

Note: in adapting classic algorithms for use with template functions and user-defined classes, the programmer has to define any operators for the class that are contained in the classic algorithms. The programmer must also replace any mentions of the data types that the classic algorithms use with parameters that will be passed into the template function. For example, the type for the variable **Extra** in Listing 6.5 is the parameter **T**.

It is important to note that since the STL's vector can be used with any kind of object, and this selection sort accepts vectors, then this sort can be used to sort anything. This is a prime example of code reuse. The user may use this sort repeatedly without having to change any code.

### Sort Performance on Object-Oriented Vectors

Because we are using an object-oriented vector and user-defined objects, the performance aspect of the sorts that rely on comparison and assignment will be dictated by the performance of the user-defined comparison and assignment operators for those objects involved. Many sort algorithms are measured relative to the number of steps that are performed in the execution of the algorithm. For instance, if a sort contains two control loops where one loop is nested in the other, and if the outer loop executes $N$ times, and the inner loop executes $M$ times, then the steps within the inner loop are executed $N * M$ times. Normally the outer loop represents the number of data items to be sorted, and the inner loop does some comparison and assignments. If the number of objects to be sorted is 1000, and the inner loop processing is 500, then there will be 500,000 comparisons and assignments times the number of comparisons or assignments that are done in the inner loop. Any attempt to calculate the performance of a sort on an object-oriented vector containing user-defined types should take this fact into consideration. Table 6.3 shows some commonly used sorts and their basic behaviors and performance.

## OBJECT-ORIENTED STACKS AND QUEUES

Whereas the vector container gives the programmer direct access to any element in the vector, the stack and queue collections provide very restricted access to the elements in the container. The stack only provides access to its top, and the queue only supplies access to its front or back. Nevertheless these are very important structures because they encapsulate the notion of *object arrival*. That is, these containers can be used to process objects based on *when* they were placed in the container. Processing a collection of objects based on *when* is in contrast to processing objects based on *what*, or *where*. Objects that are stored in a vector are processed based on *where*. The position or index of the object is the defining characteristic of the vector. When the processing depends on the sort order of the object, this is processing based on *what*. The value of the object or the value or the object's key is of primary importance in *what* processing. Collections or containers that present objects based on *when* open the door for programs that perform discrete and other types of simulation, as well as programs that require *aging relationships* between their objects.

## Object-Oriented Stacks

Stacks are containers that can hold an arbitrary number of objects. Stacks are dynamic containers. When objects are inserted into a stack the stack's size grows. When objects

**Table 6.3   Some commonly used sorts and their basic behaviors and runtime performance.**

| Types of Sorts | Description |
| --- | --- |
| **Linear Sort** | * A sort algorithm based on searching for the largest or smallest element, swapping it with the top element, and then repeating the process for all of the elements except the top element.<br>* At each iteration, the search space is reduced by one.<br>* For N number of elements, exactly N − 1 comparisons operations are performed. |
| **Bubble Sort** | * A sort algorithm in which a pair of adjacent elements are compared. If they are in correct order the next pair are compared; otherwise the element pairs are exchanged before moving to the next pair until all elements are processed.<br>* For N number of elements, exactly N − 1 comparisons are performed on the first iteration and on successive iterations the size is reduced by 1 every time. |
| **Quick Sort** | * A sort algorithm based on successive partitioning of elements, based on a key of the first element. The elements are partitioned into three groups or lists: first list contains elements that are greater than the key of the first element. This method of partitioning is continued until all sublists become singleton.<br>* A very fast method. |
| **Shell Sort** | * A sort algorithm in which elements that are x positions apart are compared and exchanged if necessary. Each iteration reduces x by 1. This process of compare and exchange continues until x becomes 1. |
| **Binary Tree Sort** | * A sort algorithm in which a binary tree is constructed where the larger (smaller) element is moved to the left subtree and the smaller (larger) element is moved to the right subtree. An in-order traversal of the tree yields a sorted list of element nodes. |
| **Selection Sort** | * A sort algorithm where the smallest element is located and then exchanged with the element in the first position. The second smallest element is located and then exchanged with the element in the second position. This continues until all elements are sorted.<br>* For N number of elements, N to the power of 2 /2 number of comparisons are performed. |
| **Insertion Sort** | * A sort algorithm in which elements are inserted in its proper place among already sorted elements. |

are removed from a stack the stack's size shrinks. The stack is a restricted-access container. Objects may only be removed from a stack one at a time. The stack is known as a *LIFO* (last-in-first-out) structure. The first item inserted into a stack is the last item removed, and the last item inserted is the first item removed. As with vectors, because the stack's functionality is encapsulated within a single unit we say that the stack is "object oriented." An object-oriented stack can only be accessed by its member functions. This means that the block of memory or storage component that the stack uses to store objects can be properly controlled through a selective implementation of member functions. The runtime version of the stack class is an object. This means that stacks can be used in the same way that any other object in the C++ environment can be used. We can use inheritance, polymorphism, and encapsulation with these stack classes to derive new collection and container classes. The runtime version of the stack class can be passed as parameters and compared with relational operators. Object-oriented stacks can be used as return values from functions. We may declare arrays of stacks or structs whose fields consist of stacks. We can have pointers to stacks, linked lists of stacks, and so on.

Figure 6.4 shows a logical view of an object-oriented stack container. The process of inserting objects into a stack is called *pushing* the stack. The process of removing or deleting objects from a stack is referred to as *popping* the stack. Objects are pushed onto the top of the stack, and objects are popped from the top of the stack. The logical notion of the stack also includes a **top()** function. This function is used to view what is on the top of a stack without popping the stack. Although the stack is only accessed from its

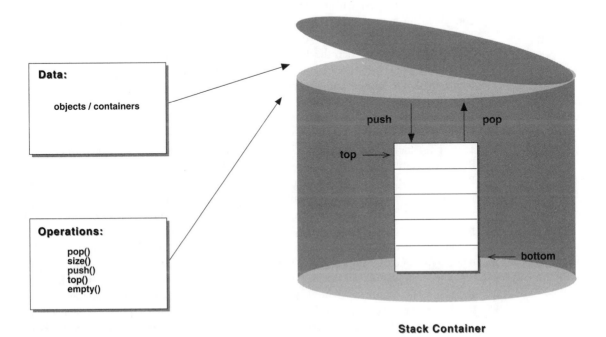

**Stack Container**

**Figure 6.4** A logical representation of an object-oriented stack container.

top, it is still considered a sequence of objects. This is because a stack does not have a hierarchical structure. It is logically construed as a sequence of objects in a linear space.

Stacks have a wide variety of applications. They are used in everything from graphical user interface processing to mathematical expression and computer language parsing. They can be used to process aging relationships also. The stack implements the notion of *when* in that it is used to process the latest element first, and then the object that arrived before that one, until it gets to the earliest element, which is processed last. Stacks permit only sequential access. If a stack contains a collection of objects, there is no way to jump into the middle of a stack to access an object. The stack must be popped the appropriate number of times before an object in the middle of the stack can be removed.

The basic operations of stack include popping the stack, pushing the stack, looking at the top member of the stack, and checking the stack for *underflow* conditions. A stack is theoretically upwardly unbounded. This means that there is no conceptual limit to how large a stack may grow. While there is no theoretical limit, there is a physical limit. The physical limit is dictated by how much computer memory is available to a stack. When a stack operation would exceed the physical limit of the memory available, the operation is said to cause a *stack overflow*. On the other hand, stacks do have a lower bound. Once the last item has been popped from a stack, no more items are available. When an operation attempts to pop an item from an empty stack, the operation is said to have caused a *stack underflow*. In the traditional data structure version of a stack, underflow and overflow are potential problems that may lead to program crashes. However, using object-oriented stacks provides the programmer with an extra level of protection. Because the memory block that implements the stack is encapsulated within the stack object, and access to that memory block is controlled by member functions; underflow and overflow conditions can be caught before they happen. That is, when a user requests a **pop()** when there are no more objects to be popped, then the stack object can decide how to respond to illegal pops. With traditional stack data structures this response must be explicitly coded everywhere the stack is used and for each type of object the stack is used on.

## THE STL'S STACK

The STL's stack is implemented by an adaptor. Adaptors are the STL versions of Stroustrup's interface classes. (See Chapter 2 for a discussion of interface classes.) Because the stack is implemented as an adaptor the programmer can change the implementation of the stack without changing the logical view of the stack. The logical view of the stack presents the programmer with **empty()**, **size()**, **top()**, **push()**, and **pop()** member functions and a last-in-first-out access order. However, to declare a stack object, the user must provide it with an implementation. An STL stack may be implemented by a vector, list, or deque container. This means that the block of memory where the objects are stored can be implemented as a vector, list, or deque container. Because vectors, lists, and deques exhibit different memory performance under different conditions, the user can pick which implementation best suits a given application. The logical view remains the same while the implementation changes. The stack adaptor provides an interface to functions that are available in the implementation containers. Table 6.4 lists which member functions are used as implementations of the stack member functions

**Table 6.4   A list of the member functions used as implementations of the stack member functions.**

| Sequence Container Member Functions | Implementation Member Functions |
| --- | --- |
| *Stack* | |
| empty () | empty() |
| size() | size() |
| top() | back() |
| push() | push_back() |
| pop() | pop_back() |

based on container. Also any user-defined class that supports the **back()**, **push_back()**, and **pop_back()** can be used as an implementation structure for the stack.

Since the stack is an adaptor it does not have its own constructors or destructors. Instead it uses the constructors and destructors of the implementation class. The operator $==$ and the operator $<$ are assumed to be implemented by any user-defined object that will be placed into the stack. Figure 6.5 shows the class relationship diagram for the stack implemented as vector, list, and deque. Notice that the relationship is containment as opposed to inheritance. This containment relationship is what allows the stack to be an effective interface class. Since a stack is an adaptor, the declaration involves

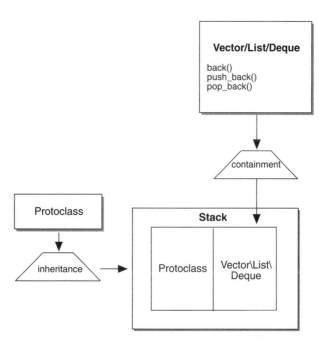

**Figure 6.5**   The class relationship diagram for a stack implemented as a vector, list, or deque.

instantiating one template with another, instantiated template. For example, to declare a stack of **doubles** implemented with a vector, the user would declare:

stack<vector<double> > MyStack

This declaration creates a stack object called **MyStack** that consists of **doubles**. The **vector<double>** argument is used to instantiate the containment relationship shown in Figure 6.5.

### Stack Member Functions

The **top()** member function returns the object at the top of the stack without removing the object. The **push(X)** member function pushes **X** onto the stack. The **pop()** member function removes the element at the top of the stack. Because the **pop()** member function is implemented by the **remove()** member function of the implementor class, the same memory management that applies to the implementor class applies to the stack. The **pop()** member function will only cause the object to be removed. The **pop()** member function does not deallocate any memory. The **size()** member function returns the number of objects that are on the stack. The **empty()** member function returns boolean true if there are no objects on the stack, and boolean false if there are objects on the stack. Any stack object can be compared to another stack object for equality using operator ==, or for greater than or less than comparisons using > or < operators.

## Object-Oriented Queues, PriorityQueues, and Deques

We are all familiar with the notion of front-to-back ordering. For instance, a line in a restaurant or the line in front of a teller at a bank is a front-to-back ordering. The people in the line are serviced based on when they entered the line. That is, they are served starting with the first person in the line and ending with the last person in the line. Queues encapsulate the notion of *when* by providing first come, first serve, last-in-line, and last served concepts. Because queues deal with objects in this fashion they are nicely suited for discrete simulation or event-driven programs. By capturing objects in a queue it is possible to simulate a *sequence of events*. The queue allows the programmer to do processing based on changes over time. Attention can be focused on the objects in the system and the simulation can be regarded as the task of following the changes that occur as the objects move from activity to activity (see Gordon 1969, 17–47). The queue structure allows the programmer to capture or simulate the history of activities as they are applied to different entities within a program or system. Any program that needs to process events based on the order in which they happen or *arrive* can use a queue. The place that an object occupies within a queue can be used to symbolically represent time of arrival or history of transaction.

A queue is a front-to-back ordering whose logical structure looks like a line. Figure 6.6 shows the logical view of an object-oriented queue. We use the phrase *logical view* or *logical representation* throughout this book in contrast to physical representation. The *logical view or representation* is conceptually how the programmer accesses or manipulates a structure or container. The *physical representation* is how and where the container

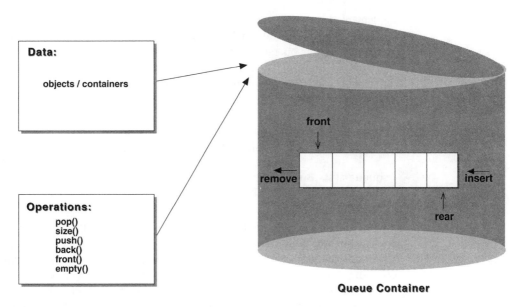

**Figure 6.6** The logical representation of an object-oriented queue.

or structure is actually stored in internal or external memory. In most cases the logical representation of a container or structure is different from its physical representation.

In a queue the items are deleted from the front and inserted into the rear of the queue. The queue is known as a *FIFO* (first-in-first-out) structure. This means that the first item that has been inserted will be the first item that will be removed. The queue can naturally represent aging relationships, because in a queue the oldest object is removed first and the youngest object is removed last. Queues are sequential structures and any method accessing a queue is a sequential access method. Queues are also *dynamic* structures. That is, they can grow or shrink during program execution. When objects are inserted into a queue, the queue grows. When objects are deleted from the queue it shrinks. The process of removing an object from a queue is known as *dequeuing*. The process of adding an object to a queue is called *enqueuing*. The notion of FIFO is encapsulated within a single unit, and is only accessible through member functions. The encapsulation together with the member-function-only access gives us an object-oriented queue. We can use inheritance, polymorphism, and encapsulation with queue classes to derive new collection and container classes. The runtime version of the queue class can be passed as parameters and compared with relational operators. Object-oriented queues can be used as return values from functions. We may declare arrays of queues or structs whose fields consist of queues. We can have pointers to queues, linked lists of queues, and so on.

## STL Queue

Like the STL stack, the STL queue is an interface class. It provides a new logical view of another embedded class. The STL refers to these interface classes as adaptors. The STL queue is implemented with either a list container or a deque. Although the queue is implemented with a list or deque, it has the logical view of a queue. The queue adaptor is declared in the *stack.h* header file. Any user-defined object that will be used with the queue must define operator $<$ and operator $==$. Any user-defined class that supports the **front()**, **push_back()**, and **pop_front()** member functions can be used as an implementation structure for the queue. A queue can be declared implemented as a list or deque using the syntax:

```
queue< list < User Defined Type> > MyQueue
queue<deque<UserDefinedType> > MyQueue
            or
queue<list<BuiltInType> > MyQueue
queue<deque<BuiltInType>> MyQueue
```

The logical view of the queue presents the programmer with six operations: **front()**, **back()**, **push()**, **pop()**, **empty()**, and **size()**. The **front()** member function returns a reference to the object that is at the front of the queue. This member function does not cause the object to be removed from the queue. The **back()** member function returns a reference to the object at the rear of the queue. The **back()** member function does not cause the object to be removed from the queue. Although the **front()** and **back()** member function return references, the programmer cannot change the value of the objects that are returned because the **front()** and **back()** member functions are const member functions. The **push(X)** member function inserts **X** at the rear of the queue. Because the queue has automatic storage management, if there is not enough space in the queue for **X**, more space will be allocated. The **pop()** member function removes the object at the front of the queue. Whereas the **front()** member function returns the object, the **pop()** member function removes the object. Note also that the **pop()** member function does not deallocate memory, it only removes the object at the front of the queue. The **empty()** member function returns boolean *true* if the queue contains zero objects and boolean *false* otherwise. The **size()** member function returns the number of objects in the queue, not the size of the queue in terms of bytes.

Table 6.5 lists which member functions are used as implementations of the queue member functions based on container. Any STL queue container can be compared with any other STL queue container using operator $==$ or operator $<$. The comparisons between elements in the queue are made using the user-defined operator $==$ for those objects. The operator $<$ does a lexicographic comparison of the objects in the queues. The lexicographical comparison of two container objects **X** $<$ **Y** causes a traversal of **X** and **Y** comparing pairs of objects **A** and **B**. If:

A $<$ B stop the traversal and return true
            or
B $<$ A stop the traversal and return false

The traversal will continue unless one of these cases is true; if the end of both containers is reached and no stopping condition has occurred then the containers are equal. If one of the containers has fewer objects than the other, the container with fewer objects is said to be less than the container with more.

---

**Table 6.5   A list of the member functions used as implementations of the queue member functions.**

| Sequence Container Member Functions | Implementation Member Functions |
|---|---|
| *Queue* | |
| empty () | empty() |
| size() | size() |
| front() | front() |
| back() | back() |
| pop() | pop_front() |
| push() | push_back() |

## PRIORITY QUEUES

A *priority queue* is an ordered queue. This means that the objects that are placed into a priority queue are sorted into some kind of order. However, this does not change the restriction of only being able to dequeue from the front of the queue and enqueue into the rear of the queue. There are two types of priority queues, *descending* priority queues and *ascending* priority queues. In a descending priority queue the objects are sorted from largest to smallest. The largest object is dequeued from the queue, and then the next largest object is dequeued, and so on. In an ascending queue the objects are stored in sequence from smallest to largest. As the objects are dequeued they begin with the smallest and proceed to the largest.

### The STL Priority Queue

Like the STL queue, the STL **priority_queue** is a adaptor or interface class. The **priority_queue** is also declared in *stack.h*. Whereas the STL queue can be implemented as a list or deque, the STL **priority_queue** can be implemented as a vector or a deque. However, any user-defined class that supports random access iterators and the **front()**, **push_back()**, and **pop_back()** can be used as an implementation structure for the **priority_queue**. The **priority_queue** supports the same set of member functions as the queue with a couple of exceptions. The **priority_queue** container cannot be compared with other priority queue containers using the operator = = or operator <, and the **priority_queue** requires a constructor. Because the priority queue maintains the elements in a sorted order it requires a comparison function object. The function object will be used to put the objects that are inserted into the queue in order. The **priority_queue** has two constructors. One constructor accepts a single function object as an argument. By changing the function objects the **priority_queue** can be set up as either a descending priority queue or as an ascending priority queue. The other constructor accepts a range of elements from another container, and a function object. Figure 6.7 shows the class relationship diagram of the **priority_queue** implemented as a vector and deque. Notice that each implementation contains a function object as a data member.

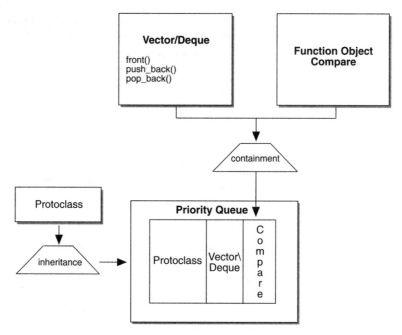

**Figure 6.7**  The class relationship diagram of the priority queue implemented as a vector and a deque. The deque contains a function object.

## DEQUES

Deques (pronounced *decks*) is a queue with the restricted access relieved a little. A queue is said to have restricted access because if there is a group of objects stored in a queue they may only be dequeued one at a time from the front of the queue. They may only be enqueued one at a time into the rear of the queue. The deque relaxes this constraint somewhat. In a deque, objects may be enqueued into either the rear of the queue or the front of the queue. Likewise objects may be dequeued from either the front of the queue or the rear of the queue. Unlike the priority queues the deques have no inherent sort order.

### The STL Deque

Whereas the STL queue and priority queue are interface classes, the deque is a concrete class. The STL deque also deviates somewhat from the traditional notion of a deque in that the STL deque provides the programmer with direct access in conjunction to sequential access. The deque class is declared in *deque.h*. Any user-defined object that will be used with a deque collection must define the operator $==$ and the operator $<$.

### Constructing the Deque

The deque has four constructors:

```
deque()
deque(site_type n, const T &value = T())
deque(const deque<T> &X)
deque(const_iterator First, const_iterator Last)
```

The first constructor is the default constructor and will construct a deque where **size()** is zero. The second constructor initialize a deque of size *n*, and initializes all the objects in the deque with **T()** or the value of some other object that is passed to the constructor. The object passed must be of the same type as the objects that the vector holds. The third constructor initialize the deque with the copy of another deque **X**. The final constructor builds a new deque from a range of elements from another container that supports **const _iterators**.

### Getting Information on the Deque

The **size()** member function returns the number of objects that are in the deque, not the deque's *size* in bytes. The **max_size()** member function returns the largest number of objects of the current type that can be inserted into the deque. The number that function returns depends on at least two things: (1) the size contained in the deque, and (2) the memory model of the operating system environment. In operating system environments such as 16-bit Microsoft Windows or MSDOS, **max_size()** will return a much smaller number than in 32-bit virtual paging operating systems such as OS/2, UNIX, VMS, Windows NT, or Windows 95. The **empty()** member function returns boolean true if there are no objects in the deque, and boolean false if **size()** is > 0.

### Inserting Objects into a Deque

The **push_front(X)** member inserts the object **X** into the front of the deque. The **push_back(X)** member function inserts the object **X** into the rear of the deque. Unfortunately these member functions do not indicate whether they were successful or not. If the memory has been exhausted, these member functions will simply quietly fail. The deque class has three **insert()** member functions. The **insert()** member functions allow the user to insert either a single object or range of objects into the deque. Whereas the **push_front(X)** and **push_back(X)** only allow insertion at the extreme ends of the deque, the **insert()** member functions allow the programmer to insert an object or objects anywhere in the deque. Objects can also be inserted into a deque using a constructor or the assignment operator.

### Removing Objects from a Deque

The **pop_front()** member function removes the object that is currently at the front of a deque. The **pop_back()** member function removes the object that is at the rear of the deque. The **erase(X)** member function erases the object that is pointed to by the iterator **X**. Unlike the other containers, the **erase(X)** member function for the deque does cause the space that the object is taking up to be released. The **erase(First,Last)** member function erases all objects that are in the range from [First,Last); this means all objects from **First** to **Last**, starting from **First**, and up to but not including **Last**.

### Accessing Objects in a Deque

The deque provides for both sequential and direct accesses. The deque can be sequentially accessed by using the **front()**, and **back()** member functions in conjunction with the **pop_front** or **pop_back()** member functions. The **front()** member function returns the object at the beginning of the deque, and the **back()** member function returns the object at the rear of the deque. Iterators can also be used to sequentially traverse through a deque. However, because the iterators are random access iterators, they support iterator arithmetic. For instance, **MyDeque** is a deque object and if **P** is an iterator supported by the deque class, then

```
P = MyDeque.begin()
P = P + 5;
cout << *P
```

will move directly to **MyDeque[5]**. Likewise **MyDeque[5]** can be used to return the same object. Because deques support random access and the [] operator, they can be used in the same places that a vector can be used. The deque then is a superset of the **vector** class.

## APPLICATION

## STACKS, QUEUES, AND SETS     INFIX EXPRESSION EVALUATION

## EVALUATING INFIX EXPRESSIONS

An infix expression is an expression where the operators are written between the operands, such as:

$$X + Y / B$$

This is in contrast to prefix expressions and postfix expressions. The same relationship in a prefix expression would be written:

$$+ X / YB$$

The same expression written as a postfix expression would be written:

$$X + YB/$$

In prefix expressions the operator appears to the left before its operands and in postfix expressions the operator appears to the right after its operands. Because of the structuring of prefix and postfix expressions there is no need to use parentheses. However, an infix expression can be ambiguous without parentheses.

For example, Table 6.6 shows that prefix and postfix expressions are unique even when the parentheses are removed. However, the infix notation is ambiguous when the parentheses are removed. We cannot tell the difference between the two infix expressions in Table 6.6, whereas we can tell the difference for the posfix and prefix expression. In general, prefix and posfix notations are *parentheses-free* notations. Compilers can easily process prefix and postfix expressions, while infix expressions are somewhat more troublesome.

There are guidelines for evaluating infix expressions without parentheses that involve operator precedence. The operator precedence is:

1. Exponentiation(**) has the highest priority.
2. (* and /) have the same priority and are higher than (+, and −).
3. (+, and −) have the same priority.

Given two operands *x* and *y*, whether *x* is an operand of * or + can be determined by taking *x* as an operand of the highest priority operator. This program accepts a simple infix expression with no parentheses and evaluates it based on operator precedence. The program uses the STL stack, queue, and set collection in order simulate how a human evaluates an infix expression without parentheses.

## USER-DEFINED OBJECTS

The program uses three user-defined classes: **operand, operator_type**, and **expression-_component**. The operand encapsulates the traditional mathematical notion of an operand. As in mathematics, our operand can be either a constant or a variable. The **operator_type** is used to encapsulate the notion of an operator. The **expression-_component** class uses multiple inheritance to create a single object that can have any purpose in an expression. Figure 6.8 shows the class relationship diagram for the expression component class.

## COLLECTIONS AND CONTAINERS

The program consists of a number of STL collections and containers. The program has two stack collections; **OperandStack** and **OperatorStack**.

**Table 6.6  This table shows that the prefix and post-fix expression are unique even when the ()'s are removed where the infix expression is ambiguous.**

|         | X + (Y * B) | (X + Y) * B |
|---------|-------------|-------------|
| **Prefix**  | + X * YB    | * + XYB     |
| **Infix**   | X + Y * B   | X + Y * B   |
| **Postfix** | XYB *+      | XY + B*     |

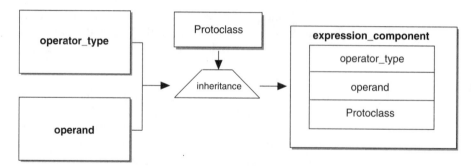

**Figure 6.8**   The class relationship diagram for the **expression_component** class.

The stacks are used to simulate operator precedence assignments. By using the rules of operator precedence, operands are combined with the proper operators and the results are placed on the **OperandStack**. The **OperatorStack** is used to hold the operators as they are parsed from the infix expression. The program consists of two queues; **ExpressionQueue** and **InstantiatedQueue**.

The **ExpressionQueue** contains operands that could be variables or constants as well as operators. The **InstantiatedQueue** only contains operands that are constants as well as operators. The program has six STL set objects: **Operands**, **Operators**, **Numbers**, **Letters**, **Variables**, and **InstantiatedSet**.

The set **Operands** contains the legal characters that can be used as operands. They are the characters (a-z, A-Z), and (0-9). The set **Operators** contains the operations that this program can perform. The set **Numbers** contains the legal numbers that this program will accept. The set **Letters** contains only characters only in the range of (A-Z,a-z). The set **Variables** contains the unknowns for any infix operation that will be evaluated. The set was a good choice here because no matter how many times a variable appears in an expression, we only needed to instantiate the variable once. The set **InstantiatedSet** contains all the variables with their user-defined values. The program contains six major functions: **initializeSets**, **parseInitialString**, **Parse2**, **InstantiateVariables**, **InstantiateQueue**, and **evaluate**. The header files *operator.h, operand.h*, and *express.h* contain the declarations for the user-defined objects. The source files *operator.cpp, operand.cpp, express.cpp*, and *parse.cpp* contain the definitions and the main program for the infix evaluator.

## SOURCE EXPLANATION

The expression generator and parser are written using C++ and STL containers. The code was tested in OS/2, MSDOS environments. The code was compiled using Borland's C++ for OS/2, IBM's CSet++, and Borland's C++ 4.5. Because the code has a console mode interface and only uses standard C++, it should be able to run in any environment that supports C++, templates, and the STL.

## PARSE.MAK

```
#==========================================
#
#
#      PARSE.MAK — Makefile PARSE.PRJ
#
#
#==========================================
.AUTODEPEND
.PATH.obj = C:\BOOK2\PROGRAMS\OS2

#==========================================
#         Translator Definitions
#==========================================

CC = bcc + PARSE.CFG
TASM = tasm.exe
TLIB = tlib.exe
TLINK = tlink
RC = brcc.exe
RB = rc.exe
LIBPATH = C:\BCOS2\LIB;c:\stl2\lib
INCLUDEPATH = c:\stl;C:\BCOS2\INCLUDE;

#==========================================
#         Implicit Rules
#==========================================
.c.obj:
$(CC) −c {$<}

.cpp.obj:
$(CC) −c {$<}

.asm.obj:
$(TASM) −Mx $*.asm,$*.obj

.rc.res:
$(RC) −r $*.rc

#==========================================
#         List Macros
#==========================================

EXE_DEPENDENCIES = \
express.obj\
parse.obj\
operator.obj\
operand.obj

#==========================================
#         Explicit Rules
#==========================================
```

```
c:\book2\programs\os2\parse.exe: parse.cfg $(EXE_DEPENDENCIES)
$(TLINK) /v /Toe /ap /L$(LIBPATH)@&&|
C:\BCOS2\LIB\CO2.OBJ+
c:\book2\programs\os2\express.obj+
c:\book2\programs\os2\parse.obj+
c:\book2\programs\os2\operator.obj+
c:\book2\programs\os2\operand.obj
c:\book2\programs\os2\parse,c:\book2\programs\os2\parse
C:\BCOS2\LIB\C2.LIB+
C:\BCOS2\LIB\OS2.LIB

#==========================================
#          Individual File Dependencies
#==========================================

express.obj: parse.cfg express.cpp

PARSE.obj: parse.cfg PARSE.CPP

OPERATOR.obj: parse.cfg OPERATOR.CPP

OPERAND.obj: parse.cfg OPERAND.CPP

#==========================================
#          Compiler Configuration File
#==========================================

parse.cfg: parse.mak
copy &&|
-R
-Vmv
-L$(LIBPATH)
-I$(INCLUDEPATH)
-nc:\book2\programs\os2
-vi-
-k-
-v
-N
|parse.cfg
```

# SOURCE LISTINGS

Note the Header Files below.

## Header Files

```
operator.h
1 // Declaration for the operator_type class
2
3 #ifndef_operator_h
4 #define_operator_h
```

```
5 class operator_type{
6 protected:
7    int Priority;
8    char Operator;
9 public:
10    operator_type(void);
11    operator_type(char N);
12    operator_type(const operator_type &N);
13    operator_type &operator=(const operator_type &N);
14    int operator>(const operator_type &N) const;
15    int operator<(const operator_type &N) const;
16    int operator==(const operator_type &N) const;
17    int operator<=(const operator_type &N) const;
18    int operator>=(const operator_type &N) const;
19    char op(void);
20    void op(char N);
21    int priority(void);
22    void priority(int Rank);
23
24 };
25
26 #endif
//==========================================
```

1 **operand.h**
```
2 // Declaration of the operand class
3
4 #ifndef_operand_h
5 #define_operand_h
6 class operand{
7 protected:
8    float Exponent;
9    double Value;
10    char Sign;
11    char Variable;
12 public:
13    operand(void);
14    operand(char X);
15    operand(double X);
16    operand(const operand &X);
17    float exponent(void);
18    void exponent(float X);
19    double value(void);
20    void value(double X);
21    char sign(void);
22    void sign(char X);
23    char variable(void);
24    void variable(char X);
25    operand &operator+(const operand &X);
26    operand &operator-(const operand &X);
```

```
27   operand &operator*(const operand &X);
28   operand &operator/(const operand &X);
29   operand &operator=(const operand &X);
30   int operator>(const operand &X) const;
31   int operator<(const operand &X) const;
32   int operator>=(const operand &X) const;
33   int operator<=(const operand &X) const;
34   int operator==(const operand &X) const;
35   int operator!=(const operand &X) const;
36 };
37
38 #endif
39
```

//============================================

```
 1 express.h
 2 // Declaration of the expression_component class
 3
 4 #include <operator.h>
 5 #include <operand.h>
 6
 7 class expression_component : public operator_type, public operand{
 8 protected:
 9   int IsOperator;
10   int IsOperand;
11 public:
12   expression_component(void);
13   expression_component(const expression_component &X);
14   expression_component &operator=(const expression_component &X);
15   int operator>(const expression_component &X) const;
16   int operator<(const expression_component &X) const;
17   int operator==(const expression_component &X) const;
18   int operator>=(expression_component &X);
19   int operator<=(expression_component &X);
20   int operator!=(expression_component &X);
21   int operator()(expression_component &X,expression_component &Y);
22    friend ostream &operator<<(ostream &Out,expression_component &X);
23   int isOperator(void);
24   void isOperator(int Bool);
25   int isOperand(void);
26   void isOperand(int X);
27   operand operand_type(void);
28   operator_type opType(void);
29 };
30
```

//============================================

## Source Definitions

```
1 operator.cpp
2
3 // Definitions for the operator_type class
4
5 #include "operator.h"
6
7 operator_type::operator_type(void)
8 {
9
10    Priority = 0;
11    Operator = '@';
12
13
14 }
15
16 operator_type::operator_type(char N)
17 {
18
19    Operator = N;
20    if((N == '+') || (N == '-')){
21       Priority = 1;
22    }
23    if((N == '*') || (N == '/')){
24       Priority = 2;
25    }
26    if(N == ''){
27       Priority = 3;
28    }
29
30 }
31
32 operator_type::operator_type(const operator_type &N)
33 {
34    Priority = N.Priority;
35    Operator = N.Operator;
36
37
38 }
39
40
41 operator_type &operator_type::operator=(const operator_type &N)
42 {
43    Priority = N.Priority;
44    Operator = N.Operator;
45    return(*this);
46 }
47
48 int operator_type::operator>(const operator_type &N) const
```

```
49 {
50    if(Priority > N.Priority){
51         return(1);
52    }
53      else{
54         return(0);
55       }
56 }
57
58
59 int operator_type::operator<(const operator_type &N) const
60 {
61      if(Priority < N.Priority){
62    return(1);
63      }
64    else{
65         return(0);
66    }
67 }
68
69
70
71
72
73 int operator_type::operator==(const operator_type &N) const
74 {
75      if(Priority == N.Priority){
76         return(1);
77      }
78      else{
79         return(0);
80       }
81
82
83 }
84
85 int operator_type::operator<=(const operator_type &N) const
86 {
87
88    if(Priority <= N.Priority){
89         return(1);
90    }
91         else{
92    return(0);
93      }
94 }
95
96 int operator_type::operator>=(const operator_type &N) const
97 {
98    if(Priority >= N.Priority){
```

```
 99    return(1);
100    }
101    else{
102    return(0);
103    }
104
105 }
106
107 char operator_type::op(void)
108 {
109    return(Operator);
110 }
111
112 void operator_type::op(char N)
113 {
114    Operator = N;
115    if((N == '+') || (N == '-')){
116        Priority = 1;
117    }
118    if((N == '*') || (N == '/')){
119    Priority = 2;
120    }
121    if(N == ''){
122        Priority = 3;
123    }
124 }
125
126 int operator_type::priority(void)
127 {
128    return(Priority);
129 }
130
131
132 void operator_type::priority(int Rank)
133 {
134        Priority = Rank;
135
136 }
//=========================================
```

```
 1 operand.cpp
 2 // Definition for the operand class
 3
 4 #include "operand.h"
 5
 6
 7 operand::operand(void)
 8 {
 9    Exponent = 1;
10    Value = 0;
```

```
11    Sign = '@';
12    Variable = '@';
13 }
14
15 operand::operand(char X)
16 {
17    Exponent = 1;
18    Value = 0;
19    Sign = '@';
20    Variable = X;
21
22 }
23
24 operand::operand(double X)
25 {
26    Exponent = 1;
27    Value = X;
28    if (X >= 0) {
29    Sign = '+';
30    }
31    else{
32    Sign = '-';
33    }
34 }
35
36
37 operand::operand(const operand &X)
38 {
39    Exponent = X.Exponent;
40    Value = X.Value;
41    Sign = X.Sign;
42    Variable = X.Variable;
43 }
44
45 float operand::exponent(void)
46 {
47    return(Exponent);
48 }
49
50 void operand::exponent(float X)
51 {
52    Exponent = X;
53 }
54
55 double operand::value(void)
56 {
57    return(Value);
58
59 }
60
```

```
61 void operand::value(double X)
62 {
63    Value = X;
64
65 }
66
67
68 char operand::sign(void)
69 {
70    return(Sign);
71
72 }
73
74 void operand::sign(char X)
75 {
76    Sign = X;
77
78 }
79
80 char operand::variable(void)
81 {
82    return(Variable);
83 }
84
85 void operand::variable(char X)
86 {
87    Variable = X;
88 }
89
90 operand &operand::operator+(const operand &X)
91 {
92
93    Value = Value + X.Value;
94    return(*this);
95 }
96
97
98 operand &operand::operator-(const operand &X)
99 {
100    Value = Value - X.Value;
101    return(*this);
102
103 }
104
105
106 operand &operand::operator*(const operand &X)
107 {
108    Value = Value * X.Value;
109    return(*this);
110 }
```

```
111
112
113 operand &operand::operator/(const operand &X)
114 {
115    if(X.Value != 0){
116    Value = Value /X.Value;
117    }
118    return(*this);
119 }
120
121 operand &operand::operator=(const operand &X)
122 {
123    Exponent = X.Exponent;
124    Value = X.Value;
125    Sign = X.Sign;
126    Variable = X.Variable;
127    return(*this);
128 }
129
130 int operand::operator>(const operand &X) const
131 {
132       if(Value > X.Value){
133    return(1);
134       }
135       else{
136       return(0);
137       }
138
139 }
140
141
142 int operand::operator<(const operand &X) const
143 {
144       if(Value < X.Value){
145    return(1);
146       }
147       else{
148       return(0);
149       }
150 }
151
152 int operand::operator>=(const operand &X) const
153 {
154    if(Value >= X.Value){
155       return(1);
156    }
157    else{
158       return(0);
159    }
160
```

```
161 }
162
163
164 int operand::operator<=(const operand &X) const
165 {
166     if(Value <= X.Value){
167   return(1);
168     }
169   else{
170       return(0);
171     }
172
173 }
174
175 int operand::operator==(const operand &X) const
176 {
177   if(Value == X.Value){
178     return(1);
179   }
180   else{
181         return(0);
182   }
183
184 }
185
186 int operand::operator!=(const operand &X) const
187 {
188
189     if(Value != X.Value){
190     return(1);
191   }
192   else{
193     return(0);
194   }
195
196 }
```
//=========================================

```
 1 express.cpp
 2 // Definition of the expression_component class
 3
 4 #include <express.h>
 5
 6 expression_component::expression_component(void)
 7 {
 8   IsOperand = 0;
 9   IsOperator = 0;
10 }
11
12 expression_component::expression_component(const expression_compo-
   nent &X)
```

```
13 {
14    Exponent = X.Exponent;
15    Value = X.Value;
16    Sign = X.Sign;
17    Variable = X.Variable;
18    Priority = X.Priority;
19    Operator = X.Operator;
20    IsOperator = X.IsOperator;
21    IsOperand = X.IsOperand;
22
23 }
24 int expression_component::isOperator(void)
25 {
26    return(IsOperator);
27 }
28
29 void expression_component::isOperator(int Bool)
30 {
31
32    IsOperator = Bool;
33 }
34
35 int expression_component::isOperand(void)
36 {
37    return(IsOperand);
38
39 }
40
41 void expression_component::isOperand(int X)
42 {
43    IsOperand = X;
44 }
45
46 expression_component &expression_component::operator=(const expres-
   sion_component &X)
47 {
48    Exponent = X.Exponent;
49    Value = X.Value;
50    Sign = X.Sign;
51    Variable = X.Variable;
52    Priority = X.Priority;
53    Operator = X.Operator;
54    IsOperator = X.IsOperator
55    IsOperand = X.IsOperand;
56    return(*this);
57
58 }
59
60 int expression_component::operator>(const expression_component &X)
   const
```

```
61 {
62     if(X.IsOperand){
63   if(Value > X.Value){
64     return(1);
65   }
66   else{
67     return(0);
68   }
69     }
70     else
71   if(Priority > X.Priority){
72     return(1);
73     }
74     else{
75        return(0);
76     }
77 }
78 int  expression_component::operator()(expression_component &X,expres-
   sion_component &Y)
79 {
80   if(X.IsOperand){
81   if(Variable < X.Variable){
82
83     return(1);
84   }
85   else{
86     return(0);
87   }
88     }
89     else
90   if((Priority < X.Priority) &&
91     (Operator < X.Operator)){
92     return(1);
93   }
94   else{
95        return(0);
96   }
97 }
98
99 int  expression_component::operator<(const  expression_component  &X)
   const
100 {
101     if(X.IsOperand){
102   if(Variable < X.Variable){
103
104     return(1);
105   }
106   else{
107     return(0);
108   }
```

```
109      }
110      else
111    if((Priority < X.Priority) &&
112      (Operator < X.Operator)){
113      return(1);
114    }
115    else{
116        return(0);
117    }
118 }
119
120 int expression_component::operator==(const expression_component &X)
    const
121 {
122      if(X.IsOperand){
123    if(Variable == X.Variable){
124      return(1);
125    }
126    else{
127      return(0);
128    }
129      }
130      else
131    if((Priority == X.Priority) &&
132      (Operator == X.Operator)){
133      return(1);
134    }
135    else{
136        return(0);
137    }
138 }
139
140 int expression_component::operator>=(expression_component &X)
141 {
142
143      if(X.IsOperand){
144    if(Value >= X.Value){
145      return(1);
146    }
147    else{
148        return(0);
149    }
150      }
151      else
152    if(Priority >= X.Priority){
153      return(1);
154    }
155    else{
156        return(0);
157      }
```

```
158
159 }
160
161 int expression_component::operator<=(expression_component &X)
162 {
163     if(X.IsOperand){
164   if(Value <= X.Value){
165     return(1);
166   }
167   else{
168       return(0);
169   }
170     }
171     else
172   if(Priority <= X.Priority){
173     return(1);
174   }
175   else{
176       return(0);
177   }
178
179 }
180
181 int expression_component::operator!=(expression_component &X)
182 {
183
184     if(X.IsOperand){
185   if(Value != X.Value){
186     return(1);
187   }
188   else{
189     return(0);
190   }
191     }
192     else
193   if(Priority != X.Priority){
194     return(1);
195   }
196   else{
197       return(0);
198   }
199 }
200
201 operand expression_component::operand_type(void)
202 {
203   operand Temp;
204   Temp.exponent(Exponent);
205   Temp.value(Value);
206   Temp.sign(Sign);
207   Temp.variable(Variable);
```

```
208    return(Temp);
209 }
210
211 operator_type expression_component::opType(void)
212 {
213    operator_type Temp;
214    Temp.priority(Priority);
215    Temp.op(Operator);
216    return(Temp);
217
218 }
219
220
221 ostream &operator<<(ostream &Out,expression_component &X)
222 {
223
224    Out << X.IsOperand << " " << X.IsOperator << endl;
225    return(Out);
226
227 }
//===========================================
```

```
 1 parse.cpp
 2 // Infix Expression Evaluation
 3
 4 #define__MINMAX_DEFINED
 5 #include <strstrea.h>
 6 #include <string.h>
 7 #include <set.h>
 8 #include <list.h>
 9 #include <stack.h>
10 #include <vector.h>
11 #include <ctype.h>
12 #include <stdlib.h>
13 #include "express.h"
14
15
16
17 typedef set<char,less<char> > set_of_char;
18 typedef set<expression_component,less<expression_component> >Expre-
   ssionSet;
19 stack < vector<operand> >OperandStack;
20 stack < vector<operator_type> > OperatorStack;
21 typedef set<expression_component,less<expression_component> >::itera-
   tor M;
22 queue<list<expression_component> >ExpressionQueue;
23 queue<list<expression_component> >InstantiatedQueue;
24 set_of_char Operands;
25 set_of_char Operators;
26 char StringOut[256] = "";
```

```
27 ostrstream Expression(StringOut,255);
28 set_of_char Numbers;
29 set_of_char Letters;
30 ExpressionSet Variables;
31 ExpressionSet InstantiatedSet;
32 operand evaluate(operand &X,operand &Y,operator_type &Op);
33
34
35 void initializeSets(void)
36 {
37
38    char Name = 'A';
39    Operators.insert('*');
40    Operators.insert('+');
41    Operators.insert('-');
42    Operators.insert('/');
43    while((Name <= 'Z') && (Name >= 'A'))
44    {
45    Operands.insert(Name);
46    Letters.insert(Name);
47    Name++;
48    }
49    Name = 'a';
50    while((Name <= 'z') && (Name >= 'a'))
51    {
52    Operands.insert(Name);
53    Letters.insert(Name);
54    Name++;
55    }
56    Name = '0';
57    while((Name >= '0') && (Name <= '9'))
58    {
59    Operands.insert(Name);
60    Numbers.insert(Name);
61    Name++;
62    }
63
64 }
65
66
67 void parseInitialString(char *Sin)
68 {
69     char Prev = '@';
70     char Curr = '@';
71     char Next = '@';
72     int Pos= 0;
73     while(Pos < strlen(Sin))
74     {
75   Curr = Sin[Pos];
76   if((Operands.count(Prev)) && (Operands.count(Curr.))){
```

```
77              Expression << "*" << Curr;
78      }
79      else
80        if(Operators.count(Curr)){
81           Expression << Curr;
82              }
83           else
84                Expression << Curr;
85      Prev = Curr;
86      Pos++;
87      }
88
89 }
90
91
92 void parse2()
93 {
94
95      expression_component Item;
96      char CnvtChar[2];
97      intN;
98      for(N = 0;N < strlen(StringOut);N++)
99      {
100     strcpy(CnvtChar," ");
101     if(Letters.count(StringOut[N])){
102        Item.isOperand(1);
103        Item.isOperator(0);
104        Item.variable(StringOut[N]);
105        Variables.insert(Item);
106     }else
107        if(Operators.count(StringOut[N])){
108           Item.isOperator(1);
109           Item.isOperand(0);
110           Item.op(StringOut[N]);
111           Item.variable('@');
112        }else
113            if(Numbers.count(StringOut[N])){
114               Item.isOperand(1);
115               Item.isOperator(0);
116               Item.variable('@');
117               CnvtChar[0] = StringOut[N];
118               CnvtChar[1] = NULL;
119               Item.value(atof(CnvtChar));
120            }
121     if(StringOut[N] != ' '){
122        ExpressionQueue.push(Item);
123     }
124      }
125
126 }
```

```
127
128
129 void instantiateVariables(expression_component Item)
130 {
131     int NthElement = 0;
132     M G = Variables.begin();
133     while(NthElement < Variables.size())
134     {
135
136   int Temp;
137   Item = *G;
138   cout << "Enter The Value for " << Item.variable() << " ";
139   cin >> Temp;
140   Item.value(Temp);
141   InstantiatedSet.insert(Item);
142   G++;
143   NthElement++;
144     }
145
146
147 }
148
149 operand evaluate(operand &X,operand &Y,operator_type &Op)
150 {
151   operand Temp;
152   if(Op.op() == '-'){
153     Temp = X - Y;
154     return(Temp);
155   }
156     if(Op.op() == '*'){
157   Temp = X * Y;
158     return(Temp);
159   }
160   if(Op.op() == '/'){
161     if(Y.value() != 0){
162   Temp = X / Y;
163   return(Temp);
164     }
165     else
166   return(Temp);
167   }
168   if(Op.op() == '+'){
169   Temp = X + Y;
170   return(Temp);
171   }
172   return(Temp);
173 }
174
175
176 void instantiateQueue(void)
```

```
177 {
178    int N = 0;
179    int Found = 0;
180    expression_component Term;
181    expression_component Temp;
182    M MyIterator = InstantiatedSet.begin();
183    while(!ExpressionQueue.empty())
184    {
185      Term.variable('@');
186      Temp.variable('@');
187      Term = ExpressionQueue.front();
188      ExpressionQueue.pop();
189      N = 0;
190      Found = 0;
191      if(Letters.count(Term.variable())){
192        while((N < InstantiatedSet.size()) && (Found == 0))
193        {
194          Temp = *MyIterator;
195          if(Term.variable() == Temp.variable()){
196            Term.value(Temp.value());
197            Found = 1;
198          }
199          N++;
200          MyIterator++;
201        }
202      }
203      MyIterator = InstantiatedSet.begin();
204      InstantiatedQueue.push(Term);
205    }
206 }
207
208 void fillOperandStack(void)
209 {
210
211    expression_component Term;
212    while(!InstantiatedQueue.empty())
213    {
214        Term = InstantiatedQueue.front();
215        InstantiatedQueue.pop();
216        OperandStack.push(Term.value());
217    }
218 }
219
220
221 operand TempOperand;
222 operator_type TempOperator;
223 operator_type CurrOperator;
224 operand Op1;
225 operand Op2;
226 double Total = 0;
```

```
227
228 void main(void)
229 {
230
231    expression_component Item;
232    char StringIn[81] = "";
233    initializeSets();
234    cout << "Enter Expression" << endl;
235    cin.getline(StringIn,80,'\n');
236    parseInitialString(StringIn);
237    cout << StringOut;
238    cout << endl;
239    parse2();
240    instantiateVariables(Item);
241    instantiateQueue();
242    while(!InstantiatedQueue.empty())
243    {
244      Item = InstantiatedQueue.front();
245      InstantiatedQueue.pop();
246      if(Item.isOperand()){
247        TempOperand = Item.operand_type();
248        OperandStack.push(TempOperand);
249      }
250      else{
251        CurrOperator = Item.opType();
252        if(!OperatorStack.empty()){
253          if(CurrOperator < OperatorStack.top()){
254            Op2 = OperandStack.top();
255            OperandStack.pop();
256            Op1 = OperandStack.top();
257            OperandStack.pop();
258            TempOperator = OperatorStack.top();
259            OperatorStack.pop();
260            OperandStack.push(evaluate(Op1,Op2,TempOperator));
261            OperatorStack.push(CurrOperator);
262          }
263          else{
264
265            OperatorStack.push(CurrOperator);
266          }
267        }
268        else{
269          OperatorStack.push(CurrOperator);
270        }
271      }
272
273    }
274    while(!OperatorStack.empty())
275    {
276        CurrOperator = OperatorStack.top();
```

```
277          OperatorStack.pop();
278          Op2 = OperandStack.top();
279          OperandStack.pop();
280          Op1 = OperandStack.top();
281          OperandStack.pop();
282          OperandStack.push(evaluate(Op1,Op2,CurrOperator));
283
284     }
285     TempOperand = OperandStack.top();
286     cout << endl << endl << "Answer is " << TempOperand.value();
287     OperandStack.pop();
288 }
```

# PROCEDURES AND FUNCTIONS

The function **initializeSets**() creates the character sets that will be used to verify the characters that are entered in for the infix expression. The **parseInitialString**() function takes a string in the form

$$7x + 5y + 9z$$

and parses it into the form:

$$7 * x + 5 * y + 9 * z$$

The function **parse2**() extracts each **expression_component** from the **string** that was generated in the **parseInitialString**() function. The **instantiateVariables**() function gets values from the user for all unknowns in the infix expression. The **instantiate-Queue**() function builds an expression with only constants and operators so that the expression can be completely evaluated. The **evaluate** function evaluates a pair of **expression_components** and returns the result.

CHAPTER 7

# RELATIONS, MAPS, AND MULTIPMAPS

IN THIS book we have shown how collections and containers can be used to store, retrieve, organize, manipulate, and search groups of objects. These are some of the primary uses for collections and containers. We now show how collections and containers can be used to relate or associate groups of objects. The relation describes a connection or association between objects. Concepts, persons, places, things, or ideas can be related with other concepts, persons, places, and ideas. How objects are related can be described in many different ways and is *context* dependent. For example, a phone number can be related to a person. If no more is said other than that the phone number is related to the person, then we do not know how the phone number is related. We only know that there is some connection between a phone number and a person. What is the connection? How are they related? The phone number could belong to that person. The phone number may belong to the person's employer. The phone number could have been the last phone number dialed by the person and so on. All of these instances describe relations the phone number can have with the person.

A relation defines a connection or association between items in a set or sets. For example, given two sets, a set of phone numbers and a set of geographical locations, we can specify a relation. The relation can be restricted to the geographic locations that are associated with specific area codes. Given the set of area codes, $\{212,215,301,707\}$, we relate cities in the United States. The phone numbers and geographic locations can be expressed in this way:

Area Codes $= \{212,215,301,707\}$
Locations $= \{\, x : x$ is a city in the United States$\}$

The relation of phone numbers to geographic location can be expressed in this way:

$$\text{Relation} \subseteq \text{Area Codes} \times \text{Locations}$$

This statement reads: *Relation* is a subset of the Cartesian product of *Area Codes* and *Locations*. This relation describes a *belonging* relation. The belonging relation in these examples associates phone numbers with certain area codes to certain geographic locations. This example also illustrates an important point about relations. Relations are normally associations between groups of objects or sets.

A set of phone numbers with certain area codes could be related to a set of residential or commercial locations. A phone number belongs to a residential or commercial location. There may be cases in which one location may have multiple phone numbers because it has separate telephone lines. In that situation, several phone numbers would be related to one location. Therefore, there may be a one-to-one correspondence between a phone number and a location or there may be a many-to-one correspondence between phone numbers and locations. Inasmuch as the phone numbers are related to locations, can locations be related to the phone numbers in the same way? Would it also be true to say that for every location there is a phone number? There may be locations without phones. Figure 7.1 illustrates possible relations between phone numbers with a 707 area code and addresses in Los Angeles, California. Determining to what extent phone numbers and locations are related helps in the description of the relation of phone numbers to locations. All relations have certain properties. Before we can describe the properties of relations we must first introduce the formal notion of a *relation*; in particular the *binary relation*.

## RELATIONS

A relation describes a connection between two groups or sets. Given a set $A$, the relation noted as $R$ would be a subset of the Cartesian product $A \times A$. The Cartesian product of $A \times A$ is all the possible ordered pairs of $A \times A$ (see Chapter 5 for a discussion of Cartesian products). The relation would be a subset of all the possible pairs. If a pair $(x, y)$ is in the relation $R$, then we would use this notation:

$$x \, R \, y$$

meaning that $x$ is related to $y$. For example, if given:

$$\text{set } A = \{ 1, 2, 3, 4 \}$$

and the relation produces the pairs:

$$R = \{(1, 2), (2, 3), (3, 4)\}$$

We would denote the pairs in $R$ as follows:

$$1 \, R \, 2$$
$$2 \, R \, 3$$
$$3 \, R \, 4$$

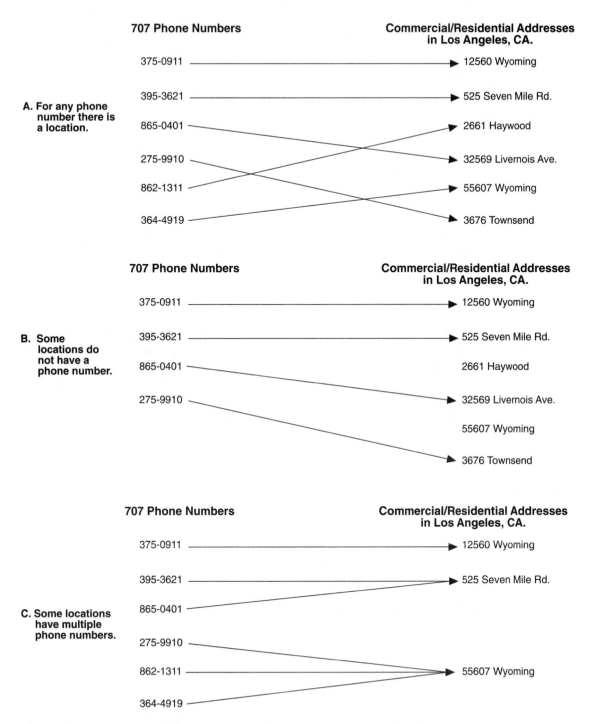

**Figure 7.1** The possible relationships between the phone numbers with a 707 area code and addresses in the Los Angeles area.

This is read: 1 is related to 2, 2 is related to 3, and 3 is related to 4 where 4 R 1, 3 R 1 are not related pairs in R.

## Properties of Relations

Relations can have certain properties that help describe their nature. Relations can be: *reflexive, symmetric, transitive,* or *equivalent*. A relation is reflexive if, given a nonempty set A and an element x in the set A, this statement is true:

$$x \, R \, x \text{ for all } x \in A$$

meaning that x is related to itself for all elements in set A. A relation can be symmetric if, given nonempty sets A and B and an element a from set A and an element b from set B, this statement is true:

$$a \, R \, b \text{ then } b \, R \, a$$

meaning if a is related to b then b is related to a. A symmetric relation can be illustrated in the relation between the phone numbers in the 707 area code, set A, and the locations in a geographic location, set C, mentioned earlier. A phone number belongs to a location in the Los Angeles, California area. The relation is symmetric because the locations in the Los Angeles, California area can belong to phone numbers with a certain area code.

Relation can be transitive if, given three nonempty sets A, C, E and an element from each set, x, y, and z, respectively, this statement is true:

$$x \, R \, y \text{ and } y \, R \, z \text{ then } x \, R \, z$$

meaning that if x is related to y and y is related to z then x is related to z. Using our phone number example, lets add an additional set E. Set E is defined as:

$$A = \{ \, x : x \text{ is a 707 area code phone number} \}$$
$$C = \{ \, x : x \text{ is a location in Los Angeles, California} \}$$
$$E = \{ \, x : x \text{ is a person who lives in Los Angeles, California} \}$$

A transitive relation can be developed between the sets A, C, and E given that:

$$x \in A$$
$$y \in C$$
$$z \in E$$
$$x \, R \, y \text{ and } y \, R \, z \text{ then } x \, R \, z$$

meaning that if a phone number in the area code 707 belongs to a location in Los Angeles, California and a location in Los Angeles, California belongs to a person who lives in Los Angeles, California, then a phone number in the 707 area code belongs to a person who lives in Los Angeles, California.

The phone number example also demonstrates that a relation can have more than one of these properties. *Irreflexive* and *antisymmetric* are also properties of relations. These properties are defined as follows:

| | |
|---|---|
| Irreflexive: | *a* not related *a* |
| Antisymmetric: | *a R b* and *b R a* then *a = b* |

An irreflexive relation is self-explanatory; *a* is not related to itself. An antisymmetric relation states that *a* is related to *b* and *b* is related to *a* because *a* and *b* are equal. A symmetric relation does not suggest that *a* and *b* are equal. For example, a phone number in the 707 area code belongs to a location in Los Angeles, California. It is also true that a location in Los Angeles, California belongs to a phone number with a 707 area code as opposed to a phone number with a 215 area code. This does not suggest that the phone number and the location are equal but that their *belonging* relation can be interpreted in either direction and is therefore symmetric. The idea that a phone number belongs to itself has no meaning. Therefore, the belonging relation in this example is irreflexive and symmetric. An *equivalent* relation is reflexive, symmetric, and transitive. Table 7.1 lists the properties of a relation and the condition in which the property exists.

## Mapping and Relations

A *mapping* is type of a relation as opposed to a property of a relation. A mapping can possess any of the aforementioned properties. A mapping is a rule that assigns to each element of a given set exactly one element of another set. If given two related sets, *A* and *B*, a mapping exists if each element of set *A* is related to exactly one element of set *B*. The

**Table 7.1  A list of the properties of relations and the conditions in which they exist.**

| Properties of Relations | Description |
|---|---|
| **Reflexive** | * If given a nonempty set **A** and an element x from set **A**, x **R** x for all x ∈ **A**. |
| **Irreflexive** | * If given a nonempty set **A** and an element a from set **A**, a is not related to a. |
| **Symmetric** | * If given nonempty sets **A** and **B** and an element a from set **A** and an element b from set **B**, a R b then b R a. |
| **Antisymmetric** | * If given nonempty sets **A** and **B** and an element a from set **A** and an element b from set **B**, a R b and b R a then a = b. |
| **Transitive** | * If given three nonempty sets **A, C, E** and an element from each set, x, y, and z respectively, x R y and y R z then x R z. |

rule that relates set $A$ to set $B$ is the function $f$. Set $A$ is the *domain* and set $B$ is the *codomain*. We use this notation to express this notion:

$$f : A \rightarrow B$$

$f$ is the rule that relates set $A$ to set $B$. Because $f$ is a relation, $f$ is a subset of the Cartesian product of $A \times B$. It is a subset of the Cartesian product because the rule that assigns elements from one set to the elements of another set may only include some of the ordered pairs while excluding others. For example, if given the sets $A$ and $B$ to be defined as:

$$A = \{-3,1,3\}$$
$$B = \{1,4,9\}$$

and let $f: A \rightarrow B$ define a rule that assigns elements of set $A$ to elements of set $B$:

$$f(a) = a * a$$

The mapping would appear as in Figure 7.2. The related set would produce these pairs:

$$\{(-3,9), (1,1), (3,9)\}$$

All other ordered pairs would be excluded. In this example set $A$ is the domain, set $B$ is the codomain. The *range* is the subset of the codomain, the set $\{1,9\}$.

## One-to-One Relationships

There are three properties that are important in describing a map. A map can be *injective*, *surjective*, or *bijective*. A mapping is said to be injective if, given sets $A$ and $B$ and elements $a$ and $b$ of set $A$, this statement is true:

$$a \neq b \text{ then } f(a) \neq f(b)$$

meaning if $a$ and $b$ of set $A$ are unequal when the rule or function is applied to elements $a$ and $b$ they would map to different elements of set $B$. An injective mapping is also called *one-to-one*. In our phone number example, in order for the mapping to be injective each phone number would belong to different locations. There could be locations without phone numbers.

A mapping is said to be surjective if, given sets $A$ and $B$ for any value $y$ in set $B$, there is at least one element $x$ in set $A$ for which this statement is true:

$$f(x) = y$$

meaning that for any value in set $B$ there is at least one value in set $A$ for which it is assigned. The important point is there is at least one value in set $A$. There can be more than one value in set $A$ for which an element in set $B$ is assigned. For example, if a single

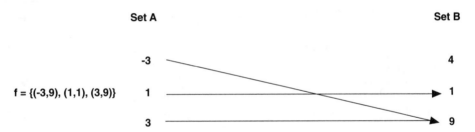

**Figure 7.2**   The mapping of set **A** to set **B**.

residential or commercial location had more than one phone number then the mapping or relation would be surjective.

Mapping can be both injective and surjective. This is called a *bijection* or a *one-to-one correspondence*. Considering our phone number example again; If each phone number was assigned or belonged to either a single commercial or residential location and each residence and commercial location had only one phone number then this would be bijection. Figure 7.3 illustrates an injective, surjective, and bijective mapping. Table 7.2 lists the types of mappings and a brief description. Relations associate elements of one set to elements of another set. Those relations can be described to have certain properties: reflexive, symmetric, transitive, and equivalent. Mappings are a type of relation. It is a specific type of relation that associates one element of a set to one element of another set. Mappings can be described as injective, surjective, or bijective. Simple associations do not suggest any type of rigor or assist in the enumeration and development of the sets that are to be associated. With mappings, the sets have to be clearly defined. Considering the properties of the mappings will help in the determinations of the usage and manipulations of the sets and their relations. In the C++ language, the relations and properties of relations are not constructs of the language but can be implemented using the object-oriented features that the language provides.

## MAP COLLECTION CLASS

The *map* collection is a special type of *set*. The map collection, also called a *dictionary* or *associative array*, is used to create a collection of *related* pairs. The map collection associates the elements of one set to the elements of another set. The map collection is an indexed structure similar to a vector. Where a vector uses integers as the index value, a map collection can use any type as the index value. The map collection consists of related ordered pairs. The first element of the pair serves as the *key* and the other element the *value*. The value can be accessed by using the key as the index value within a subscript operator. The key and the value can be of the same type or any mix of types. Map collections are associative structures where the key is one dimension and the value is another. It can be considered multidimensional. Figure 7.4 shows the logical view of a map collection.

Map collections are also nonlinear structures. The objects that it contains cannot be

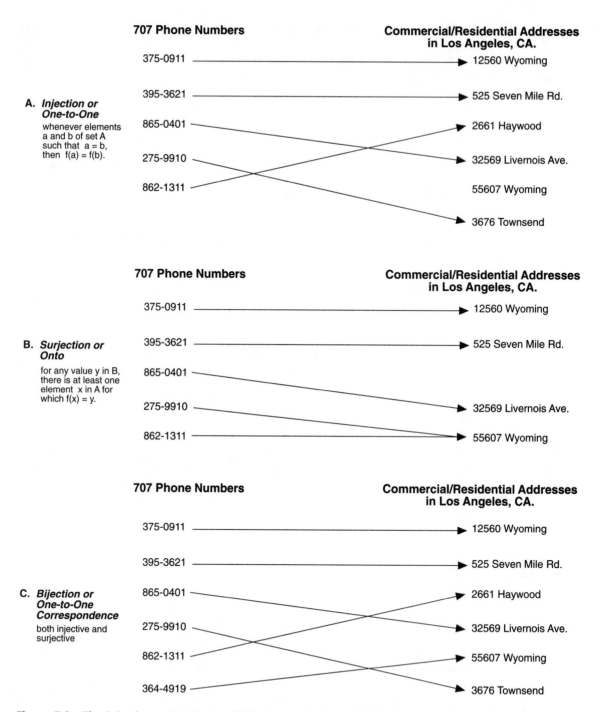

**Figure 7.3** The injective, surjective, and bijective mappings of 707 phone numbers to locations in Los Angeles, CA.

**Table 7.2** A list of the types of mappings and a brief description of each type.

| Types of Mappings | Description |
| --- | --- |
| Injection | * Given a set **A** and a set **B**, elements a and b of **A** such that a ≠ b, then f(a) ≠ f(b); different elements will always have different images. |
| Surjection | * For any value y in set **B**, there is at least one element x in set A for which f(x) = y; an arbitrary element b in set **B** and by using a formula or applying a function or rule there exist an element a in set **A** such that b= f(a). |
| Bijection | * Both injective and surjective, also called a *one-to-one correspondence*; for every element there is an unique image and for every image there is a unique element. |

thought of as consisting of a sequence of objects. Map collections utilize both direct and relational access methods. It uses direct access because an object can be retrieved from any position within the collection without the need of processing other objects first. Map collections use relational access methods. This means that storage, retrieval, and access of one object (value) are dependent upon its relationship with another object (key).

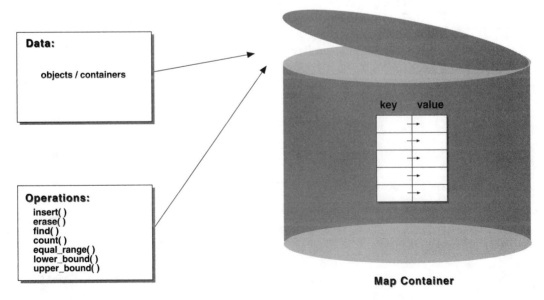

**Figure 7.4** A logical representation of an object-oriented map collection.

## THE STL MAP COLLECTION

The STL map collection is an associative *set* collection that allows unique keys of a given type to be associated with a value of the same or another type. It is an unordered collection by definition but the implementer has the liberty to designate an order by supplying the function object.

The map collection is declared in *map.h*. The map collection is a template class. The user must supply the template with certain arguments in order to declare a map class. The user must supply the type of object that will serve as the key for the map, the type of object that will serve as the value the key is associated with and the function object that specifies the *sort order*. The sort order is imposed on the key as opposed to the values. Elements of the map collection are stored in pairs. Each map contains at the most one pair (key + value) for each key value. A key cannot be associated with more than one value. Figure 7.5 illustrates the type of mapping used in the map collection.

### Client Responsibilities for Built-In Types and User-Defined Types

Since the sort order is imposed on the key, the < operator and the == operator should be defined for the key type. If the key type is a built-in data type, the < operator and the == operator is already defined for all built-in data types. Therefore, if built-in data types are used for the key types, the user or client does not have to be concerned with the operator requirements. The STL provides the **less** (<) and the **greater** (>) function objects that can be used with any of the built-in data types. These function objects are also templates and must be passed the data type.

If the map collection is declared using the **less** function object then the key values of the map would be sorted from the smallest to the largest. If the map collection is declared using the **greater** function object then the key values of the map would be sorted from the largest to the smallest. For example, to declare a map collection using the built-in

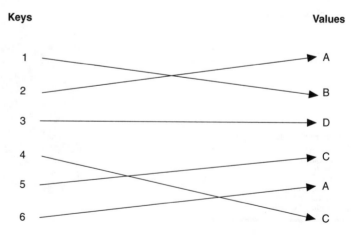

**Figure 7.5**  The type of mapping used in the map collection.

data type **int** for the key values and **string** for the values sorted in descending order, the code would look like this:

```
#include<map.h>
#include<cstring.h>

.
.
.

map<int,string,greater<int> > MapA;
```

The **greater()** function object is used for descending order of the key values. The **greater** template is passed the same type as the key type: **greater<int>**. If the key type was a **double** or a **string**, the template would be passed a **double** or a **string**, respectively: **greater<double>** or **greater<string>**.

When using user-defined objects as the key type, the user or client must provide the definition of the < operator and the definition of the == operator. The user or client must also provide the map collection declaration with a function object that will be used to designate the sort order on the key values. For example, to declare a map collection with the key values of the user-defined type **clock_time** and values of type **string** in ascending order, the code would look like this:

```
#include<map.h>
#include <cstring.h>
#include "clktime.h"

.
.
.

map<clock_time, string, less<clock_time> > MapB;
```

The function object uses the STL's built-in **less** function object. This is permissible because the class **clock_time** has defined the < operator.

Note: The client responsibilities for built-in types and user-defined types also apply to the multimap collection.

## Map Construction

The STL's map collection has three constructors:

```
map(const Compare& comp = Compare())

map(const map<Key, T, Compare>& x)

map(const value_type* first, const value_type* last, const Compare& comp =
    Compare())
```

The first constructor is the default constructor; it constructs an empty map. The **comp** function object is passed as a parameter. The **comp** is a comparison function object used to order the key elements of the map collection. As mentioned earlier, in order to instantiate a map collection, the function object is passed to the template before the constructor is called. It may be convenient to use the **typedef** declaration when instantiating a map collection. The **typedef** declaration is used when the declaration of an object is complex or long. The **typedef** declaration supplies a shortcut when numerous instantiations will occur. A **typedef** could be used in the instantiation of a map collection:

```
typedef map<clock_time, string, less<clock_time> > Map;
```

The **typedef** is used as shortcut for specifying the map **map<clock_time, string, less<clock_time> >**. Every time an object is declared using the identifier **Map**, the compiler knows to use **map<clock_time, string, less<clock_time> >**. This is convenient when a list of **Map** type objects is declared, for example:

```
Map MapA;
Map MapB;
Map MapC(greater<clock_time);
```

These maps all contain **clock_time** objects. The maps **MapA** and **MapB** contain **clock_time** objects in which the keys are sorted in ascending order based on the function object **less<clock_time>** according to the **typedefMap**. The map **MapC** uses the same **typedef** but supplies the **greater** function object. Therefore, **MapC** keys will be sorted in descending order. This is one convenience provided by this constructor.

The second constructor accepts another map collection as the argument. This is the map copy constructor. When this constructor is used, the map being constructed will be initialized with copies of the elements of the map in its argument.

The third constructor constructs an empty map and initializes it with copies of the elements in the range [**first, last**). This constructor accepts three arguments. The first and second arguments:

```
const value_type* first
const value_type* last
```

are pointers to the types of objects that will be stored in the map. **value_type** represents the elements stored in the map. **value_type** is the **typedef** identifier for **pair<const Key, T>**, which associates a key of **Key** type with a value of **T** type. The definition for **pair** object can be found in *pair.h*. The range [**first, last**) supplies the range of objects that will be copied to the map collection. The range is an *open-ended* interval, meaning the range includes **first** and up to but not including **last**. For example, in Listing 7.1, a map collection is constructed using the user-defined type **clock_time** as the key and **string** as the values. The map collection is initialized with copies of elements from a vector of object pairs. The third argument, **comp**, is the function object that is used to order the keys of the map. It defaults to the function object that was used to instantiate the template.

### Listing 7.1

```
1 // Listing 7.1
2 // This program demonstrates how a map collection can
3 // be initialized using the constructor that initializes
4 // an empty map with the elements of a range supplied by
5 // a vector of pairs. This map collection uses the user-
```

```
 6 // defined class clock_time as the key and a string
 7 // as the value.
 8
 9
10 #include<cstring.h>
11 #include<map.h>
12 #include<iostream.h>
13 #include"clktime.h"
14
15
16   clock_time Time1(140);
17   clock_time Time2(230);
18   clock_time Time3(1156);
19   pair<clock_time,string> Object1(Time1,"Bobby");
20   pair<clock_time,string> Object2(Time2,"Sally");
21   pair<clock_time,string> Object3(Time3,"Greg");
22   pair<clock_time,string> Group[3];
23   pair<clock_time,string> Temp;
24
25
26 void main(void)
27 {
28   Group[0] = Object1;
29   Group[1] = Object2;
30   Group[2] = Object3;
31   map<clock_time,string,less<clock_time> > MapA(Group,Group+3);
32   map<clock_time,string,less<clock_time> >::iterator P = MapA.begin();
33   while(P != MapA.end())
34   {
35     Temp = *P;
36     cout << "The key for MapA is " << Temp.first << endl;
37     cout << "The value for MapA is " << Temp.second << endl;
38     P++;
39   }
40
41 }
```

The program in Listing 7.1 creates a map collection and initializes the map with a range of elements. The constructor creates an empty map, then it inserts the elements in the range or interval **[first,last)** into the map collection. The range is the starting and ending address of a vector of pairs called **Group**. The map collection, called **MapA**, uses the **clock_time** class as the key type and **string** types as the value. Then the keys and the values of the map collection are displayed.

## Map Destruction

The map destructor ~**map()** is called when a map collection leaves scope or when the delete function is called. All the space that was allocated by the map is returned. Before the space is returned, any members that were in the map collection are erased. The destructors for the members are called individually.

## Map Collection Information Member Functions

There are four member functions that supply information about the map collection and its objects. They are **empty()**, **size()**, **max_size()**, and **count()**. The **empty()** member function returns a boolean type. It returns a true if the map is empty and false otherwise. The **size()** member function returns the number of elements in the map collection. The **max_size()** member function returns the maximum possible size of the map collection. It does not return the amount of space or the size of the map collection. The **max_size()** member function will return at least **size()**\* the *real* size of the objects that are being stored in the collection. The **count()** member function accepts an argument **x** of **key-_type. key_type** represents the type of the keys of the map collection. The **count()** member function will return the number of elements that have a key equal to **x**. Since the map collection has only unique keys, if the key has been inserted into the map collection, the **count()** member function will return a 1; otherwise it will return a 0.

## Adding Objects to the Map Collection

There are three ways to add objects into the map collection: through constructors, assignment operation, and the **insert()** member functions. Two of the three constructors can initialize an empty map collection. One constructor:

    map(const map<Key, T, Compare>& x)

adds objects from one map collection to a newly constructed map collection. The other constructor:

    map(const value_type* first, const value_type* last, const Compare&
        comp = Compare())

adds objects in the range [**first, last**) to a newly constructed map collection.

The assignment operation is defined for the map collection. This is another way to copy elements from one map to another:

    MapA = MapB

After this operation is performed, the elements of **MapB** are copied to **MapA**.

There are three **insert()** member functions. One of the **insert()** member function accepts an iterator and an argument *x* of **value_type**. The value *x* is inserted into the map collection if not already inserted. The iterator argument tells where the **insert()** member function should begin its search. An iterator is returned that points to the element with the key equal to the key of *x*. An **insert()** member function inserts the *x* value into the map if it is not already present. It returns a pair object that has an iterator and a **bool** component. The iterator points to the element that has a key equal to the key of *x*. The **bool** component indicates whether the insertion of the *x* value has taken place. Another **insert()** member function accepts two arguments. They are pointers to the same object type that is stored in the map collection. These pointers represent a range of elements. The elements in the range [**first,last**) are inserted into the map collection. This **insert()** member function has no return value.

## Removing Objects from the Map Collection

The map collection has three **erase()** member functions that remove objects from a map collection. One of the **erase()** member functions accepts an iterator that points to the element that is to be removed from the map collection. Another **erase()** member function accepts a value of the key type. It removes all the pairs that have a key equal the value of its argument. This **erase()** member function returns the number of elements that was erased. Since the map collection only has unique keys, this value will always be 1 if the key is present in the collection; otherwise, it will return a 0. There is an **erase()** member function that erases elements in a range. This **erase()** member function accepts two iterators that are assumed to point to elements in the map collection. The iterators point to the first and last elements of the range [**first, last**). All the elements in that range are removed from the map collection. This **erase()** member function has no return value.

## Object Visitation in the Map Collection

The map collection supplies a number of ways to perform object visitation. This can be performed with iterators, subscript operator, and numerous member functions. The map collection supports bidirectional and reverse iterators. The iterators allow us to visit one object at a time forward or backward using the bidirectional iterators, and front to back, back to front using the reverse iterators of the map collection.

The map collection has four member functions that return iterators: **begin()**, **end()**, **rbegin()**, and **rend()**. The **begin()** and **end()** member functions return an iterator of bidirectional type. The **rbegin()** and **rend()** member functions return **reverse_iterator** of reverse type. The **begin()** member functions returns a bidirectional iterator that can be used to begin the traversal through all the locations of the map collection. The **end()** member function returns a bidirectional iterator that is used in a comparison to end the traversal through the map collection. The **rbegin()** member function returns the reverse iterator that can be used to begin the traversal to all locations in the map collection in the reverse order. The **rend()** member function returns a reverse iterator that can be used in a comparison for ending a *reverse-the-direction* traversal through all the locations on the map collection.

One way to traverse through the elements of a map collection is to use the map **iterator** or **reverse_iterator** objects. An iterator object is declared:

```
map<clock_time, string, less<clock_time> >:: iterator P;
map<clock_time, string, less<clock_time> >:: reverse_iterator R;
```

The first is a bidirectional iterator and the second is a reverse iterator. These iterators are used with a map collection that has **clock_time** types for the keys and **string** types for the values. Once the appropriate type of iterator is declared, the user can initialize them with iterators that point to elements in the map collection with a call to the appropriate member functions mentioned earlier. For example:

```
P = MapA.begin();
  or
P = MapA.end();

PR = MapA.rbegin();
  or
PR = MapA.rend();
```

Since the **begin()** and **end()** member functions both return the bidirectional type of iterators and **rbegin()** and **rend()** member functions both return reverse iterators, then these would be appropriate assignments. The incrementation or decrementation of pointers can be used with the iterators to sequentially traverse through the map collection. When the iterator is dereferenced, the value is not a single element but a pair.

The subscript operator can be used to visit elements in the map collection. A key value is used and the operator will return the object that is associated with that key. Unlike the subscript operators for vectors, if the map does not contain the key and its associated element, it will insert the pair into the map. Therefore, the subscript operator can be used to access objects or insert elements into the map collection. The subscript operator is used to directly access a single object or provide total object visitation. The program in Listing 7.2 demonstrates the usage of iterators and subscript operator for object visitation of a map collection. The program also demonstrates how the **insert()** member function can be used to initialize a map.

### Listing 7.2

```
 1 // Listing 7.2
 2 // This program demonstrates how a map collection can
 3 // be initialized using the insert member function. It
 4 // also demonstrates how objects in a map collection can
 5 // be visited using the iterator and the subscript
 6 // operator. This map collection uses the user-defined
 7 // class clock_time as the key and a string as the value.
 8
 9
10 #include<cstring.h>
11 #include<map.h>
12 #include<iostream.h>
13 #include"clktime.h"
14
15
16    clock_time Time1(140);
17    clock_time Time2(230);
18    clock_time Time3(1156);
19    string TempStr;
20    pair<clock_time,string> Object1(Time1,"Bobby");
21    pair<clock_time,string> Object2(Time2,"Sally");
22    pair<clock_time,string> Object3(Time3,"Greg");
23    pair<clock_time,string> Group[3];
24    pair<clock_time,string> Temp;
```

```
25
26
27 void main(void)
28 {
29   Group[0] = Object1;
30   Group[1] = Object2;
31   Group[2] = Object3;
32   map<clock_time,string,less<clock_time> > MapA;
33   MapA.insert(Group,Group+3);
34    map<clock_time,string,less<clock_time> >::iterator P = MapA.begin();
35   while(P != MapA.end())
36   {
37     Temp = *P;
38     cout << "The key for MapA is " << Temp.first << endl;
39     P++;
40   }
41   for(int N = 0;N <= 2;N++)
42   {
43     TempStr = MapA[Group[N].first];
44     cout << "The value for MapA is " << TempStr << endl;
45   }
46 }
47
```

In Listing 7.2, **MapA** is initialized by using the **insert()** member function. The **insert()** member function is passed an interval **[first, last)**. The interval is the beginning and ending address of a vector of pairs called **Group**. An iterator, **P1**, is created and initialized with an iterator that points to the beginning of the collection. This is done by calling the **begin()** member function. The iterator that points to the end of the collection is used as the termination value to end the traversal through the map in the while loop. The iterator points to the elements in the collection that are pairs. When the iterator **P1** is deferenced, the pair is assigned to a pair object called **Temp. Temp.first** returns the key value, which is displayed. A for loop is used to demonstrate the subscript operator. **Group[N].first** is used as the key for the subscript operator. **MapA[Group[N].first]** returns a value whose key is equal to **Group[N].first**. The values are displayed.

Objects in the collection can also be accessed by using the **find()** member functions. These member functions locate elements in the map collection. The **find()** member function locates an element that is equal to the key supplied by its argument. It accepts an argument $x$ of the key type of the map collection. If the element is present, the **find()** member function will return an iterator pointing to that element. Otherwise an iterator pointing to the end of the map collection is returned.

The member functions **lower_bound()**, **upper_bound()**, and **equal_range()** all accept an argument $x$ of the key type. All of these member functions can be used to retrieve a specific element from the map collection. The **lower_bound()** member function searches the map collection for the first element whose key is not less than $x$ key. It searches for the first element whose key satisfies this statement:

$$y \geq x$$

If the element is present in the map collection, the member function will return an iterator pointing to that element. The **upper_bound()** member function searches for the first element whose key is greater than *x* key. It searches for the first element whose key satisfies this statement:

$$y > x$$

If the element is present in the map collection, the member function will return an iterator pointing to that element. If the element is not present in the collection, the **lower_bound()** and **upper_bound()** member functions will return the iterator that points to the end of the collection. The **equal_range()** member function will return the pair **lower_bound()** and **upper_bound()**. Table 7.3 lists the descriptions and the performance of these member functions.

## Map Collection Operators and Operations

The map collection supports the relational operators: $==, !=, <, >, <\div<=, >=$. If given two maps, **MapA** and **MapB**, relational comparisons such as

```
MapA > MapB
MapB == MapA
```

**Table 7.3   A list of the descriptions and runtime performance of the special map operations upper_bound, lower_bound, and equal_range.**

| Member Function | Description | Performance |
|---|---|---|
| **upper_bound(x)** | * Accepts a key x of key type.<br>* Returns an iterator which points to the first element with a key greater than x.<br>* If there is no such element, end() is returned. | 0(logN) where N is the number of elements in the map. |
| **lower_bound(x)** | * Accepts a key x of key type.<br>* Returns an iterator which points to the first element with a key greater than or equal to key x.<br>* If there is no such element, end() is returned. | 0(logN) where N is the number of elements in the map. |
| **equal_range(x)** | * Accepts a key x of key type.<br>* Returns the values of **upper_bound()** and **lower_bound()** member functions as a pair. | 0(logN) where N is the number of elements in the map. |

can be performed. These comparisons will return a **bool** value *true* if the statement is true and a **bool** *false* if the statement is not true.

The map collection can be viewed as a set of pairs. Because the map collection can be viewed in this way, it would be appropriate to use set operations on the map collection. As mentioned earlier, the set operations **includes, set_union, set_intersection, set _difference**, and **set_symmetric_difference** are all STL generic algorithms that can be used on any sorted structure. The map collection is sorted based on the function objects passed to the template during instantiation or during construction of the map collection. The set operations are discussed in Chapter 5. The **includes** set operation returns a **bool** value. It accepts two ranges represented as four input iterators. The first two input iterators point to the beginning and the end of the second range and the last two input iterators point to the beginning and end of the first range. The **includes** set operation returns a *true* if every element in the first range is contained in the second range. Otherwise, it returns a *false*. In other words, if the first range is represented as **MapA** and the second range is represented as **MapB**, the **includes** set operation would determine if this statement is true:

**SetA ⊂ SetB**

The **includes** set operation can determine if a range of elements in one map is within a range of elements in another map. The program in Listing 7.3 demonstrates how the includes set operation can be used on a map collection.

### Listing 7.3

```
 1 // Listing 7.3
 2 // This program demonstrates how set operations can be
 3 // used with a map collection. The includes set
 4 // operation is used to determine whether a map
 5 // is the subset of another map. Both the map
 6 // collections use the user-defined
 7 // class clock_time as the key and a string as
 8 // the value.
 9
10
11 #include<set.h>
12 #include<algo.h>
13 #include<cstring.h>
14 #include<map.h>
15 #include<iostream.h>
16 #include"clktime.h"
17
18
19    clock_time Time1(140);
20    clock_time Time2(230);
21    clock_time Time3(1156);
22    clock_time Time4(140);
23    clock_time Time5(123);
```

```
24    string TempStr;
25    pair<clock_time,string> Object1(Time1,"Bobby");
26    pair<clock_time,string> Object2(Time2,"Sally");
27    pair<clock_time,string> Object3(Time3,"Greg");
28    pair<clock_time,string> Object4(Time2,"Dick");
29    pair<clock_time,string> Object5(Time4,"Sue");
30    pair<clock_time,string> Group1[3];
31    pair<clock_time,string> Group2[5];
32    pair<clock_time,string> Temp;
33
34
35
36 void main(void)
37 {
38    Group1[0] = Object1;
39    Group1[1] = Object2;
40    Group1[2] = Object3;
41    map<clock_time,string,less<clock_time> >MapA;
42    MapA.insert(Group1,Group1+3);
43     map<clock_time,string,less<clock_time> >::iterator M = MapA.begin();
44    map<clock_time,string,less<clock_time> >::iterator P = MapA.end();
45    Group2[0] = Object1;
46    Group2[1] = Object2;
47    Group2[2] = Object3;
48    Group2[3] = Object4;
49    Group2[4] = Object5;
50    map<clock_time,string,less<clock_time> > MapB;
51    MapB.insert(Group2,Group2+5);
52    map<clock_time,string,less<clock_time> >::iterator Q = MapB.begin();
53    map<clock_time,string,less<clock_time> >::iterator R = MapB.end();
54    if(includes(Q,R,M,P)){
55       cout << "MapA is a subset of MapB" << endl;
56    }
57    else {
58       cout << "MapA is not a subset of MapB" << endl;
59    }
60 }
```

The program in Listing 7.3 constructs two map collections that are initialized with copies of elements from a vector of pairs by using the **insert()** member function. The keys for both maps are of the user-defined type **clock_time** and the values are **string** types. The **includes()** set operation is used to determine if **MapA** is a subset of **MapB**. The **includes** set operation accepts two ranges of elements. They are represented as iterators of the map collections. The **includes** set operation returns a **bool** value *true* if every element in the range [first2,last2) is contained in the range [first1,last1), and a *false* value otherwise. The **includes()** member function returns a *true*, therefore **MapA** is a subset of **MapB**.

# MULTIMAP COLLECTION CLASS

The multimap collection is a special type of multiset. The multimap collection is used to create a collection of related pairs. Whereas the map includes the unique pairs of related items, the multimap may include duplicate pairs. The multimap collection associates the elements of one set to the elements of another set. Multimap collections are structured in the same way as the map collection. The elements in the collection are pairs. The difference between a multimap and a map collection is that the multimap collection allows key duplication. In other words, the same key can be associated with different values. Figure 7.6 illustrates the type of mapping used in a multimap collection. Considering our phone number example using the locations as keys and phone numbers as values of the multimap, a single location with more than one phone can be mapped to different phone numbers.

# THE STL MULTIMAP COLLECTION

The STL multimap collection is an associative collection that allows duplicate keys of a given type to be associated with different values of another type. The multimap collection is declared in *multimap.h*. It is declared and instantiated in the same way as the map collection. The user supplies the type of object that will serve as the key, the type of object that will serve as the values, and the function object. Each multimap contains as many pairs as desired (key + value) for each key value. The multimap collection does not define the subscript operator. This is logical considering there may be more than one value associated with a key.

## Client Responsibilities for Built-In Types and User-Defined Types

Since the sort order is imposed on the key, the < operator and the == operator should be defined for the key type. If the key type is a built-in data type, the < operator and the

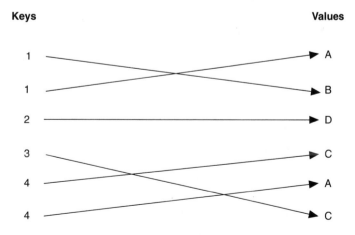

**Figure 7.6** The type of mapping used in the multimap collection.

== operator is already defined for all built-in data types. Therefore, if built-in data types are used for the key types, the user or client does not have to be concerned with the operator requirements. The STL provides the **less** (<) and the **greater** (>) function objects that can be used with any of the built-in data types. These function objects are also templates and must be passed the data type.

If the map collection is declared using the **less** function object, then the key values of the map would be sorted from the smallest to the largest. If the map collection is declared using the **greater** function object, then the key values of the map would be sorted from the largest to the smallest. For example, to declare a map collection using the built-in data type **int** for the key values and **string** for the values sorted in descending order, the code would look like this:

```
#include<map.h>
#include<cstring.h>

  .
  .
  .

map<int,string,greater<int> > MapA;
```

The **greater** function object is used for descending order of the key values. The **greater** template is passed the same type as the key type: **greater<int>**. If the key type was a **double** or a **string**, the template would be passed a **double** or a **string**, respectively: **greater<double>** or **greater<string>**.

When using user-defined objects as the key type, the user or client must provide the definition of the < operator and the definition of the == operator. The user or client must also provide the map collection declaration with a function object that will be used to designate the sort order on the key values. For example, to declare a map collection with the key values of the user-defined type **clock_time** and values of type **string** in ascending order, the code would look like this:

```
#include<map.h>
#include <cstring.h>
#include "clktime.h"

  .
  .
  .

map<clock_time, string, less<clock_time> > MapB;
```

The function object uses the STL's built-in **less()** function object. This is permissible because the class **clock_time** has defined the **less** operation.

## Multimap Construction

The STL's multimap collection has three constructors:

```
multimap(const Compare& comp = Compare())

multimap(const multimap<Key, T, Compare>& x)

multimap(const value_type* first, const value_type* last, const
    Compare& comp = Compare())
```

The first constructor is the default constructor; it constructs an empty multimap. The **comp** function object is passed as a parameter. The **comp** is a comparison function object used to order the key elements of the multimap collection. This constructor can also be used with a **typedef** declaration. The second constructor accepts another multimap collection as the argument. This is the multimap copy constructor. When this constructor is used, the multimap is initialized with copies of the elements of the multimap in its argument. The third constructor constructs an empty multimap and initializes it with copies of the elements in the range [**first, last**). The third argument **comp** is the function object that is used to order the keys of the map. Even though the multimap may have duplicate keys, no sort on the values is performed on pairs with the same keys.

## Multimap Destruction

The multimap destructor ~**multimap()** is called when a multimap collection leaves scope or when the delete function is called. All the space that was allocated by the multimap is returned. Before the space is returned, any members that were in the multimap collection are erased. The destructors for the members are called individually.

## Multimap Collection Information Member Functions

The multimap collection has the same member functions as the map collection for supplying information about the multimap collection and its objects: **empty()**, **size()**, **max_size()**, and **count()**. The **empty()**, **size()**, and **max_size()** member functions perform in the same manner for multimap collections as they do for map collections. As for the **count()** member function, it will return the number of all pairs with keys equal to *x*. Since the multimap collection may have duplicate keys, each pair is counted separately. If the pair duplications also have the same values, they will also be counted as individual pairs.

## Adding Objects to the Multimap Collection

There are three ways to add objects into the multimap collection: through constructors, assignment operation, and the **insert()** member functions. Two of the three constructors can initialize an empty multimap collection. One constructor:

```
multimap(const multimap<Key, T, Compare>& x)
```

adds objects from one multimap collection to a newly constructed multimap collection. The other constructor:

```
multimap(const value_type* first, const value_type* last, const
    Compare& comp = Compare())
```

adds objects in the range [**first, last**) to a newly constructed map collection.

The assignment operation is defined for the multimap collection: **MultimapA = MultimapB**. After this operation is performed, the elements of **MultimapB** are copied to **MultimapA**.

There are three **insert()** member functions defined for the multimap collection. They perform differently from their map collection counterparts. It is important to note that all the **insert()** member functions for multimaps will always insert the pair element into the collection. Two of the **insert()** member functions for map collections will only insert the element under the condition that the key is not already present in the collection. It searches the collection for an occurrence of the key; if the key is present then the pair is not inserted. Because the multimap collection allows for duplicate keys, the element will always be inserted when using the **insert()** member functions. The member function only considers the keys and not the values. Therefore, pairs with duplicate keys and identical values as pairs already present in the collection will be inserted as well. When the **insert()** member function is passed a pair element, it does not execute the **insert()** member function that returns a pair object as with the map collection. The iterator that points to the newly inserted pair element is returned.

## Removing Objects from the Multimap Collection

The multimap collection has three **erase()** member functions that remove objects from a multimap collection. They accept the same argments and have the same return types as the map collection versions. When the **erase()** member function is passed a key, then all pairs with that key will be erased. The number of element pairs erased is returned.

## Object Visitation in the Multimap Collection

Object visitation for the multimap collection can be performed with iterators and a number of member functions. The multimap collection supports bidirectional and reverse iterators; therefore the **begin()**, **end()**, **rbegin()**, and **rend()** member functions can be used with the multimap.

Objects in multimap collection can also be accessed by using the **find()** member function. This member function locates elements in the multimap collection. The **find()** member function accepts an argument $x$ of the key type of the map collection. It locates the element with a key equal to $x$. If the element is present, the **find()** member function will return an iterator pointing to that element. Otherwise an iterator pointing to the end of the map collection is returned. If there is more than one element with a key equal to $x$, the **find()** member function will return an iterator pointing to one of those elements.

The member functions **lower_bound()**, **upper_bound()** are very useful when processing through elements with equal keys. They can be used to retrieve a specific element from the multimap collection. The **lower_bound()** member function searches the multimap collection for the first element whose key is not less than $x$ key. For duplicate keys, this will be the first occurrence. Then the iterator that is returned can be used to traverse through the remaining elements. The **upper_bound()** member function can be used to end the traversal. It searches for the first element whose key is greater than $x$ key.

## Multimap Collection Operators and Operations

The multimap collection supports the relational operators: $==$, $!=$, $<$, $>$, $<\div<=$, $>=$. If given two multimaps, **MultimapA** and **MultimapB**, relational comparisons such as

MultimapA > MultimapB
MultimapB == MultimapA

can be performed. Since the multimap collections are multisets, it would be appropriate to use set operations on multimap collections. The set operations **includes, set_union, set_intersection, set_difference**, and **set_symmetric_difference** are all STL generic algorithms that can be used on any sorted structure that supports input, output, and forward iterators and has a function object. These algorithms, along with any of the generic algorithms that require input, output, and forward iterators, can be used with the multimap collection.

## MAPPING AND RELATIONS REVISITED

A *mapping* relates the elements of one set to the elements of another set. A map can be injective, surjective, or bijective. A mapping is a type of relation. Relations possess a number of properties: transitive, symmetric, and reflexive. The map and the multimap collections can be used to construct mappings that reflect the properties of mapping and relations. For example, the program in Listing 7.4 demonstrates how a map is used to create a surjective mapping and how that map along with a multimap is used to create a transitive relation.

### Listing 7.4

```
1 // Listing 7.4
2 // This program demonstrates how the map and
3 // multimap collections can be used to simulate
4 // a surjective mapping and a transitive relation.
5
6
7 #include<multimap.h>
8 #include<map.h>
9 #include<pair.h>
10 #include<cstring.h>
11 #include"clktime.h"
```

```
12 #include<algo.h>
13 #include<iostream.h>
14
15
16    pair<string,string> Temp1;
17    pair<string,string> Temp2;
18    pair<string,string> Group1[14];
19    pair<string,string> Group2[9];
20
21 void main(void)
22 {
23
24    Group1[0].first = "Input";
25    Group1[0].second= "equal";
26    Group1[1].first = "Output";
27    Group1[1].second= "reverse_copy";
28    Group1[2].first = "Forward";
29    Group1[2].second= "equal";
30    Group1[3].first = "Forward";
31    Group1[3].second= "stable_sort";
32    Group1[4].first= "Bidirectional";
33    Group1[4].second= "reverse_copy";
34    Group1[5].first = "Random";
35    Group1[5].second= "stable_sort";
36    Group2[0].first = "equal";
37    Group2[0].second= "non_mutating";
38    Group2[1].first = "reverse_copy";
39    Group2[1].second= "mutating";
40    Group2[2].first = "stable_sort";
41    Group2[2].second= "sort";
42    multimap<string,string,less<string> > MapA(Group1,Group1+5);
43    multimap<string,string,less<string> >::iterator M = MapA.begin();
44    multimap<string,string,less<string> >::iterator P = MapA.end();
45    map<string,string,less<string> > MapB(Group2,Group2+3);
46    map<string,string,less<string> >::iterator Q = MapB.begin();
47    map<string,string,less<string> >::iterator R = MapB.end();
48    while(M != MapA.end())
49    {
50      Temp1 = *M;
51      cout << Temp1.first << " iterator is related to ";
52      cout << Temp1.second << " algorithm." << endl;
53      Temp2 = *Q;
54      cout << Temp2.first << " algorithm is related to ";
55      cout << Temp2.second << " algorithm type." << endl;
56      cout << "Therefore, " << Temp1.first;
57      cout << " iterator is related to " << Temp2.second;
58      cout << " algorithm type." << endl << endl;
59      M++;
60    }
61 }
```

The program in Listing 7.4 creates a multimap, **MapA**, that simulates a surjective relation between types of iterators and generic algorithms. Iterators are related to generic algorithms because certain types of iterators are used with specific generic algorithms. A map, **MapB**, is created that relates the generic algorithms with the algorithm type. Table 7.4 lists the multimap **MapA** and map **MapB** element pairs. The multimap and the map together are used to simulate a transitive relation between types of iterators and algorithm types. This transitive relation implies that certain iterator types are used with certain types of algorithms. This can also be expressed this way:

Iterators = { x : x is an iterator type}
Algorithms = { x : x is a generic algorithm}
Algorithm Types = { x : x is an algorithm type}
a ∈ Iterators
b ∈ Algorithms
c ∈ Algorithm Types
a R b and b R c then a R c

Figure 7.7 illustrates multimap **MapA**'s surjective mapping of iterators to generic algorithms and map **MapB**'s mapping of algorithms to their algorithm type. Finally, the transitive relation is shown between the types of iterators and the algorithm types.

**Table 7.4   The input pairs for the map and multimap collections for the program in Listing 7.4**

*Input Pairs for Map and Multimap Collections for Program Listing 7.4*

| **Map Pairs:** | **MapA** | |
|---|---|---|
| | Input | equal |
| | Output | reverse_copy |
| | Forward | equal |
| | Forward | stable_sort |
| | Bidirectional | reverse_copy |
| | Random | stable_sort |
| | | |
| **Multimap Pairs:** | **MapB** | |
| | equal | nonmutating |
| | reverse_copy | mutating |
| | stable_sort | sort |

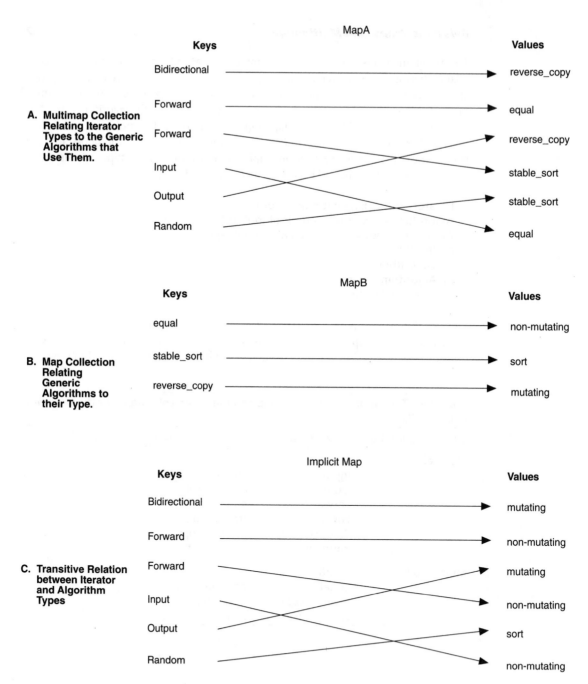

**Figure 7.7** The map and multimap relations created in Program Listing 7.4.

CHAPTER 8

# GRAPH OBJECTS

THE TERM *graph* has different meanings in mathematics and in computer science. We are all familiar with the notion of a graph that is a pictorial representation of numerical data, as in a bar chart or pie chart. The notion of graphing curves, lines, and functions in the Cartesian or polar coordinate system is also a familiar usage of the term graph. However, when we use graph in this book we are referring to a kind of *structure*, not a pictorial representation. The graph structure consists of only two things: a set of objects called *nodes* or *vertices*, and a set of connected or related objects called *edges*. A good example of a graph is the structure of a *family*. A family structure consists of two sets. The first set is a collection of people. The second set is a collection of relationships or connections between those people. The connections are described by relationships between the people in the family, like brother, sister, mother, cousin, nephew, and so on. The people in the family are the vertices or nodes of the graph. The relationships or connections between the people are the edges of the graph.

Just as the set collection is not classified as a linear or hierarchical structure, the graph is not described as a linear or hierarchical structure. When objects are stored in sequential or linear structures, they are accessed by either sequential access or direct access methods. When objects are stored in hierarchical structures, the hierarchy of the structure dictates how the objects can be accessed. However, when objects are stored in graphs, the objects are accessed based on their connection, or relationship, with other objects in the graph. The graph has *relational access methods* as opposed to sequential, linear, or direct access methods. The logical view of vectors, stacks, queues, lists, and deques includes the notion of top, bottom, front, back, head, tail, first, or last. The graph structure does not have a first, last, top, or bottom. There is no unique entry point into a graph. There is no unique exit point from a graph. The graph is somewhat of a free-form structure. For this reason it is perhaps the most flexible structure available to the computer programmer.

The primary purpose of collections and containers is to hold an object or group of objects. When the object or group of objects needs to be retrieved in some specific manner, or stored in some specific manner, then we pick an appropriate collection object or container object to store the group. When the manner in which we store or visit objects in a container is an important part of the solution to some programming problem, then the selection of the appropriate collection or container is of even more concern. The graph structure provides the programmer with a collection that is capable of storing groups of objects and relationships between that group of objects. Almost any scenario imaginable can be described as some group of objects and their relationships. Any problem can be described as a pathfinding problem; see (Kowalski 1979, 75). This means that the graph structure is an extremely powerful programming construct. Once a collection of objects has been stored in a graph, and the direct connections between the objects have been stored in the graph, the graph can be used to find any direct or indirect connection or relationship between those objects. The graph becomes a *search space*. The graph can be searched for all the direct connections as well as all the indirect connections. The indirect connections may be the result of long chains of direct connections. For instance, the connection between a great-great grandfather and his grandson is a chain of relationship connections. The son is not immediately the son of the great-great grandfather, but instead is indirectly connected through a chain of *son of* relationships. The primary uses of graphs involve path or connection finding. In pathfinding, the goal is to determine how one object in the graph can be reached from another object in the graph.

In our designation of collections and containers, the graph is a collection. It has an extremely rich interface and a vast repertoire of algorithms, and even a moderate explanation of graph theory is beyond the scope of this book. We can only hope to introduce the most basic vocabulary, definitions, and algorithms that come from graph theory, and how we can use C++ and the STL to construct graph objects. For a complete introduction to algorithmic graph theory and how graphs are used in computer science, see *Algorithmic Graph Theory* (1987) by Alan Gibbons.

## SOME GRAPH VOCABULARY AND DEFINITIONS

A graph $G$ is a structure $G = \{V, E\}$ that consists of a nonempty set V of points (called vertices) and a set $E$ of segments (called edges) such that each edge $e$ contains exactly two vertices, one vertex at each endpoint of the segment. The edges of set $E$ may consist of ordered pairs or unordered pairs. Set $E$ may also be empty! When two vertices in set $V$ are connected or related to each other they are said to be *adjacent*. When two vertices are adjacent they serve as *endpoints* of the edge, or endpoints of the connection. When a vertex is an endpoint of an edge it is said to be *incident* with the edge. Hence every edge has two endpoints and both endpoints are said to be incident with the edge, and the edge is said to be incident with the endpoints. Two edges $e$ and $f$ that are both incident with vertex $n$ are said to be adjacent at $n$.

The degree of a vertex is the number of edges that are incident to it. The *indegree* of a vertex $n$ is the number of edges that have $n$ as the head, and the *outdegree* of a vertex $n$ is the number of edges that have $n$ as the tail. If a vertex $n$ is adjacent to a vertex $m$ then there is an edge from $m$ to $n$. If $n$ is adjacent to $m$, then $n$ is called the successor of $m$, and $m$ is called a predecessor of $n$.

## Graph Connections

A *walk* W between vertices $v^0$ and $v^k$ is a finite, nonempty sequence of adjacent vertices and edges of the form:

$$v^0, e^1, v^1, e^2, \ldots, v^{k-1}, e^k, v^k$$

The length of the walk W is k. The vertices and the edges may or may not be distinct. That is, a vertex may start with itself and end with itself. A walk describes and unrestricted traversal in which vertices and edges can be traversed repeatedly in any direction.

A *trail* T in G is a *walk* W in which the edges $e^i$ and $e^j$ are distinct whenever $i \approx j$. That is, no edge of T is traversed more than once. A trail that returns to its starting vertex is called a *circuit*. A *path* P in G is a trail T in which the vertices $v^i$ and $v^j$ are distinct whenever $i \approx j$. Hence, no edge in P is repeated, nor does P return to any vertex previously visited. A simple circuit M in N is a walk W of the form

$$v^0, e^1, v^1, e^2, \ldots, v^{k-1}, e^k, v^0$$

in which $e^1 \approx e^j$ and $v^i \approx v^j$ whenever $i \approx j$. In other words, a simple circuit is a walk that returns to its starting vertex without traversing any edge more than once and without passing through any intermediate vertex more than once.

So then, a graph structure defines several connections between vertices or nodes. Graph structures support walks, trails, paths, and circuits. The walks, trails, paths, and circuits are the means in which we move from one object in the graph to another object in the graph. Much of the work done with graph structures involves finding walks, trails, paths, and circuits between objects in a graph. In fact, the very nature of most problem-solving techniques can be described as a walk or a trail through a graph. Table 8.1 shows some of the common types of trails and circuits used on graph structures.

## Types of Graphs

Graphs come in many flavors. One of the most common types of graphs is the tree. There are connected graphs, bipartite graphs, transport networks, multigraphs, weighted graphs, directed graphs, and planar graphs. Table 8.2 shows the properties of some of the graphs that are commonly found in computer programming.

# OBJECT-ORIENTED GRAPHS

A graph is a *polylithic* collection. That is, a graph is a structure that requires other structures to complete its definition. The fact that a graph is a collection that consists of two sets, a set of vertices and a set of edges, makes it polylithic. That means the graph is a *superstructure* because it is a collection that is built from another collection. The object-oriented graph is not to be confused with the notion of a *pictorial graph*. This is not to say

**Table 8.1    Some of the common types of trails and circuits used on graphs.**

| Trail/Circuit Type | Description |
| --- | --- |
| **Path** | * A type of trail in which the edges are distinct, and no edge is traversed more than once. |
| **Simple Circuit** | * A walk that returns to the starting vertex without traversing an edge more than once and without passing through any intermediate vertex more than once. |
| **Proper Circuit** | * A simple circuit of length 1 or greater in which no edge is repeated. |
| **Euler Trail** | * A trail that covers each edge exactly once. |
| **Euler Circuit** | * A Euler trail that ends at its starting vertex. |
| **Hamilton Path** | * A path that passes through each vertex exactly once. |
| **Hamilton Circuit** | * A simple circuit that passes through each vertex exactly once. |

that graphs cannot be represented visually. Figure 8.1 shows an example of how a graph could be depicted. The graph, like the set, is an extremely expressive collection. Note that sets and graphs represent good examples of collections, because they have personality that goes above and beyond the objects they contain. This is in contrast to containers that simply provide holding areas, and whose characteristics and behavior provide only basic insertion, deletion, and access. Collections have powerful characteristics and behaviors apart from the objects they contain. The logical view of the graph consists of a free-form structure that provides several member functions. Table 8.3 shows the core services that a graph collection will provide and their descriptions: insert, remove, vertex, edge, incident, adjacent, indegree, and outdegree.

Two common relational comparisons between graphs are *isomorphic* comparison, and *homeomorphic* comparison. These types of comparisons tell how similar two graphs are.

## The Graph Collection Class

We can use the object-oriented features in the C++ language to encapsulate the notion of a graph and create a graph collection class. One of the first decisions that must be made is how the vertices and the edges should be implemented. Figure 8.2 shows some of the common implementations of the graph structure in traditional programming languages. The adjacency matrix and adjacency list are two of the most efficient methods of representing vertices and edges. However, we use the STL set collection to implement the set of vertices and edges to demonstrate how the STL can be used to implement new collections. Because we use STL set objects that can contain user-defined objects, we remove some of the restrictions of the adjacency matrix and adjacency list representation. The efficiency of a graph collection that is built on two sets will be largely determined by the implementation of the sets, and the relational and assignment operators that are defined on the objects that are in the sets. In this case we are using the

**Table 8.2  Some of the graphs commonly used in computer programming and their base properties.**

| Types of Graphs | Description |
|---|---|
| **Connected** | * A graph that only has one component; two nodes are of the same component if there is a path between them. |
| **Disconnected** | * A graph that has more than one component. |
| **Empty** | * A graph that has *m* vertices and no edges; each vertex is a component. |
| **Simple** | * A graph with no self-loops and no parallel edges (edges that have the same endnodes). |
| **Bipartite** | * A graph in which the set of vertices is divided into two nonempty sets; the set of vertices is the union of the two sets and there are no elements of the sets that intersect; each edge of the graph connects a vertex of one set to a vertex of the other set. |
| **Transport Networks** | * A finite connected digraph in which one vertex is called the source of the network and another vertex is called the sink of the network. |
| **Multigraphs** | * A graph with parallel edges but no self-loops. |
| **Weighted** | * A graph in which a number is associated with each arc; the number or weight is the remainder obtained by dividing the integer at the head of the arc by the integer at the tail. |
| **Directed or Digraph** | * A graph in which the nodes of the graph are ordered pairs. |
| **Planar** | * A graph that can be drawn in a plane with no intersecting edges. |

STL set, which is implemented by a red black tree structure. We have made no specific attempt to optimize the performance of the relational and assignment operators for our user-defined objects. Our graph class is a simplified version of a much more complex structure that is utilized at CTEST labs.

Listing 8.1 shows the class declaration for our graph class.

### Listing 8.1

```
// Listing 8.1
// Declaration for a simple graph class

1 template<class T, class V, class U, class Q> class graph{
2 protected:
3    set<U,Q> Edges;
```

```
 4    set<T,V> Vertices;
 5    queue<list<U> > Path;
 6    void noPath(void);
 7    int LenthOfPath;
 8 public:
 9    graph(void);
10    graph(char *FileOfVertices, char *FileOfEdges);
11    graph(set<T,V> SetOfVertices, set<U,Q> SetOfEdges);
12    virtual int adjacent(T &X, T &Y);
13    virtual int findPath(T Predecessor, T Successor);
14    virtual int inDegree(T X);
15    virtual int outDegree(T X);
16    set<U,Q> edges(void);
17    int edges(U X);
18    int vertices(V X);
19    set<T,V> vertices(void);
20    void reset(char *FileOfVertices, char *FileOfEdges);
21    void reset(set<T,V> SetOfVertices,set<U,Q> SetOfEdges);
22    int length(void);
23    U edge(void);
24    void displayPath(ostream &Destiny);
25 };
26
```

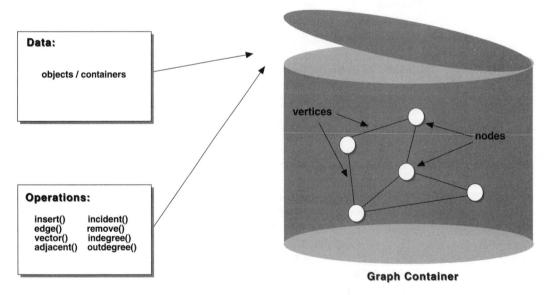

**Figure 8.1**   A logical representation of an object-oriented graph container.

Table 8.3  A list of the core services that a graph collection will provide and a brief description of each.

| Core Graph Services | Description |
| --- | --- |
| insert | * Inserts nodes or edges to the graph. |
| remove | * removes nodes or edges from the graph. |
| vertex | * Adds a node to the graph. |
| edge | * Adds an edge to the graph; each arc is specified by a pair of nodes or vertices. |
| incident | * A node is incident to an arc if the node is one of the endnodes to the arc; two arcs are incident to a node if the node is an endnode to both arcs. |
| adjacent | * A node is adjacent to another node if there is an arc between them; two arcs are adjacent to each other if there is a node between them. |
| indegree | * The number of edges in which a node serves as the head or the predecessor vertex. |
| outdegree | * The number of edges in which a node serves as the tail or successor vertex. |

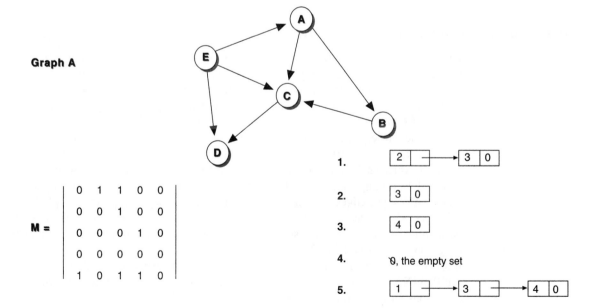

Graph A

$$M = \begin{vmatrix} 0 & 1 & 1 & 0 & 0 \\ 0 & 0 & 1 & 0 & 0 \\ 0 & 0 & 0 & 1 & 0 \\ 0 & 0 & 0 & 0 & 0 \\ 1 & 0 & 1 & 1 & 0 \end{vmatrix}$$

A. Adjacency Matrix for Graph A

B. Adjacency List for Graph A

Figure 8.2  Some common implementations of a graph structure in traditional programming languages.

This graph class provides just enough functionality to demonstrate how a graph collection can be constructed. Every collection or container object will encapsulate some block of memory. The block of memory is where the objects that will be inserted are stored. The block of memory will be either internal (residing in RAM) or external (residing on disk). How the block of memory is accessed is called the *implementation*. How the class is accessed is called the logical view. However, the polylithic or superstructure complicates this distinction somewhat. Since a superstructure is a class that contains at least one collection or container, the programmer has more than one layer of abstraction between the class interface of the superstructure and the memory blocks that implement the superstructure. For instance, the simple graph declaration in Listing 8.1 shows a graph collection that contains two STL set collections, and an STL queue. The sets and the queue are also high-level structures and are implemented by other structures.

Although the sets and the queue are encapsulated within the graph class, the programmer depends on the logical view of the sets and the queue to properly use the graph class. This demonstrates that for superstructures there are usually *multiple layers* of logical views that are available before access to the implementation layer is available. Figure 8.3 shows the multiple layers of the graph collection class. The list of services that the user of the graph collection class sees is implemented by set collections. The set collections are implemented by red black trees. The red black trees directly access the internal or virtual memory blocks where the objects that are placed into the graph will be stored. The layers of abstraction between the computer memory and the list of services that the class provides are increased with collections and containers that contain other collections and containers.

## The Graph Collection Member Functions

The graph class provides three constructors. The first constructor builds a graph that has two empty sets. The second constructor gets the sets of vertices and edges from two files. The third constructor gets the set of edges and vertices from two STL sets. The **adjacent(X,Y)** member function returns 1 if $X$ and $Y$ are adjacent and 0 otherwise. The **indegree(X)** member function returns the number of edges that has $X$ as a *predecessor* vertex. The **outdegree(X)** member function returns the number of edges that has $X$ as a *successor* vertex. The **vertices(X)** member function is used to add a node to the graph. Since the **vertices(X)** member function is implemented using a set insert operation, there will be no duplicate nodes. The **vertices()** member function returns a copy of the set of vertices. The **edges(X)** member function is used to add an edge to the graph. Since the **edges(X)** member function is implemented using a set insertion operation, there will be no duplicate edges. The **edges()** member function returns a copy of the set of edges in the graph. The **findPath(X,Y)** member function attempts to find a *walk* between $X$ and $Y$. If a walk is found, the edges of the walk are stored in the queue called **Path**. The **findPath(X,Y)** returns a 1 if a path is found and a 0 otherwise. Listing 8.2 shows the definitions for the graph collection class.

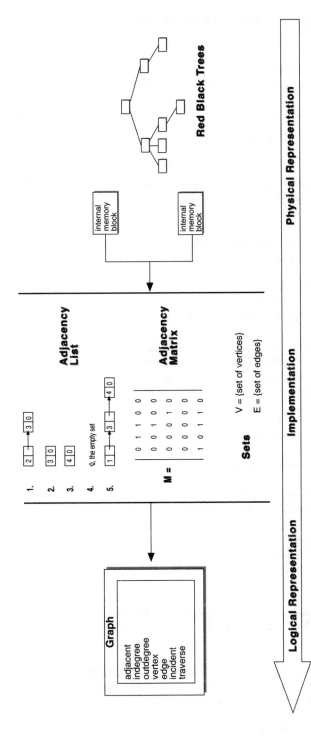

**Figure 8.3** The layers of abstraction showing the physical representation, implementation, and logical representation of an object-oriented set.

**Listing 8.2**

```
1 // Listing 8.2
2 // Definitions for the graph collection class
3
4 template <class T, class V, class U, class Q> graph <T,V,U,Q>::graph(void)
5 {
6    LengthOfPath = 0;
7 }
8
9 template <class T, class V, class U, class Q> graph<T,V,U,Q>::graph(char *FileOf
  Vertices, char *FileOfEdges)
10 {
11
12    ifstream In(FileOfEdges);
13    T Vertex;
14    T Predecessor;
15    T Successor;
16    U TempFrame;
17    while(!In.eof() && In.good())
18    {
19      In >> Predecessor >> Successor;
20      TempFrame.origin(Predecessor);
21      TempFrame.destination(Successor);
22      Edges.insert(TempFrame);
23    }
24    In.close();
25    In.open(FileOfVertices);
26
27    while(!In.eof() && In.good())
28    {
29      In >> Vertex;
30      Vertices.insert(Vertex);
31    }
32    In.close();
33    LengthOfPath = 0;
34
35 }
36
37 template <class T, class V, class U,class Q>
38 graph<T,V,U,Q>::graph(set<T,V> SetOfVertices, set<U,Q> SetOfEdges)
39 {
40
41    set<T,V>::iterator S = SetOfVertices.begin();
42    set<U,Q>::iterator R = SetOfEdges.begin();
43    while(S != SetOfVertices.end())
44    {
45    Vertices.insert(*S);
46    S++;
47    }
```

```
48    while (R != SetOfEdges.end())
49    {
50    Edges.insert(*R);
51    R++;
52    }
53    LengthOfPath = 0;
54 }
55
56
57 template <class T, class V, class U, class Q> int graph<T,V,U,Q>::length(void)
58 {
59    return(Path.size());
60 }
61
62 template <class T, class V, class U,class Q>
63 graph<T,V,U,Q>::inDegree(T X)
64 {
65
66    U Edge;
67    int Count = 0;
68    set<U,Q>::iterator R = Edges.begin();
69    while(R != Edges.end())
70    {
71    Edge = *R;
72    if(Edge.origin() == X){
73       Count++;
74    }
75    R++;
76    }
77    return(Count);
78 }
79
80 template <class T, class V, class U,class Q>
81 graph<T,V,U,Q>::outDegree(T X)
82 {
83    U Edge;
84    int Count = 0;
85    set<U,Q>::iterator R = Edges.begin();
86    while(R != Edges.end())
87    {
88    Edge = *R;
89    if(Edge.destination() == X){
90       Count++;
91    }
92    R++;
93    }
94    return(Count);
95 }
96
```

```
 97 template <class T, class V, class U,class Q> set<U,Q> graph<T,V,U,Q>::
    edges(void)
 98 {
 99   return(Edges);
100 }
101
102 template <class T, class V, class U,class Q> int graph<T,V,U,Q>::edges(U X)
103 {
104   pair<set<U,Q>::iterator,int> Result;
105   Result = Edges.insert(X);
106   return(Result.second);
107 }
108
109
110 template <class T, class V, class U,class Q> set<T,V> graph<T,V,U,Q>::
    vertices(void)
111 {
112   return(Vertices);
113 }
114
115 template <class T, class V, class U,class Q> int graph<T,V,U,Q>::vertices(T X)
116 {
117   pair<set<T,V>::iterator,int> Result;
118   Result = Vertices.insert(X);
119   return(Result.second);
120 }
121
122
123
124 template<class T, class V, class U,class Q> U graph<T,V,U,Q>::edge(void)
125 {
126   U Temp;
127   Temp = Path.front();
128   Path.pop();
129   return(Temp);
130
131 }
132
133
134 template<class T, class V, class U, class Q>
135 void graph<T,V,U,Q>::reset(set<T,V> SetOfVertices,set<U,Q> SetOfEdges)
136 {
137   set<T,V>::iterator S = SetOfVertices.begin();
138   set<U,Q>::iterator R = SetOfEdges.begin();
139   while(S != SetOfVertices.end())
140   {
141   Vertices.insert(*S);
142   S++;
143   }
144   while (R != SetOfEdges.end())
```

```
145    {
146    Edges.insert(*R);
147    R++;
148    }
149
150 }
151
152 template<class T, class V, class U, class Q>
153 void graph<T,V,U,Q>::reset(char *FileOfVertices, char *FileOfEdges)
154 {
155
156    ifstream In(FileOfEdges);
157    T Vertex;
158    U TempFrame;
159    T Successor;
160    T Predecessor;
161    Edges.erase(Edges.begin(),Edges.end());
162    Vertices.erase(Vertices.begin(), Vertices.end());
163    while(!In.eof() && In.good())
164    {
165       In >> Predecessor >> Successor;
166       TempFrame.origin(Predecessor);
167       TempFrame.destination(Successor);
168       Edges.insert(TempFrame);
169    }
170    In.close();
171    In.open(FileOfVertices);
172    while(!In.eof() && In.good())
173    {
174       In >> Vertex;
175       Vertices.insert(Vertex);
176    }
177    In.close();
178 }
179
180
181 template<class T, class V, class U, class Q> void graph<T,V,U,Q>::noPath(void)
182 {
183    Path.pop();
184    while(!Path.empty())
185    {
186       Edges.insert(Path.front());
187       Path.pop();
188
189    }
190 }
191
192
193 template<class T, class V, class U, class Q> int graph<T,V,U,Q>::findPath(T
    Predecessor, T Successor)
```

```
194 {
195   int DirectMatch = 0;
196   int VertexFound = 1;
197   set<U,Q>::iterator E = Edges.begin();
198   set<U,Q>::iterator F = Edges.begin();
199   U TempVertex;
200   T Vertex1 = Predecessor;
201   int Found = 0;
202   int MoreStartNodes = 1;
203   DirectMatch = 0;
204   DirectMatch = adjacent(Predecessor,Successor);
205   TempVertex.origin(Predecessor);
206   TempVertex.destination(Successor);
207   while((F != Edges.end()) &&(DirectMatch == 0) && (MoreStartNodes))
208   {
209   DirectMatch = 0;
210   while((F != Edges.end()) && (DirectMatch == 0) &&(MoreStartNodes))
211   {
212       E = F;
213       Found = 0;
214       VertexFound = 0;
215       while((E != Edges.end()) && (Found == 0))
216       {
217
218         TempVertex = *E;
219         if(Vertex1 == TempVertex.origin()){
220         Path.push(TempVertex);
221         Vertex1 = TempVertex.destination();
222         Found = 1;
223         VertexFound = 1;
224       }
225     E++;
226   }
227   F++;
228   if(VertexFound){
229     DirectMatch = adjacent(Vertex1,Successor);
230   }
231   else{
232       noPath();
233       if(Vertex1 == Predecessor){
234         MoreStartNodes = 0;
235       }
236       Vertex1 = Predecessor;
237     }
238   }
239
240   }
241
242   if(DirectMatch){
243 TempVertex.origin(Vertex1);
```

```
244    TempVertex.destination(Successor);
245    Path.push(TempVertex);
246    return(1);
247       }
248      else{
249    return(0);
250    }
251
252 }
253
254 template<class T, class V, class U, class Q>
255 int graph<T,V,U,Q>::adjacent(T &X, T &Y)
256 {
257
258    U TempEdge;
259    int Adjacent = 0;
260    set<U,Q>::iterator E = Edges.begin();
261    while((E != Edges.end()) && (Adjacent == 0))
262    {
263    TempEdge = *E;
264    if((X == TempEdge.origin()) && (Y == TempEdge.destination())){
265       Adjacent = 1;
266    }
267    E++;
268    }
269    return(Adjacent);
270 }
271
272 template <class T, class V, class U, class Q>
273 void graph<T,V,U,Q>::displayPath(ostream &Destiny)
274 {
275
276    U TempVertex;
277    while(!Path.empty())
278    {
279
280    TempVertex = Path.front();
281    Destiny << TempVertex << endl;
282    Path.pop();
283
284    }
285 }
```

The graph collection defines four member functions as virtual:

```
virtual int adjacent(T &X, T &Y);
virtual int findPath(T Predecessor, T Successor);
virtual int inDegree(T X);
virtual int outDegree(T X);
```

These member functions are defined as virtual so that the programmer can override these member functions with more desirable algorithms. This graph class makes certain assumptions about the structure of the edges that are used. Specifically, the edges are assumed to have at least two data members, one representing each node in an edge. Also the edges are assumed to have an **origin()** and a **destination()** member function. These member functions will return the predecessor and successor vertices respectively. The **adjacent()** member function can be overridden and therefore the user can use whatever representation for edges may be appropriate. The **pair<X,Y>** class in the STL is a good candidate for this purpose. Since the **edges()** and **vertices()** member functions return their respective sets, the programmer can find a particular vertex or edge by using the STL set iterators. The set iterators can be used to visit each vertex in the set of vertices and each edge in the set of edges. This is possible because of the construction of the graph collection class. Figure 8.4 shows the class relationship diagram for the graph collection class. Notice that the sets have a contained-in relationship as opposed to an inheritance relationship. The contained-in relationship allows the graph collection to redefine and combine set member functions for new purposes. This is similar to what an interface class does.

## Searching the Graph Collection

One of the most powerful member functions or generic algorithms that a graph collection can have is **findPath(X,Y)**, where X, and Y are two vertices in a graph. The

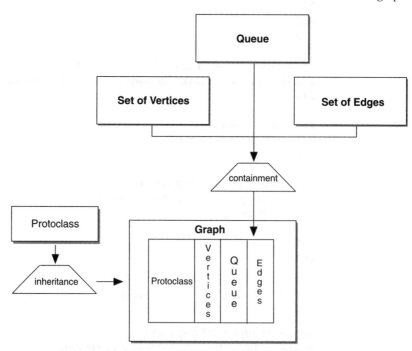

**Figure 8.4**  A class relationship diagram for the graph collection class. It contains a set of edges, a set of vertices, and a queue.

**findPath(X,Y)** member function can be used to find either a *walk*, a *trail*, or a *circuit* between vertices in a graph. Since graphs provide only relational access methods, the **findPath(X,Y)** member function is used to traverse the graph based on relationships between vertices. Finding a path in a relation may be as simple as finding two things that are associated, for instance, a telephone number and a location. The **findPath(X,Y)** algorithm can also be used to find complex indirect relationships, like a path from a piece of DNA to a particular class of people. Because graphs are so flexible and free form, there is no one right way to approach finding paths within graphs. In fact, pathfinding continues to be one of the hottest areas of research in computer science. Since the **findPath(X,Y)** member function is virtual in our graph collection, the user can override this member function and supply any technique that is desired. The **findPath(X,Y)** member function for this graph collection uses a simple walk traversal to determine if there is a path from *X* to *Y*. The walk uses a type of search classified as *depth first*. Sometimes the goal of graph traversal is total object visitation. In other words it may be desirable to visit each object in the graph. At other times it may be necessary only to find a particular object or objects in a graph. Traversal is still required in this case, but not necessarily total traversal. Finally, it may be desirable to find a path or paths from one object to another. This case also requires traversal. Finding a path from one object to another may involve total object visitation. Most iteration involving graphs can be classified as searches because to iterate through a graph we must find adjacency and incidence of vertices.

In graph processing, *traversals* imply the search for vertices that are adjacent and edges that are incident. There are two commonly used techniques to search or traverse a graph. The first is called *depth-first* search. The second is called *breadth-first* search. These two types of searches can be further divided into depth-first search of edges and depth-first search of vertices, and breadth-first search of edges and breadth-first search of vertices. If the traversal only seeks to visit each *vertex once* it is referred to as a *Hamiltonian* path or trail. If the traversal only seeks to visit each *edge once* it is referred to as a *Eulerian* path or trail. There are depth- and breadth-first Hamiltonian trails, and there are depth- and breadth-first Eulerian trails. The paths that may visit a vertex or edge more than once are called walks.

## CONNECTED AND DISCONNECTED GRAPHS

The type of search used is dictated by what the graph is used for. If the graph is connected and *X* and *Y* are vertices in the graph, then we know that there is a path from *X* to *Y*. It is simply a matter of finding a walk or trail between *X* and *Y*. However, if the graph is not connected we do not know whether there is a path from *X* to *Y*. In this case much processing could be expended only to find that there is no relationship or connection between *X* and *Y*. When a graph is *connected,* there is a path between any two vertices in the graph. A connected graph is considered to be one component. The paths in a connected graph may be the result of adjacent vertices or of walks or trails between two vertices that are indirectly connected. When a graph is not connected it consists of two or more components, and it is possible to find two vertices in that graph that cannot be connected. Figure 8.5 shows a connected graph and a graph that is not connected.

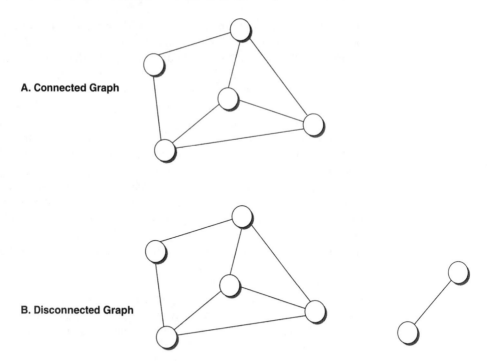

**A. Connected Graph**

**B. Disconnected Graph**

**Figure 8.5**   A connected graph and a graph that is not connected.

## BREADTH-FIRST OBJECT VISITATION

There are many ways to achieve a breadth-first traversal of a graph. However, most breadth-first techniques involve a common core of processing. Let's say that $V$ is any vertex in a graph $G$. We could begin a breadth-first search in $G$ by starting with $V$ and searching all the vertices that are adjacent to $V$. Once we have searched all the vertices that are adjacent to $V$, we would pick some other vertex, let's say $X$, that had not yet been visited. We would then visit all the vertices that are adjacent to $X$ that had not previously been visited. Once we had visited all the vertices adjacent to $X$, we would pick another vertex, let's call it $Y$, that had not been visited, and the traversal would proceed until every vertex in the graph had been visited or until the object that was being sought had been found. Most breadth-first traversal techniques use some variation on this scheme.

## DEPTH-FIRST OBJECT VISITATION

There are as many ways to do a depth-first traversal of a graph as there are ways to do a breadth-first traversal. Just as the breadth-first traversals have a common core of processing, most depth-first traversals have a common underlining principle. Lets say that $V$ is any vertex in a graph $G$. We could do a depth-first traversal of $G$ by starting with $V$ and finding a vertex $X$ that is adjacent with $V$. We would then find a vertex $Y$ that is adjacent with $X$. We would then find a vertex $Z$ that is adjacent with $Y$. We would continue this process until we had a vertex $M$ that did not have any adjacent vertex. We would then pick another vertex Q that had not been visited. We would then find a vertex that is adjacent to Q; let's call it R. We would then find a vertex adjacent to R; let's call it S. We would continue this process until we had visited every vertex in the graph. Whereas the breadth-first traversal visits all the vertices that are adjacent to the vertex in question, the depth-first search builds a path, sometimes called a *spanning tree*. Most depth-first search techniques use some variation on path-building traversal.

The **findPath(X,Y)** member function of our graph collection class from Listing 8.2 uses a variation of the depth-first search. The **findPath(X,Y)** member function starts with X and finds a vertex, call it M, that is adjacent to X. It then checks to see if M is equal to Y; if not, the algorithm tries to find a vertex adjacent to M; call it N. It then checks to see if N is equal to Y. The processing continues in this fashion looking for a vertex equal to Y, in the process building a path from X to Y. Our **findPath(X,Y)** member function may visit a vertex more than once. Some depth-first traversal methods only allow a vertex to be visited once.

### Visit by Hamilton or Visit by Euler

Traversals are often classified by how they traverse through vertices or edges, and whether they are allowed to visit an edge or a vertex more than once. Let G be a graph. A path that passes through each *vertex* in G exactly once is called a *Hamiltonian path*. A simple circuit that passes through each vertex of G exactly once is called a *Hamiltonian circuit*. Some breadth-first and depth-first traversals form Hamiltonian paths. A trail that covers each *edge* of the graph G exactly once is called a *Euler trail*. A Euler trail that ends at its starting vertex is called a *Euler circuit*, whereas a Hamiltonian visitation moves from vertex to vertex. A Eulerian visitation moves from edge to edge. The graph collection class supports both Hamiltonian and Eulerian visitation.

This chapter provides only an introductory discussion of the graph structure and the object-oriented graph. The application sidebar that follows presents a simple graph collection class, and an example application of how an object-oriented graph using STL collections and containers can be used to represent a problem, and the solution to the problem.

## APPLICATION

## The Path Finder          Graphs and Sets

## PROBLEM SOLVING

Problem solving can be described as the movement from some initial state to some desired final state, by applying certain information, technique, skills, heuristics, rules, operators, operations, or processes to the initial state. Making a touchdown in the game of football is a good example of problem solving. The problem for the team on offense is how to move the ball past the defensive team into the end zone of the defensive team. The offense starts out with the ball at a certain position on the football field. Ideally, the offense moves the ball from that position into the defense's end zone. Once the ball is in the end zone a touchdown is declared and the problem is solved. The position where the offense initially receives the ball is the initial state. Making a touchdown is the final state or goal state. The process of passing, running, and kicking to advance the ball toward the defense's end zone are the operations that transform the initial state to the final state. Virtually any problem-solving process involves these three components: initial state, final state, and operators. Knowing this about problem solving we can devise computer programs that can solve problems.

To design a computer program that solves problems we need three components. The first component is a data structure where we can store the initial state, the final state, and other relevant information that might be encountered. This data structure is normally a database, knowledge base, or some other group of collections and containers. The second component we need is a set of operators that can transform or advance the initial state toward the final state. This set of operators may be algorithms, functions, rules, or maps. The third component that we need is a control strategy. The control strategy determines how, when, and where we should apply the operators to the initial state. In this application sidebar we use the STL's set and queue structure to create a graph collection. The graph collection is used to model the *problem context*. The problem context contains the initial state, the goal state, and any other information that may be encountered in trying to move from the initial state to the goal state. We use the graph collection to store the problem context. Since the solution to any problem often involves many steps, we use a queue structure to store intermediate results of our problem-solving process. We also use a queue structure to store the final sequence of steps that were used in solving the problem. We use a version of depth-first search as our control strategy. Using the depth-first search and the set *Edges* represented by an STL set collection we are able to create a path from our initial state to our goal state. Hence a computer program uses a problem-solving technique.

## USING GRAPH OBJECTS TO SOLVE PROBLEMS

The edges in a graph are used to represent either connections or relationships between objects. These relationships can represent simple associations or complex connections that are determined by intricate rules, conditions, or operations. When edges are used to represent relationship or connections, and vertices are used to represent objects, a graph collection can be used to simulate transactions in virtually any scenario or situation. This suggests that graph collections can be used to solve real-world problems. Most real-world problems can be described as a set of objects (vertices) and a set of relationships between those objects (edges). In general, problem solving can be described as trying to find a path from some initial state to some required state (see Kowalski 1979, 75–93). The challenges, uncertainty, constraints, and conflicts of how to move from the initial state to the desired final state are what makes a problem a problem.

The graph collection can be used to represent the items from the problem. Each item is represented by a vertex. Each item in the problem is related in some way. Problem solving will involve moving from the objects and their initial relationships (initial state) to other objects and their relationships (final state). When two objects *a*, *b* are in an edge, a path exists between those objects. The path between *a* and *b* may be a transformation of *a* to *b* by some operation, or *a* may be related to *b* by some relational operation. The path may represent that *b* is necessary for *a* and so on. Whatever the case, the edges represent the relationships between the objects in the problem. A traversal from some object or objects (the initial state) to some other object or objects (final state) represents a solution to the problem. For a detailed introduction to graphs and problem solving, see the *The Handbook of Artificial Intelligence*, edited by Avron Barr and Edward A. Feigenbaum and *Logic for Problem Solving* by Robert Kowalski.

In this application, we need to electronically transfer a file from one location to another. Sometimes we have a direct line between the locations. Sometimes we don't. Our task is to identify a route for transferring files between locations, even when we don't have a direct line. We have eight locations represented by **SiteA**, **SiteB**, **SiteC**, through **SiteH**. Each site has a list of computers that they can receive information from, and a list of computers that they can send information to. Given any two of our eight sites, we want to be able to determine what route can be taken (if any) to electronically transfer a file between them. Our graph collection is used to demonstrate how graphs can be used to solve such a problem.

## USER-DEFINED OBJECTS

This graph example uses three user-defined objects: **transmission_frame**, **vertex**, and **graph**. The **transmission_frame** object is a simple model of a data packet. A data packet is a unit of data that is transferrable between computers on a network or across telephone lines. Our data packet only has an origin and destination. The **vertex** class is used to model a Cartesian coordinate position on a graph. The **vertex** class has an *x* position, *y* position, a label, and a **bitmap-id**. If the graph collection contains a solution to our routing problem it will display the solution using lines and vertex objects. The graph object is a user-defined collection. The graph collection is a superstructure because it consists of three metastructures. The graph collection consists of two sets and one queue (see Figure 8.4). The metastructures in the graph collection class are implemented by STL sets and an STL queue.

## SOURCE EXPLANATIONS

The disk accompanying this book contains an OS/2 Presentation Manager, Text Mode, and Windows version of the graph application. The Text Mode version can be used in the UNIX or VMS environments. We show the OS2 version in this application sidebar. The application requires six files: *vertex.h*, *frame.h*, *stlgraph.cpp*, *gdld1os2.cpp*, *dgrafos2.cpp*, and *contos2.rc*.

## OS2GRAPH.MAK

```
#===============================================
#
#
#   OS2GRAPH.MAK - Makefile for project
#
#
#===============================================

.AUTODEPEND

#===============================================
#         Translator Definitions
#===============================================

CC = bcc +OS2GRAPH.CFG
TASM = tasm.exe
TLIB = tlib.exe
TLINK = tlink
RC = brcc.exe
RB = rc.exe
LIBPATH = C:\BCOS2\LIB
INCLUDEPATH = C:\BCOS2\INCLUDE;c:\stl

#===============================================
#         Implicit Rules
#===============================================

.c.obj:
$(CC) −c {$< }

.cpp.obj:
$(CC) −c {$< }

.asm.obj:
$(TASM) −Mx $*.asm,$*.obj

.rc.res:
$(RC) −r $*.rc

#===============================================
#         List Macros
#===============================================

LINK_EXCLUDE = \
contos2.res
```

```
LINK_INCLUDE = \
gmainosb.obj \
dgrafos2.obj \
vertex.obj \
frame.obj \
gdlg1os2.obj


#=========================================
#        Explicit Rules
#=========================================

os2graph.exe: os2graph.cfg $(LINK_INCLUDE) $(LINK_EXCLUDE)
$(TLINK) /v /x /Toe /aa /L$(LIBPATH) @&&|
C:\BCOS2\LIB\CO2.OBJ+
gmainosb.obj+
dgrafos2.obj+
vertex.obj+
frame.obj+
gdlg1os2.obj
os2graph
        # no map file
C:\BCOS2\LIB\C2.LIB+
C:\BCOS2\LIB\OS2.LIB

|
rc.exe CONTOS2.res os2graph.exe


#=========================================
#        Individual File Dependencies
#=========================================

CONTOS2.res: os2graph.cfg CONTOS2.RC
        brcc.exe −R −I$(INCLUDEPATH) −FO CONTOS2.res CONTOS2.RC

GMAINOSB.obj: os2graph.cfg GMAINOSB.CPP

DGRAFOS2.obj: os2graph.cfg DGRAFOS2.CPP

VERTEX.obj: os2graph.cfg VERTEX.CPP

FRAME.obj: os2graph.cfg FRAME.CPP

GDLG1OS2.obj: os2graph.cfg GDLG10S2.CPP


#=========================================
#        Compiler Configuration File
#=========================================

os2graph.cfg: os2graph.mak
  copy &&|
```

```
-R
-D__MINMAX_DEFINED
-L$(LIBPATH)
-I$(INCLUDEPATH)
-vi-
-v
-w-inl
|os2graph.cfg
```

## Header Files

// **frame.h**

```
 1 #include <iostream.h>
 2 #include <cstring.h>
 3
 4
 5 class transmission_frame{
 6 protected:
 7    string Origin;
 8    string Destination;
 9
10 public:
11    transmission_frame(void);
12    transmission_frame(const transmission_frame &X);
13    transmission_frame &operator=(const transmission_frame &X);
14    int operator<(const transmission_frame &X) const;
15    int operator>(const transmission_frame &X) const;
16    int operator!=(const transmission_frame &X) const;
17    int operator==(const transmission_frame &X) const;
18    int operator>=(const transmission_frame &X) const;
19    int operator<=(const transmission_frame &X) const;
20    int operator()(const transmission_frame &X, const transmission_frame &Y)
       const;
21    string origin(void);
22    string destination(void);
23    void origin(string X);
24    void destination(string X);
25    friend ostream &operator<<(ostream &Out,transmission_frame &X);
26
27
28 };
29
```

// **vertex.h**

```
 1 #include <cstring.h>
 2
 3 class vertex{
 4 protected:
 5    string Name;
```

```
 6    int XLoc;
 7    int YLoc;
 8    int BitmapId;
 9 public:
10    vertex(void);
11    vertex(const vertex &X);
12    vertex &operator=(const vertex &X);
13    int operator>(const vertex &X) const;
14    int operator<(const vertex &X) const;
15    int operator>=(const vertex &X) const;
16    int operator<=(const vertex &X) const;
17    int operator==(const vertex &X) const;
18    int operator!=(const vertex &X) const;
19    string name(void);
20    void name(string &X);
21    int xLocation(void);
22    int yLocation(void);
23    void xLocation(int XX);
24    void yLocation(int YY);
25    void bitmap(int BMap);
26    int bitmap(void);
27 };
28
// gdlg1os2.h

 1 MRESULT EXPENTRY graphDialog(HWND WindowHandle,
 2                     ULONG Msg,
 3                     MPARAM MessParm1,
 4                     MPARAM MessParm2);
```

## Source Definitions

```
// frame.cpp

 1 #include "frame.h"
 2
 3
 4 transmission_frame::transmission_frame(void)
 5 {
 6    Origin = "
 7    Destination = ";
 8
 9
10 }
11
12
13 transmission_frame::transmission_frame(const transmission_frame &X)
14 {
15    Origin = X.Origin;
16    Destination = X.Destination;
```

```
17
18 }
19
20
21
22  transmission_frame  &transmission_frame::operator=(const  transmission
    _frame & X)
23
24  Origin = X.Origin;
25  Destination = X.Destination;
26  return(*this)
27
28 }
29
30
31 int transmission_frame::operator<(const transmission_frame & X) const
32 {
33   if(Orgin < X.Origin){
34     return(1);
35   }
36   else{
37       return(0);
38   }
39 }
40
41  int  transmission_frame::operator()(const  transmission_frame  &X,  const
    transmission_frame &Y) const
42 {
43 string YTemp;
44 string XTemp;
45 YTemp = Y.Origin + Y.Destination;
46 XTemp = X.Origin + X.Destination;
47   if(XTemp < YTemp){
48     return(1);
49   }
50   else{
51   return(0);
52   }
53 }
54
55
56 int transmission_frame::operator>(const transmission_frame &X) const
57 {
58
59   if(Origin > X.Origin){
60     return(1);
61   }
62   else{
63   return(0);
```

```
64    }
65 }
66 int transmission_frame::operator!=(const transmission_frame &X) const
67 {
68    if(Origin != X.Origin){
69       return(1);
70    }
71    else{
72    return(0);
73    }}
74
75
76 int transmission_frame::operator==(const transmission_frame &X) const
77 {
78
79    if((Origin == X.Origin) && (Destination == X.Destination)){
80       return(1);
81    }
82    else{
83    return(0);
84    }
85
86 }
87
88
89 int transmission_frame::operator>=(const transmission_frame &X) const
90 {
91
92    if(Origin >= X.Origin){
93       return(1);
94    }
95    else{
96    return(0);
97    }
98 }
99
100
101 int transmission_frame::operator<=(const transmission_frame &X) const
102 {
103    if(Origin <= X.Origin){
104       return(1);
105    }
106    else{
107    return(0);
108    }
109
110
111 }
112
113
```

```
114 string transmission_frame::origin(void)
115 {
116
117    return(Origin);
118
119 }
120
121 string transmission_frame::destination(void)
122 {
123
124      return(Destination);
125
126 }
127
128 void transmission_frame::origin(string X)
129 {
130      Origin = X;
131
132 }
133
134
135 void transmission_frame::destination(string X)
136 {
137
138      Destination = X;
139 }
140
141
142
143
144
145 ostream &operator<<(ostream &Out,transmission_frame &X)
146 {
147
148    Out << X.Origin << "->" << X.Destination;
149    return(Out);
150 }
151
152
153
```

// **vertex.cpp**

```
1 #include "vertex.h"
2
3 vertex::vertex(void)
4 {
5    XLoc = 0;
6    YLoc = 0;
7    Name = " ";
8    BitmapId = 0;
```

```
 9
10 }
11
12 vertex::vertex(const vertex &X)
13 {
14   XLoc = X.XLoc;
15   YLoc = X.YLoc;
16   Name = X.Name;
17   BitmapId = X.BitmapId;
18
19 }
20
21
22 string vertex::name(void)
23 {
24   return(Name);
25 }
26
27
28 void vertex::name(string &X)
29 {
30   Name = X;
31 }
32
33 int vertex::bitmap(void)
34 {
35   return(BitmapId);
36 }
37
38 void vertex::bitmap(int BMap)
39 {
40   BitmapId = BMap;
41 }
42
43
44 vertex &vertex::operator=(const vertex &X)
45 {
46   XLoc = X.XLoc;
47   YLoc = X.YLoc;
48   Name = X.Name;
49   BitmapId = X.BitmapId;
50   return(*this);
51
52 }
53
54
55
56 int vertex::operator>(const vertex &X) const
57 {
58   if(Name > X.Name){
```

```
59      return(1);
60    }
61    else{
62    return(0);
63    }
64
65 }
66
67 int vertex::operator<(const vertex &X) const
68 {
69    if(Name < X.Name){
70        return(1);
71    }
72    else{
73    return(0);
74    }
75
76
77 }
78
79
80 int vertex::operator>=(const vertex &X) const
81 {
82
83    if(Name >= X.Name){
84        return(1);
85    }
86    else{
87    return(0);
88    }
89
90 }
91
92
93 int vertex::operator<=(const vertex &X) const
94 {
95    if(Name <= X.Name){
96        return(1);
97    }
98    else{
99    return(0);
100    }
101
102 }
103
104
105 int vertex::operator==(const vertex &X) const
106 {
107    if(Name == X.Name){
108        return(1);
```

```
109    }
110    else{
111    return(0);
112    }
113
114
115 }
116
117 int vertex::operator!=(const vertex &X) const
118 {
119
120    if(Name != X.Name){
121       return(1);
122    }
123    else{
124    return(0);
125    }
126
127 }
128
129
130 int vertex::xLocation(void)
131 {
132
133       return(XLoc);
134 }
135
136 int vertex::yLocation(void)
137 {
138
139    return(YLoc);
140
141 }
142
143 void vertex::xLocation(int XX)
144 {
145    XLoc = XX;
146 }
147
148 void vertex::yLocation(int YY)
149 {
150    YLoc= YY;
151 }
152
```

// **gdlg1os2.cpp**

```
1 #define INCL_WIN
2 #define INCL_GPI
3 #include <os2.h>
4 #include <cstring.h>
```

```
 5 #include <vector.h>
 6 #include "graphres.h"
 7 #include "vertex.h"
 8 #include "gdlg1os2.h"
 9
10
11
12 extern vector<vertex> Nodes;
13 extern int Start;
14 extern int Stop;
15
16
17
18
19 MRESULT EXPENTRY graphDialog(HWND WindowHandle,
20      ULONG Msg,
21      MPARAM MessParm1,
22      MPARAM MessParm2)
23 {
24   HWND List1;
25   HWND List2;
26   int N = 0;
27   int NumElements = 0;
28   vertex Vertex;
29   string Name;
30
31   switch(Msg){
32   case WM_INITDLG:
33   List1 = WinWindowFromID(WindowHandle,ListBox1Ctl);
34   List2 = WinWindowFromID(WindowHandle,ListBox2Ctl);
35   NumElements = Nodes.size();
36   for(N = 0; N < NumElements;N++)
37   {
38     Vertex = Nodes[N];
39     Name = Vertex.name();
40     WinInsertLboxItem(List1,LIT_END,Name.c_str());
41     WinInsertLboxItem(List2,LIT_END,Name.c_str());
42   }
43   break;
44   case WM_COMMAND:
45   switch(SHORT1FROMMP(MessParm1))
46   {
47     case GraphDialogOkCtl:
48       Start = (short) WinSendDlgItemMsg(WindowHandle,ListBox1Ctl,LM
   _QUERYSELECTION,0,0);
49       Stop = (short) WinSendDlgItemMsg(WindowHandle,ListBox2Ctl,LM
   _QUERYSELECTION,0,0);
50       break;
51     case GraphDialogCancelCtl:
52       WinDismissDlg(WindowHandle,GraphDialogCancelCtl);
```

```
53      Start = −1;
54      Stop = −1;
55      break;
56    }
57    default:
58      return(WinDefDlgProc(WindowHandle,Msg,MessParm1,MessParm2));
59    }
60    return(MRESULT) 0;
61
62 }
63
```

## // dgrafos2.cpp

```
 1 #define INCL_WIN
 2 #define INCL_GPI
 3 #include <os2.h>
 4 #include <cstring.h>
 5 #include <vector.h>
 6 #include "vertex.h"
 7 #include "stlgraph.cpp"
 8
 9
10
11
12 extern vector<vertex> Nodes;
13 extern graph<string,less<string>,transmission_frame,transmission_frame>
   NetGraph;
14
15 void displayGraph(HWND Handle);
16
17 void displayGraph(HWND Handle)
18 {
19   vertex Vertex;
20   int N = 0;
21   int Found = 0;
22   POINTL Coord;
23   int Elements;
24   HPS PSpace;
25   PSpace = WinGetPS(Handle);
26   transmission_frame Edge;
27   int Walk = NetGraph.length();
28   int First = 1;
29   Elements = Nodes.size();
30
31   while(Walk)
32   {
33     Edge = NetGraph.edge();
34     Found = 0;
35     N = 0;
36     while((N < Elements) && (!Found))
```

```
37     {
38
39   Vertex = Nodes[N];
40   if(Edge.origin() == Vertex.name()){
41     Coord.x = Vertex.xLocation();
42     Coord.y = Vertex.yLocation();
43     if(First){
44     GpiMove(PSpace,&Coord);
45     }
46     GpiLine(PSpace,&Coord);
47     Found = 1;
48     First = 0;
49   }
50   N++;
51     }
52     N = 0;
53     Found = 0;
54     while((N < Elements) && (!Found))
55     {
56
57   Vertex = Nodes[N];
58   if(Edge.destination() == Vertex.name()){
59     Coord.x = Vertex.xLocation();
60     Coord.y = Vertex.yLocation();
61     GpiLine(PSpace,&Coord);
62     Found = 1;
63   }
64   N++;
65     }
66
67
68     Walk--;
69   }
70   WinReleasePS(PSpace);
71
72 }
```

// **stlgraph.cpp**

```
 1 #define__MINMAX_DEFINED
 2 #include "frame.h"
 3 #include <fstream.h>
 4 #include <set.h>
 5 #include <stack.h>
 6 #include <list.h>
 7
 8 template<class T, class V, class U, class Q> class graph{
 9 protected:
10   set<U,Q> Edges;
11   set<T,V> Vertices;
12   queue<list<U> > Path;
```

```
13    void noPath(void);
14    int LenthOfPath;
15 public:
16    graph(void);
17    graph(char *FileOfVertices, char *FileOfEdges);
18    graph(set<T,V> SetOfVertices, set<U,Q> SetOfEdges);
19    virtual int adjacent(T &X, T &Y);
20    virtual int findPath(T Predecessor, T Successor);
21    virtual int inDegree(T X);
22    virtual int outDegree(T X);
23    set<U,Q> edges(void);
24    int edges(U X);
25    int vertices(V X);
26    set<T,V> vertices(void);
27    void reset(char *FileOfVertices, char *FileOfEdges);
28    void reset(set<T,V> SetOfVertices,set<U,Q> SetOfEdges);
29    int length(void);
30    U edge(void);
31    void displayPath(ostream &Destiny);
32 };
33
34
35 template <class T, class V, class U, class Q> graph<T,V,U,Q>::graph(void)
36 {
37    LengthOfPath = 0;
38 }
39
40 template <class T, class V, class U, class Q> graph<T,V,U,Q>::graph(char
     *FileOfVertices, char *FileOfEdges)
41 {
42
43    ifstream In(FileOfEdges);
44    T Vertex;
45    T Predecessor;
46    T Successor;
47    U TempFrame;
48    while(!In.eof() && In.good())
49    {
50      In >> Predecessor >> Successor;
51      TempFrame.origin(Predecessor);
52      TempFrame.destination(Successor);
53      Edges.insert(TempFrame);
54    }
55    In.close();
56    In.open(FileOfVertices);
57
58    while(!In.eof() && In.good())
59    {
60      In >> Vertex;
61      Vertices.insert(Vertex);
```

```
62    }
63    In.close();
64    LengthOfPath = 0;
65
66 }
67
68 template <class T, class V, class U,class Q>
69 graph<T,V,U,Q>::graph(set<T,V> SetOfVertices, set<U,Q> SetOfEdges)
70 {
71
72    set<T,V>::iterator S = SetOfVertices.begin();
73    set<U,Q>::iterator R = SetOfEdges.begin();
74    while(S != SetOfVertices.end())
75    {
76    Vertices.insert(*S);
77    S++;
78    }
79    while (R != SetOfEdges.end())
80    {
81    Edges.insert(*R);
82    R++;
83    }
84    LengthOfPath = 0;
85 }
86
87
88 template <class T, class V, class U, class Q> int graph<T,V,U,Q>::length(void)
89 {
90    return(Path.size());
91 }
92
93 template <class T, class V, class U,class Q>
94 graph<T,V,U,Q>::inDegree(T X)
95 {
96
97      U Edge;
98      int Count = 0;
99      set<U,Q>::iterator R = Edges.begin();
100     while(R != Edges.end())
101     {
102    Edge = *R;
103    if(Edge.origin() == X){
104      Count++;
105    }
106    R++;
107     }
108     return(Count);
109 }
110
111 template <class T, class V, class U,class Q>
```

```
112 graph<T,V,U,Q>::outDegree(T X)
113 {
114
115   U Edge;
116   int Count = 0;
117   set<U,Q>::iterator R = Edges.begin();
118   while(R != Edges.end())
119   {
120   Edge = *R;
121   if(Edge.destination() == X){
122     Count++;
123   }
124   R++;
125     }
126     return(Count);
127 }
128
129 template <class T, class V, class U,class Q> set<U,Q> graph<T,V,U,Q>::
    edges(void)
130 {
131   return(Edges);
132 }
133
134 template <class T, class V, class U,class Q> int graph<T,V,U,Q>::edges(U X)
135 {
136   pair<set<U,Q>::iterator,int> Result;
137   Result = Edges.insert(X);
138   return(Result.second);
139 }
140
141
142 template <class T, class V, class U,class Q> set<T,V> graph<T,V,U,Q>::
    vertices(void)
143 {
144   return(Vertices);
145 }
146
147 template <class T, class V, class U,class Q> int graph<T,V,U,Q>::vertices(T X)
148 {
149   pair<set<T,V>::iterator,int> Result;
150   Result = Vertices.insert(X);
151   return(Result.second);
152 }
153
154
155
156 template<class T,class V, class U,class Q> U graph<T,V,U,Q>::edge(void)
157 {
158   U Temp;
159   Temp = Path.front();
```

```
160    Path.pop();
161    return(Temp);
162
163 }
164
165
166 template<class T, class V, class U, class Q>
167 void graph<T,V,U,Q>::reset(set<T,V> SetOfVertices,set<U,Q> SetOfEdges)
168 {
169
170    set<T,V>::iterator S = SetOfVertices.begin();
171    set<U,Q>::iterator R = SetOfEdges.begin();
172    while(S != SetOfVertices.end())
173    {
174    Vertices.insert(*S);
175    S++;
176    }
177    while (R != SetOfEdges.end())
178    {
179 Edges.insert(*R);
180 R++;
181    }
182
183 }
184
185 template<class T, class V, class U, class Q>
186 void graph<T,V,U,Q>::reset(char *FileOfVertices, char *FileOfEdges)
187 {
188
189    ifstream In(FileOfEdges);
190    T Vertex;
191    U TempFrame;
192    T Successor;
193    T Predecessor;
194    Edges.erase(Edges.begin(),Edges.end());
195    Vertices.erase(Vertices.begin(), Vertices.end());
196    while(!In.eof() && In.good())
197    {
198      In >> Predecessor >> Successor;
199      TempFrame.origin(Predecessor);
200      TempFrame.destination(Successor);
201      Edges.insert(TempFrame);
202    }
203    In.close();
204    In.open(FileOfVertices);
205    while(!In.eof() && In.good())
206    {
207      In >> Vertex;
208      Vertices.insert(Vertex);
209    }
```

```
210   In.close();
211 }
212
213
214 template<class T, class V, class U, class Q> void graph<T,V,U,Q>::noPath(void)
215 {
216   Path.pop();
217   while(!Path.empty())
218   {
219     Edges.insert(Path.front());
220     Path.pop();
221
222   }
223 }
224
225
226 template<class T, class V, class U, class Q> int graph<T,V,U,Q>::findPath(T
      Predecessor, T Successor)
227 {
228   int DirectMatch = 0;
229   int VertexFound = 1;
230   set<U,Q>::iterator E = Edges.begin();
231   set<U,Q>::iterator F = Edges.begin();
232   U Temp Vertex;
233   T Vertex1 = Predecessor;
234   int Found = 0;
235   int MoreStartNodes = 1;
236   DirectMatch = 0;
237   DirectMatch = adjacent(Predecessor,Successor);
238   TempVertex.origin(Predecessor);
239   TempVertex.destination(Successor);
240   while((F != Edges.end()) &&(DirectMatch == 0) && (MoreStartNodes))
241   {
242   DirectMatch = 0;
243   while((F != Edges.end()) && (DirectMatch == 0) &&(MoreStartNodes))
244   {
245       E = F;
246       Found = 0;
247       VertexFound = 0;
248       while((E != Edges.end()) && (Found == 0))
249       {
250
251         TempVertex = *E;
252         if(Vertex1 == TempVertex.origin()){
253           Path.push(TempVertex);
254           Vertex1 = TempVertex.destination();
255           Found = 1;
256           VertexFound = 1;
257         }
258         E++;
```

```
259      }
260      F++;
261        if(VertexFound){
262           DirectMatch = adjacent(Vertex1,Successor);
263        }
264        else{
265            noPath();
266            if(Vertex1 == Predecessor){
267               MoreStartNodes = 0;
268            }
269            Vertex1 = Predecessor;
270         }
271      }
272
273      }
274
275      if(DirectMatch){
276   TempVertex.origin(Vertex1);
277   TempVertex.destination(Successor);
278   Path.push(TempVertex);
279   return(1);
280      }
281      else{
282   return(0);
283      }
284
285
286 }
287
288
289
290
291
292 template<class T, class V, class U, class Q>
293 int graph<T,V,U,Q>::adjacent(T &X, T &Y)
294 {
295
296   U TempEdge;
297   int Adjacent = 0;
298   set<U,Q>::iterator E = Edges.begin();
299   while((E != Edges.end()) && (Adjacent == 0))
300   {
301   TempEdge = *E;
302   if((X == TempEdge.origin()) && (Y == TempEdge.destination())){
303     Adjacent = 1;
304   }
305   E++;
306   }
307   return(Adjacent);
308 }
```

```
309
310
311 template<class T, class V, class U, class Q>
312 void graph<T,V,U,Q>::displayPath(ostream &Destiny)
313 {
314
315    U TempVertex;
316    while(!Path.empty())
317    {
318
319    TempVertex = Path.front();
320    Destiny << TempVertex << endl;
321    Path.pop();
322
323    }
324 }
```

## // gmainosb.cpp

```
 1 #define INCL_WIN
 2 #define INCL_GPI
 3 #include <os2.h>
 4 #include <stdlib.h>
 5 #include <fstream.h>
 6 #include <strstream.h>
 7 #include <vector.h>
 8 #include <algo.h>
 9 #include "stlgraph.cpp"
10 #include "vertex.h"
11 #include <cstring.h>
12 #include <string.h>
13 #include "graphres.h"
14 #include "gdlglos2.h"
15
16
17
18
19
20 vector<vertex> Nodes;
21  graph<string,less<string>,transmission_frame,transmission_frame>  Net-
    Graph("vertex.txt","edges.txt");
22
23
24
25 int Start = 0;
26 int Stop = 0;
27 void displayGraph(HWND Handle);
28 string Origin;
29 string.Destination;
30
31
```

```
32
33
34 MRESULT EXPENTRY graphMain(HWND WindowHandle,
35                    ULONG Msg,
36                    MPARAM MessParm1,
37                    MPARAM MessParm2);
38
39
40
41
42 MRESULT EXPENTRY graphMain(HWND WindowHandle,
43                    ULONG Msg,
44                    MPARAM MessParm1,
45                    MPARAM MessParm2)
46
47 {
48    HPS PSpace;
49    ifstream In("vertex.txt");
50    ostrstream ResultMsg;
51    string Name;
52    int X = 0;
53    int Y = 0;
54    int N = 0;
55    int BitMapId = 0;
56    int Elements = 0;
57    POINTL Location;
58    HBITMAP BitMapHandle;
59    char LocationName[50] = "";
60    vertex Vertex;
61    switch(Msg)
62    {
63
64    case WM_ERASEBACKGROUND:
65      return(MRESULT) TRUE;
66    case WM_CREATE:
67            while(!In.eof() && In.good())
68            {
69               In >> Name >> X >> Y >>BitMapId;
70               Vertex.name(Name);
71               Vertex.xLocation(X);
72               Vertex.yLocation(Y);
73               Vertex.bitmap(BitMapId);
74               if(!In.eof()){
75                   Nodes.push_back(Vertex);
76               }
77            }
78            sort(Nodes.begin(),Nodes.end());
79            In.close();
80            return(0);
81    case WM_PAINT:
```

```
82              N = 0;
83              Elements = Nodes.size();
84              PSpace = WinGetPS(WindowHandle);
85              Location.x = 100;
86              Location.y = 100;
87
88              if(NetGraph.length()){
89                 displayGraph(WindowHandle);
90              }
91              else{
92                 while(N < Elements)
93                   {
94                      Vertex = Nodes[N];
95                      Location.x = Vertex.xLocation();
96                      Location.y = Vertex.yLocation();
97                      Name = Vertex.name();
98                      strcpy(LocationName,Name.c_str());
99
GpiCharStringAt(PSpace,&Location,strlen(LocationName),LocationName);
100             BitMapHandle = GpiLoadBitmap(PSpace,0,Vertex.bitmap(),
    32,32);
101
WinDrawBitmap(PSpace,BitMapHandle,NULL,&Location,0L,0L,DBM_NORMAL);
102                GpiDeleteBitmap(BitMapHandle);
103                N++;
104              }
105           }
106      WinReleasePS(PSpace);
107      break;
108
109   case WM_COMMAND:
110     switch(SHORT1FROMMP(MessParm1))
111     {
112       case GraphCtl:
113             WinDlgBox(HWND_DESKTOP,WindowHandle,graphDialog,0,
    DLG1,0);
114             Vertex = Nodes[Start];
115             Origin = Vertex.name();
116             Vertex = Nodes[Stop];
117             Destination = Vertex.name();
118             if(NetGraph.findPath(Origin,Destination)){
119                displayGraph(WindowHandle);
120             }
121             else{
122
123                   ResultMsg << "No Path From " << Origin << " TO " <<
    Destination;
124
WinMessageBox(HWND_DESKTOP,WindowHandle,"",ResultMsg.str(),0,MB_OK);
125           }
```

```
126             NetGraph.reset("vertex.txt","edges.txt");
127             break;
128     case ClrGraphCtl:
129             PSpace = WinGetPS(WindowHandle);
130             GpiErase(PSpace);
131             WinReleasePS(PSpace);
132             WinSendMsg(WindowHandle,WM_PAINT,0L,0L);
133             break;
134     case ExitGraphCtl:
135             WinSendMsg(WindowHandle,WM_CLOSE,0L,0L);
136             return 0;
137
138     }
139
140
141
142   default:
143     return(WinDefWindowProc(WindowHandle,Msg,MessParm1,Mess
    Parm2));
144     }
145
146     return(WinDefWindowProc(WindowHandle,Msg,MessParm1,Mess
    Parm2));
147
148 }
149
150
151 int main(void)
152 {
153
154   HAB Anchor;
155   ULONG UlFlags;
156   HMQ MessQueueHandle;
157   HWND FrameHandle;
158   HWND ClientHandle;
159   QMSG MessageQueue;
160   unsigned char WinClass[] = "ExampleClass";
161
162   UlFlags = FCF_MENU|
163     FCF_TITLEBAR |
164     FCF_SIZEBORDER |
165     FCF_MINMAX |
166     FCF_SYSMENU |
167     FCF_VERTSCROLL |
168     FCF_HORZSCROLL |
169     FCF_SHELLPOSITION |
170     FCF_TASKLIST;
171 Anchor = WinInitialize(0);
172 MessQueueHandle = WinCreateMsgQueue(Anchor,0);
173 if(!WinRegisterClass(Anchor,(PSZ)WinClass,graphMain,CS_SIZEREDRAW,0)){
```

```
174        exit(1);
175        }
176        FrameHandle = WinCreateStdWindow(HWND_DESKTOP,
177                        WS_VISIBLE,
178                    &UlFlags,
179                        WinClass,
180                        "Graph Collection Class",
181                        WS_VISIBLE,
182                        0,
183                        1,
184                        NULL);
185        while(WinGetMsg(Anchor,&MessageQueue,0L,0,0))
186        {
187        WinDispatchMsg(Anchor,&MessageQueue);
188        }
189        WinDestroyWindow(FrameHandle);
190        WinDestroyMsgQueue(MessQueueHandle);
191        WinTerminate(Anchor);
192        return(0);
193
194
195 }
```

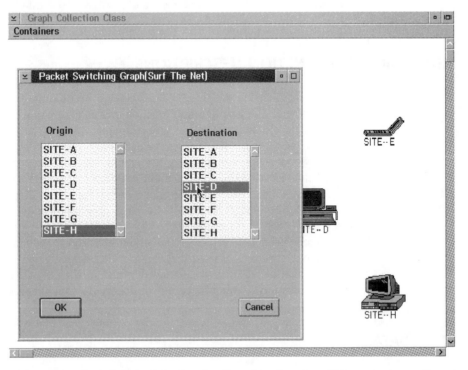

**Figure 8.6** The origin and destination lists that the user will have to choose from in the graph application.

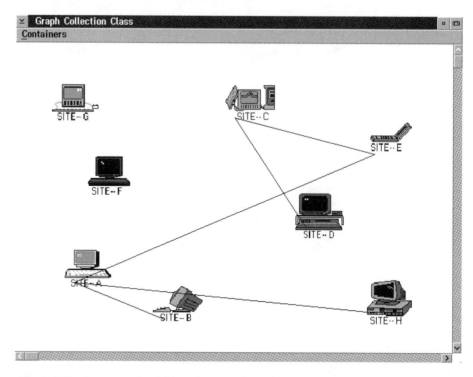

**Figure 8.7**   An example of how the program plots a route.

## PROCEDURE AND FUNCTION DESCRIPTIONS

The graph application has three main functions: **graphMain()**, **displayGraph()**, and **graphDialog()**. The **graphMain()** function creates the main windows and dispatches the incoming and outgoing messages for this application. It is declared in *gmainos2.cpp*. The **displayGraph()** function takes the path that was found between the two sites and displays a route depicting the path. The graph collection class has a component called **Path**. This object stores the results of **findPath(X,Y)** requests. If a path is found between *X* and *Y*, it will be stored in the queue object **Path**. The **displayGraph()** uses the contents of the queue object **Path** as the edges. The **graphDialog()** function is a dialog that gets the two sites from the user. The user is presented with a list of origins and destinations. The user can select an origin and a destination. Once an origin and destination have been chosen, the user clicks OK, and the graph collection will attempt to find a path between the origin and destination that the user has chosen. If a path exists, the **displayGraph()** function will display the route between the origin and the destination.

## INPUT DATA

The graph application reads two files. The first file is called *vertex.txt* and contains an entry for each of the sites. The second file *edges.txt* contains the allowable connections between particular computers. Figure 8.6 shows the origin and destination lists that the user will have to choose from. The origin and destination lists contain the input data for the graph program.

## PROGRAM OUTPUT

Figure 8.7 shows an example how the program plots a route between two computers.

CHAPTER 9

# PERSISTENT OBJECTS

The C++ language has two *declarable storage classes*. A storage class is a *duration specifier*. The storage class specifies how long an object exists. An object can have a declared storage class of either *automatic* or *static*. An automatic object exists only during the invocation of a block. This means that space and values that the object has only exist within a block. Once the flow of control has left that block, the object ceases to exist. On the other hand, a static object exists and retains values throughout the execution of the entire program. There is a third option in C++ that utilizes the notion of a *dynamically* allocated object. A dynamically allocated object can have less than automatic existence and no more than static existence. The programmer has complete control over when a dynamically created object is created and destroyed. The programmer can create a dynamic object upon entering a block, and destroy that object before the block is exited. In this case, the object is less than automatic. The programmer creates a dynamic object at runtime that may exist for the entire execution of a program. In this case, the object is like a static object. Basically, the C++ language only has declarable storage classes that apply to life spans of objects during program execution. Unfortunately, C++ does not have a declarable storage class that specifies object existence beyond the execution of a program.

Persistent objects are objects that can exist beyond the execution of the program in which they were created. Beware! Persistence is not necessarily synonymous with storage to disk. Operating systems that support virtual storage, such as UNIX or OS/2, may store automatic or static objects to disk (virtual memory) during program execution. However, after the program is over, these objects are destroyed. In this instance, these objects are not persistent (although they did spend time on disk). On the other hand, some persistent objects live only in internal memory. For instance, objects that are created in network or distributed environments may be electronically passed between programs or sessions, never seeing storage to a disk. While the program that originally created the object terminates, the object may persist on other workstations and in other programs. Whereas *storage class* and *duration* refer to objects during the execution of a program or session, *persistence* refers to objects that exist before or after the execution of a program or session. In general, persistent objects are artificially divided into two broad categories:

object-oriented databases and persistent collections or containers. As we shall see, these categories are really just two sides to the same coin.

# OBJECT-ORIENTED DATABASES

Strictly speaking, a database is a collection of files. A database management system (DBMS) is an encapsulation of those files that provides a logical view as well as a list of services on the data that is encapsulated. The physical structure of the files in a database is unimportant. The list of services that is provided on the database defines the value of the DBMS. The core services that a DBMS will provide are as follows:

Intersection
Union
Selection
Join
Projection
Product
Insertion
Set Difference
Query and Relation Semantics
Sorting and Searching
Implementation Independence
Security Protocols
Integrity Protocols
Deletion

In this sense, a DBMS is similar to an object. A object encapsulates its internal structure and code into a single unit. The object provides the user with a list of services on the data that the object contains. The internal structure or implementation of the services is unimportant to the user of the object. The list of services on the object provides the user with the complete interface to the object. The list of services that a DBMS provides performs a similar function. Traditionally, databases consist of data types that represent strings, characters, integers, and floating point numbers. These data types are organized into records. The object-oriented database is an application of object orientation to the concept of a database. Whereas the smallest unit of information in a traditional database is one of the fundamental data types, that is, strings, characters, integers, or floating point numbers, the object-oriented database extends this list to include objects. The single unit may be an object or a record that consists of a collection of objects.

The file is the operating system's primary method of providing persistence. Because databases consist of collections of files, the database itself is persistent. A database exists before the start of a given program that uses its data and will endure beyond the termination of that program.

# PERSISTENT COLLECTIONS AND CONTAINERS

Persistent collections and containers are *external* objects that contain or hold other groups of objects. We use the term external here to emphasize that the collection or container lives beyond the program or session that created it. The persistent collection or container may live on disk or in virtual memory. Any of the collections or containers that we've discussed in this book can have a *persistent* version. That is, we may have persistent sets, maps, graphs, stacks, queues, lists, trees, and so on. Although the C++ language and the STL lack ready-made persistent collection or container classes, they do provide the building blocks for persistent collections, containers, and object-oriented databases. It should be noted that although object-oriented databases represent an entire area of study, they are, in fact, just another type of persistent collection. While the list of services that the object-oriented database requires is demanding, the object-oriented database still can be and should be classified as a persistent collection. Therefore, we include object-oriented databases in our list of persistent collections and containers. When we discuss persistence, we make no distinction between an object-oriented database and any other persistent collection or container class.

# APPROACHES TO OBJECT-ORIENTED PERSISTENCE IN C++

There are several strategies for implementing object persistence in C++. The strategy that is used is dictated by the type of collection or container that needs to persist, as well as tradeoffs between implementation complexity and class hierarchy interface policies. In other words, if all that is needed is a flat file collection consisting of simple objects, then persistence is approached one way. On the other hand, if a database collection is needed that supports versioning, concurrency, on-line transaction processing, external deep copy, and object recovery, then implementing object persistence will be more complex and require considerably more effort. Currently, there are no *one-size-fits-all* techniques for implementing persistence. There are several reasons for this. First, C++ does not offer a persistence storage class or persistence keyword. Persistence in C++ must be built from the ground up. Second, there are so many different uses for persistence that cover such a wide area of requirements that a *one-size-fits-all* approach would most likely produce code too big and too slow to be effective. Third, persistence means different things to different applications. What counts as persistent in a distributed network environment may not count as persistent in a single user nonvirtual storage environment. With this in mind, the designers of C++ chose not to try to provide persistence but rather suggest that object persistence is best provided as a collection of components to be mixed and matched by the user (see Stroustrup's *The Design and Evolution of C++ 1994*).

There are four broad categories that persistence strategies fit into. The first category includes the *session savers*. The session saver persistence strategies implement persistence by using various techniques to capture the entire state of memory and all the objects within it, along with their relationships, pointer values, virtual tables, and so forth, to disk or some other external medium. These sessions can then be restored to their active states at a later time. The second category includes the *dual object representations*. This category implements persistence by separating the in-memory representation of an object from its external representation. Object data members that consist of pointers are replaced by relative disk locations, object ids, absolute disk locations, and so on. The dual object representation addresses the *external deep copy* problem that we shall discuss later. The third category uses object-based schemes. In Chapter 3 we discussed a technique for implementing collections and containers that involves using a common ancestor for all collections or containers. The persistence strategy that uses object-based schemes employs the same technique. The basic idea is to have every object that needs to persist inherit some object that already has persistence operations defined. The fourth persistence strategy attempts to provide persistence through extending the language by means of special-purpose libraries and the C++ preprocessor. Most persistence strategies that use object-oriented features in C++ can be grouped into one of these four categories.

## Policy-Based Persistence

Another approach to persistence that is a hybrid of the object-based strategy and the dual-object representation is the *policy-based strategy*. The policy-based persistence strategies are effective in closed environments. If the persistent collections, containers, and objects to be placed into them all originate within a cooperative group, organization, corporation, or institution, a persistence policy can be built into each object in the same way that copy constructors are generally supplied for most objects. The policy is usually a minimum interface that the suppliers of persistent classes must adhere to. The interface will usually include definitions for specific operators and member functions. Although policy-based persistence strategies normally produce larger objects, and add more responsibilities to the class suppliers, they have the virtue of being simpler to implement and more generic than some of the other approaches. Because policy-based persistence is an easy entry level into object persistence, this chapter will focus on policy-based persistence strategies. For a detailed discussion of persistence and C++, see Jiri Soukup's (1994) *Taming C++ Pattern Classes and Persistence for Large Projects*.

Before we can begin our discussion of policy-based persistence, we must first discuss the two primary building blocks of object-oriented input and output in C++. The first building block is the set of **iostream** classes that are part of the C++ environment. The second building block is the generic algorithms, **istream_iterators**, and **ostream _iterators** from the STL.

# THE IOSTREAM CLASSES—BUILDING BLOCKS FOR PERSISTENCE

The **iostream** classes are a set of C++ classes used to implement an object-oriented model of input and output. The **iostream** facilities packaged as a standard component with all C++ compilers is an object-oriented input and output facility providing access to unbuffered (low-level) as well as buffered I/O operations. Because the **iostream** classes have full support for the object-oriented paradigm, they can be extended through polymorphism and inheritance. This makes the **iostream** classes well suited to the task of building persistent objects and persistent collections. In this chapter, we present only enough information on the **iostream** classes to demonstrate their use as building blocks for persistent collections and containers. (For a detailed discussion of the **iostream** classes see *Object-Oriented I/O Using C++ Iostreams* by Hughes, Hamilton, and Hughes, and *C++ IOStreams Handbook* by Teale.)

The **iostreams** are made of three fundamental components: the **ios** class, the **streambuf** family of classes, and the **istream** and **ostream** family of classes.

These three components work together in patterns to produce an *object-oriented input* and *output stream*. This object-oriented stream represents a generic sequence of bytes moving into and out of some generic file. The generic file is normally attached to some device such as disk drive, console display, or printer. The *object-oriented stream* encompasses both the generic sequences of bytes and the generic files they are read from and written to. Since the goals of persistence are to have some way to store objects beyond the execution of a program and to be able to retrieve those objects later, the object-oriented stream will be a major component of our persistence strategy. The class relationship diagram in Figure 9.1 shows the fundamental relationship among the three types of classes. Notice the buffer class has a containment relationship as opposed to an inheritance relationship with the object-oriented stream.

## The ios (Stream State) Class

The **ios** class contains the condition of the object-oriented stream at any given point or time. The **iostream** has several predefined states. The **iostream** classes also support user-defined states. The stream may be in a *good* state, signaling that the previous operation on the stream was successful and the next operation on the stream can be attempted. The stream may be in a *fail* or *bad* state, signaling that the previous operations failed and

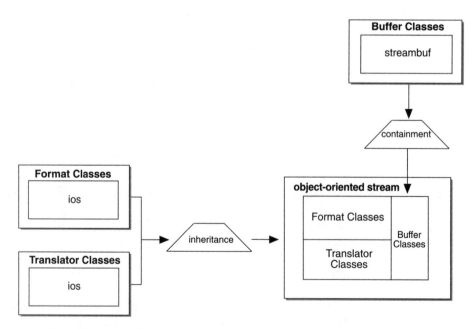

**Figure 9.1** The fundamental relationship between the three types of classes; **ios, streambuf,** and an object-oriented stream.

unless action is taken any following operations will fail. When using **iostream** classes, it is a good idea to check the state of the stream after input or output operations. The **ios** class also contains specifications that represent the format of how data should be interpreted coming into or going out of the stream. For instance, the **ios** class will dictate whether the data should be interpreted as binary or text or whether certain values are represented as hexadecimal, octal, or decimal. The **ios** class also has specifications for whether numeric values are represented as fixed point or as scientific notation. The **ios** class is important to our persistence strategy because the **ios** class can determine whether a persistent object is being written in a binary or text format or whether the persistent object is being read from a binary or text format. Table 9.1 gives a list of the **ios** member functions and public data members.

The **ios** class contains information about how the stream has been opened. For instance, the **ios** class contains information on whether the object stream has been opened in the *append mode* or whether the stream can be read or written to. Some streams are read only and some streams are write only. Some streams can be opened for both *read* and *write* operations. The **ios** class holds the information that designates the attached stream as a binary stream or a text stream. The **ios** class encapsulates the information that determines the base the numbers will be formatted to when inserted

**Table 9.1    A list of the *ios* member functions and public data members.**

| Class | Public Member Functions | Public Data Members |
|-------|-------------------------|---------------------|
| **ios** | ios() | seek_dir |
| | ~ios() | open_mode |
| | bad() | adjustfield |
| | bitalloc() | basefield |
| | clear() | floatfield |
| | eof() | io_state |
| | fail() | |
| | fill() | |
| | flags() | |
| | good() | |
| | precision() | |
| | rdbuf() | |
| | setf() | |
| | unsetf() | |
| | sync_with_stdio() | |
| | tie() | |
| | width() | |
| | xalloc() | |
| | skip() | |
| | rdstate() | |
| | iword() | |
| | pword() | |
| | operator!() | |

into a stream or when extracted from a stream. The **ios** class also controls precision information for numbers entering or exiting a stream. So then, the **ios** class represents the control and format specification for the **iostream** classes.

## The streambuf Family

The **streambuf** family of classes are *buffer* classes. They specify generic holding areas for the data while it is in transit from an input device or to an output device. The **streambuf** class has the capability of processing generic sequences of bytes. The **streambuf** class has methods that get bytes, put bytes, skip bytes, put bytes back, and so on. The **streambuf** classes have both get pointers and put pointers. The **streambuf** class has the functionality that controls what happens with stream overflow or stream underflow conditions. From the **streambuf** class other classes are derived to deal with file buffers, generic memory processing, and **stdio** synchronization. The **streambuf** class is usually contained as a data member of one of the other **iostream** classes.

There are three basic types of buffers represented by the **streambuf** family. The **streambuf** class is the buffer that generally contains bytes that are going to the console and coming from the keyboard. The **strstreambuf** class is the buffer that generally contains bytes going to an internal memory block and coming from an internal memory block. The **filebuf** class is the buffer that contains a sequence of bytes moving to and from the devices that have been opened as files. The **strstreambuf** and the **filebuf** classes are of special interest to us here because persistence is generally implemented on disk storage or in virtual memory. The **filebuf** class will be useful in disk storage implementations of persistence. The **strstreambuf** class will be useful in virtual memory implementations of persistence. The buffer classes encapsulate generic holding areas. These areas simply hold sequences of bytes. The buffer classes contain the specifications for the operations that can be performed on the data in the generic holding area. The buffer classes specify position designators (get and put pointers) that determine where the next character in the holding area will be read from or where in the holding area the next character will be written to. Table 9.2 contains the list of public member functions and data members for **filebuf** and **strstreambuf**.

## istream and ostream Family of Classes

The **istream** and **ostream** family of classes are conversion or translation classes. The **istream** family (**istream**, **istrstream**, and **ifstream**) are objects that encapsulate *input* functionality. The **ostream** family (**ostream**, **ostrstream**, and **ofstream**) are objects that encapsulate *output* functionality. These classes either convert the data types to a generic sequence of bytes on the output stream or translate a generic sequence of bytes from the input stream into either user-defined data types or built-in data types. The **istream** and **ostream** classes are largely responsible for giving the programmer the device-independent look and feel that the **iostreams** have. Just as there are three basic types of **streambuf** classes, there are three basic types of translation classes. Table 9.3 shows the three types of **streambuf** classes and their corresponding **istream** and **ostream** classes. Each type of translation class has an input version and an output version. The **istream** class does conversions coming from the console. The **istrstream** class does conversions

**Table 9.2   A list of the public member functions and data members for *filebuf* and *strstreambuf* classes.**

| Class | Derived From | Public Member Functions | Public Data Members |
|---|---|---|---|
| **strstrteambuf** | streambuf | strstreambuf()<br>~strstreambuf()<br>freeze()<br>seekoff()<br>setbuf()<br>sync()<br>overflow()<br>underflow()<br>str()<br>doallocate() | None |
| **filebuf** | streambuf | filebuf()<br>filebuf()<br>is_open()<br>fd()<br>open()<br>close()<br>attach()<br>overflow()<br>underflow()<br>sync()<br>seekoff()<br>setbuf()<br>lock()<br>unlock() | openprot |

coming from an internal block of memory, that is, a character array. The **ifstream** class does conversions on sequences of bytes that come from files. The files can represent devices such as disk drives, CDROMS, tapes, printers, and so on. The **ostream** class does conversion going to the display console. The **ostrstream** class does conversions going to an internal block of memory. The **ofstream** class does conversions on sequences of bytes that are going to a file. Table 9.4 shows the public member functions and data members of the **istream** family and **ostream** family.

**Table 9.3   A list of the three types of *streambuf* classes and their corresponding *istream* and *ostream* classes.**

| Types of streambuf Classes | istream Class | ostream Class | Both |
|---|---|---|---|
| **filebuf** | ifstream | ofstream | fstream |
| **strstreambuf** | istrstream | ostrstream | strstream |
| **streambuf** | istream | ostream | iostream |

**Table 9.4**  **A list of the public member functions and data members of the istream and ostream family of classes.**

| Class | Derived From | Public Member Functions | Public Data Members |
|---|---|---|---|
| **istream** | ios | istream() <br> ~istream() <br> ipfx() <br> isfx() <br> seekg() <br> tellg() <br> get() <br> getline() <br> peek() <br> ignore() <br> read() <br> gcount() <br> putback() <br> sync() <br> operator>>() | None |
| **ifstream** | istream <br> fstreambase | ifstream() <br> ~ifstream <br> open() <br> rdbuff() | None |
| **istrstream** | istream <br> strstreambase | istrstream() <br> ~istrstream() | None |
| **ostream** | ios | ostream() <br> ~ostream() <br> opfx() <br> osfx() <br> seekp() <br> tellp() <br> put() <br> write() <br> operator<<() | None |
| **ofstream** | ostream <br> fstreambase | ofstream() <br> ~ofstream() <br> open() <br> rdbuff() | None |
| **ostrstream** | ostream <br> strstreambase | ostrstream() <br> ~ostrstream() <br> str() <br> pcount() | None |

Together the **istream** and **ostream** classes encapsulate the base functionality of the entire family of **iostream** classes. The **istream** and the **ostream** classes are base classes for most of the other classes in the **iostream** hierarchy. Most **iostream** implementations have used multiple inheritance to derive a single class called **iostream** that is derived from **istream** and **ostream**. The reader should not confuse the **iostream** class with the **iostream** family of classes. The **iostream** class is a single entity that has been derived from an **istream** class and an **ostream** class. The **iostream** classes represent the entire object-oriented network of classes in the C++ environment that includes the **ios** class, **streambuf** family, **ostream** family, **istream** family, and the manipulators.

## iostream Class Hierarchy

These classes are interconnected through inheritance and possession. The conversion classes are usually descendants of a **ios** class. The **ios** class possesses a buffer class. The buffer class may have buffer ancestors, and so on. Because the **iostreams** are a set of classes (not functions!), all the concepts and advantages of object orientation can be applied. Figure 9.2 shows the class relationship diagram for the **iostream** family of classes. It is important to keep in mind the entire class hierarchy of the **iostreams** when building persistence because the **iostreams** already encapsulate most of the functionality needed to implement persistent collections and containers.

### THE INSERTION AND EXTRACTION OPERATIONS

The **iostreams** support a common interface for reading and writing objects both built-in and user-defined. The common interface simplifies what a programmer has to remember when doing input and output on objects. The common interface is a considerable improvement over the **printf()**, **scanf()**, **fprintf()**, **sscanf()**, **vscanf()**, and **sprintf()** functions that are supplied in the standard C++ library. When using the non–object-oriented standard C++ I/O routines, if input and output are coming from and going to the console, one set of functions is used. If input and output are coming from and going to files, an entirely different set of functions is used. In the **iostream** class library, the *single-interface, multiple-implementation* benefit of polymorphism relieves some of the complexity that would be required to implement persistence with the I/O functions of the C++ standard library. The **iostreams**' interface uses either overloaded <<, >> operators, or **read()** and **write()** member functions to perform all types of input and output regardless of the data type involved. Reading objects from a stream is called *extraction*. Writing objects to a stream is called *insertion*.

The **iostream** classes define the << and >> operators for all the built-in classes. The << operator is called an *inserter*. The >> operator is called an *extractor*. The **istream** family of classes uses the extractor. Objects are *inserted* into an output stream and *extracted* from an input stream. The **ostream** family of classes uses the inserter. For instance, this little program inserts an integer, character, and float value into the predefined **ostream** class **cout**:

```
#include <iostream.h>
int Num1 = 10;
```

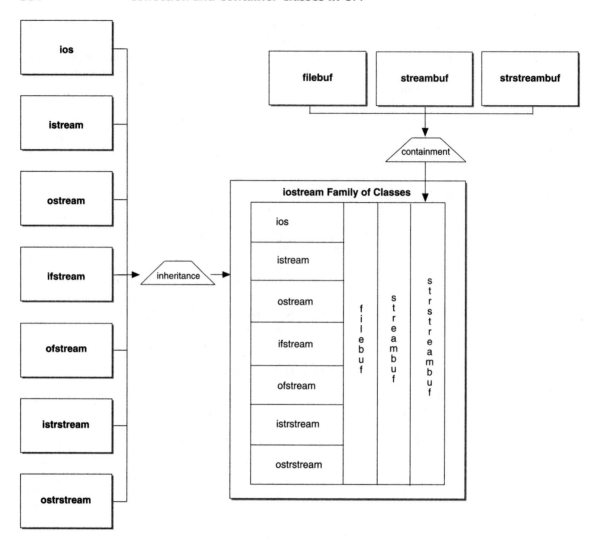

**Figure 9.2**  The class relationship diagram for the **iostream** family of classes.

```
                    char Letter = 'A';
                    float Dollars = 34.3;
                    void main(void)
            {
                    cout << Num1 << Letter << Dollars;
            }
```

Although the inserter is used with different data types, the interface is the same. The **cout** object knows how to insert each data type. This is accomplished by providing a definition of the << operator for every built-in type. The inserter translates built-in types or user-defined types into generic sequences of bytes. The bytes are then placed into their respective buffers and are eventually sent to the destination device. Figure 9.3 shows the process that inserters and extractors use. The inserter and extractor operators can also be defined for user-defined types and classes. This is where our object-oriented persistence strategy begins. Because the **iostreams** can be extended to include user-defined objects, we can define persistence for any object.

### *Defining Operators << and >> for User-Defined Classes*

The $<<$ operator and the $>>$ operator are shift operators. These operators are over-loaded to perform object insertion and extraction for the **iostream** classes. Any user-defined class can include insertion and extraction by defining the $<<$ operator and $>>$ operator as member functions for that class. These member functions should be declared as friend functions. For instance, our user-defined class **rational** in Listing 9.1 has inserter and extractor member functions defined.

**Listing 9.1**

```
1 #include <iostream.h>
2
3 class rational{
4    protected:
5    long Numerator;
6    long Denominator;
7    public:
8    rational(long Num = 0,long Den = 1);
9    void assign(long X, long Y);
10   rational operator*(rational X);
11   rational operator+(rational X);
12   rational operator=(rational X);
13   rational operator-(rational X);
14   rational operator/(rational X);
```

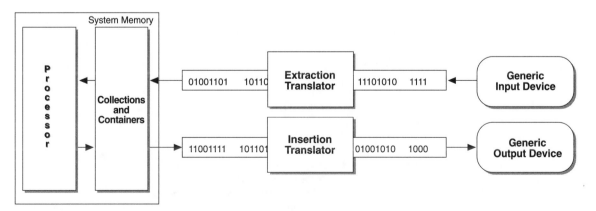

**Figure 9.3**　The process that inserters and extractors use to send a stream of bytes to or from a generic device.

```
15   boolean operator==(rational X);
16   long numerator(void);
17   long denominator(void);
18   void reduce(void);
19   friend ostream &operator<<(ostream &out, rational &X);
20   friend istream &operator>>(istream &in, rational &X);
21 };
```

The inserter and extractor member functions are declared with:

```
friend ostream &operator<<(ostream &out, rational &X);
friend istream &operator>>(istream &in, rational &X);
```

The inserter and extractor member functions take two arguments. The first argument is a reference to an **iostream** class. The second argument is a reference to a class of type **rational**. We could have defined the inserter to take an argument of type **ofstream** and the extractor to take an argument of type **ifstream**. However, by using **ostream** and **istream** objects, we can insert or extract our **rational** class from any of the **iostream** classes. This is because all **istream** classes have **istream** as a base class. All **ostream** classes have **ostream** as a base class and C++ allows a reference to a base class to access any derived class. Our inserter and extractor member function will also work on any descendant of the **rational** class for the same reason. Listing 9.2 contains the definitions for our inserter and extractor member functions.

### Listing 9.2

```
1 // Definitions for the inserter and extractor of the rational class
2
3 ostream &operator<<(ostream& out,rational X)
4 {
5 if(X.Denominator < 0){
6     X.Denominator *= -1;
7     X.Numerator *= -1;
8   }
9   if(X.Numerator == X.Denominator){
10    out << 1;
11    return out;
12  }
13    else
14    if(X.Denominator == 1){
15   out << X.Numerator;
16   return out;
17    }
18   else
19   if(X.Numerator != X.Denominator){
20     out << X.Numerator << "/" << X.Denominator;
21     return out;
22  }
23 }
```

```
24
25
26 istream &operator>>(istream& in,rational &X)
27 {
28      char Ascii;
29      In >> X.Numerator >> Ascii >> X.Denominator;
30   return(In);
31      }
32 }
33
```

With these definitions, we now have persistence for the **rational** class. The program in Listing 9.3 creates two **rational** objects and inserts them into an **ofstream** object called **Out**. The **ofstream** object is attached to a file called *fract.txt*. The program then creates an **ifstream** object called **In** and attaches it to *fract.txt*. The **rational** objects that are in that file are extracted and placed into the **rational** objects **Num1** and **Num2**. **Num1** and **Num2** are then inserted into the **cout** object.

### Listing 9.3

```
 1 // This program demonstrates how
 2 // user-defined objects can be
 3 // made persistent using inserter
 4 // and extractor member functions.
 5
 6 #include <fstream.h>
 7 #include "rational.h"
 8
 9
10 void main(void)
11 {
12
13   ofstream Out("fract.txt");
14   rational Num1(3,2);
15   rational Num2(2,4);
16   Out << Num1 << " " << Num2;
17   Out.close();
18   ifstream In("fract.txt");
19   In >> Num1 >> Num2;
20   cout << Num1 << " " << Num2 << endl;
21   In.close();
22
23 }
```

Defining the << operator and the >> operator for the user-defined class is the easiest way to make user-defined objects persist. However, simply defining these operators provides only the crudest method of storing and retrieving user-defined objects. This method makes many assumptions and has several limitations. This method assumes that the file will be homogeneous. That is, only one kind of object will be stored in the file. The method assumes that every object written to the file is the same size. We could not write **rational** objects with varying lengths to this file. Furthermore, it assumes that the file is in text mode and therefore depends on ASCII representations. To retrieve a **rational** object from *fract.txt* we would have to process the file sequentially. There are no **search()** or **find()** member functions in the **iostream** hierarchy. Also, because the << operator and >> operator have been defined for built-in types, it is possible to inadvertently write other types of objects to *fract.txt*, making it difficult to later retrieve the **rational** objects. This method is not type safe. However, if all that is needed is a method of storing and retrieving fixed-length homogenous objects, then simply defining << operator and >> operator will give the programmer base-level persistence.

It should be noted that in this example the container is a file. The objects are stored in a text file. This is part of the dual-object representation that makes up the policy-based persistence strategy. Objects will have one structure during program execution and an entirely different structure in their persistent form. The *flat* file is the simplest external container available. It is only used to store and retrieve objects. It has no special **search()** and **retrieval()** functions. Although flat files only offer the basics, they continue to be important containers and are in wide use. For instance, many operating system configuration files, ini files, batch files, and so on are nothing more than flat files. As long as the programmer knows how these files are structured, they can be very useful and convenient.

### *Text Mode and Binary Mode Persistence*

Using the **iostream** classes, the programmer can open a stream in either text mode or binary mode. This is specified using the **open()** member function:

```
ofstream Out;
Out.open("fract.txt");
Out.open("fract.txt",ios::binary);
```

The first **open()** member function opens the file in text mode. The second **open()** member function opens the file in binary mode using a data member from the **ios** class. When a stream is opened in text mode, the objects that are inserted or extracted are translated into an ASCII or in some rare cases EBCDIC format. In text mode, every object is written out as a stream of characters. For instance, if we were to insert the number 165 into a text mode stream, three characters would be sent to the stream. The first character would be the ASCII representation of 1, the second character would be the ASCII representation of 6, and the third character would be the ASCII representation of 5. It should be noted that the text mode versus binary mode distinction is somewhat misleading. Data written in either text mode or binary mode will both be stored as series of binary digits, or bytes. The distinction requires that text mode uses certain patterns of bits and numbers of bytes to represent data while the binary mode requires other patterns of bits and numbers of bytes to represent data. In this sense, both text mode and binary mode store their data in a binary format. For example, the number 165 in text mode might look something like this:

00110001 00110110 00110101

where each series of 8 bits represents one character. That is:

00110001 = '1'
00110110 = '6'
00110101 = '5'

However, the binary mode representation of 165 will look much different. Binary 165 looks like this:

10100101

Whereas the text mode representation required three bytes to represent 165 (one byte for each number), the binary mode representation only requires one byte. This illustrates an important difference between text mode and binary mode files. In general, the text mode file will be much larger than its binary equivalent, especially when numbers make up part of the data. So then a binary file will most likely have a different file size than its text file representation. The text mode treats '\n' differently than binary mode does. The text mode will translate this character into a carriage return character plus a line feed character upon output and will translate these two characters to '\n' upon input. This means that the in-memory version of the file will be a different size and consist of a different content than the output version of the file. There are several other differences between binary mode and text mode. Whereas control characters like '\n', '\b', '\f' have specific meaning in text mode, they are treated as any other piece of data in binary mode. It is important to know that there is a distinction between binary mode and text mode streams. The two are not interchangeable.

### Using Read and Write Member Functions with User-Defined Classes

The **read()** and **write()** member functions can be used to read and write blocks of data in binary mode. The **read()** and **write()** member functions perform unformatted extractions and insertions on the streams that they are used with. The **read()** member function is a member of the **istream** family of classes. The **write()** member function is a member of the **ostream** family of classes. These member functions are best used on streams that have been opened in a binary mode. The **read()** and **write()** member functions can be used to insert and extract variable-length objects from a file of homogenous objects. The **read()** and **write()** member functions can also be used to insert and extract fixed or variable-length objects from a file containing heterogeneous objects. This is possible because these member functions take the size of a block of memory as one of their parameters. For instance:

```
char Bitmap[128000];
ofstream Out("MyFile.txt",ios::binary);
Out.close();
Out.write(Bitmap,128000);
```

```
ifstream In("MyFile.txt",ios::binary);
In.read(Bitmap,128000);
In.close();
```

inserts 128,000 bytes into the **Out ofstream** object. If the programmer keeps track of the size of the objects that have been inserted and the positions where they have been inserted, then the **read()** and **write()** member functions can be used to store objects of any size and any type together. There are a couple of simplistic ways to do this. First, the programmer can store the relative positions and sizes and possibly object ids of the objects in a second file and use the second file as an index. Then, whenever an object needs to be retrieved the index would be used to determine where the object is in the file and how big the object is. The second method stores the size of each object within the initial bytes of the object and the relative location of the next object. This creates a kind of linked list on disk. Both methods are simple entry-level techniques that can accomplish object persistence.

User-defined insertion and extraction operations can make use of << operator, >> operator, **read()** member function, and **write()** member function. For instance, for a class **Bitmap**, we could define an insertion operation:

```
ostream &operator<<(ostream &Out, Bitmap &X)
{
    Out << Bitmap.size;
    Out << Bitmap.id;
    Out.write(Bitmap,Bitmap.size);
    return(Out);
}
```

Hint: By using the **istream**'s **seekg()** and **tellg()** and the **ostream**'s **seekp()** and **tellp()**, the programmer can design direct access methods to store and retrieve variable-length objects in hetereogenous or homogenous files. These member functions can be used in conjunction with the an index file to design very effective persistence strategies.

### Objects that Contain Pointers

Designing persistence strategies for objects that involve pointers is somewhat more troublesome. However, they should be approached as variable-length objects. Therefore, it is necessary to have a size data member for every pointer data member that an object has, for instance:

```
class MyObject{
protected:
  long SizeBitmapA;
  long Length ListA
  int ObjectID
  char *BitmapA
  int *ListA;
};
```

The class **MyObject** has two pointers to components that can vary in length; **BitmapA**, and **ListA**. In order to know how big the **BitmapA** is or how long the list of integers is, we store size data members for both components. Therefore, when defining the $<<$ operator or $>>$ operator for **MyObject**, we will know how to read and write the object. This is a part of the policy-based persistence strategy that makes the objects larger. Every component in the object that can vary in size must have a corresponding size data member. This is one of the policies in policy-based persistence. Another policy in policy-based persistence requires every object that needs to persist to define its own $<<$ operator and $>>$ operator.

Since we have access to size data members for every variable-length component, we can use the **read()** and **write()** member functions to retrieve and store objects that vary in size. Also these objects can be constructed from disk by employing the **read()** and **write()** member functions within the constructors of the user-defined objects. Using the **read()** and **write()** member functions along with maintaining size data members for every variable-length component in an object allows the programmer to achieve *external deep* copies between objects within a program and objects external to a program. The external deep copies between transient and persistent objects are what create most of the difficulty in creating persistent collections and containers. Policy-based persistence attempts to minimize the difficulty by requiring certain interfaces to be maintained for all objects that need to persist.

### GUIDELINES OF POLICY-BASED PERSISTENCE

Now that we have a cursory understanding of how objects can be made persistent using the **iostream** classes, we can state the guidelines for our policy-based persistence strategy:

1. Every object that needs to persist must define operator $<<$ and operator $>>$.
2. Data members that hold size should be included for each data member that can have a variable length.
3. Binary and text mode insertion should be defined for each object where necessary.
4. For objects that have pointers or variable length members, the size data members should come first in the declaration of the object. This is necessary so that the size of a variable-length object can be retrieved prior to retrieving its block of data when extracting the object from a file.
5. The insertion operation should insert the sizes of all variable-length data members before the values for the variable length members are inserted.
6. The extraction operation should mirror the insertion operator. That is, the extraction operator should read the objects in the same order that the objects were written.

Although these guidelines create larger objects and add more responsibility to the class supplier, they make the implementation of persistence simpler. The policy-based strategies will work in environments where every class that is used obeys the persistence guidelines that have been set. We have only touched the surface of the **iostream** classes; however, enough has been said to demonstrate where persistence and the **iostreams** are connected. Next we shall discuss how the STL **istream_iterators**, **ostream_iterators**, and generic algorithms can be combined with the **iostream** classes to provide the building blocks for persistent collections and containers.

# THE STL STREAM ITERATORS

The STL has two stream iterators: **ostream_iterator** and **istream_iterator**. The **ostream_iterator** works with the **ostream** family of classes. The **istream_iterator** works with the **istream** family. These two iterators are our connection between the **iostream** classes and the STL collections and containers. We use the **iostream** classes to help us build persistent objects. We use the STL stream iterators and generic algorithms in conjunction with the persistent objects to form persistent collections and containers. The **ostream_iterator** is a descendant of **output_iterator**. The **istream_iterator** is a descendant of type **input_iterator**. Figure 9.4 shows the class relationship diagrams for **ostream_iterator** and **istream_iterator**. Notice that **istream_iterator** contains an **istream** object and **ostream_iterator** contains an **ostream** object.

Since the **istream_iterator** is sufficient for an **input_iterator**, any algorithm that accepts input iterators can be used with the **istream** family of classes. Since the **ostream_iterator** is sufficient for an **output_iterator**, any algorithm that accepts output iterators can be used with the **ostream** family of classes.

## The istream_iterator

The **istream_iterator** is declared in *iterator.h*. The **istream_iterator** has three constructors. The default constructor constructs an end-of-stream iterator value. The second constructor takes a reference to **istream** or one of its descendants. The **istream_iterator** will get its values from this **istream** object. The third constructor is a copy constructor. To construct an **istream_iterator** that would point to an **ifstream** object that contains our user-defined type **rational**, we would declare the iterator as:

```
ifstream In("Myfile.txt");
istream_iterator<rational,ptrdiff_t> P(In);
istream_iterator<rational,ptrdiff_t> Eos;
```

**P** could then be used to iterator through the stream. Also **P** could be used as an argument to any STL generic algorithm that accepts an **input_iterator**. **Eos** is an **istream_iterator** that contains an end-of-stream value. This value can be used in the same fashion that the **end()** member function is used in the STL containers. The **istream_iterator** supports ++operator. This can be used to iterate through the **istream** class. The **istream_iterator** assumes that operator>> has been defined for the elements that are in the **istream** object. Note that this was one of our guidelines for policy-based persistence. Since the **istream_iterator** is an **input_iterator**, the same restrictions that apply to **input_iterators** apply to **istream_iterators**.

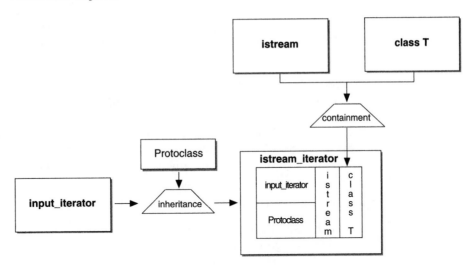

**A. istream_iterator**

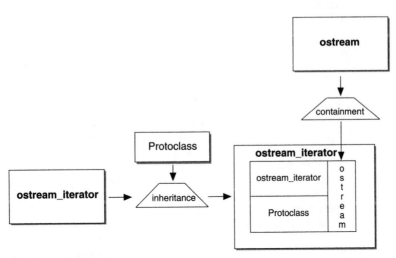

**B. ostream_iterator**

**Figure 9.4** The class relationship diagram for the **ostream_iterator** and **istream _iterator.**

## The ostream_iterator

The **ostream_iterator** is declared in *iterator.h*. The **ostream_iterator** has two constructors. The first constructor accepts a reference $X$ to an **ostream** or one of its descendants. The iterator can then be used to write the stream $X$. The second constructor accepts a reference $X$ to an **ostream** or one of its descendants and a char * **Delim. Delim** will be written out to $X$ after each insertion. **Delim** can be any string including the control characters "\n", "\f", "\t", "\b". To construct an **ostream_iterator** that would point to an **ofstream** object that contains our user-defined type **rational**, we would declare the iterator as:

```
ofstream Out("Myfile.txt");
ostream_iterator<rational,ptrdiff_t> P(Out,"\n");
```

The **ostream_iterator** also supports the ++operator used for traversing through the **ostream** objects. Since **ostream_iterator** is a type of **output_iterator**, the same restrictions that apply to **output_iterators** apply to **ostream_iterators**.

## Using the Stream Iterators with the Generic Algorithms

Table 9.5 lists all the generic algorithms that accept input iterators or output iterators. Any of these algorithms can be used with the stream iterators. The stream iterators allow external collections to be compared, copied, intersected, and merged with in-memory containers. Persistent collections can be freely mixed with transient collections. The program in Listing 9.4 demonstrates how the stream iterators can be used to tie persistent objects with STL containers and algorithms.

**Table 9.5    A list of all the generic algorithms that accept input or output iterators.**

| Algorithms | Input/Output Iterator | Algorithms | Input/Output Iterator |
|---|---|---|---|
| for_each | Input | partial_sort_copy | Input |
| merge | Both | includes | Input |
| set_union | Both | set_intersection | Both |
| set_difference | Both | set_symmetric_difference | Both |
| max_element | Input | min_element | Input |
| lexicographical_compare | Input | accumulate | Input |
| inner_product | Input | partial_sum | Both |
| adjacent_difference | Both | find | Input |
| find_if | Input | count | Input |
| count_if | Input | mismatch | Input |
| equal | Input | copy | Both |
| transform | Both | replace_copy | Both |
| remove_copy | Both | remove_copy_if | Both |
| unique_copy | Both | rotate_copy | Output |

### Listing 9.4

```
1 // This program demonstrates how
2 // user persistent objects can be used with STL containers
3 // and algorithms through the usage of stream iterators.
4 //
5
```

```
 6 #include <fstream.h>
 7 #include <vector.h>
 8 #include "rational.h"
 9 #include <iterator.h>
10 #include <algo.h>
11 #include <multiset.h>
12
13
14
15 void main(void)
16 {
17
18    vector<rational> MyVect;
19    multiset<rational, less<rational> > MySet;
20    ofstream Out("fract.txt");
21    rational Num1(3,2);
22    rational Num2(2,4);
23    rational Num3(5,3);
24    rational Num4(7,9);
25    rational Num5(12,5);
26    MyVect.push_back(Num3);
27    MyVect.push_back(Num4);
28    MyVect.push_back(Num5);
29    sort(MyVect.begin(),MyVect.end(),Num1);
30    Out << Num1 << " " << Num2;
31    Out.close();
32    ifstream In("fract.txt");
33    istream_iterator<rational,ptrdiff_t> P(In);
34    istream_iterator<rational,ptrdiff_t> EndOfFile;
35    ofstream Out2("merge.txt");
36    ostream_iterator<rational> S(Out2," ");
37    ostream_iterator<rational> Console(cout,"\n");
38    merge(P,EndOfFile,MyVect.begin(),MyVect.end(),S);
39    Out2.close();
40    In.close();
41    In.open("merge.txt");
42    while(In)
43    {
44    In >> Num1;
45    if(!In.eof()){
46    MySet.insert(Num1);
47    }
48    }
49    In.close();
50    copy(MySet.begin(),MySet.end(),Console);
51    Out2.open("diff2.txt");
52    ostream_iterator<rational> M(Out2," ");
53    set_difference(MySet.begin(), MySet.end(), MyVect.begin(),
54         MyVect.end(),M);
55    Out2.close();
```

```
56   In.open("diff2.txt");
57   cout << endl << "The set difference " << endl;
58   while(!In.eof())
59   {
60
61     if(!In.eof()){
62   In >> Num1;
63   cout << Num1 << endl;
64     }
65   }
66   In.close();
67
68
69
70 }
```

The program in Listing 9.4 uses a set of **rationals** and a vector of **rationals** to demonstrate how our persistent **rational** class can be used with STL containers. The **merge()** algorithm on line 38 merges an **ifstream** object containing **rational** objects with a vector of **rational** objects. The result is stored in an **ostream** object that is connected to the text file *merge.txt*. The results of the **merge()** algorithm are then extracted from an **ifstream** object called **In** and placed into a set called **MySet**. The **copy()** algorithm is then used to copy the elements of **MySet** to **Console**. Console is an **ostream_iterator** that is tied to the predefined **ostream** object **cout**. The program then performs a set difference between **MySet** and **MyVect** and the resulting set is stored in an **ofstream** object called **Out2**. The results of the **set_difference()** algorithm are then extracted from the **ifstream** object **In** and displayed. Table 9.6 shows the output from this program.

**Table 9.6   Output from program Listing 9.4 demonstrates the persistent rational class. The program performs a set difference between MySet and MyVect and the resulting set is displayed.**

*Output from Program Listing 9.4*

7/9
2/4
3/2
5/3
12/5

The set difference
2/4
5/3
5/3

# FROM THE IOSTREAM CLASSES AND STL ALGORITHMS TO PERSISTENCE

This chapter demonstrates how the **iostreams** can be used as building blocks for persistent objects. We've only scratched the surface with our policy-based persistence. There are many more considerations when designing persistent classes. Object ids, versioning, object aggregates, and storage efficiency are just a few of the important issues that must be addressed when implementing complete object persistence. However, the techniques presented in this chapter offer a start. The STL **istream_iterator** and **ostream_iterator** bridge the gap between the **iostream** classes and the STL containers. The program in Listing 9.4 illustrates how the **iostreams** and the STL containers can be mixed to achieve object persistence. By applying the generic algorithms to **ofstream** and **ifstream** objects, the **ofstream** and **ifstream** objects become effective persistent containers. We are able to call the **find()** algorithm, the set algorithms, the **copy()** and **replace()** algorithms to work with the **iostream** objects. This allows us to approach sophisticated collections and containers without the need for preprocessor tricks or artificial extensions to the language. In Chapter 10, we use the **iostream** classes as storage components and demonstrate how even higher-level persistence classes can be built.

| No matter where you go, there you are. . . .  Tautology |
| --- |

# BUILDING YOUR OWN COLLECTIONS AND CONTAINERS

THE COLLECTION and container classes that we've discussed so far are taken from the traditional data structures in computer science. Implementations of stacks, queues, vectors, lists, sets, deques, and graphs can be found as data structures in non–object-oriented languages and environments. However, the application of object-oriented techniques to these traditional structures transform them from data structures to meta-structures. We call these metastructures collection and container classes. The number and type of collection and container classes are in no way limited to the structures discussed in this book. In practice, many exotic collections and containers are found, such as: garage, bank, cell, crowd, village, group, ring, transport, box, 3D space, scenario, timeline, knowledge base, room, field, transfinite set, cabinets, neural net, and organism.

Most of these containers are domain specific. That is, they are used only in certain areas, whereas the collections and containers that are discussed in this book are more generic and have broader application. In many situations the traditional collection and container will be appropriate. In other situations, for instance, in modeling or simulation, more exotic collections or containers may be necessary. The choice of whether to build or reuse constantly presents itself in programming, and especially in C++. This choice will present itself with respect to the new STL that has been added to the C++ language. The STL contains seven basic containers and more than 30 algorithms that can work with those containers. However, these containers only offer the basics. There will be many occasions when the programmer will find them incomplete, inadequate, or aesthetically wrong for the job at hand. When this happens, the choice is either to find other prebuilt collections and containers or to construct new ones. In this chapter, we present some of the issues that the programmer should consider when preparing to build a collection or container class.

# BUILD OR REUSE?

It is rarely necessary to build a collection or container class from scratch. While the container libraries that come with C++ compilers are not always adequate, they usually offer at least the building blocks that are needed. The STL offers several basic containers and more than 30 algorithms that work on those containers. These components can be used as building blocks for your own collection or container classes. The first step in building your own collection or container class is to determine what components are available in the environment you use. After you have taken careful inventory of the components that are available in your C++ environment, it is a good idea to see if these components can be combined in ways that supply the container functionality that is needed. The goal is to let the existing components do as much of the work as possible. Ask yourself: Can the components be extended through inheritance to provide the functionality that is needed?

Another important consideration when deciding whether to reuse or build is the assumption that suppliers of the components made about the users. Were the components designed to be extended, or were they designed as self-contained units of functionality that can't be extended because critical data members and member functions are made private or const. If the components were designed as self-contained units, can you reasonably plug them into your collection or container class? If the components are part of the ANSI/ISO standard for C++, then they are fairly stable and any code built from these components is under your control. However, if the components come as part of a vendor-specific offering, then they are subject to change and the vendors have control over any code that is built using these components. Sometimes a market-driven implementation is desirable; many times it is not. Do the suppliers of the components assume that you will use templates? Does the supplier of the collections or containers assume that an object-based hierarchy is acceptable? Are the components that you are considering known to be tested and robust? Will the components work in the memory model that you are using? Some collection and container classes assume virtual memory, while others can't take advantage of virtual memory.

Making the determination of whether to build or reuse should always involve a careful consideration of the target environment as well as the development environment. In most cases there will be reusable components available. Today's C++ environments have a rich entree of collection and container classes and components. In these environments the real question is not whether to reuse but how much to reuse. Therefore, in building your own collection and container classes don't start from scratch, unless you are doing so for academic or other more noble reasons.

# COLLECTION OR CONTAINER?

Throughout this text we've tried to separate the terms *collection* and *container* where appropriate, and there is a distinction. If all that is needed is an object that will provide storage, retrieval, and removal, then what you want is a container. On the other hand, if the holding object has to have special characteristics like sorted, unique elements, special operations, explicit methods for object insertion, object deletion, and specific traversal methods, then a collection is required. In general, containers are easier to build and have generic fat interfaces (see Stroustrup 1991, 452). Collections require more rigor and have highly specific interfaces. Collection interfaces have highly specific semantics. That means that the naming conventions of the member functions and data members are important. It also means that the protocols used when interacting with the class have very specific meanings. Many collections are either established mathematical notions or domain-specific models. The interface will determine whether you are building a collection or container. In general, containers are generic holders with fat interfaces, and collections are groupings with highly semantic interfaces.

## OBJECT BASED OR TEMPLATE BASED?

There are several possibilities for implementing collections and containers. In Chapter 3 we discussed object-based and template-based architectures. The object-based strategy requires that any object that needs to be used with containers be derived from some common *object*, and that any user-defined container be derived from some common collection class. In this way the designer of the collection class could depend on runtime polymorphism. For instance:

```
class Container{
protected:
    char *Memory;
public:
    virtual void add(Object &X);
};
void Container::add(Object &X)
{
    Memory[N] = X;
}
```

The **add()** member function will store **Object X** and any of its descendants. If a class is not descended from **Object**, that is, **int, char, float**, and **double**, then it cannot be added to the container. This poses several problems. The primary problem is that adding built-in data types to containers requires workarounds. However, for storing families of objects this method is acceptable. Runtime polymorphism allows **Object &** to accept any derived type. Runtime polymorphism also allows the **add()** member function to be overridden to supply a more appropriate **add()** member function. Object-based architectures are acceptable when the combination of *content + object* has semantic importance within a program. For example, if in a bank application we have a container called **coin-holder** that is designed to hold various types of coins, then requiring that all the objects that can be placed into **coin-holder** be derived from **coin** is acceptable and preferable. Furthermore, we would like to prevent the user from attempting to add dollars, or savings bonds, or credit cards to our **coin-holder** container. Using object-based architectures can preserve the semantics of objects and their relationships to other objects within an application.

Object-based architectures are best used when the programmer needs to model or simulate domains with particular attention to detail. Maintaining the meaning of an object and the relationship between that object and other objects within the framework of an application is important when performing modeling and simulation. Properly defined object hierarchies contain both meaning and knowledge. For example, if an object is in our **coin_holder**, then we know the object is a type of **coin** as opposed to some other type of object. Depending upon where in the **coin_holder** our object is, we can infer things about its value, size, composition, and so on. For instance, if the object is in the **coin_holder** and fits into the **dime_slot**, we can infer that the object is not a quarter, or made of copper. Furthermore, it makes sense for a coin to be in a **coin_holder**. This is the strength of object-based containers. They tie the type of object to the type of container! However, object-based containers are not good architectures for generic containers. Martin Carroll and Margaret Ellis give an interesting argument against using object-based containers in their (1995) book *Designing and Coding Reusable C++*. As a rule, if the relationship between the container and the object is unimportant, or if the container needs to be able to hold any possible kind of object, then object-based architectures are unacceptable. On the other hand, if the relationship between the object and the container has semantic significance, and the container is not a general-purpose container, then an object-based architecture is acceptable and sometimes preferable.

When generic containers that can hold any kind of object are required, then the method of choice is template-based containers. Because the template is parameterized, it can hold any kind of object. This allows you to implement the container once and for all. When a template is used the container does not have to be implemented again for different types. This is one of the downfalls of object-based containers. If an object-based container is properly designed it will only work for certain families of objects. The container must be recoded for each new family of objects that will be stored. The template-based architecture is leaner (Carroll, Ellis 1995, 195). The template-based approach tends to produce horizontal container families, whereas the object-based approach tends to produce highly vertical container families. The template-based architecture emphasizes genericity, while the object-based architecture emphasizes relationship and meaning. Template-based containers and collections are generally domain independent and have broad application. Object-based containers and collections are normally domain specific. In a large application there will probably be room for both types. As the programmer moves closer to the domain of an application, object-based collections and containers become more important. When the programmer needs to emphasize reuse, then template-based containers and collections are more important.

## A Note on Genericity

Keep in mind that while genericity is normally desirable for reusability, it can wreak havoc in system testing and maintenance. Good test plans depend upon the relationships between objects and their meanings in a program. Genericity and fat interfaces degrade these relationships and can obscure object meaning, making testing and debugging more difficult. Furthermore, when genericity is taken to the nth degree, programs become extremely difficult to maintain, even for those that created them. The programmer that has to try to make sense of someone else's zeal for genericity is bound for many late nights at the office. As a rule of thumb, make your collections and containers as generic as necessary and no more.

## IMPLEMENTATION DECISIONS

Once you have decided that you will have to implement your own collection or container class, and you've decided whether it will have an object-based or template-based architecture, then you must decide the implementation of the storage component for the collection or container. Every collection and container must have a storage component. The storage component is where the user's objects get stored. Recall the stack adaptor from Chapter 6. The stack adaptor is a stack whose storage component is implemented by another container. For instance, the STL stack can be implemented by a vector, list, or deque. This means that while the user sees the **push()**, **pop()**, and LIFO attributes of a stack, the objects are actually being stored in either a vector, list, or deque.

In this case the stack adaptor is an interface class. It does not define any new functionality; it only renames member functions of other containers. When building your own collection or container class you must determine whether providing a new interface for an existing class is sufficient, or whether you will have to use an existing class and supply all new member functions. This is the distinction between an interface class and a new class based on an existing class. An interface class simply provides new member function names that wrap functions from some existing class; whereas the new class that has an existing class as a component defines new member functions. For instance, we could define an **external_vector** by using a **fstream** class as our storage component. The program in Listing 10.1 declares an **external_vector** and then demonstrates the use of the [] operator to iterate through the **external_vector**.

**Listing 10.1**

```
1 // Listing 10.1
2 // Example of a persistent container built
3 // with a fstream storage component
4
5 #include <fstream.h>
6
7 template <class T> class external_vector{
8 protected:
9    int Size;
10   fstream V;
11 public:
12   external_vector(char *Vector,int Mode);
13   ~external_vector(void);
14   T operator[](int N);
15   void add(T X);
16   int size(void);
17 };
```

```
18
19
20 template <class T> external_vector<T>::external_vector(char *Vector,int
   Mode)
21 {
22   Size = 0;
23   V.open(Vector,Mode);
24 }
25
26
27 template <class T> external_vector<T>::~external_vector(void)
28 {
29   V.close();
30 }
31
32
33 template <class T> void external_vector<T>::add(T X)
34 {
35   V.write((char *)&X,sizeof(T));
36   Size++;
37 }
38
39
40 template <class T> T external_vector<T>::operator[](int N)
41 {
42   T X;
43   V.seekg(0,ios::beg);
44   V.seekg((N * sizeof(T)),ios::beg);
45   V.read((char *) &X,sizeof(T));
46   return(X);
47 }
48
49
50 template <class T> int external_vector<T>::size(void)
51 {
52   return(Size);
53 }
54
55 void main(void)
56 {
57   external_vector<double> MyVect("VectA.txt",ios::binary | ios::out | ios::in);
58   MyVect.add(5.3);
59   MyVect.add(6.4);
60   MyVect.add(9.1);
61   MyVect.add(22.1);
62   int N;
63   for(N = 0;N < MyVect.size();N++)
64   {
65     cout << MyVect[N] << endl;
66   }
```

```
67
68 }
69
```

The **fstream** object provides the storage component. We can, therefore, store as many objects as available disk space will allow. The **external_vector** is a simple example of a persistent container that is implemented by reusing the **fstream** class. The [ ] operator and the **add()** member function demonstrate the advantages of using an existing class. We are able to take advantage of **fstream**'s **seekg()** member function to locate our objects, and **fstream**'s **write()** member function to add our objects to the **external_vector**.

It is important to note that the performance of your collection and container will be constrained by the implementation of the storage component. If access to objects in your storage component is restricted to sequential access, then your collection or container's performance will reflect that fact. In the case of our **external_vector** we can achieve direct access, because the implementation of our storage component supports direct access with the **seekg()** member function. Also how many objects your collection or container will be able to store is dependent on the storage component you select. If your storage component is restricted to a maximum size of 64 K, then your collection or container will only be able to access 64 K. In the case of our **external_vector** we used an **fstream** storage component; therefore our container can access available disk storage.

Many collections and containers allow multiple implementation of the storage component. For instance, the STL stack, queue, and **priority_queue** containers provide a choice of storage components. The user is free to choose whichever component offers the best performance for the application. When building your own collection and container classes this is certainly an option. However, one word of caution is required: Supplying multiple implementations for collections and containers is similar to optimizing programs. Just as it is advisable to get the program to work properly before optimizing it, it is advisable to make sure the collection or container is functionally correct before providing multiple implementations.

## HOW WILL OBJECT VISITATION BE ACHIEVED?

A collection or container class that does not provide a means for the user to visit each object in the container violates the core responsibilities of collection or container classes. There are two basic methods that are used to provide access to the objects within a container. The first method defines a set of member functions for the container, for example, **next()**, **previous()**, **current()**, or the [] operator. These member functions can be used to visit each object in the container. Every collection or container must provide a means of total object visitation or iteration. For instance, in the **external_vector** in Listing 10.1, the [] operator was defined. The user can use the [] operator to access any object in the **external-_vector**. Providing member functions that allow object visitation is the simplest method. However, it has one major restriction. The user has limited access to the number of objects that can be visited simultaneously. That is, there is only one **current()** object, or one **next()** object, or one **previous()** object. If the user wants to visit objects at different locations within the collection or container concurrently, member functions are prohibitive.

This brings us to the *iterator*, the second method of providing visitation in a collection or container. The iterator is a class that is separate from the collection or container but has access to the collection or container's storage component. For example, we could declare an **external_vector_iterator** to work with our **external_vector** from Listing 10.1 as:

```
template <class T> class external_vector_iterator{
private:
  fstream Data;
public:
  external_vector_iterator(fstream &X);
  T operator[](int N);
};

template  <class  T>  external_vector_iterator<T>::external_vector_itera-
tor(fstream &X)
{
    Data.attach(X.rdbuf()->fd());
}

template <class T> T external_vector_iterator<T>::operator[](int N)
{
    T X;
    Data.seekg(0,ios::beg);
    Data.seekg((N * sizeof(T)),ios::beg);
    Data.read((char *) &X,sizeof(T));
    return(X);
}
```

Once this iterator is defined we could declare more than one object of type **external-_vector_iterator.** This would allow us to directly access multiple locations within the vector concurrently. This is because the iterator has access to the storage component of the container. In this case, the constructor for **external_vector iterator** gains access to the storage component of the **external_vector** class with the **fstream's attach()** member function. Once the iterator has access to the storage component, then we can use the iterator to visit each object in the container. We may have different iterators visiting different objects within the same container. This is the advantage of iterators over member functions. They allow the programmer to access multiple locations within a collection or container class simultaneously. Each iterator maintains or accesses a different position. The program in Listing 10.2 demonstrates how the iterator concept works with our **external_vector** class.

### Listing 10.2

```
1 // Listing 10.2
2 // Example of a persistent container built
3 // with a fstream storage component. The iterator
4 // external_vector_iterator is an example of a
5 // separate iterator class for a user-defined
```

```
 6 // type.
 7
 8
 9 #include <fstream.h>
10
11 template <class T> class external_vector{
12 protected:
13    int Size;
14    fstream V;
15 public:
16    external_vector(char *Vector,int Mode);
17    ~external_vector(void);
18    fstream &operator()(void);
19    T operator[](int N);
20    void add(T X);
21    int size(void);
22 };
23
24
25 template <class T> external_vector<T>::external_vector(char *Vector,int
   Mode)
26 {
27    Size = 0;
28    V.open(Vector,Mode);
29 }
30
31
32 template <class T> external_vector<T>::~external_vector(void)
33 {
34    V.close();
35 }
36
37
38 template <class T> void external_vector<T>::add(T X)
39 {
40    V.write((char *)&X,sizeof(T));
41    Size++;
42 }
43
44
45 template <class T> T external_vector<T>::operator[](int N)
46 {
47    T X;
48    V.seekg(0,ios::beg);
49    V.seekg((N * sizeof(T)),ios::beg);
50    V.read((char *) &X,sizeof(T));
51    return(X);
52 }
53
54
```

```
55 template <class T> int external_vector<T>::size(void)
56 {
57    return(Size);
58 }
59
60 template <class T> fstream &external_vector<T>::operator()(void)
61 {
62    return(V);
63 }
64
65 template <class T> class external_vector_iterator{
66 private:
67    fstream Data;
68 public:
69    external_vector_iterator(fstream &X);
70    T operator[](int N);
71 };
72
73 template <class T> external_vector_iterator<T>::external_vector_itera-
   tor(fstream &X)
74 {
75    Data.attach(X.rdbuf()->fd());
76 }
77
78
79 template <class T> T external_vector_iterator<T>::operator[](int N)
80 {
81    T X;
82    Data.seekg(0,ios::beg);
83    Data.seekg((N * sizeof(T)),ios::beg);
84    Data.read((char *) &X,sizeof(T));
85    return(X);
86 }
87
88 void main(void)
89 {
90     external_vector<double>  MyVect("VectA.txt",ios::binary | ios::out |
    ios::in);
91    external_vector_iterator<double> M(MyVect());
92    external_vector_iterator<double> N(MyVect());
93    external_vector_iterator<double> P(MyVect());
94    MyVect.add(5.3);
95    MyVect.add(6.4);
96    MyVect.add(9.1);
97    MyVect.add(22.1);
98    MyVect.add(15.2);
99    MyVect.add(231.54);
100   MyVect.add(-77.1);
101   cout << M[3] << endl;
102   cout << P[0] << endl;
```

```
103    cout << N[6] << endl;
104 }
105
```

Keep in mind that the classes **external_vector** and **external_vector_iterator** are extreme oversimplifications of a persistent vector. In practice, there are many issues that we simply did not deal with in this example, such as buffering, file-locking, and exception handling. These examples are meant only to provide you with a broad outline of how to approach designing your own collection and container classes.

While iterators do provide the most flexible method of object visitation, you must address several sensitive areas. A policy for iterator destruction must be implemented. It is undesirable to have an iterator that points to a collection or container that no longer exists. That is, avoid policies that lead to iterators that have longer life spans than the collection or containers they are assigned to. Ideally the iterator should be destroyed either before or at the same time the collection or container is destroyed. Also, you must decide whether the iterator will allow the user to read, write, or modify the objects in the collection or container. The STL solves this problem by providing input, output, forward, bidirectional, and random access iterators. If you are designing your own iterator classes you will have to make similar categories of iterators.

## TRANSIENT OR PERSISTENT COLLECTIONS?

Transient collections and containers can only exist during the execution of a program they are created in. Persistent collections and containers can exist outside the program they were created in. When determining what type of implementation your collection and container will have, consider whether the collection or container needs to be persistent, or whether a transient implementation will do. The implementation of the storage component is dependent upon whether the collection is a transient or persistent collection. Table 10.1 shows some of the common storage components for transient collections and containers, and some of the common storage components for persistent collections and containers. The memory management policy will also depend on whether the storage component is transient or persistent. Ownership of the objects within the containers is also largely determined by whether the container has a transient or persistent storage component.

## SOME FINAL THOUGHTS

The C++ language and its support for object-oriented programming and generic programming provides the programmer with powerful tools of expression. The programmer is able to implement virtual communities of objects that resemble real-world tasks, processes, or ideas. The collection and container classes give the programmer a means to organize those objects into meaningful and comprehensible groups. As the program or system grows, the collection and container classes allow the programmer to effectively deal with complexity issues. The introduction of the STL into the C++ environment

**Table 10.1.  Some of the common storage components for the transient and persistent collections and containers.**
EXAMPLE STORAGE COMPONENTS

| *Transient Collections/Containers* | *Persistent Collections/Containers* |
| --- | --- |
| Queue | B-Tree |
| Vector | Flat File |
| Adjacency Matrix | Ascii File |
| Adjacency List | Database |

relieves the programmer from the drudgery of implementing fundamental data structures from scratch. The collection and container classes that are available promote code reuse, thereby making C++ programmers and developers more productive. Now that we have powerful methods for developing and modeling objects and groups of objects and their relationships we can effectively tackle the programming problems that are presented in developing object-oriented databases, client/server systems, knowledge-based systems, natural language processing systems, discrete simulation, expert systems, and parallel processing systems. Frameworks, pattern classes, class libraries, and collection and container classes provide the C++ programmer with an arsenal of tools for modeling, simulation, and problem solving. In this book we introduced the collection and container class in C++ as a technique of organization and abstraction. We introduced the Standard Template Library and how it can be used to manage groups of objects. We also provided some of the theoretical foundations for the set, relation (map), and graph collections. C++ has become the most widely used object-oriented programming language in the world. Collection and container classes can be used to help the productivity and effectiveness of every C++ programmer who uses them.

# APPENDIX A

# THE STANDARD TEMPLATE LIBRARY

## ALEXANDER STEPANOV
## AND MENG LEE

*Hewlett-Packard Laboratories*
*1501 Page Mill Road*
*Palo Alto, CA 94304*
*February 7, 1995*

# 1  INTRODUCTION

The Standard Template Library provides a set of well structured generic C++ components that work together in a seamless way. Special care has been taken to ensure that all the template algorithms work not only on the data structures in the library, but also on built-in C++ data structures. For example, all the algorithms work on regular pointers. The orthogonal design of the library allows programmers to use library data structures with their own algorithms, and to use library algorithms with their own data structures. The well specified semantic and complexity requirements guarantee that a user component will work with the library, and that it will work efficiently. This flexibility ensures the widespread utility of the library.

Another important consideration is efficiency. C++ is successful because it combines expressive power with efficiency. Much effort has been spent to verify that every template component in the library has a generic implementation that performs within a few percentage points of the efficiency of the corresponding hand coded routine.

The third consideration in the design has been to develop a library structure that, while being natural and easy to grasp, is based on a firm theoretical foundation.

# 2  STRUCTURE OF THE LIBRARY

The library contains five main kinds of components:

 algorithm: defines a computational procedure.
 container: manages a set of memory locations.
 iterator: provides a means for an algorithm to traverse through a container.
 function object: encapsulates a function in an object for use by other components.
 adaptor: adapts a component to provide a different interface.

Such decomposition allows us to dramatically reduce the component space. For example, instead of providing a search member function for every kind of container we provide a single version that works with all of them as long as a basic set of requirements is satisfied.

The following description helps clarify the structure of the library. If software components are tabulated as a three-dimensional array, where one dimension represents different data types (e.g., int, double), the second dimension represents different containers (e.g., vector, linked-list, file), and the third dimension represents different algorithms on the containers (e.g., searching, sorting, rotation), if i, j, and k are the size of the dimensions, then i*j*k different versions of code have to be designed. By using template functions that are parameterized by a data type, we need only j*k versions. Further, by making our algorithms work on different containers, we need merely j+k versions. This significantly simplifies software design work and also makes it possible to use components in the library together with user defined components in a very flexible way. A user may easily define a specialized container class and use the library's sort function to sort it. A user may provide a different comparison function for the sort either as a regular pointer to a comparison function, or as a function object (an object with an `operator()` defined) that does the comparisons. If a user needs to iterate through a container in the reverse direction, the `reverse_iterator` adaptor allows that.

The library extends the basic C++ paradigms in a consistent way, so it is easy for a C/C++ programmer to start using the library. For example, the library contains a merge template function. When a user has two arrays a and b to be merged into c it can be done with:

```
int a[1000];
int b[2000];
int c[3000];
. . .
merge (a, a + 1000, b, b + 2000, c);
```

When a user wants to merge a vector and a list (both of which are template classes in the library) and put the result into a freshly allocated uninitialized storage it can be done with:

```
vector<Employee> a;
list<Employee> b;
. . .
Employee* c = allocate(a.size() + b.size(), (Employee*)0);
merge(a.begin(), a.end(), b.begin(), b.end(),
    raw_storage_iterator<Employee*, Employee>(c));
```

where `begin()` and `end()` are member functions of containers that return the right types of iterators or pointer-like objects that allow the merge to do the job and `raw_storage_iterator` is an adapter that allows algorithms to put results directly into uninitialized memory by calling the appropriate copy constructor.

In many cases it is useful to iterate through input/output streams in the same way as through regular data structures. For example, if we want to merge two data structures and then store them in a file, it would be nice to avoid creation of an auxiliary data structure for the result, instead storing the result directly into the corresponding file. The library provides both `istream_iterator` and `ostream_iterator` template classes to make many of the library algorithms work with I/O streams that represent homogenous aggregates of data. Here is a program that reads a file of integers from the standard input, removes all those that are divisible by its command argument, and writes the result to the standard output:

```
main(int argc, char** argv) {
    if (argc @= 2) throw ("usage: remove_if_divides integer\n");
    remove_copy_if(istream_iterator<int>(cin), istream_iterator<int>(),
        ostream_iterator<int>(cout, "\n"),
        not1 (bind2nd(modulus<int>(), atoi (argv[1]))));
}
```

All the work is done by `remove_copy_if` which reads integers one by one until the input iterator becomes equal to the *end-of-stream* iterator that is constructed by the constructor with no arguments. (In general, all the algorithms work in a "from here to there" fashion taking two iterators that signify the beginning and the end of the input.) Then `remove_copy_if` writes the integers that pass the test onto the output stream through the output iterator that is bound to `cout`. As a predicate, `remove_copy_if` uses a function object constructed from a function object, `modulus<int>`, which takes i and j and returns i%j, as a binary predicate and makes it into a unary predicate by using `bind2nd` to bind the second argument to the command line argument, `atoi (argv[1])`. Then the negation of this unary predicate is obtained using function adaptor `not1`.

A somewhat more realistic example is a filter program that takes a file and randomly shuffles its lines.

```
main(int argc, char**) {
    if (argc != 1) throw(``usage: shuffle\n'');
    vector<string> v;
    copy(istream_iterator<string>(cin), istream_iterator<string>(),
        inserter (v, v.end()));
    random_shuffle(v.begin(), v.end());
    copy(v.begin(), v.end(), ostream_iterator<string>(cout));
}
```

In this example, copy moves lines from the standard input into a vector, but since the vector is not pre-allocated it uses an insert iterator to insert the lines one by one into the vector. (This technique allows all of the copying functions to work in the usual overwrite mode as well as in the insert mode.) Then random-_shuffle shuffles the vector and another call to copy copies it onto the cout stream.

## 3  REQUIREMENTS

To ensure that the different components in a library work together, they must satisfy some basic requirements. Requirements should be as general as possible, so instead of saying "class x has to define a member function operator++ ( )," we say "for any object x of class x, ++x is defined." (It is unspecified whether the operator is a member or a global function.) Requirements are stated in terms of well-defined expressions, which define valid terms of the types that satisfy the requirements. For every set of requirements there is a table that specifies an initial set of the valid expressions and their semantics. Any generic algorithm that uses the requirements has to be written in terms of the valid expressions for its formal type parameters.

   If an operation is required to be linear time, it means no worse than linear time, and a constant time operation satisfies the requirement.

   In some cases we present the semantic requirements using C++ code. Such code is intended as a specification of equivalence of a construct to another construct, not necessarily as the way the construct must be implemented (although in some cases the code given is unambiguously the optimum implementation).

## 4  CORE COMPONENTS

This section contains some basic template functions and classes that are used throughout the rest of the library.

### 4.1  Operators

To avoid redundant definitions of operator != out of operator == and operators>, <=, and >= out of operator< the library provides the following:

```
template <class T>
inline bool operator!=(const T& x, const T& y) {
    return !(x == y);
}

template <class T>
inline bool operator>(const T& x, const T& y) {
```

```
        return y < x;
}

template <class T>
inline bool operator<= (const T& x, const T& y) {
    return ! (y < x);
}

template <class T>
inline bool operator>= (const T& x, const T& y) {
    return ! (x < y);
}
```

## 4.2   Pair

The library includes templates for heterogeneous pairs of values.

```
template <class T1, class T2>
struct pair {
    T1 first:
    T2 second;
    pair(const T1& x, const T2& y) : first(x), second(y) {}
};

template <class T1, class T2>
inline bool operator== (const pair<T1, T2>& x, const pair<T1, T2>& y) {
    return x.first == y.first && x.second == y.second;
}

template <class T1, class T2>
inline bool operator< (const pair<T1, T2>& x, const pair<T1, T2>& y) {
    return x.first < y.first || (! (y.first < x.first) && x.second < y.second);
}
```

The library provides a matching template function `make_pair` to simplify their construction. Instead of saying, for example,

```
return pair<int, double>(5, 3.1415926); // explicit types
```

one may say

```
return make_pair(5, 3.1415926); // types are deduced
```

```
template <class T1, class T2>
inline pair<T1, T2> make_pair(const T1& x, const T2& y) {
    return pair<T1, T2>(x, y);
```

## 5   ITERATORS

Iterators are a generalization of pointers that allow a programmer to work with different data structures (containers) in a uniform manner. To be able to construct template algorithms that work correctly and efficiently on different types of data structures, we need to formalize not just the interfaces but also the semantics and complexity assumptions of iterators. Iterators are objects that have `operator*` returning a value of some class or built-in type T called a *value type* of the iterator. For every iterator type X for which equality is defined, there is a corresponding signed integral type called the *distance type* of the iterator.

Since iterators are a generalization of pointers, their semantics is a generalization of the semantics of pointers in C++. This assures that every template function that takes iterators works with regular pointers. Depending on the operations defined on them, there are five categories of iterators: *input iterators, output iterators, forward iterators, bidirectional iterators* and *random access iterators*. Forward iterators satisfy all the requirements of the input and output iterators and can be used whenever either kind is specified. Bidirectional iterators satisfy all the requirements of the forward iterators and can be used whenever a forward iterator is specified. Random access iterators satisfy all the requirements of bidirectional iterators and can be used whenever a bidirectional iterator is specified. There is an additional attribute that forward, bidirectional and random access iterators might have, that is, they can be *mutable* or *constant* depending on whether the result of the `operator*` behaves as a reference or as a reference to a constant. Constant iterators do not satisfy the requirements for output iterators.

### Table A-1   Relations Among Iterator Categories

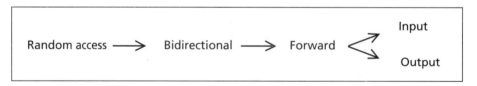

Just as a regular pointer to an array guarantees that there is a pointer value pointing past the last element of the array, so for any iterator type there is an iterator value that points past the last element of a corresponding container. These values are called *past-the-end* values. Values of the iterator for which the `operator*` is defined are called *dereferenceable*. The library never assumes that past-the-end values are dereferenceable. Iterators might also have *singular* values that are not associated with any container. For example, after the declaration of an uninitialized pointer x (as with `int* x;`), x should always be assumed to have a singular value of a pointer. Results of most expressions are undefined for singular values. The only exception is an assignment of a nonsingular value to an iterator that holds a singular value. In this case the singular value is overwritten the same way as any other value. Dereferenceable and past-the-end values are always nonsingular.

An iterator j is called *reachable* from an iterator i if and only if there is a finite sequence of applications of `operator++` to i that makes i == j. If i and j refer to the same container, then either j is reachable from i, or i is reachable from j, or both (i == j).

Most of the library's algorithmic templates that operate on data structures have interfaces that use ranges. A range is a pair of iterators that designate the beginning and end of the computation. A range [i, i) is an empty range; in general, a range [i, j) refers to the elements in the data structure starting with the one pointed to by i and up to but not including the one pointed to by j. Range [i, j) is valid if and only if j is reachable from i. The result of the application of the algorithms in the library to invalid ranges is undefined.

All the categories of iterators require only those functions that are realizable for a given category in constant time (amortized). Therefore, requirement tables for the iterators do not have a complexity column.

In the following sections, we assume: a and b are values of x, n is a value of the distance type `Distance`, u, tmp, and m are identifiers, r and s are lvalues of x, t is a value of value type T.

## 5.1   Input iterators

A class or a built-in type X satisfies the requirements of an input iterator for the value type T if the following expressions are valid:

**Table A2   Input Iterator Requirements**

| expression | return type | operational semantics | assertion/note pre/post-condition |
|---|---|---|---|
| X(a) | | | a == X(a).<br>note: a destructor is assumed. |
| X u(a);<br>X u = a; | | | post: u == a. |
| a == b | convertible to bool | | == is an equivalence relation. |
| a != b | convertible to bool | ! (a == b) | |
| *a | convertible to T | | pre: a is dereferenceable.<br>a == b implies *a == *b. |
| ++r | X& | | pre: r is dereferenceable.<br>post: r is dereferenceable or r is past-the-end.<br>&r == &++r. |
| r++ | X | { X tmp = r;<br>++r;<br>return tmp; } | |

**NOTE:**  For input iterators, r == s does not imply ++r == ++s. (Equality does not guarantee the substitution property or referential transparency.) Algorithms on input iterators should never attempt to pass through the same iterator twice. They should be *single pass* algorithms. *Value type T is not required to be an lvalue type.* These algorithms can be used with istreams as the source of the input data through the `istream_iterator class`.

## 5.2   Output iterators

A class or a built-in type X satisfies the requirements of an output iterator if the following expressions are valid:

**Table A3   Output Iterator Requirements**

| expression | return type | operational semantics | assertion/note pre/post-condition |
|---|---|---|---|
| X(a) | | | *a=t is equivalent to *X(a) +t. note: a destructor is assumed. |
| X u(a); X u = a; | | | |
| *a = t | result is not used | | |
| ++r | X& | | |
| r++ | X or X& | | |

**NOTE:** The only valid use of an `operator*` is on the left side of the assignment statement. *Assignment through the same value of the iterator happens only once.* Algorithms on out put iterators should never attempt to pass through the same iterator twice. They should be *single pass* algorithms. Equality and inequality are not necessarily defined. Algorithms that take output iterators can be used with ostreams as the destination for placing data through the `ostream_iterator` class as well as with insert iterators and insert pointers. In particular, the following two conditions should hold: first, any iterator value should be assigned through before it is incremented (this is, for an output iterator i, i++; i++; is not a valid code sequence); second, any value of an output iterator may have at most one active copy at any given time (for example, i = j; *++i = a; *j = b; is not a valid code sequence).

## 5.3   Forward iterators

A class or a built-in type X satisfies the requirements of a forward iterator if the following expressions are valid:

**Table A4   Forward Iterator Requirements**

| expression | return type | operational semantics | assertion/note pre/post-condition |
|---|---|---|---|
| X u; | | | note: u might have a singular value. note: a destructor is assumed. |
| X() | | | note: X() might be singular. |
| X(a) | | | a == X(a). |
| X u(a); X u = a; | | X u; u = a; | post: u == a. |
| a == b | convertible to bool | | == is an equivalence relation. |
| a != b | convertible to bool | ! (a == b) | |
| r = a | X& | | post: r == a. |
| *a | convertible to T | | pre: a is dereferenceable. a == b implies *a == *b. If X is mutable, *a = t is valid. |
| ++r | X& | | pre: r is dereferenceable. post: r is dereferenceable or r is past-the-end. r == s and r is dereferenceable implies ++r == ++s. &r == &++r. |
| r++ | X | { X tmp = r; ++r; return tmp; } | |

**NOTE:** The fact that r == s implies ++r == ++s (which is not true for input and output iterators) and the removal on the restrictions on the number of the assignments through the iterator (which applies to output iterators) allows the use of multipass one-directional algorithms with forward iterators.

## 5.4　Bidirectional iterators

A class or a built-in type X satisfies the requirements of a bidirectional iterator if to the table that specifies forward iterators we add the following lines:

**Table A5　Bidirectional Iterator Requirements (in addition to forward iterator)**

| expression | return type | operational semantics | assertion/note pre/post-condition |
|---|---|---|---|
| --r | X& |  | pre: there exists s such that $r == ++s$.<br>post: s is dereferenceable.<br>$--(++r) == r$.<br>$--r == --s$ implies $r == s$.<br>$\&r == \&--r$. |
| r-- | X | { X tmp = r;<br>--r;<br>return tmp; } |  |

NOTE: Bidirectional iterators allow algorithms to move iterators backward as well as forward.

## 5.5   Random access iterators

A class or a built-in type X satisfies the requirements of a random access iterator if to the table that specifies bidirectional iterators we add the following lines:

**Table A6   Random Access Iterator Requirements (in addition to bidirectional iterator)**

| expression | return type | operational semantics | assertion/note pre/post-condition |
|---|---|---|---|
| r += n | X& | { Distance m = n;<br>if (m >= 0)<br>   while (m−−) ++r;<br>else<br>   while (m++) −−r;<br>return r; } | |
| a + n<br>n + a | X | { X tmp = a;<br>return tmp += n; } | a + n == n + a. |
| r −= n | X& | return r += −n; | |
| a − n | X | { X tmp = a;<br>return tmp −= n; } | |
| b − a | Distance | | pre: there exists a value n of Distance such that a + n = b.<br>b == a + (b − a) . |
| a [n] | convertible to T | * (a + n) | |
| a < b | convertible to bool | b − a > 0 | < is a total ordering relation |
| a > b | convertible to bool | b < a | > is a total ordering relation opposite to <. |
| a >= b | convertible to bool | ! (a < b) | |
| a <= b | convertible to bool | ! (a > b) | |

## 5.6   Iterator tags

To implement algorithms only in terms of iterators, it is often necessary to infer both of the value type and the distance type from the iterator. To enable this task it is required that for an iterator i of any category other than output iterator, the expression `value_type(i)` returns `(T*) (0)` and the expression `distance _type(i)` returns `(Distance*) (0)`. For output iterators, these expressions are not required.

### 5.6.1   EXAMPLES OF USING ITERATOR TAGS

For all the regular pointer types we can define `value_type` and `distance_type` with the help of:

```
template <class T>
inline T* value_type(const T*) { return (T*) (0); }

template <class T>
inline ptrdiff_t* distance_type(const T*) { return (ptrdiff_t*) (0); }
```

Then, if we want to implement a generic `reverse` function, we do the following:

```
template <class BidirectionalIterator>
inline void reverse(BidirectionalIterator first, BidirectionalIterator last) {
    _reverse(first, last, value_type(first), distance_type(first));
```

where_reverse is defined as:

```
template <class BidirectionalIterator, class T, class Distance>
void_reverse(bidirectionalIterator first, BidirectionalIterator last, T*,
        Distance*) {
    Distance n;
    distance(first, last, ni); // see Iterator operations section
    --n;
    while (n > 0) {
        T tmp = *first;
        *first++ = *--last;
        *last = tmp;
        n -= 2;
    }
}
```

If there is an additional pointer type_huge such that the difference of two_huge pointers is of the type `long long`, we define:

```
template <class T>
inline T* value_type(const T_huge *) { return (T*) (0); }

template <class T>
inline long long* distance_type(const T_huge *) { return (long long*) (0); }
```

It is often desirable for a template function to find out what is the most specific category of its iterator argument, so that the function can select the most efficiency algorithm at compile time. To facilitate this, the library introduces *category tag* classes which are used as compile time tags for algorithm selection. They are: `input_iterator_tag`, `output_iterator_tag`, `forward_iterator_tag`, `bidirectional_iterator_tag` and `random_access_iterator_tag`. Every iterator i must have an expression `iterator_category(i)` defined on it that returns the most specific category tag that describes its behavior. For example, we define that all the pointer types are in the random access iterator category by:

```
template <class T>
inline random_access_iterator_tag iterator_category(const T*) {
    return random_access_iterator_tag();
```

For a user-defined iterator `BinaryTreeIterator`, it can be included into the bidirectional iterator category by saying:

```
template <class T>
inline bidirectional_iterator_tag iterator_category(
        const BinaryTreeIterator<T>&) {
    return bidirectional_iterator_tag();
```

If a template function `evolve` is well defined for bidirectional iterators, but can be implemented more efficiently for random access iterators, then the implementation is like:

```
template <class BidirectionalIterator>
inline void evolve(BidirectionalIterator first, BidirectionalIterator last)
    evolve(first, last, iterator_category(first));
}
template <class BidirectionalIterator>
void evolve(BidirectionalIterator first, BidirectionalIterator last,
        bidirectional_iterator_tag) {
    // . . . more generic, but less efficient algorithm
}
template <class RandomAccessIterator>
void evolve (RandomAccessIterator first, RandomAccessIterator last,
        random_access_iterator_tag) {
    // . . . more efficient, but less generic algorithm
}
```

## 5.6.2 LIBRARY DEFINED PRIMITIVES

To simplify the task of defining the `iterator_category`, `value_type` and `distance_type` for user definable iterators, the library provides the following predefined classes and functions:

```
// iterator tags

struct input_iterator_tag {};
struct output_iterator_tag {};
```

```
struct forward_iterator_tag {};
struct bidirectional_iterator_tag {};
struct random_access_iterator_tag {};

// iterator bases

template <class T, class Distance = ptrdiff_t> struct input_iterator {};
struct output_iterator {};
// output_iterator is not a template because output iterators
// do not have either value type or distance type defined.
template <class T, class Distance = ptrdiff_t> struct forward_iterator {};
template <class T, class Distance = ptrdiff_t> struct bidirectional_iterator {};
template <class T, class Distance = ptrdiff_t> struct random_access_iterator {};

// iterator_category

template <class T, class Distance>
inline input_iterator_tag
iterator_category(const input_iterator<T, Distance>&) {
    return input_iterator_tag();
}
inline output_iterator_tag iterator_category(const output_iterator&) {
    return forward_iterator_tag();
}
template <class T, class Distance>
inline bidirectional iterator_tag
iterator_category(const bidirectional_iterator<T, Distance>&) {
    return forward_iterator_tag();
}
template <class T, class Distance>
inline bidirectional_iterator_tag
iterator_category(const bidirectional_iterator<T, Distance>&) {
    return bidirectional_iterator_tag();
}
template <class T, class Distance>
inline random_access_iterator_tag
iterator_category(const random_access_iterator<T, Distance>& {
    return random_access_iterator_tag();
}
template <class T>
inline random_access_iterator_tag iterator_category(const T*) {
    return random_access_iterator_tag();
}

// value_type of iterator

template <class T, class Distance>
inline T* value_type(const input_iterator<T, Distance>&) {
    return (T*) (0);
}
template <class T, class Distance>
inline T* value_type(const forward_iterator<T, Distance>&) {
    return (T*) (0);
```

```
}
template <class T, class Distance>
inline T* value_type(const bidirectional_iterator<T, Distance>&) {
    return (T*)(0);
}
template <class T, class Distance>
inline T* value_type(const random_access_iterator<T, Distance>&) {
    return (T*)(0);
}
template <class T>
inline T* value_type(const T*) { return (T*)(0); }

// distance_type of iterator

template <class T, class Distance>
inline Distance* distance_type(const input_iterator<T, Distance>&) {
    return (Distance*)(0);
}
template <class T, class Distance>
inline Distance* distance_type(const forward_iterator<T, Distance>&) {
    return (Distance*)(0);
}
template <class T, class Distance>
inline Distance* distance_type(const bidirectional_iterator<T, Distance>&) {
    return (Distance*)(0);
}
template <class T, class Distance>
inline Distance* distance_type(const random_access_iterator<T, Distance>&) {
    return (Distance*)(0);
}
template <class T>
inline ptrdiff_t* distance_type(const T*) { return (ptrdiff_t*)(0); }
```

If a user wants to define a bidirectional iterator for some data structure containing `double` and such that it works on a large memory model of a computer, it can be done by defining:

```
class MyIterator : public bidirectional_iterator<double, long> {
    //code implementing ++, etc.
};
```

Then there is no need to define `iterator_category`, `value_type`, and `distance_type` on `MyIterator`.

## 5.7　Iterator operations

Since only random access iterators provide + and − operators, the library provides two template functions `advance` and `distance`. These functions use + and − for random access iterators (and are, therefore, constant time for them); for input, forward and bidirectional iterators they use ++ to provide linear time implementations. `advance` takes a negative argument n for random access and bidirectional iterators only.

advance increments (or decrements for negative n) iterator reference i by n. distance increments n by the number of times it takes to get from `first` to `last`.

```
template <class InputIterator, class Distance>
inline void advance(InputIterator& i, Distance n);

template <class InputIterator, class Distance>
inline void distance(Input Iterator first, InputIterator last, Distance& n);
```

distance must be a three argument function storing the result into a reference instead of returning the result because the distance type cannot be deduced from built-in iterator types such as `int*`.

## 6   FUNCTION OBJECTS

Function objects are objects with an `operator()` defined. They are important for the effective use of the library. In the places where one would expect to pass a pointer to a function to an algorithmic template, the interface is specified to accept an object with an `operator()` defined. This not only makes algorithmic templates work with pointers to functions, but also enables them to work with arbitrary function objects. Using function objects together with function templates increases the expressive power of the library as well as making the resulting code much more efficient. For example, if we want to have a by-element addition of two vectors a and b containing `double` and put the result into a we can do:

```
transform(a.begin(), a.end(), b.begin(), a.begin(), plus<double>());
```

If we want to negate every element of a we can do:

```
transform(a.begin(), a.end(), a.begin(), negate<double>());
```

The corresponding functions will inline the addition and the negation.

To enable adaptors and other components to manipulate function objects that take one or two arguments it is required that they correspondingly provide typedefs `argument_type` and `result_type` for function objects that take one argument and `first_argument_type`, `second_argument_type`, and `result_type` for function objects that take two arguments.

### 6.1   Base

The following classes are provided to simplify the typedefs of the argument and result types:

```
template <class Arg, class Result>
struct unary_function {
    typedef Arg argument_type:
typedef Result result_type;
};

template <class Arg1, class Arg2, class Result>
struct binary_function {
    typedef Arg1 first_argument_type;
```

```
    typedef Arg2 second_argument_type;
    typedef Result result_type;
};
```

## 6.2  Arithmetic operations

The library provides basic function object classes for all of the arithmetic operators in the language.

```
template <class T>
struct plus : binary_function<T, T, T> {
    T operator() (const T& x, const T& y) const { return x + y; }
};

template <class T>
struct minus : binary_function<T, T, T> {
    T operator() (const T& x, const T& y) const { return x - y; }
};

template <class T>
struct times: binary_function<T, T, T> {
    T operator() (const T& x, const T& y) const { return x * y; }
};

template <class T>
struct divides : binary_function<T, T, T> {
    T operator() (const T& x, const T& y) const { return x / y; }
};

template <class T>
struct modulus : binary_function<T, T, T> {
    T operator() (const T& x, const T& y) const { return x % y; }
};

template <class T>
struct negate : unary_function<T, T> {
    T operator() (const T& x) const { return -x; }
};
```

## 6.3  Comparisons

The library provides basic function object classes for all of the comparison operators in the language.

```
template <class T>
struct equal_to : binary_function<T, T, bool> {
    bool operator() (const T& x, const T& y) const { return x == y; }
};

template <class T>
struct not_equal_to : binary_function<T, T, bool> {
    bool operator() (const T& x, const T& y) const { return x != y; }
};
```

```
template <class T>
struct greater : binary_function<T, T, bool> {
    bool operator() (const T& x, const T& y) const { return x > y; }
};

template <class T>
struct less : binary_function<T, T, bool> {
    bool operator() (const T& x, const T& y) const { return x <= y; }
};

template <class T>
struct greater_equal : binary_function<T, T, bool> {
    bool operator() (const T& x, const T& y) const { return x >= y; }
};
template <class T>
struct less_equal : binary_function<T, T, bool> {
    bool operator() (const T& x, const T& y) const { return x <= y; }
};
```

## 6.4   Logical operations

```
template <class T>
struct logical_and : binary_function<T, T, bool> {
    bool operator() (const T& x, const T& y) const { return x && y; }
};

template <class T>
struct logical_or : binary_function<T, T, bool> {
    bool operator() (const T& x, const T& y) const { return x || y; }
};

template <class T>
struct logical_not : unary_function<T, bool> {
    bool operator() (const T& x) const { return !x; }
};
```

# 7   ALLOCATORS

One of the common problems in portability is to be able to encapsulate the information about the memory model. This information includes the knowledge of pointer types, the type of their difference, the type of the size of objects in this memory model, as well as the memory allocation and deallocation primitives for it.

STL addresses this problem by providing a standard set of requirements for *allocators*, which are objects that encapsulate this information. All of the containers in STL are parameterized in terms of allocators. That dramatically simplifies the task of dealing with multiple memory models.

## 7.1   Allocator requirements

In the following table, we assume X is an allocator class for objects of type T, a is a value of X, n is of type X::size_type, p is of type X::pointer, r is of type X::reference and s is of type X::const _reference.

All the operations on the allocators are expected to be amortized constant time.

**Table A7   Allocator Requirements**

| expression | return type | assertion/note pre/post-condition |
|---|---|---|
| X::value_type | T | |
| X::reference | lvalue of T | |
| X::const_reference | const lvalue of T | |
| X::pointer | pointer to T type | the result of operator* of values of X::pointer is of reference. |
| X::const_pointer | pointer to const T type | the result of operator* of values of X::const_pointer is of const_reference; it is the same type of pointer as X::pointer, in particular, sizeof(X::const_pointer) == sizeof(X::pointer). |
| X::size_type | unsigned integral type | the type that can represent the size of the largest object in the memory model. |
| X::difference_type | signed integral type | the type that can represent the difference between any two pointers in the memory model. |
| X a; | | note: a destructor is assumed. |
| a.address(r) | pointer | *(a.address(r)) == r. |
| a.const_address(s) | const_pointer | *(a.address(s)) == s. |
| a.allocate(n) | X::pointer | memory is allocated for n objects of type T but objects are not constructed. allocate may raise an appropriate exception. |
| a.deallocate(p) | result is not used | all the objects in the area pointed by p should be destroyed prior to the call of the deallocate. |
| construct(p, a) | void | post: *p == a. |
| destroy(p) | void | the value pointed by p is destroyed. |
| a.init_page_size() | X::size_type | the returned value is the optimal value for an initial buffer size of the given type. It is assumed that if k is returned by init_page_size, t is the construction time for T, and u is the time that it takes to do allocate(k), then k * t is much greater than u. |
| a.max_size() | X::size_type | the largest positive value of X::difference _type |

pointer belongs to the category of mutable random access iterators referring to T. const_pointer belongs to the category of constant random access iterators referring to T. There is a conversion defined from pointer to const_pointer.

For any allocator template Alloc there is a specialization for type void. Alloc<void> has only constructor, destructor, and Alloc<void>::pointer defined. Conversions are defined from any instance of Alloc<T>::pointer into Alloc<void>::pointer and back so that for any p, p == Alloc<T>::pointer (Alloc<void>::pointer (p)).

## 7.2   The default allocator

```
template <class T>
class allocator {
public:
    typedef T* pointer;
    typedef const T* const_pointer;
    typedef T& reference;
    typedef const T& const_reference;
    typedef T value_type;
    typedef size_t size_type;
    typedef ptrdiff_t difference_type;
    allocator();
    ~allocator();
    pointer address(reference x);
    const_pointer const_address(const_reference x);
    pointer allocate(size_type n);
    void deallocate(pointer p);
    size_type init_page_size();
    size_type max_size();
};

class allocator<void> {
public:
    typedef void* pointer;
    allocator();
    ~allocator();
};
```

In addition to allocator the library vendors are expected to provide allocators for all supported memory models.

## 8   CONTAINERS

Containers are objects that store other objects. They control allocation and deallocation of these objects through constructors, destructors, insert and erase operations.

In the following table, we assume X is a container class containing objects of type T, a and b are values of X, u is an identifier and r is a value of X&.

## Table A8  Container Requirements

| expression | return type | operational semantics | assertion/note pre/post-condition | complexity |
|---|---|---|---|---|
| `X::value_type` | T | | | compile time |
| `X::reference` | | | | compile time |
| `X::const_reference` | | | | compile time |
| `X::pointer` | a pointer type pointing to `X::refer-ence` | | pointer to T in the memory model used by the container | compile time |
| `X::iterator` | iterator type pointing to `X::refer-ence` | | an iterator of any iterator category except output iterator. | compile time |
| `X::const_iterator` | iterator type pointing to `X::const_reference` | | a constant iterator of any iterator category except output iterator. | compile tile |
| `X::difference_type` | signed integral type | | is identical to the distance type of `X::iterator` and `X::const_iterator` | compile time |
| `X::size_type` | unsigned integral type | | `size_type` can represent any non-negative value of `difference_type` | compile time |
| `X u;` | | | post: `u.size() == 0`. | constant |
| `X()` | | | `X().size() == 0`. | constant |
| `X(a)` | | | `a == X(a)`. | linear |
| `X u(a);`<br>`X u = a;` | | `X u; u = a;` | post: `u == a`. | linear |
| `(&a)->~X()` | result is not used | | post: `a.size() == 0`. note: the destructor is applied to every element of a and all the memory is returned. | linear |
| `a.begin()` | iterator; const_iterator for constant a | | | constant |

**Table A8   Container Requirements (*continued*)**

| expression | return type | operational semantics | assertion/note pre/post-condition | complexity |
|---|---|---|---|---|
| `a.end()` | `iterator;` `const_` `iterator` for constant `a` | | | constant |
| `a == b` | convertible to `bool` | `a.size() ==` `b.size() &&` `etual(a.begin(),` `a.end(),` `b.begin())` | `==` is an equivalence re-lation. note: `equal` is defined in the algorithms section. | linear |
| `a != b` | convertible to `bool` | `!(a == b)` | | linear |
| `r = a` | `X&` | `if (&r != &a) {` `(&r) ->X::~X();` `new (&r) X(a);` `return r; }` | post: `r == a`. | linear |
| `a.size()` | `size_type` | `a.end() -` `a.begin()` | | constant |
| `a.max_size()` | `size_type` | | `size()` of the largest possible container. | constant |
| `a.empty()` | convertible to `bool` | `a.size() == 0` | | constant |
| `a < b` | convertible to `bool` | `lexicographical` `_compare` `(a.begin(),` `a.end(),` `b.begin(),` `b.end()).` | pre: `<` is defined for values of `T`. `<` is a total ordering relation. `lexicographical` `_compare` is defined in the algorithms section. | linear |
| `a > b` | convertible to `bool` | `b < a` | | linear |
| `a <= b` | convertible to `bool` | `!(a > b)` | | linear |
| `a >= b` | convertible to `bool` | `!(a < b)` | | linear |
| `a.swap(b)` | `void` | `swap(a,b)` | | constant |

The member function `size()` returns the number of elements in the container. Its semantics is defined by the rules of constructors, inserts, and erases.

begin() returns an iterator referring to the first element in the container. end() returns an iterator which is the past-the-end value.

If the iterator type of a container belongs to the bidirectional or random access iterator categories, the container is called `reversible` and satisfies the following additional requirements:

**Table A9   Reversible Container Requirements (in addition to container)**

| expression | return type | operational semantics | complexity |
|---|---|---|---|
| X::reverse _iterator | | reverse_iterator<iterator, value_type, reference, difference_type> **for random access iterator** reverse_bidirectional_ iterator<iterator, value_type, reference, difference_type> **for bidirectional iterator** | compile time |
| X::const _reverse _iterator | | reverse_iterator<const_iterator, value_type, const_reference, difference_type> **for random access iterator** reverse_bidirectional_iterator< const_iterator, value_type, const_reference, difference_type> **for bidirectional iterator** | compile time |
| a.rbegin() | reverse_ iterator; const _reverse_ iterator **for** constant a | reverse_iterator(end()) | constant |
| a.rend() | reverse_ iterator; const _reverse_ iterator **for** constant a | reverse_iterator(begin()) | constant |

## 8.1   Sequences

A sequence is a kind of container that organizes a finite set of objects, all of the same type, into a strictly linear arrangement. The library provides three basic kinds of sequence containers: vector, list, and deque. It also provides container adaptors that make it easy to construct abstract data types, such as stacks or queues, out of the basic sequence kinds (or out of other kinds of sequences that the user might define).

In the following two tables, X is a sequence class, a is value of X, i and j satisfy input iterator requirements, [i, j) is a valid range, n is a value of X::size_type, p is a valid iterator to a, q, q1 and q2 are valid dereferenceable iterators to a, [q1, q2) is a valid range, t is a value of X::value_type.

The complexities of the expressions are sequence dependent.

**Table A10   Sequence Requirements (in addition to container)**

| expression | return type | assertion/note<br>pre/post-condition |
|---|---|---|
| `X(n, t)`<br>`X a(n, t);` | | post: `size()==n`.<br>constructs a sequence with n copies of `t`. |
| `X(i, j)`<br>`X a(i, j);` | | post: `size() ==` distance between `i` and `j`.<br>constructs a sequence equal to the range `[i, j)`. |
| `a.insert(p, t)` | `iterator` | inserts a copy of `t` before `p`.<br>the return value points to the inserted copy. |
| `a.insert(p, n, t)` | result is not used | inserts n copies of `t` before `p`. |
| `a.insert(p, i, j)` | result is not used | inserts copies of elements in `[i, j)` before `p`. |
| `a.erase(q)` | result is not used | erases the element pointed to by `q`. |
| `a.erase(q1, q2)` | result is not used | erases the elements in the range `(q1, q2)`. |

`vector`, `list`, and `deque` offer the programmer different complexity trade-offs and should be used accordingly. `vector` is the type of sequence that should be used by default. `list` should be used when there are frequent insertions and deletions from the middle of the sequence. `deque` is the data structure of choice when most insertions and deletions take place at the beginning or at the end of the sequence.

`iterator` and `const_iterator` types for sequences have to be at least of the forward iterator category.

**Table A11  Optional Sequence Operations**

| expression | return type | operational semantics | container |
|---|---|---|---|
| `a.front()` | `reference;`<br>`const_reference`<br>for constant `a` | `*a.begin()` | `vector, list, deque` |
| `a.back()` | `reference;`<br>`const_reference`<br>for constant `a` | `*a.(--end())` | `vector, list, deque` |
| `a.push_front(x)` | `void` | `a.insert(a.begin(), x)` | `list, deque` |
| `a.push_back(x)` | `void` | `a.insert(a.end(), x)` | `vector, list, deque` |
| `a.pop_front()` | `void` | `a.erase(a.begin())` | `list, deque` |
| `a.pop_back()` | `void` | `a.erase(--a.end())` | `vector, list, deque` |
| `a[n]` | `reference;`<br>`const_reference`<br>for constant `a` | `*(a.begin() + n)` | `vector, deque` |

All the operations in the above table are provided only for the containers for which they take constant time.

## 8.1.1   VECTOR

vector is a kind of sequence that supports random access iterators. In addition, it supports (amortized) constant time insert and erase operations at the end; insert and erase in the middle take linear time. Storage management is handled automatically, though hints can be given to improve efficiency.

```
template <class T, template <class U> class Allocator = allocator>
class vector {
public:

// typedefs:

    typedef iterator;
    typedef const_iterator;
    typedef Allocator<T>::pointer pointer;
    typedef Allocator<T>::reference reference;
    typedef Allocator<T>::const_reference const_reference;
    typedef size_type;
    typedef difference_type;
    typedef T value_type;
    typedef reverse_iterator;
    typedef const_reverse_iterator;

// allocation/deallocation:

    vector();
    vector(size_type n, const T& value = T());
    vector(const vector<T, Allocator>& x);
    template <class InputIterator>
    vector (InputIterator first, InputIterator last);
    ~vector();
    vector<T, Allocator>& operator=(const vector<T, Allocator>& x);
    void reserve(size_type n);
    void swap(vector<T, Allocator>& x);

// accessors:
    iterator begin();
    const_iterator begin() const;
    iterator end();
    const_iterator end() const;
    reverse_iterator rbegin();
    const_reverse_iterator rbegin();
    reverse_iterator rend();
    const_reverse_iterator rend();
    size_type size() const;
    size_type max_size() const;
    size_type capacity() const;
    bool empty() const;
    reference operator[] (size_type n);
    const_reference operator[] (size_type n) const;
    reference front();
    const_reference front() const;
```

```
    reference back();
    const_reference back() const;

// insert/erase:

    void push_back (const T& x);
    iterator insert(iterator position, const T& x = T());
    void insert(iterator position, size_type n, const T& x);
    template <class InputIterator>
    void insert(iterator position, InputIterator first, InputIterator last);
    void pop_back();
    void erase(iterator position);
    void erase(iterator first, iterator last);
};

template <class T, class Allocator>
bool operator<(const vector<T, Allocator>& x, const vector<T, Allocator>& y);
```

`iterator` is a random access iterator referring to T. The exact type is implementation dependent and determined by `Allocator`.

`const_iterator` is a constant random access iterator referring to `const` T. The exact type is implementation dependent and determined by `Allocator`. It is guaranteed that there is a constructor for `const_iterator` out of `iterator`.

`size_type` is an unsigned integral type. The exact type is implementation dependent and determined by `Allocator`.

`difference_type` is a signed integral type. The exact type is implementation dependent and determined by `Allocator`.

The constructor `template <class InputIterator> vector(InputIterator first, InputIterator last)` makes only N calls to the copy constructor of T (where N is the distance between `first` and `last`) and no reallocations if iterators `first` and `last` are of forward, bidirectional, or random access categories. It does at most 2N calls to the copy constructor of T and logN reallocations if they are just input iterators, since it is impossible to determine the distance between `first` and `last` and then do copying.

The member function `capacity` returns the size of the allocated storage in the vector. The member function `reserve` is a directive that informs `vector` of a planned change in size, so that it can manage the storage allocation accordingly. It does not change the size of the sequence and takes at most linear time in the size of the sequence. Reallocation happens at this point if and only if the current capacity is less than the argument of `reserve`. After `reserve`, `capacity` is greater or equal to the argument of `reserve` if reallocation happens; and equal to the previous value of `capacity` otherwise. Reallocation invalidates all the references, pointers, and iterators referring to the elements in the sequence. It is guaranteed that no reallocation takes place during the insertions that happen after `reserve` takes place till the time when the size of the vector reaches the size specified by `reserve`.

`insert` causes reallocation if the new size is greater than the old capacity. If no reallocation happens, all the iterators and references before the insertion point remain valid. Inserting a single element into a vector is linear in the distance from the insertion point to the end of the vector. The amortized complexity over the lifetime of a vector of inserting a single ement at its end is constant. Insertion of multiple elements into a vector with a single call of the insert member function is linear in the sum of the number of elements plus the distance to the end of the vector. In other words, it is much faster to insert many elements into the middle of a vector at once than to do the insertion one at a time. The insert template member function preallocates enough storage for the insertion if the iterators `first` and `last` are of forward, bidirectional or random access category. Otherwise, it does insert elements one by one and should not be used for inserting into the middle of vectors.

   `erase` invalidates all the iterators and references after the point of the erase. The destructor of T is called the number of times equal to the number of the elements erased, but the assignment operator of T is called the number of times equal to the number of elements in the vector after the erased elements.

   To optimize space allocation, a specialization for `bool` is provided:

```
class vector<bool, allocator> {
public:

// bit reference:

    class reference {
    public:
        ~reference();
        operator bool() const;
        reference& operator=(const bool x);
        void flip();        // flips the bit
    };

// typedefs:

    typedef bool const_reference;
    typedef iterator;
    typedef const_iterator;
    typedef size_t size_type;
    typedef ptrdiff_t difference_type;
    typedef bool value_type;
    typedef reverse_iterator;
    typedef const_reverse_iterator;

// allocation/deallocation:

    ~vector();
    vector(size_type n, const bool& value = bool());
    vector(const vector<bool, allocator>& x);
    template <class InputIterator>
    vector(InputIterator first, InputIterator last);
    vector();
    vector<bool, allocator>& operator=(const vector<bool, allocator>& x);
    void reserve(size_type n);
    void swap(vector<vector<bool, allocator>& x);

// accessors:

    iterator begin();
    const_iterator begin() const;
    iterator end();
    const_iterator end() const;
    reverse_iterator rbegin();
    const_reverse_iterator rbegin();
```

```
    reverse_iterator rend();
    const_reverse_iterator rend();
    size_type size() const;
    size_type max_size() const;
    size_type capacity() const;
    bool empty() const;
    reference operator[] (size_type n);
    const_reference operator[] (size_type n) const;
    reference front();
    const_reference front() const;
    reference back();
    const_reference back() const;
```

```
// insert/erase:
```

```
    void push_back(const bool& x);
    iterator insert(iterator position, const bool& x = bool());
    void insert (iterator position, size_type n, const bool& x);
    template <class InputIterator>
    void insert (iterator position, InputIterator first, InputIterator last);
    void pop_back();
    void erase(iterator position);
    void erase(iterator first, iterator last);
};
```

```
void swap(vector<bool, allocator>::reference x,
    vector<bool, allocator>::reference y);
```

```
bool operator==(const vector<bool, allocator>& x,
        const vector<bool, allocator>& y);
```

```
bool operator<(const vector<bool, allocator>& x,
        const vector<bool, allocator>& y);
```

`reference` is a class that simulates the behavior of references of a single bit in `vector<bool>`.

Every implementation is expected to provide specializations of `vector<bool>` for all supported memory models.

---

At present, it is not possible to templatize a specialization. That is, we cannot write:

```
    template <template <class U> class Allocator = allocator>
    class vector<bool, Allocator> { /* . . . */ };
```

Therefore, only `vector<bool, allocator>` is provided.

---

### 8.1.2  LIST

`list` is a kind of sequence that supports bidirectional iterators and allows constant time insert and erase operations anywhere within the sequence, with storage management handled automatically. Unlike vectors and deques, fast random access to list elements is not supported, but many algorithms only need sequential access anyway.

```
template <class T, template <class U> class Allocator = allocator>
class list {
public:

// typedefs:

    typedef iterator;
    typedef const_iterator;
    typedef Allocator<T>::pointer pointer;
    typedef Allocator<T>::reference reference;
    typedef Allocator<T>::const_reference const_reference;
    typedef size_type;
    typedef difference_type;
    typedef T value_type;
    typedef reverse_iterator;
    typedef const_reverse_iterator;

// allocation/deallocation:

    list();
    list(size_type n, const T& value = T());
    template <class InputIterator>
    list(InputIterator first, InputIterator last);
    list(const list<T, Allocator>& x);
    ~list();
    list<T, Allocator>& operator=(const list<T, Allocator>& x);
    void swap(list<T, Allocator>& x);

// accessors:

    iterator begin();
    const_iterator begin() const;
    iterator end();
    const_iterator end() const;
    reverse_iterator rbegin();
    const_reverse_iterator rbegin();
    reverse_iterator rend();
    const_reverse_iterator rend();
    bool empty() const;
    size_type size() const;
    size_type max_size() const;
    reference front();
    const_reference front() const;
    reference back();
    const_reference back() const;

// insert/erase:

    void push_front(const T& x);
    void push_back(const T& x);
```

```
    iterator insert(iterator position, const T& x = T());
    void insert(iterator position, size_type n, const T& x);
    template <class InputIterator>
    void insert(iterator position, InputIterator first, InputIterator last);
    void pop_front();
    void pop_back();
    void erase(iterator position);
    void erase(iterator first, iterator last);

// special mutative operations on list:

    void splice(iterator position, list<T, Allocator>& x);
    void splice(iterator position, list<T, Allocator>& x, iterator i);
    void splice(iterator position, list<T, Allocator>& x, iterator first,
        iterator last);
    void remove(const T& value);
    template <class Predicate> void remove_if(Predicate pred);
    void unique();
    template <class BinaryPredicate> void unique(BinaryPredicate binary_pred);
    void merge(list<T, Allocator>& x);
    template <class Compare> void merge(list<T, Allocator>& x, Compare comp);
    void reverse();
    void sort();
    template <class Compare> void sort(Compare comp);
};

template <class T, class Allocator>
bool operator==(const list<T, Allocator>& x, const list<T, Allocator>& y);

template <class T, class Allocator>
bool operator<(const list<T, Allocator>& x, const list<T, Allocator>& y);
```

`iterator` is a bidirectional iterator referring to `T`. The exact type is implementation dependent and determined by `Allocator`.

`const_iterator` is a constant bidirectional iterator referring to `const T`. The exact type is implementation dependent and determined by `Allocator`. It is guaranteed that there is a constructor for `const_iterator` out of `iterator`.

`size_type` is an unsigned integral type. The exact type is implementation dependent and determined by `Allocator`.

`difference_type` is a signed integral type. The exact type is implementation dependent and determined by `Allocator`.

`insert` does not affect the validity of iterators and references. Insertion of a single element into a list takes constant time and exactly one call to the copy constructor of `T`. Insertion of multiple elements into a list is linear in the number of elements inserted, and the number of calls to the copy constructor of `T` is exactly equal to the number of elements inserted.

`erase` invalidates only the iterators and references to the erased elements. Erasing a single element is a constant time operation with a single call to the destructor of `T`. Erasing a range in a list is linear time in the size of the range and the number of calls to the destructor of type `T` is exactly equal to the size of the range.

Since lists allow fast insertion and erasing from the middle of a list, certain operations are provided specifically for them:

list provides three splice operations that destructively move elements from one list to another:

void splice(iterator position, list<T, Allocator>& x) inserts the contents of x before position and x becomes empty. It takes constant time. The result is undefined if &x == this.

void splice(iterator position, list<T, Allocators>& x, iterator i) inserts an element pointed to by i from list x before position and removes the element from x. It takes constant time. i is a valid dereferenceable iterator of x. The result is unchanged if position == i or position == ++i.

void splice(iterator position, list<T, Allocator>& x, iterator first, iterator last) inserts elements in the range [first, last) before position and removes the elements from x. It takes constant time if &x == this; otherwise, it takes linear time. [first, last) is a valid range in x. The result is undefined if position is an iterator in the range [first, last).

remove erases all the elements in the list referred by the list iterator i for which the following conditions hold: *i == value, pred(*i) == true. remove is stable, that is, the relative order of the elements that are not removed is the same as their relative order in the original list. Exactly size() applications of the corresponding predicate are done.

unique erases all but the first element from every consecutive group of equal elements in the list. Exactly size() − 1 applications of the corresponding binary predicate are done.

merge merges the argument list into the list (both are assumed to be sorted). The merge is stable, that is, for equal elements in the two lists, the elements from the list always precede the elements from the argument list. x is empty after the merge. At most size() + x.size() − 1 comparisons are done.

reverse reverses the order of the elements in the list. It is linear time.

sort sorts the list according to the operator< or a compare function object. It is stable, that is, the relative order of the equal elements is preserved. Approximately NlogN comparisons are done where N is equal to size().

### 8.1.3 DEQUE

deque is a kind of sequence that, like a vector, supports random access iterators. In addition, it supports constant time insert and erase operations at the beginning or the end; insert and erase in the middle take linear time. As with vectors, storage management is handled automatically.

```
template <class T, template <class U> class Allocator = allocator>
class deque {
public:

// typedefs:

    typedef iterator;
    typedef const_iterator;
    typedef Allocator<T>::pointer pointer;
    typedef Allocator<T>::reference reference;
    typedef Allocator<T>::const_reference const_reference;
    typedef size_type;
    typedef difference_type;
    typedef T value_type;
```

```
    typedef reverse_iterator;
    typedef const_reverse_iterator;

// allocation/deallocation:

    deque();
    deque(size_type n, const T& value = T());
    deque (const deque<T, Allocator>& x);
    template <class InputIterator>
    deque(InputIterator first, InputIterator last);
    ~deque();
    deque<T, Allocator>& operator=(const deque<T, Allocator>& x);
    void swap(deque<T, Allocator>& x);

//accessors:

    iterator begin();
    const_iterator begin() const;
    iterator end();
    const_iterator end() const;
    reverse_iterator rbegin();
    const_reverse_iterator rbegin();
    reverse_iterator rend();
    const_reverse_iterator rend();
    size_type size() const;
    size_type max_size() const;
    bool empty() const;
    reference operator[] (size_type n);
    const_reference operator[] (size_type n) const;
    reference front();
    const_reference front() const;
    reference back();
    const_reference back() const;

//insert/erase:

    void push_front(const T& x);
    void push_back(const T& x);
    iterator insert(iterator position, const T& x = T());
    void insert (iterator position, size_type n, const T& x);
    template <class InputIterator>
    void insert (iterator position, InputIterator first, InputIterator last);
    void pop_front();
    void pop_back();
    void erase(iterator position);
    void erase(iterator first, iterator last);
};

template <class T, class Allocator>
bool operator==(const deque<T, Allocator>& x, const deque<T, Allocator>& y);
```

```
template <class T, class Allocator>
bool operator<(const deque<T, Allocator>& x, const deque<T, Allocator>& y);
```

`iterator` is a random access iterator referring to T. The exact type is implementation dependent and determined by `Allocator`.

`const_iterator` is a constant random access iterator referring to `const` T. The exact type is implementation dependent and determined by `Allocator`. It is guaranteed that there is a constructor for `const_iterator` out of `iterator`.

`size_type` is an unsigned integral type. The exact type is implementation dependent and determined by `Allocator`.

`difference_type` is a signed integral type. The exact type is implementation dependent and determined by `Allocator`.

`insert` and `push` invalidate all the iterators and references to the deque. In the worst case, inserting a single element into a deque takes time linear in the minimum of the distance from the insertion point to the beginning of the deque and the distance from the insertion point to the end of the deque. Inserting a single element either at the beginning or end of a deque always takes constant time and causes a single call to the copy constructor of T. That is, a deque is especially optimized for pushing and popping elements at the beginning and end.

`erase` and `pop` invalidate all the iterators and references to the deque. The number of calls to the destructor is the same as the number of elements erased, but the number of the calls to the assignment operator is equal to the minimum of the number of elements before the erased elements and the number of elements after the erased elements.

## 8.2   Associative containers

Associative containers provide an ability for fast retrieval of data based on keys. The library provides four basic kinds of associative containers: `set`, `multiset`, `map` and `multimap`.

All of them are parameterized on `Key` and an ordering relation `Compare` that induces a total ordering on elements of `Key`. In addition, `map` and `multimap` associate an arbitrary type T with the `Key`. The object of type `Compare` is called the *comparison object* of a container.

In this section when we talk about equality of keys we mean the equivalence relation imposed by the comparison and *not* the `operator==` on keys. That is, two keys k1 and k2 are considered to be equal if for the comparison object comp, `comp(k1, k2) == false && comp(k2, k1) == false`.

An associative container supports *unique keys* if it may contain at most one element for each key. Otherwise, it supports *equal keys*. `set` and `map` support unique keys. `multiset` and `multimap` support equal keys.

For `set` and `multiset` the value type is the same as the key type. For `map` and `multimap` it is equal to `pair<const Key, T>`.

`iterator` of an associative container is of the bidirectional iterator category. `insert` does not affect the validity of iterators and references to the container, and `erase` invalidates only the iterators and references to the erased elements.

In the following table, X is an associative container class, a is a value of X, a_uniq is a value of X when X supports unique keys, and a_eq is a value of X when X supports multiple keys, i and j satisfy input iterator requirements and refer to elements of `value_type`, [i, j) is a valid range, p is a valid iterator to a, q, q1 and q2 are valid dereferenceable iterators to a, [q1, q2) is a valid range, t is a value of X::value _type and k is a value of X::key_type.

**Table A12   Associative Container Requirements (in addition to container)**

| expression | return type | assertion/note pre/post-condition | complexity |
|---|---|---|---|
| `X::key_type` | `Key` | | compile time |
| `X::key_compare` | `Compare` | defaults to `less<key_type>`. | compile time |
| `X::value_compare` | a binary predicate type | is the same as `key_compare` for `set` and `multiset`; is an ordering relation on pairs induced by the first component (i.e. Key) for `map` and `multimap`. | compile time |
| `X(c)` `X a(c);` | | constructs an empty container; uses `c` as a comparison object. | constant |
| `X()` `X a;` | | constructs an empty container; uses `Compare()` as a comparison object. | constant |
| `X(i, j, c)` `X a(i, j, c);` | | constructs an empty container and inserts elements from the range `[i, j)` into it; uses `c` as a comparison object. | `NlogN` in general (`N` is the distance from `i` to `j`); linear if `[i, j)` is sorted with `value_comp()` |
| `X(i, j)` `X a(i, j);` | | same as above, but uses `Compare()` as a comparison object. | same as above |
| `a.key_comp()` | `X::key_compare` | returns the comparison object out of which `a` was constructed. | constant |
| `a.value_comp()` | `X::value_compare` | returns an object of `value_compare` constructed out of the comparison object. | constant |
| `a_uniq.insert(t)` | `pair<iterator, bool>` | inserts `t` if and only if there is no element in the container with key equal to the key of `t`. The `bool` component of the returned pair indicates whether the insertion takes place and the `iterator` component of the pair points to the element with key equal to the key of `t`. | logarithmic |
| `a_eq.insert(t)` | `iterator` | inserts `t` and returns the iterator pointing to the newly inserted element. | logarithmic |

| expression | return type | assertion/note<br>pre/post-condition | complexity |
|---|---|---|---|
| `a.insert(p, t)` | `iterator` | inserts `t` if and only if there is no element with key equal to the key of `t` in containers with unique keys; always inserts `t` in containers with equal keys. always returns the iterator pointing to the element with key equal to the key of `t`. iterator `p` is a hint pointing to where the insert should start to search. | logarithmic in general, but amortized constant if `t` is inserted right after `p`. |
| `a.insert(i, j)` | result is not used | inserts the elements from the range `[i, j)` into the container. | `Nlog(size()+N)` (N is the distance from `i` to `j`) in general; linear if `[i, j)` is sorted according to `value_comp()` |
| `a.erase(k)` | `size_type` | erases all the elements in the container with key equal to `k`. returns the number of erased elements. | `log(size()) + count(k)` |
| `a.erase(q)` | result is not used | erases the element pointed to by `q`. | amortized constant |
| `a.erase(q1, q2)` | result is not used | erases all the elements in the range `[q1, q2)`. | `log(size())+N` where `N` is the distance from `q1` to `q2`. |
| `a.find(k)` | `iterator`; `const_iterator` for constant `a` | returns an iterator pointing to an element with the key equal to `k`, or `a.end()` if such an element is not found. | logarithmic |
| `a.count(k)` | `size_type` | returns the number of elements with key equal to `k`. | `log(size())+ count(k)` |
| `a.lower_bound(k)` | `iterator`; `const_iterator` for constant `a` | returns an iterator pointing to the first element with key not less than `k`. | logarithmic |
| `a.upper_bound(k)` | `iterator`; `const_iterator` for constant `a` | returns an iterator pointing to the first element with key greater than `k`. | logarithmic |
| `a.equal_range(k)` | `pair<iterator, iterator>`; `pair<const_iterator, const_iterator>` for constant `a` | equivalent to `make_pair(a.lower_bound(k), a.upper_bound(k))`. | logarithmic |

The fundamental property of iterators of associative containers is that they iterate through the containers in the nondescending order of keys where nondescending is defined by the comparison that was used to construct them. For any two dereferenceable iterators i and j such that distance from i to j is positive,

```
value_comp(*j, *i) == false
```

For associative containers with unique keys the stronger condition holds,

```
value_comp(*i, *j) == true.
```

## 8.2.1  SET

set is a kind of associative container that supports unique keys (contains at most one of each key value) and provides for fast retrieval of the keys themselves.

```
template <class Key, class Compare = less<Key>,
      template <class U> class Allocator = allocator>
class set {
public:

// typedefs:

    typedef Key key_type;
    typedef Key value_type;
    typedef Allocator<Key>::pointer pointer;
    typedef Allocator<Key>::reference reference;
    typedef Allocator<Key>::const_reference const_reference;
    typedef Compare key_compare;
    typedef Compare value_compare;
    typedef iterator;
    typedef iterator const_iterator;
    typedef size_type;
    typedef difference_type;
    typedef reverse_iterator;
    typedef const_reverse_iterator;

// allocation/deallocation:

    set(const Compare& comp = Compare());
    template <class InputIterator>
    set(InputIterator first, InputIterator last,
        const Compare& comp = Compare());
    set(const set<Key, Compare, Allocator>& x);
    ~set();
    set<Key, Compare, Allocator>& operator=(const set<Key, Compare,
        Allocator>& x);
    void swap(set<Key, Compare, Allocator>& x);

// accessors:

    key_compare key_comp() const;
    value_compare value_comp() const;
```

```
    iterator begin() const;
    iterator end() const;
    reverse_iterator rbegin() const;
    reverse_iterator rend() const;
    bool empty() const;
    size_type size() const;
    size_type max_size() const;

// insert/erase:

    pair<iterator, bool> insert(const value_type& x);
    iterator insert(iterator position, const value_type& x);
    template <class InputIterator>
    void insert (InputIterator first, InputIterator last);
    void erase(iterator position);
    size_type erase(const key_type& x);
    void erase(iterator first, iterator last);

// set operations:

    iterator find(const key_type& x) const;
    size_type count(const key_type& x) const;
    iterator lower_bound(const key_type& x) const;
    iterator upper_bound(const key_type& x) const;
    pair<iterator, iterator> equal_range(const key_type& x) const;
};
template <class Key, class Compare, class Allocator>
bool operator==(const set<Key, Compare, Allocator>& x,
        const set<Key, Compare, Allocator>& y);

template <class Key, class Compare, class Allocator>
bool operator<(const set<Key, Compare, Allocator>& x,
        const set<Key, Compare, Allocator>& y);
```

`iterator` is a constant bidirectional iterator referring to `const value_type`. The exact type is implementation dependent and determined by `Allocator`.

`const_iterator` is the same type as `iterator`.

`size_type` is an unsigned integral type. The exact type is implementation dependent and determined by `Allocator`.

`difference_type` is a signed integral type. The exact type is implementation dependent and determined by `Allocator`.

## 8.2.2   MULTISET

`multiset` is a kind of associative container that supports equal keys (possibly contains multiple copies of the same key value) and provides for fast retrieval of the keys themselves.

```
template <class Key, class Compare = less<Key>,
       template <class U> class Allocator = allocator>
class multiset {
public:

// typedefs:

    typedef Key key_type;
    typedef Key value_type;
    typedef Allocator<Key>::pointer pointer;
    typedef Allocator<Key>::reference reference;
    typedef Allocator<Key>::const_reference const_reference;
    typedef Compare key_compare;
    typedef Compare value_compare;
    typedef iterator;
    typedef iterator const_iterator;
    typedef size_type;
    typedef difference_type;
    typedef reverse_iterator;
    typedef const_reverse_iterator;

// allocation/deallocation:

    multiset(const Compare& comp = Compare());
    template <class InputIterator>
    multiset(InputIterator first, InputIterator last,
        const Compare& comp = Compare());
    multiset(const multiset<Key, Compare, Allocator>& x);
    ~multiset();
    multiset<Key, Compare, Allocator>& operator=(const multiset<Key, Compare,
        Allocator>& x);
    void swap(multiset<Key, Compare, Allocator>& x);

// accessors:

    key_compare key_comp() const;
    value_compare value_comp() const;
    iterator begin() const;
    iterator end() const;
    reverse_iterator rbegin();
    reverse_iterator rend();
  bool empty() const;
    size_type size() const;
    size_type max_size() const;
```

```
// insert/erase:

    iterator insert(const value_type& x);
    iterator insert(iterator position, const value_type& x);
    template <class InputIterator>
    void insert(InputIterator first, InputIterator last);
    void erase(iterator position);
    size_type erase(const key_type& x);
    void erase(iterator first, iterator last);

// multiset operations:

    iterator find(const key_type& x) const;
    size_type count(const key_type& x) const;
    iterator lower_bound(const key_type& x) const;
    iterator upper_bound(const key_type& x) const;
    pair<iterator, iterator> equal_range(const key_type& x) const;
};

template <class Key, class Compare, class Allocator>
bool operator==(const multiset<Key, Compare, Allocator>& x,
        const multiset<Key, Compare, Allocator>& y);

template <class Key, class Compare, class Allocator>
bool operator<(const multiset<Key, Compare, Allocator>& x,
        const multiset<Key, Compare, Allocator>& y);
```

`iterator` is a constant bidirectional iterator referring to `const value_type`. The exact type is implementation dependent and determined by `Allocator`.

  `const_iterator` is the same type as `iterator`.

  `size_type` is an unsigned integral type. The exact type is implementation dependent and determined by `Allocator`.

  `difference_type` is a signed integral type. The exact type is implementation dependent and determined by `Allocator`.

## 8.2.3   MAP

map is a kind of associative container that supports unique keys (contains at most one of each key value) and provides for fast retrieval of values of another type T based on the keys.

```
template <class Key, class T, class Compare = less<Key>,
        template <class U> class Allocator = allocator>
class map {
public:

// typedefs:

    typedef Key key_type;
    typedef pair<const Key, T> value_type;
    typedef Compare key_compare;
    class value_compare
        : public binary_function<value_type, value_type, bool> {
```

```
    friend class map;
protected:
    Compare comp;
value_compare(Compare c) : comp(c) {}
public:
    bool operator() (const value_type& x, const value_type& y) {
        return comp(x.first, y.first);
    }
};
typedef iterator;
typedef const_iterator;
typedef Allocator<value_type>::pointer pointer;
typedef Allocator<value_type>::reference reference;
typedef Allocator<value_type>::const_reference const_reference;
typedef size_type;
typedef difference_type;
typedef reverse_iterator;
typedef const_reverse_iterator;
// allocation/deallocation:
map(const Compare& comp = Compare());
template <class InputIterator>
map(InputIterator first, InputIterator last,
    const Compare& comp = Compare());
map(const map<Key, T, Compare, Allocator>& x);
~map();
map<Key, T, Compare, Allocator>&
    operator=(const map<Key, T, Compare, Allocator>& x);
void swap(map<Key, T, Compare, Allocator>& x);
// accessors:
key_compare key_comp() const;
value_compare value_comp() const;
iterator begin();
const_iterator begin() const;
iterator end();
const_iterator end() const;
reverse_iterator rbegin();
const_reverse_iterator rbegin();
reverse_iterator rend();
const_reverse_iterator rend();
bool empty() const;
size_type size() const;
size_type max_size() const;
Allocator<T>::reference operator[] (const key_type& x);
// insert/erase:
pair<iterator, bool> insert(const value_type& x);
iterator insert(iterator position, const value_type& x);
template <class InputIterator>
```

```
    void insert(InputIterator first, InputIterator last);
    void erase(iterator position);
    size_type erase(const key_type& x);
    void erase(iterator first, iterator last);
```

```
// map operations:
```

```
    iterator find(const key_type& x);
    const_iterator find(const key_type& x) const;
    size_type count(const key_type& x) const;
    iterator lower_bound(const key_type& x);
    const_iterator lower_bound(const key_type& x) const;
    iterator upper_bound(const key_type& x);
    const_iterator upper_bound(const key_type& x) const;
    pair<iterator, iterator> equal_range(const key_type& x);
    pair<const_iterator, const_iterator> equal_range(const key_type& x) const;
};
```

```
template <class Key, class T, class Compare, class Allocator>
bool operator==(const map<Key, T, Compare, Allocator>& x,
        const map<Key, T, Compare, Allocator>& y);
```

```
template <class Key, class T, class Compare, class Allocator>
bool operator==(const map<Key, T, Compare, Allocator>& x,
        const map<Key, T, Compare, Allocator>& y);
```

iterator is a bidirectional iterator referring to value_type. The exact type is implementation dependent and determined by Allocator.

const_iterator is a constant bidirectional iterator referring to const value_type. The exact type is implementation dependent and determined by Allocator. It is guaranteed that there is a constructor for const_iterator out of iterator.

size_type is an unsigned integral type. The exact type is implementation dependent and determined by Allocator.

difference_type is a signed integral type. The exact type is implementation dependent and determined by Allocator.

In addition to the standard set of member functions of associative containers, map provides Allocator<T>::reference operator[] (const key_type&). For a map m and key k, m[k] is semantically equivalent to (*((m.insert(make_pair(k, T()))).first)).second.

## 8.2.4 Multimap

multimap is a kind of associative container that supports equal keys (possibly contains multiple copies of the same key value) and provides for fast retrieval of values of another type T based on the keys.

```
template <class Key, class T, class Compare = less<Key>,
        template <class U> class Allocator = allocator>
class multiset {
public:
```

```
// typedefs:
```

```
    typedef Key key_type;
    typedef pair<const Key, T> value_type;
    typedef Compare key_compare;
    class value_compare
        : public binary_function<value_type, value_type, bool> {
    friend class map;
    protected:
        Compare comp;
        value_compare(Compare c) : comp(c) {}
    public:
        bool operator() (const value_type& x, const value_type& y) {
            return comp(x.first, y.first);
        }
    };
    typedef iterator;
    typedef const_iterator;
    typedef Allocator<value_type>::pointer pointer;
    typedef Allocator<value_type>::reference reference;
    typedef Allocator<value_type>::const_reference const_reference;
    typedef size_type;
    typedef difference_type;
    typedef reverse_iterator;
    typedef const_reverse_iterator;

// allocation/deallocation:

    multimap(const Compare& comp = Compare());
    template <class InputIterator>
    multimap(InputIterator first, InputIterator last,
        const Compare& comp = Compare());
    multimap(const multimap<Key, T, Compare, Allocator>& x);
    ~multimap();
    multimap<Key, T, Compare, Allocator>&
        operator=(const multimap<Key, T, Compare, Allocator>& x);
    void swap(multimap<Key, T, Compare, Allocator>& x);

// accessors:

    key_compare key_comp() const;
    value_compare value_comp() const;
    iterator begin();
    const_iterator begin() const;
    iterator end();
    const_iterator end() const;
    reverse_iterator rbegin();
    const_reverse_iterator rbegin();
    reverse_iterator rend();
    const_reverse_iterator rend();
    bool empty() const;
    size_type size() const;
    size_type max_size() const;
```

```
// insert/erase:

    iterator insert(const value_type& x);
    iterator insert(iterator position, const value_type& x);
    template <class InputIterator>
    void insert(InputIterator first, InputIterator last);
    void erase(iterator position);
    size_type erase(const key_type& x);
    void erase(iterator first, iterator last);

// multimap operations:

    iterator find(const key_type& x);
    const_iterator find(const key_type& x) const;
    size_type count(const key_type& x) const;
    iterator lower_bound(const key_type& x);
    const_iterator lower_bound(const key_type& x) const;
    iterator upper_bound(const key_type& x);
    const_iterator upper_bound(const key_type& x) const;
    pair<iterator, iterator> equal_range(const key_type& x);
    pair<const_iterator, const_iterator> equal_range(const key_type& x) const;
};

template <class Key, class T, class Compare, class Allocator>
bool operator==(const multimap<Key, T, Compare, Allocator>& x,
        const multimap<Key, T, Compare, Allocator>& y);

template <class Key, class T, class Compare, class Allocator>
bool operator==(const multimap<Key, T, Compare, Allocator>& x,
        const multimap<Key, T, Compare, Allocator>& y);
```

`iterator` is a bidirectional iterator referring to `value_type`. The exact type is implementation dependent and determined by `Allocator`.

`const_iterator` is the a constant bidirectional iterator referring to `const value_type`. The exact type is implementation dependent and determined by `Allocator`. It is guaranteed that there is a constructor for `const_iterator` out of `iterator`.

`size_type` is an unsigned integral type. The exact type is implementation dependent and determined by `Allocator`.

`difference_type` is a signed integral type. The exact type is implementation dependent and determined by `Allocator`.

# 9   STREAM ITERATOR

To make it possible for algorithmic templates to work directly with input/output streams, appropriate iteratorlike template classes are provided. For example,

```
partial_sum_copy(istream_iterator<double>(cin),istream_iterator<double>(),
        ostream_iterator<double>(cout, "\n"));
```

reads a file containing floating point numbers from `cin`, and prints the partial sums onto `cout`.

## 9.1 Istream Iterator

istream_iterator<T> reads (using operator>>) successive elements from the input stream for which it was constructed. After it is constructed, and every time ++ is used, the iterator reads and stores a value of T. If the end of stream is reached (operator void*() on the stream returns false), the iterator becomes equal to the *end-of-stream* iterator value. The constructor with no arguments istream_iterator() always constructs an end of stream input iterator object, which is the only legitimate iterator to be used for the end condition. The result of operator* on an end of stream is not defined. For any other iterator value a const T& is returned. It is impossible to store things into istream iterators. The main peculiarity of the istream iterators is the fact that ++ operators are not equality preserving, that is, i == j does not guarantee at all that ++i == ++j. Every time ++ is used a new value is read.

The practical consequence of this fact is that istream iterators can be used only for one-pass algorithms, which actually makes perfect sense, since for multipass algorithms it is always more appropriate to use in-memory data structures. Two end-of-stream iterators are always equal. An end-of-stream iterator is not equal to a non-end-of-stream iterator. Two non-end-of-stream iterators are equal when they are constructed from the same stream.

```
template <class T, class Distance = ptrdiff_t>
class istream_iterator : public input_iterator<T, Distance> {
friend bool operator==(const istream_iterator<T, Distance>& x,
                       const istream_iterator<T, Distance>& y);
public:
    istream_iterator();
    istream_iterator(istream& s);
    istream_iterator(const istream_iterator<T, Distance>& x);
    ~istream_iterator();
    const T& operator*() const;
    istream_iterator<T, Distance>& operator++();
    istream_iterator<T, Distance> operator++(int);
};
template <class T, class Distance>
bool operator==(const istream_iterator<T, Distance>& x,
        const istream_iterator<T, Distance>& y);
```

## 9.2 Ostream iterator

ostream_iterator<T> writes (using operator<<) successive elements onto the output stream from which it was constructed. If it was constructed with char* as a constructor argument, this string, called a *delimiter string*, is written to the stream after every T is written. It is not possible to get a value out of the output iterator. Its only use is as an output iterator in situations like

```
while (first != last) *result++ = *first++;
```

ostream_iterator is defined as

```
    template <class T>
    class ostream_iterator : public output_iterator {
```

```
public:
    ostream_iterator(ostream& s);
    ostream_iterator(ostream& s, const char* delimiter);
    ostream_iterator(const ostream_iterator<T>& x);
    ~ostream_iterator();
    ostream_iterator<T>& operator=(const T& value);
    ostream_iterator<T>& operator*();
    ostream_iterator<T>& operator++();
    ostream_iterator<T>& operator++(int);
};
```

# 10  ALGORITHMS

All of the algorithms are separated from the particular implementations of data structures and are parameterized by iterator types. Because of this, they can work with user defined data structures, as long as these data structures have iterator types satisfying the assumptions on the algorithms.

Both in-place and copying versions are provided for certain algorithms. The decision whether to include a copying version was usually based on complexity considerations. When the cost of doing the operation dominates the cost of copy, the copying version is not included. For example, sort_copy is not included since the cost of sorting is much more significant, and users might as well do copy followed by sort. When such a version is provided for *algorithm* it is called *algorithm*_copy. Algorithms that take predicates end with the suffix _if (which follows the suffix _copy).

The Predicate class is used whenever an algorithm expects a function object that when applied to the result of dereferencing the corresponding iterator returns a value testable as true. In other words, if an algorithm takes Predicate pred as its argument and first as its iterator argument, it should work correctly in the construct if (pred(*first)) { . . . }. The function object pred is assumed not to apply any non-constant function through the dereferenced iterator.

The BinaryPredicate class is used whenever an algorithm expects a function object that when applied to the result of dereferencing two corresponding iterators or to dereferencing an iterator and type T when T is part of the signature returns a value testable as true. In other words, if an algorithm takes BinaryPredicate binary_pred as its argument and first1 and first2 as its iterator arguments, it should work correctly in the construct if (binary_pred(*first, *first2)) { . . . }. BinaryPredicate always takes the first iterator type as its first argument, that is, in those cases when T value is part of the signature, it should work correctly in the context of if (binary_pred(*first, value)) { . . . }. It is expected that binary_pred will not apply any nonconstant function through the dereferenced iterators.

In the description of the algorithms operators + and − are used for some of the iterator categories for which they do not have to be defined. In these cases the semantics of a+n is the same as that of { X tmp = a; advance(tmp, n); return tmp; } and that of a-b is the same as that of { Distance n; distance(a, b, n); return n; }.

## 10.1  Nonmutating sequence operations

### 10.1.1  FOR EACH

```
template <class InputIterator, class Function>
Function for_each(InputIterator first, InputIterator last, Function f);
```

`for_each` applies `f` to the result of dereferencing every iterator in the range `[first, last)` and returns `f`. `f` is assumed not to apply any nonconstant function through the dereferenced iterator. `f` is applied exactly `last − first` times. If `f` returns a result, the result is ignored.

### 10.1.2  FIND

```
template <class InputIterator, class T>
InputIterator find(InputIterator first, InputIterator last, const T& value);
```

```
template <class InputIterator, class Predicate>
InputIterator find_if(InputIterator first, InputIterator last, Predicate pred);
```

`find` returns the first iterator `i` in the range `[first, last)` for which the following corresponding conditions hold: `*i == value`, `pred(*i) == true`. If no such iterator is found, `last` is returned. Exactly `find(first, last, value) − first` applications of the corresponding predicate are done.

### 10.1.3  ADJACENT FIND

```
template <class InputIterator>
InputIterator adjacent_find(InputIterator first, InputIterator last);
```

```
template <class InputIterator, class BinaryPredicate<
InputIterator adjacent_find(InputIterator first, InputIterator last,
        BinaryPredicate binary_pred);
```

`adjacent_find` returns the first iterator `i` such that both `i` and `i + 1` are in the range `[first, last)` for which the following corresponding conditions hold: `*i == *(i +1)`, `binary_pred(*i, *(i +1)) == true`. If no such iterator `i` is found, `last` is returned. At most `max((last − first) − 1, 0)` applications of the corresponding predicate are done.

### 10.1.4  COUNT

```
template <class InputIterator, class T, class Size>
void count (InputIterator first, InputIterator last, const T& value, Size& n);
```

```
template <class InputIterator, class Predicate, class Size<
void count_if(InputIterator first, InputIterator last, Predicate pred, Size& n);
```

`count` adds to `n` the number of iterators `i` in the range `[first, last)` for which the following corresponding conditions hold: `*i == value`, `pred(*i) == true`. Exactly `last − first` applications of the corresponding predicate are done.

`count` must store the result into a reference argument instead of returning the result because the size type cannot be deduced from built-in iterator types such as `int *`.

### 10.1.5  MISMATCH

```
template <class InputIterator1, class InputIterator2>
pair<InputIterator1, InputIterator2> mismatch (InputIterator1 first1,
        InputIterator1 last1, InputIterator2 first2);
```

```
template <class InputIterator1, class InputIterator2, class BinaryPredicate>
pair<InputIterator1, InputIterator2> mismatch (InputIterator1 first1,
      InputIterator1 last1, InputIterator2 first2),
      Binary Predicate binary_pred);
```

mismatch returns a pair of iterators i and j such that j == first2 + (i − first1) and i is the first iterator in the range (first1, last1) for which the following corresponding conditions hold: ! (*i == *(first2 + (i − first1))), binary_pred(*i, *(first2 + (i − first1))) == false. If such an iterator i is not found, a pair of last1 and first2 + (last 1 − first1) is returned. At most last1 − first1 applications of the corresponding predicate are done.

### 10.1.6  EQUAL

```
template <class InputIterator1, class InputIterator2>
bool equal<InputIterator1 first 1, InputIterator1 last1, InputIterator2 first 2);
```

```
template <class InputIterator1, class InputIterator2, class BinaryPredicate>
bool equal(InputIterator1 first 1, InputIterator1 last1, InputIterator2 first 2,
      BinaryPredicate binary_pred);
```

equal returns true if for every iterator i in the range [first1, last1) the following corresponding conditions hold: *i == *(first2 + (i − first 1)), binary_pred(*i, *(first2 + (i − first1))) = = true. Otherwise, it returns false. At most last1 − first1 applications of the corresponding predicate are done.

### 10.1.7  SEARCH

```
template <class ForwardIterator1, class ForwardIterator2>
ForwardIterator1 search(forwardIterator1 first1, ForwardIterator1 last1,
      ForwardIterator2 first2, ForwardIterator2 last2);
```

```
template <class ForwardIterator1, class ForwardIterator2, class BinaryPredicate>
ForwardIterator1 search(ForwardIterator1 first1, ForwardIterator1 last1,
      ForwardIterator2 first2, ForwardIterator2 last2, BinaryPredicate
      binary_pred);
```

search finds a subsequence of equal values in a sequence. search returns the first iterator i in the range [first1, last1 − (last 2 − first2)) such that for any non-negative integer n less than last 2 − first2 the following corresponding conditions hold: *(i + n) == *(first2 + n), binary _pred(*(i + n), *(first2 + n)) == true. If no such iterator is found, last1 is returned. At most (last1 − first1) * (last2 − first2) applications of the corresponding predicate are done. The quadratic behavior, however, is highly unlikely.

## 10.2  Mutating sequence operations

### 10.2.1  COPY

```
template <class InputIterator, class OutputIterator>
OutputIterator copy(InputIterator first, InputIterator last,
      OutputIterator result);
```

copy copies elements. For each non-negative integer n < (last − first), *(result + n) = *(first + n) is performed. copy returns result + (last − first). Exactly last − first assignments are done. The result of copy is undefined if result is in the range [first, last).

```
template <class BidirectionalIterator1, class BidirectionalIterator2>
BidirectionalIterator2 copy_backward(BidirectionalIterator1 first,
        BidirectionalIterator1 last, BidirectionalIterator2 result);
```

copy_backward copies elements in the range [first, last) into the range [result − (last − first), result) starting from last − 1 and proceeding to first. It should be used instead of copy when last is in the range [result − (last − first), result). For each positive integer n <= (last − first), *(result − n) = *(last − n) is performed. copy_backward returns result − (last − first). Exactly last − first assignments are done. The result of copy _backward is undefined if result is in the range [first, last).

### 10.2.2 SWAP

```
template <class T>
void swap(T& a, T& b);
```

swap exchanges values stored in two locations.

```
template <class ForwardIterator1, class ForwardIterator2>
void iter_swap(ForwardIterator1 a, Forward Iterator2 b);
```

iter_swap exchanges values pointed by the two iterators a and b.

```
template <class ForwardIterator1, class ForwardIterator2>
ForwardIterator2 swap_ranges(ForwardIterator1 first1, ForwardIterator1 last1,
        ForwardIterator2 first2);
```

For each nonnegative integer n < (last1 − first1) the swap is performed: swap(*(first1 + n), *(first2 + n)). swap_ranges returns first2 + (last1 − first1). Exactly last1 − first1 swaps are done. The result of swap_ranges is undefined if the two ranges [first1, last1) and [first2, first2 + (last1 − first1)) overlap.

### 10.2.3 TRANSFORM

```
template <class InputIterator, class OutputIterator, class UnaryOperation>
OutputIterator transform(InputIterator first, InputIterator last,
        Output Iterator result, UnaryOperation op);

template >class InputIterator1, class InputIterator2, class OutputIterator,
        class BinaryOperation>
OutputIterator transform(InputIterator1 first1, InputIterator1 last1,
        InputIterator2 first2, OutputIterator result,
        BinaryOperation binary_op);
```

transform assigns through every iterator i in the range [result, result + (last1 − first1)) a new corresponding value equal to op(*(first1 + (i − result))) or binary_op(*(first1 + (i − result), *(first2 + (i − result)))). transform returns result + (last1 − first1). Exactly last1 − first1 applications of op or binary_op are performed. op and binary_op are expected not to have any side effects. result may be equal to first in case of unary transform, or to first1 or first2 in case of binary transform.

### 10.2.4 REPLACE

```
template <class ForwardIterator, class T>
void replace(ForwardIterator first, ForwardIterator last, const T& old_value,
        const T& new_value);
template <class ForwardIterator, class Predicate, class T>
void replace_if(ForwardIterator first, ForwardIterator last, Predicate pred,
        const T& new_value);
```

replace substitutes elements referred by the iterator i in the range [first, last) with new_value, when the following corresponding conditions hold: *i == old_value, pred(*i) == true. Exactly last − first applications of the corresponding predicate are done.

```
template <class InputIterator, class OutputIterator, class T>
OutputIterator replace_copy(InputIterator first, InputIterator last,
        OutputIterator result, const T& old_value, const T& new_value);
```

```
template <class Iterator, class OutputIterator, class Predicate, class T>
OutputIterator replace_copy_if(Iterator first, Iterator last,
        OutputIterator result, Predicate pred, const T& new_value);
```

replace_copy assigns to every iterator i in the range [result, result + (last − first)) either new_value or *(first + (i − result)) depending on whether the following corresponding conditions hold: *(first + (i − result)) == old_value, pred(*(first + (i − result))) == true. replace_copy returns result + (last − first). Exactly last − first applications of the corresponding predicate are done.

### 10.2.5 FILL

```
template <class ForwardIterator, class T>
void fill(ForwardIterator first, ForwardIterator last, const T& value);
```

```
template <class OutputIterator, class Size, class T>
void fill_n(OutputIterator first, Size n, const T& value);
```

fill assigns value through all the iterators in the range [first, last) or [first, first + n). Exactly last − first (or n) assignments are done.

### 10.2.6  GENERATE

```
template <class ForwardIterator, class Generator>
void generate(ForwardIterator first, ForwardIterator last, Generator gen);

template <class OutputIterator, class Size, class Generator<
void generate_n(OutputIterator first, Size n, Generator gen);
```

generate invokes the function object gen and assigns the return value of gen through all the iterators in the range [first, last) or [first, first + n). gen takes no arguments. Exactly last − first (or n) invocations of gen and assignments are done.

### 10.2.7  REMOVE

```
template <class ForwardIterator, class T>
ForwardIterator remove(ForwardIterator first, ForwardIterator last,
        const T& value);

template <class ForwardIterator, class Predicate>
ForwardIterator remove_if(ForwardIterator first, ForwardIterator last,
        Predicate pred);
```

remove eliminates all the elements referred to by iterator i in the range [first, last) for which the following corresponding conditions hold: *i == value, pred(*i) == true. remove returns the end of the resulting range. remove is stable, that is, the relative order of the elements that are not removed is the same as their relative order in the original range. Exactly last − first applications of the corresponding predicate are done.

```
template <class InputIterator, class OutputIterator, class T>
OutputIterator remove_copy (InputIterator first, InputIterator last,
        OutputIterator result, const T& value);

template <class InputIterator, class OutputIterator, class Predicate>
OutputIterator remove_copy_if(InputIterator first, InputIterator last,
        OutputIterator result, Predicate pred);
```

remove_copy copies all the elements referred to by the iterator i in the range [first, last) for which the following corresponding conditions do not hold: *i == value, pred(*i)== true. remove _copy returns the end of the resulting range. remove_copy is stable, that is, the relative order of the elements in the resulting range is the same as their relative order in the original range. Exactly last − first applications of the corresponding predicate are done.

### 10.2.8  UNIQUE

```
template <class ForwardIterator>
ForwardIterator unique(ForwardIterator first, ForwardIterator last);

template <class ForwardIterator, class BinaryPredicate>
ForwardIterator unique(ForwardIterator first, ForwardIterator last,
        BinaryPredicate binary_pred);
```

unique eliminates all but the first element from every consecutive group of equal elements referred to by the iterator i in the range [first, last) for which the following corresponding conditions hold: *i == *(i −1) or binary_pred(*i, *(i − 1)) == true. unique returns the end of the result range. Exactly (last − first) − 1 applications of the corresponding predicate are done.

```
template <class InputIterator, class OutputIterator>
OutputIterator unique_copy(InputIterator first, InputIterator last,
        OutputIterator result);
```

```
template <class InputIterator, class OutputIterator, class BinaryPredicate>
OutputIterator unique_copy(InputIterator first, InputIterator last,
        OutputIterator result, BinaryPredicate binary_pred);
```

unique_copy copies only the first element from every consecutive group of equal elements referred to by the iterator i in the range [first, last) for which the following corresponding conditions hold: *i == *(i − 1) or binary_pred(*i, *(i − 1)) == true. unique_copy returns the end of the resulting range. Exactly last − first applications of the corresponding predicate are done.

### 10.2.9 REVERSE

```
template <class BidirectionalIterator>
void reverse(BidirectionalIterator first, BidirectionalIterator last);
```

For each nonnegative integer i <= (last − first)/2, reverse applies swap to all pairs of iterators first + i, (last − i) − 1. Exactly (last − first)/2 swaps are performed.

```
template <class BidirectionalIterator, class OutputIterator>
OutputIterator reverse_copy(BidirectionalIterator first,
        BidirectionalIterator last, OutputIterator result);
```

reverse_copy copies the range [first, last) to the range [result, result + (last − first)) such that for any nonnegative integer i < (last − first) the following assignment takes place: *(result + (last − first) − i) = *(first + i). reverse_copy returns result + (last − first). Exactly last − first assignments are done. The result of reverse_copy is undefined if [first, last) and [result, result + (last − first)) overlap.

### 10.2.10 ROTATE

```
template <class ForwardIterator>
void rotate(ForwardIterator first, ForwardIterator middle, ForwardIterator last);
```

For each nonnegative integer i < (last − first), rotate places the element from the position first + i into position first + (last − middle)) % (last − first). [first, middle) and [middle, last) are valid ranges. At most last − first swaps are done.

```
template <class ForwardIterator, class OutputIterator>
OutputIterator rotate_copy(ForwardIterator first, ForwardIterator middle,
        ForwardIterator last, OutputIterator result);
```

rotate_copy copies the range [first, last) to the range [result, result + (last − first)) such that for each nonnegative integer i < (last − first) the following assignment takes place: *(result + (i + (last − middle)) % (last − first)) = *(first + i). rotate _copy returns result + (last − first). Exactly last − first assignments are done. The result of rotate_copy is undefined if [first, last) and [result, result + (last − first)) overlap.

### 10.2.11  RANDOM SHUFFLE

```
template <class RandomAccessIterator>
void random_shuffle(RandomAccessIterator first, RandomAccessIterator last);
```

```
template <class RandomAccessIterator, class RandomNumberGenerator>
void random_shuffle(RandomAccessIterator first, RandomAccessIterator last,
     RandomNumber Generator& rand);
```

random_shuffle shuffles the elements in the range [first, last) with uniform distribution. Exactly (last − first) − 1 swaps are done. random_shuffle can take a particular random number generating function object rand such that rand takes a positive argument n of distance type of the RandomAccessIterator and returns a randomly chosen value between 0 and n−1.

### 10.2.12 PARTITIONS

```
template <class BidirectionalIterator, class Predicate>
BidirectionalIterator partition(BidirectionalIterator first,
     BidirectionalIterator last, Predicate pred);
```

partition places all the elements in the range [first, last) that satisfy pred before all the elements that do not satisfy it. It returns an iterator i such that for any iterator j in the range [first, i), pred(*j) == true, and for any iterator k in the range [i, last), pred(*j) == false. It does at most (last − first)/2 swaps. Exactly last − first applications of the predicate is done.

```
template <class BidirectionalIterator, class Predicate>
BidirectionalIterator stable_partition(BidirectionalIterator first,
     BidirectionalIterator last, Predicate pred);
```

stable_partition places all the elements in the range [first, last) that satisfy pred before all the elements that do not satisfy it. It returns an iterator i such that for any iterator j in the range [first, i), pred(*j) == true, and for any iterator k in the range [i, last), pred(*j) == false. The relative order of the elements in both groups is preserved. It does at most (last − first) * log(last − first) swaps, but only linear number of swaps if there is enough extra memory. Exactly last − first applications of the predicate are done.

## 10.3   Sorting and related operations

All the operations in this section have two versions: one that takes a function object of type Compare and one that uses an operator>.

Compare is used as a function object which returns true if the first argument is less than the second, and false otherwise. Compare comp is used throughout for algorithms assuming an ordering relation. It is assumed that comp will not apply any nonconstant function through the dereferenced iterator. For all algorithms that take Compare, there is a version that uses operator< instead. That is, comp(*i, *j) == true defaults to *i < *j == true. For the algorithms to work correctly, comp has to induce a total ordering on the values.

A sequence is sorted with respect to a comparator comp if for any iterator i pointing to the sequence and any nonnegative integer n such that i + n is a valid iterator pointing to an element of the sequence, comp(*(i + n), *i) == false.

In the descriptions of the functions that deal with ordering relationships we frequently use a notion of equality to describe concepts such as stability. The equality to which we refer is not necessarily an operator==, but an equality relation induced by the total ordering. That is, two elements a and b are considered equal if and only if !(a < b) && !(b <a).

## 10.3.1 SORT

```
template <class RandomAccessIterator>
void sort(RandomAccessIterator first, RandomAccessIterator last);

template <class RandomAccessIterator, class Compare>
void sort (RandomAccessIterator first, RandomAccessIterator last, Compare comp);
```

sort sorts the elements in the range [first, last). It does approximately NlogN (where N equals to last - first) comparisons on the average. If the worst case behavior is important stable_sort or partial_sort should be used.

```
template <class RandomAccessIterator>
void stable_sort (RandomAccessIterator first, RandomAccessIterator last);

template <class RandomAccessIterator, class Compare>
void stable_sort (RandomAccessIterator first, RandomAccessIterator last), Compare comp;
```

stable_sort sorts the elements in the range [first, last). It is stable, that is, the relative order of the equal elements is preserved. It does at most $N(\log N)^2$ (where N equals to $last - first$) comparisons; if enough extra money is available, it is NlogN.

```
template <class RandomAccessIterator>
void partial_sort(RandomAccessIterator first, RandomAccessIterator middle,
      RandomAccessIterator last);

template <class RandomAccessIterator, class Compare>
void partial_sortRandomAccessIterator first, RandomAccessIterator middle,
      RandomAccessIterator last, Compare comp);
```

partial_sort places the first middle − first sorted elements from the range [first, last) into the range [first, middle). The rest of the elements in the range [middle, last) are placed in an undefined order. It takes approximately (last − first) * log(middle − first) comparisons.

```
template <class InputIterator, class RandomAccessIterator>
RandomAccessIterator partial_sort_copy(InputIterator first, InputIterator last,
        RandomAccessIterator result_first, RandomAccessIterator
        result_last);
```

```
template <class InputIterator, class RandomAccessIterator, class Compare>
RandomAccessIterator partial_sort_copy(InputIterator first, InputIterator last,
        RandomAccessIterator result_first, RandomAccessIterator
        result_last, Compare comp);
```

partial_sort_copy places the first min(last − first, result_last − result_first) sorted elements into the range [result_first, result_first + min(last − first, result_last − result_first)). It returns either result_last or result_first + (last − first), whichever is smaller. It takes approximately (last − first) * log(min(last − first, result_last − result_first)) comparisons.

### 10.3.2  NTH ELEMENT

```
template <class RandomAccessIterator>
void nth_element(RandomAccessIterator first, RandomAccessIterator nth,
        RandomAccessIterator last);
```

```
template <class RandomAccessIterator, class Compare>
void nth_element(RandomAccessIterator first, RandomAccessIterator nth,
        RandomAccessIterator last, Compare comp);
```

After nth_element the element in the position pointed to by nth is the element that would be in that position if the whole range were sorted. Also for any iterator i in the range [first, nth) and any iterator j in the range [nth, last) it holds that !(*i > *j) or comp(*i, *j) == false. It is linear on the average.

### 10.3.3  BINARY SEARCH

All of the algorithms in this section are versions of binary search. They work on nonrandom access iterators minimizing the number of comparisons, which will be logarithmic for all types of iterators. They are especially appropriate for random access iterators, since these algorithms do a logarithmic number of steps through the data structure. For nonrandom access iterators they execute a linear number of steps.

```
template <class ForwardIterator, class T>
ForwardIterator lower_bound(ForwardIterator first, ForwardIterator last,
        const T& value);
```

```
template <class ForwardIterator, class T, class Compare>
ForwardIterator lower_bound(ForwardIterator first, ForwardIterator last,
        const T& value, Compare comp);
```

lower_bound finds the first position into which value can be inserted without violating the ordering. lower_bound returns the furthermost iterator i in the range [first, last) such that for any iterator j in the range [first, i) the following corresponding conditions hold: *j < value or comp(*j, value) == true. At most log(last − first) + 1 comparisons are done.

```
template <class ForwardIterator, class T>
ForwardIterator upper_bound(ForwardIterator first, ForwardIterator last,
        const T& value);
```

```
template <class ForwardIterator, class T, class Compare>
ForwardIterator upper_bound(ForwardIterator first, ForwardIterator last,
        const T& value, Compare comp);
```

upper_bound finds the furthermost position into which value can be inserted without violating the ordering. upper_bound returns the furthermost iterator i in the range [first, last) such that for any iterator j in the range [first, i) the following corresponding conditions hold: !(value < *j) or comp(value, *j) == false. At most log(last − first) + 1 comparisons are done.

```
template <class ForwardIterator, class T>
pair<ForwardIterator, ForwardIterator> equal_range(ForwardIterator first,
        ForwardIterator last, const T& value);
```

```
template <class ForwardIterator, class T, class Compare>
pair<ForwardIterator, ForwardIterator> equal_range(ForwardIterator first,
        ForwardIterator last, const T& value, Compare comp);
```

equal_range finds the largest subrange [i, j) such that the value can be inserted at any iterator k in it. k satisfies the corresponding conditions: !(*k < value) && !(value < *k) or comp(*k, value) == false && comp(value, *k) == false. At most 2 * log(last − first) + 1 comparisons are done.

```
template <class ForwardIterator, class T>
bool binary_search(ForwardIterator first, ForwardIterator last, const T& value);
```

```
template <class ForwardIterator, class T, class Compare>
bool binary_search(ForwardIterator first, ForwardIterator last, const T& value);
        Compare comp);
```

binary_search returns true if there is an iterator i in the range [first last) that satisfies the corresponding conditions: !(*i < value) && !(value < *i) or comp(*i, value) == false && comp(value, *i) == false. At most log(last − first) + 2 comparisons are done.

## 10.3.4  MERGE

```
template <class InputIterator1, class InputIterator2, class OutputIterator>
OutputIterator merge(InputIterator1 first1, InputIterator1 last1,
        InputIterator2 first2, InputIterator2 last2,
        OutputIterator result);
```

```
template <class InputIterator1, class InputIterator2, class OutputIterator,
    class Compare>
```

```
OutputIterator merge(InputIterator1 first1, InputIterator1 last1,
      InputIterator2 first2, InputIterator2 last2,
      OutputIterator result, Compare comp);
```

merge merges two sorted ranges [first1, last1) and [first2, last2) into the range [result, result + (last1 − first1) + (last2 − first2)). The merge is *stable*, that is, for equal elements in the two ranges, the elements from the first range always precede the elements from the second. merge returns result + (last1 − first1) + (last2 − first2). At most (last1 − first1) + (last2 − first2) − 1 comparisons are performed. The result of merge is undefined if the resulting range overlaps with either of the original ranges.

```
template <class BidirectionalIterator>
void inplace_merge(BidirectionalIterator first, BidirectionalIterator middle,
      BidirectionalIterator last);

template <class BidirectionalIterator, class Compare>
void inplace_merge(BidirectionalIterator first, BidirectionalIterator middle,
      BidirectionalIterator last, Compare comp);
```

inplace_merge merges two sorted consecutive ranges [first, middle) and [middle, last) putting the result of the merge into the range [first, last). The merge is *stable*, that is, for equal elements in the two ranges, the elements from the first range always precede the elements from the second. When enough additional memory is available, at most (last − first) − 1 comparisons are performed. If no additional memory is available, an algorithm with O(NlogN) complexity may be used.

### 10.3.5   SET OPERATIONS ON SORTED STRUCTURES

This section defines all the basic set operations on sorted structures. They even work with multisets containing multiple copies of equal elements. The semantics of the set operations is generalized to multisets in a standard way by defining union to contain the maximum number of occurrences of every element, intersection to contain the minimum, and so on.

```
template <class InputIterator1, class InputIterator2>
bool includes(InputIterator1 first1, InputIterator1 last 1,
      InputIterator2 first 2, InputIterator2 last2);

template <class InputIterator1, class InputIterator2, class Compare>
bool includes(InputIterator1, first1, InputIterator1 last1,
      InputIterator2 first2, InputIterator2 last2, Compare comp);
```

includes returns true if every element in the range [first2, last2) is contained in the range [first1, last1). It returns false otherwise. At most ((last1 − first1) + (last2 − first2)) * 2 − 1 comparisons are performed.

```
template <class InputIterator1, class InputIterator2, class OutputIterator>
OutputIterator set_union(InputIterator1, first1, InputIterator1 last1,
      InputIterator2 first2, InputIterator2 last2,
      OutputIterator result);
```

```
template <class InputIterator1, class InputIterator2, class OutputIterator, class
    Compare>
OutputIterator set_union(InputIterator1 first1, InputIterator1 last1,
    InputIterator2 first2, InputIterator2 last2,
    OutputIterator result, Compare comp);
```

set_union constructs a sorted union of the elements from the two ranges. It returns the end of the constructed range. set_union is stable, that is, if an element is present in both ranges, the one from the first range is copied. At most ((last1 − first1) + (last2 − first2)) * 2 − 1 comparisons are performed. The result of set_union is undefined if the resulting range overlaps with either of the original ranges.

```
template <class InputIterator1, class InputIterator2, classOutputIterator>
OutputIterator set_intersection(InputIterator1 first1, InputIterator1, last1,
    InputIterator2 first2, InputIterator2 last2,
    OutputIterator result);

template <class InputIterator1, class InputIterator2, class OutputIterator,
    class Compare>
OutputIterator set_intersection(InputIterator1 first1, InputIterator1 last1,
    InputIterator2 first2, InputIterator2 last2, OutputIterator result,
    Compare comp);
```

set_intersection constructs a sorted intersection of the elements from the two ranges. It returns the end of the constructed range. set_intersection is guaranteed to be stable, that is, if an element is present in both ranges, the one from the first range is copied. At most ((last1 − first1) + (last2 − first2)) * 2 − 1 comparisons are performed. The result of set_intersection is undefined if the resulting range overlaps with either of the original ranges.

```
template <class InputIterator1, class InputIterator2, class OutputIterator>
OutputIterator set_difference(InputIterator1 first1, InputIterator1 last1,
    InputIterator2 first2, InputIterator2 last2,
    OutputIterator result);

template <class InputIterator1, class InputIterator2, classOutputIterator,
    class Compare>
OutputIterator set_difference(InputIterator1 first1, InputIterator1 last1,
    InputIterator2 first2, InputIterator2 last2,
    OutputIterator result, Compare comp);
```

set_difference constructs a sorted difference of the elements from the two ranges. It returns the end of the constructed range. At most ((last1 − first1) + (last2 − first2)) * 2 − 1 comparisons are performed. The result of set_difference is undefined if the resulting range overlaps with either of the original ranges.

```
template <class InputIterator1, class InputIterator2, class OutputIterator>
OutputIterator set_symmetric_difference(InputIterator1 first1, InputIterator1
    last1, InputIterator2 first2, InputIterator2 last2,
    OutputIterator result);
```

```
template <class InputIterator1, class InputIterator2, class OutputIterator,
        class Compare>
OutputIterator set_symmetric_difference(InputIterator1 first1, InputIterator1
        last1, InputIterator2 first2, InputIterator2 last2,
        OutputIterator result, Compare comp);
```

set_symmetric_difference constructs a sorted symmetric difference of the elements from the two ranges. It returns the end of the constructed range. At most ((last1 − first1) − (last2 − first2)) * 2 − 1 comparisons are performed. The result of set_symmetric_difference is undefined if the resulting range overlaps with either of the original ranges.

### 10.3.6   HEAP OPERATIONS

A heap is a particular organization of elements in a range between two random access iterators [a, b). Its two key properties are: (1) *a is the largest element in the range and (2) *a may be removed by pop_heap, or a new element added by push_heap, in O(logN) time. These properties make heaps useful as priority queues. make_heap converts a range into a heap and sort_heap turns a heap into a sorted sequence.

```
template <class RandomAccessIterator>
void push_heap(RandomAccessIterator first, RandomAccessIterator last);
```

```
template <class RandomAccessIterator, class Compare>
void push_heap(RandomAccessIterator first, RandomAccessIterator last,
        Compare comp);
```

push_heap assumes the range [first, last − 1) is a valid heap and properly places the value in the location last − 1 into the resulting heap [first, last). At most log(last − first) comparisons are performed.

```
template <class RandomAccessIterator>
void pop_heap(RandomAccessIterator first, RandomAccessIterator last);
```

```
template <class RandomAccessIterator, class Compare>
void pop_heap(RandomAccessIterator first, RandomAccessIterator last,
        Compare comp);
```

pop_heap assumes the range [first, last) is a valid heap, then swaps the value in the location first with the value in the location last − 1 and makes [first, last − 1) into a heap. At most 2 * log(last − first) comparisons are performed.

```
template <class RandomAccessIterator>
void make_heap(RandomAccessIterator first, RandomAccessIterator last);
```

```
template <class RandomAccessIterator, class Compare>
void make_heap(RandomAccessIterator first, RandomAccessIterator last,
        Compare comp);
```

make_heap constructs a heap out of the range [first, last). At most 3*(last − first) comparisons are performed.

```
template <class RandomAccessIterator>
void sort_heap(RandomAccessIterator first, RandomAccessIterator last);

template <class RandomAccessIterator, class Compare>
void sort_heap(RandomAccessIterator first, RandomAccessIterator last,
        Compare comp);
```

sort_heap sorts elements in the heap [first, last). At most NlogN comparisons are performed where N is equal to last − first. sort_heap is not stable.

### 10.3.7 MINIMUM AND MAXIMUM

```
template <class T>
const T& min(const T& a, const T& b);

template <class T, class Compare>
const T& min(const T& a, const T& b, Compare comp);

template <class T>
const T& max(const T& a, const T& b);

template <class T, class Compare>
const T& max(const T& a, const T& b, Compare comp);
```

min returns the smaller and max the larger. min and max return the first argument when their arguments are equal.

```
template <class InputIterator>
InputIterator max_element(InputIterator first, InputIterator last);

template <class InputIterator, class Compare>
InputIterator max_element(InputIterator first, InputIterator last, Compare comp);
```

max_element returns the first iterator i in the range [first, last) such that for any iterator j in the range [first, last) the following corresponding conditions hold: !(*i < *j) or comp(*i, *j) == false. Exactly max((last − first) − 1, 0) applications of the corresponding comparisons are done.

```
template <class InputIterator>
InputIterator min_element(InputIterator first, InputIterator last);

template <class InputIterator, class Compare>
InputIterator min_element(InputIterator first, InputIterator last, Compare comp);
```

min_element returns the first iterator i in the range [first, last) such that for any iterator j in the range [first, last) the following corresponding conditions hold: !(*j < *i) or comp(*j, *i) == false. Exactly max((last − first) − 1, 0) applications of the corresponding comparisons are done.

### 10.3.8  Lexicographical comparison

```
template <class InputIterator1, class InputIterator2>
bool lexicographical_compare(InputIterator1 first1, InputIterator1, last1,
        InputIterator2 first2, InputIterator2 last2);

template <class InputIterator1, class InputIterator2, class Compare>
bool lexicographical_compare(InputIterator1 first1, InputIterator1 last1,
        InputIterator2 first2, InputIterator2 last2, Compare comp);
```

`lexicographical_compare` returns `true` if the sequence of elements defined by the range `[first1, last1)` is lexicographically less than the sequence of elements defined by the range `[first2, last2)`. It returns `false` otherwise. At most `min((last1 − first1), (last2 − first2))` applications of the corresponding comparison are done.

### 10.3.9  Permutation generators

```
template <class BidirectionalIterator>
bool next_permutation(BidirectionalIterator first, BidirectionalIterator last);

template <class BidirectionalIterator, class Compare>
bool next_permutation(BidirectionalIterator first, BidirectionalIterator last,
        Compare comp);
```

`next_permutation` takes a sequence defined by the range `[first, last)` and transforms it into the *next* permutation. The next permutation is found by assuming that the set of all permutations is lexicographically sorted with respect to `operator<` or `comp`. If such a permutation exists, it returns `true`. Otherwise, it transforms the sequence into the smallest permutation, that is, the ascendingly sorted one, and returns `false`. At most `(last − first)/2` swaps are performed.

```
template <class BidirectionalIterator>
bool prev_permutation(BidirectionalIterator first, BidirectionalIterator last);

template <class BidirectionalIterator, class Compare>
bool prev_permutation(BidirectionalIterator first, BidirectionalIterator last,
        Compare comp);
```

`prev_permutation` takes a sequence defined by the range `[first, last)` and transforms it into the *previous* permutation. The previous permutation is found by assuming that the set of all permutations is lexicographically sorted with respect to `operator<` or `comp`. If such a permutation exists, it returns `true`. Otherwise, it transforms the sequence into the largest permutation, that is, the descendingly sorted one, and returns `false`. At most `(last − first)/2` swaps are performed.

## 10.4  Generalized numeric operations

### 10.4.1  Accumulate

```
template <class InputIterator, class T>
T accumulate(InputIterator first, InputIterator last, T init);
```

```
template <class InputIterator, class T, class BinaryOperation>
T accumulate(InputIterator first, InputIterator last, T init,
      BinaryOperation binary_op);
```

accumulate is similar to the APL *reduction* operator and Common Lisp *reduce* function, but it avoids the difficulty of defining the result of reduction on an empty sequence by always requiring an initial value. Accumulation is done by initializing the accumulator acc with the initial value init and then modifying it with acc = acc + *i or acc = binary_op(acc, *i) for every iterator i in the range [first, last) in order. binary_op is assumed not to cause side effects.

### 10.4.2 INNER PRODUCT

```
template <class InputIterator1, class InputIterator2, class T>
T inner_product(InputIterator1 first1, InputIterator1 last1,
      InputIterator2 first2, T init);

template <class InputIterator1, class InputIterator2, class T,
      class BinaryOperation1, class BinaryOperation2>
T inner_product(InputIterator1 first1, InputIterator1, last1,
      InputIterator2 first2, T init,
      BinaryOperation1, binary_op1, BinaryOperation2 binary_op2);
```

inner_product computes its result by initializing the accumulator acc with the initial value init and then modifying it with acc = acc + (*i1) * (*i2) or acc = binary_op!(acc, binary _op2(*i1, *i2)) for every iterator i1 in the range [first, last) and iterator i2 in the range [first2, first2 + (last − first)) in order. binary_op1 and binary_op2 are assumed not to cause side effects.

### 10.4.3 PARTIAL SUM

```
template <class InputIterator, class OutputIterator>
OutputIterator partial_sum(InputIterator first, InputIterator last,
      OutputIterator result);

template <class InputIterator, class OutputIterator, class BinaryOperation>
OutputIterator partial_sum(InputIterator first, InputIterator last,
      OutputIterator result, BinaryOperation binary_op);
```

partial_sum assigns to every iterator i in the range [result, result + (last − first)) a value correspondingly equal to ((. . . (*first + *(first +1)) + . . . )+ *(first + (i − result))) or binary_op(binary_op(. . ., binary_op(*first, *(first +1)),. . .), *(first + (i − result))). partial_sum returns result + (last − first). Exactly (last − first) − 1 applications of binary_op are performed. binary_op is expected not to have any side effects. result may be equal to first.

### 10.4.4 ADJACENT DIFFERENCE

```
template <class InputIterator, class OutputIterator>
OutputIterator adjacent_difference(InputIterator first, InputIterator last,
      OutputIterator result);
```

```
template <class InputIterator, class OutputIterator, class BinaryOperation>
OutputIterator adjacent_difference(InputIterator first, InputIterator last,
      OutputIterator result, BinaryOperation binary_op);
```

adjacent_difference assigns to every element referred to by iterator i in the range [result + 1, result + (last − first)) a value correspondingly equal to *(first + (i − result)) − *(first + (i − result) − 1) or binary_op(*(first + (i − result)), *(first + (i − result) − 1)). result gets the value of *first. adjacent_difference returns result + (last − first). Exactly (last − first) − 1 applications of binary_op are performed. binary_op is expected not to have any side effects. result may be equal to first.

# 11   ADAPTORS

Adaptors are template classes that provide interface mappings. For example, insert_iterator provides a container with an output iterator interface.

## 11.1   Container adaptors

It is often useful to provide restricted interfaces to containers. The library provides stack, queue and priority_queue through the adaptors that can work with different sequence types.

### 11.1.1   STACK

Any sequence supporting operations back, push_back and pop_back can be used to instantiate stack. In particular, vector, list and deque can be used.

```
template <class Container>
class stack {
friend bool operator==(const stack<Container>& x, const stack<Container>& y);
friend bool operator<(const stack<Container>& x, const stack<Container>& y);
public:
    typedef Container::value_type value_type;
    typedef Container::size_type size_type;
protected:
    Container c;
public:
    bool empty() const { return c.empty(); }
    size_type size() const { return c.size(); }
    value_type& top() { return c.back(); }
    const value_type& top() const { return c.back(); }
    void push(const value_type& x) { c.push_back(x); }
    void pop() { c.pop_back(); }
};

template <class Container>
bool operator==(const stack<Container>& x, const stack<Container>& y) {
    return x.c == y.c;
}
```

```
template <class Container>
bool operator<(const stack<Container>& x, const stack<Container>& y) {
    return x.c < y.c;
}
```

For example, stack<vector<int> > is an integer stack made out of vector, and stack <deque<char> > is a character stack made out of deque.

## 11.1.2   QUEUE

Any sequence supporting operations front, back, push_back and pop_front can be used to instantiate queue. In particular, list and deque can be used.

```
template <class Container>
class queue {
friend bool operator==(const queue<Container>& x, const queue<Container>& y);
friend bool operator<(const queue<Container>& x, const queue<Container>& y);
public:
    typedef Container::value_type value_type;
    typedef Container::size_type size_type;
protected:
    Container c;
public:
    bool empty() const { return c.empty(); }
    size_type size() const { return c.size(); }
    value_type& front() { return c.front(); }
    const value_type& front() const { return c.front(); }
    value_type& back() { return c.back(); }
    const value_type& back() const { return c.back(); }
    void push(const value_type& x) { c.push_back(x); }
    void pop() { c.pop_front(); }
};
template <class Container>
bool operator==(const queue<Container>& x, const queue<Container>& y) {
    return x.c == y.c;
}
template <class Container>
bool operator<(const queue<Container>& x, const queue<Container>& y) {
    return x.c < y.c;
}
```

## 11.1.3   PRIORITY QUEUE

Any sequence with random access iterator and supporting operations front, push_back and pop_back can be used to instantiate priority_queue. In particular, vector and deque can be used.

```
template <class Container, class Compare = less<Container::value_type> >
class priority_queue {
```

```
public:
    typedef Container::value_type value_type;
    typedef Container::size_type size_type;
protected:
    Container c;
    Compare comp;
public:
    priority_queue(const Compare& x = Compare()) : c(), comp(x) {}
    template <class InputIterator>
    priority_queue(InputIterator first, InputIterator last,
            const Compare& x = Compare()) : c(first, last), comp(x) {
        make_heap(c.begin(), c.end(), comp);
    }
    bool empty() const { return c.empty(); }
    size_type size() const { return c.size(); }
    const value_type& top() const { return c.front(); }
    void push(const value_type& x) {
        c.push_back(x);
        push_heap(c.begin(), c.end(), comp);
    }
    void pop() {
        pop_heap(c.begin(), c.end(), comp);
        c.pop_back();
    }
};
```

// no equality is provided


## 11.2   Iterator adaptors

### 11.2.1   REVERSE ITERATORS

Bidirectional and random access iterators have corresponding reverse iterator adaptors that iterate through the data structure in the opposite direction. They have the same signatures as the corresponding iterators. The fundamental relation between a reverse iterator and its corresponding iterator i is established by the identity

```
&*(reverse_iterator(i)) == &*(i − 1).
```

This mapping is dictated by the fact that while there is always a pointer past the end of an array, there might not be a valid pointer before the beginning of an array.

```
template <class BidirectionalIterator, class T, class Reference = T&,
    class Distance = ptrdiff_t>
class reverse_bidirectional_iterator
    : public bidirectional_iterator<T, Distance> {
    typedef reverse_bidirectional_iterator<BidirectionalIterator, T,
                Reference, Distance> self;
    friend bool operator==(const self& x, const self& y);
protected:
    BidirectionalIterator current;
```

```
public:
    reverse_bidirectional_iterator() {}
    reverse_bidirectional_iterator(BidirectionalIterator x) : current(x) {}
    BidirectionalIterator base() { return current; }
    Reference operator*() const {
        BidirectionalIterator tmp = current;
        return *--tmp;
    }
    self& operator++() {
        --current;
        return *this;
    }
    self operator++(int) {
        self tmp = *this;
        --current;
        return tmp;
    }
    self& operator--() {
        ++current;
        return *this;
    }
    self operator--(int) {
        self tmp = *this;
        ++current;
        return tmp;
    }
};

template <class BidirectionalIterator, class T, class Reference, class Distance>
inline bool operator==(
        const reverse_bidirectional_iterator<BidirectionalIterator, T,
                Reference, Distance>& x,
        const reverse_bidirectional_iterator<BidirectionalIterator, T,
                Reference, Distance>& y) {
    return x.current == y.current;
    }

template <class RandomAccessIterator, class T, class Reference = T&,
    class Distance = ptrdiff_t>
class reverse_iterator : public random_access_iterator<T, Distance> {
    typedef reverse_iterator<RandomAccessIterator, T, Reference, Distance>
        self;
    friend bool operator==(const self& x, const self& y);
    friend bool operator<(const self& x, const self& y);
    friend Distance operator-(const self& x, const self& y);
    friend self operator+(Distance n, const self& x);
protected:
    RandomAccessIterator current;
public:
    reverse_iterator() {}
    reverse_iterator(RandomAccessIterator x) : current(x) {}
```

```
    RandomAccessIterator base() { return current; }
    Reference operator*() const {
        RandomAccessIterator tmp = current;
        return *--tmp;
    }
    self& operator++() {
        --current;
        return *this;
    }
    self operator++(int) {
        self tmp = *this;
        --current;
        return tmp;
    }
    self& operator--() {
        ++current;
        return *this;
    }
    self operator--(int) {
        self tmp = *this;
        ++current;
        return tmp;
    }
    self operator+(Distance n) const {
        return self(current - n);
    }
    self& operator+=(Distance n) {
        current -= n;
        return *this;
    }
    self operator-(Distance n) const {
        return self(current + n);
    }
    self& operator-=(Distance n) {
        current += n;
        return *this;
    }
    Reference operator[] (Distance n) { return *(*this +n); }
};

template <class RandomAccessIterator, class T, class Reference, class Distance>
inline bool operator==(
    const reverse_iterator<RandomAccessIterator, T, Reference, Distance>& x,
    const reverse_iterator<RandomAccessIterator, T, Reference, Distance>& y) {
    return x.current == y.current;
}

template <class RandomAccessIterator, class T, class Reference, class Distance>
inline bool operator<(
    const reverse_iterator<RandomAccessIterator, T, Reference, Distance>& x,
    const reverse_iterator<RandomAccessIterator, T, Reference, Distance>& y) {
```

```
        return y.current < x.current;
}

template <class RandomAccessIterator, class T, class Reference, class Distance>
inline Distance operator−(
    const reverse_iterator<RandomAccessIterator, T, Reference, Distance>& x,
    const reverse_iterator<RandomAccessIterator, T, Reference, Distance>& y) {
    return y.current − x.current;
}

template <class RandomAccessIterator, class T, class Reference, class Distance>
inline reverse_iterator<RandomAccessIterator, T, Reference, Distance> operator+(
    Distance n,
    const reverse_iterator<RandomAccessIterator, T, Reference, Distance>& x) {
    const reverse_iterator<RandomAccessIterator, T, Reference, Distance>
(x. current − n);
}
```

## 11.2.2 INSERT ITERATORS

To make it possible to deal with insertion in the same way as writing into an array, a special kind of iterator adaptors, called *insert iterators*, are provided in the library. With regular iterator classes,

```
while (first != last) *result++ = *first++;
```

causes a range [first, last) to be copied into a range starting with result. The same code with result being an insert iterator will insert corresponding elements into the container. This device allows all of the copying algorithms in the library to work in the *insert mode* instead of the regular overwrite mode.

An insert iterator is constructed from a container and possibly one of its iterators pointing to where insertion takes place if it is neither at the beginning nor at the end of the container. Insert iterators satisfy the requirements of output iterators. operator* returns the insert iterator itself. The assignment operator=(const T& x) is defined on insert iterators to allow writing into them, it inserts x right before where the insert iterator is pointing. In other words, an insert iterator is like a cursor pointing into the container where the insertion takes place. back_insert_iterator inserts elements at the end of a container, front_insert_iterator inserts elements at the beginning of a container, and insert_iterator inserts elements where the iterator points to in a container. back_inserter, front_inserter, and inserter are three functions making the insert iterators out of a container.

```
template <class Container>
class back_insert_iterator : public output_iterator {
protected:
    Container& container;
public:
    back_insert_iterator(Container& x) : container(x) {}
    back_insert_iterator<Container>&
    operator=(const Container::value_type& value) {
        container.push_back(value);
        return *this;
    }
```

```cpp
    back_insert_iterator<Container>& operator*() { return *this; }
    back_insert_iterator<Container>& operator++() { return *this; }
    back_insert_iterator<Container>& operator++(int) { return *this; }
};
template <class Container>
back_insert_iterator<Container> back_inserter(Container& x) {
    return back_insert_iterator<Container>(x);
}

template <class Container>
class front_insert_iterator : public output_iterator {
protected:
    Container& container;
public:
    front_insert_iterator(Container& x) : container(x) {}
    front_insert_iterator<Container>&
    operator=(const Container::value_type& value) {
        container.push_front(value);
        return *this;
    }
    front_insert_iterator<Container>& operator*() { return *this; }
    front_insert_iterator<Container>& operator++() { return *this; }
    front_insert_iterator<Container>& operator++(int) { return *this; }
};

template <class Container<
front_insert_iterator<Container> front_inserter(Container& x) {
    return front_insert_iterator<Container>(x);
}

template <class Container>
class insert_iterator : public output_iterator {
protected:
    Container& container;
    Container::iterator iter;
public:
    insert_iterator(Container& x, Container::iterator i)
        : container(x), iter(i) {}
    insert_iterator<Container>& operator=(const Container::value_type& value) {
        iter = container.insert(iter, value);
        ++iter;
        return *this;
    }
    insert_iterator<Container>& operator*() { return *this; }
    insert_iterator<Container>& operator++() { return *this; }
    insert_iterator<Container>& operator++(int) { return *this; }
};

template <class Container, class Iterator>
insert_iterator<Container> inserter(Container& x, Iterator i) {
    return insert_iterator<Container>(x, Container::iterator(i));
}
```

### 11.2.3 RAW STORAGE ITERATOR

`raw_storage_iterator` is provided to enable algorithms to store the results into uninitialized memory. The formal template parameter `OutputIterator` is required to have `construct(OutputIterator, const T&)` defined.

```
template <class OutputIterator, class T>
class raw_storage_iterator : public output_iterator {
protected:
    OutputIterator iter;
public:
    raw_storage_iterator(OutputIterator x) : iter(x) {}
    raw_storage_iterator<OutputIterator, T>& operator*() { return *this; }
    raw_storage_iterator<OutputIterator, T>& operator=(const T& element) {
        construct(iter, element);
        return *this;
    }
    raw_storage_iterator<OutputIterator, T>& operator++() {
        ++iter;
        return *this;
    }
    raw_storage_iterator<OutputIterator, T> operator++(int) {
        raw_storage_iterator<OutputIterator, T> tmp = *this;
        ++iter;
        return tmp;
    }
};
```

## 11.3 Function adaptors

Function adaptors work only with function object classes with argument types and result type defined.

### 11.3.1 NEGATORS

Negators `not1` and `not2` take a unary and a binary predicate correspondingly and return their complements.

```
template <class Predicate>
class unary_negate : public unary_function<Predicate::argument_type, bool> {
protected:
    Predicate pred;
public:
    unary_negate(const Predicate& x) : pred(x) {}
    bool operator() (const argument_type& x) const { return !pred(x); }
};

template <class Predicate>
unary_negate<Predicate> not1(const Predicate& pred) {
    return unary_negate<Predicate>(pred);
}
```

```
template <class Predicate>
class binary_negate : public binary_function<Predicate::first_argument_type,
             Predicate::second_argument_type, bool> {
protected:
   Predicate pred;
public:
   binary_negate(const Predicate& x) : pred(x) {}
   bool operator() (const first_argument_type& x,
          const second_argument_type& y) const {
      return !pred(x, y);
   }
};

template <class Predicate>
binary_negate<Predicate> not2(const Predicate& pred) {
   return binary_negate<Predicate>(pred);
}
```

## 11.3.2 Binders

Binders `bind1st` and `bind2nd` take a function object `f` of two arguments and a value `x` and return a function object of one argument constructed out of `f` with the first or second argument correspondingly bound to `x`.

```
template <class Operation>
class binder1st : public unary_function<Operation::second_argument_type,
                                         Operation::result_type> {
protected:
   Operation op;
   Operation::first_argument_type value;
public:
   binder1st(const Operation& x, const Operation::first_argument_type& y)
      : op(x), value(y) {}
   result_type operator() (const argument_type& x) const {
      return op(value, x);
   }
};

template<class Operation, class T>
binder1st<Operation> bind1st(const Operation& op, const T& x) {
   return binder1st<Operation>(op, Operation::first_argument_type(x));
}

template <class Operation>
class binder2nd : public unary_function<Operation::first_argument_type,
                                         Operation::result_type> {
protected:
   Operation op;
   Operation::second_argument_type value;
public:
   binder2nd(const Operation& x, const Operation::second_argument_type& y)
```

```
        : op(x), value(y) {}
    result_type operator() (const argument_type& x) const {
        return op(x, value);
    }
};

template <class Operation, class T>
binder2nd<Operation> bind2nd(const Operation& op, const T& x) {
    return binder2nd<Operation>(op, Operation::second_argument_type(x));
}
```

For example, `find_if(v.begin(), v.end(), bind2nd(greater<int>(), 5))` finds the first integer in vector v greater than 5; `find_if(v.begin(), v.end(), bind1st(greater<int>(), 5))` finds the first integer in v less than 5.

### 11.3.3   ADAPTORS FOR POINTERS TO FUNCTIONS

To allow pointers to (unary and binary) functions to work with function adaptors the library provides:

```
template <class Arg, class Result>
class pointer_to_unary_function : public unary_function<Arg, Result> {
protected:
    Result (*ptr) (Arg);
public:
    pointer_to_unary_function(Result (*x) (Arg)) : ptr(x) {}
    Result operator() (Arg x) const { return ptr(x); }
};

template <class Arg, class Result>
pointer_to_unary_function<Arg, Result> ptr_fun(Result (*x) (Arg)) {
    return pointer_to_unary_function<Arg, Result>(x);
}

template <class Arg1, class Arg2, class Result>
class pointer_to_binary_function : public binary_function<Arg1, Arg2, Result> {
protected:
    Result (*ptr) (Arg1, Arg2);
Public:
    pointer_to_binary_function(Result (*x) (Arg1, Arg2)) : ptr(x) {}
    Result operator() (Arg1 x, Arg2 y) const { return ptr(x, y); }
};

template <class Arg1, class Arg2, class Result>
pointer_to_binary_function<Arg1, Arg2, Result
ptr_fun(Result (*x) (Arg1, Arg2)) {
    return pointer_to_binary_function<Arg1, Arg2, Result>(x);
}
```

For example, `replace_if(v.begin(), v.end(), not1(bind2nd(ptr_funstrcmp), "C")), "C++")` replaces all the "C" with "C++" in sequence v.

Compilation systems that have multiple pointer to function types have to provide additional `ptr_fun` template functions.

## 12   MEMORY HANDLING

### 12.1   Primitives

To obtain a typed pointer to an uninitialized memory buffer of a given size the following function is defined:

```
template <class T>
inline T* allocate(ptrdiff_t n, T*); // n <= 0
```

The size (in bytes) of the allocated buffer is no less than `n*sizeof(T)`.

For every memory model there is a corresponding `allocate` template function defined with the first argument type being the distance type of the pointers in the memory model.

For example, if a compilation system supports _huge pointers with the distance type being `long, long`, the following template function is provided:

```
template <class T>
inline T _huge* allocate(long long n, T _huge *);
```

Also, the following functions are provided:

```
template <class T>
inline void deallocate(T* buffer);

template <class T1, class T2>
inline void construct(T1* p, const T2& value) {
    new (p) T1(value);
}

template <class T>
inline void destroy(T* pointer) {
    pointer-<~T();
}
```

`deallocate` frees the buffer allocated by `allocate`. For every memory model there are corresponding `deallocate`, `construct` and `destroy` template functions defined with the first argument type being the pointer type of the memory model.

```
template <class T>
pair<T*, ptrdiff_t> get_temporary_buffer(ptrdiff_t n, T*);

template <class T>
void return_temporary_buffer(T* p);
```

`get_temporary_buffer` finds the largest buffer not greater than `n*sizeof(T)`, and returns a pair consisting of the address and the capacity (in the units of `sizeof(T)`) of the buffer. `return_temporary` `_buffer` returns the buffer allocated by `get_temporary_buffer`.

## 12.2   Specialized algorithms

All the iterators that are used as formal template parameters in the following algorithms are required to have `construct(ForwardIterator, const T&)` defined.

```
template <class ForwardIterator>
void destroy(ForwardIterator first, ForwardIterator last) {
    while (first != last) destroy(first++);
}

template <class InputIterator, class ForwardIterator>
ForwardIterator uninitialized_copy(InputIterator first, InputIterator last,
          ForwardIterator result) {
    while (first != last) construct(result++, *first++);
    return result;
}

template <class ForwardIterator, class T>
void uninitialized_fill(ForwardIterator first, ForwardIterator last,
        const T& x) {
    while (first != last) construct(first++, x);
}

template <class ForwardIterator, class Size, class T>
void uninitialized_fill_n(ForwardIterator first, Size n, const T& x) {
    while (n--) construct(first++, x);
}
```

## 13   ACKNOWLEDGMENTS

The following people contributed to the design of STL:

Pete Becker, David Jacobson, Mehdi Jazayeri, Tom Keffer, Andy Koenig, Milon Mackey, Doug Morgan, Dave Musser, Nathan Myers, Larry Podmolik, Bob Shaw, Carl Staelin, Bjarne Stroustrup, Mark Terribile, Parthasarathy Tirumalai, Mike Vilot, John Wilkes.

The present library is a descendant of several earlier libraries (in Scheme, Ada, and C++) which were designed jointly with Dave Musser. He contributed to all the aspects of the STL work: design of the overall structure, semantic requirements, algorithm design, complexity analysis and performance measurements.

Andy Koenig is responsible for explaining to us that C++ has an underlying abstract machine and that the generic library should fit this machine. He also convinced us that we should attempt to turn our work into a C++ standard proposal.

During the writing of the proposal Bjarne Stroustrup has been a constant supporter and has been giving us a lot of technical advice especially on the language dependent parts of the library.

Andy and Bjarne have answered literally hundreds of "urgent" messages and phone calls of the form: "Could we do this?"

Dan Fishman and Mary Loomis created the environment where we were able to concentrate on the design without any distractions.

Bill Worley is responsible for starting this project and supporting it throughout his tenure as our lab director.

Rick Amerson and Dmitry Lenkov have given us advice and support.

## 14  BIBLIOGRAPHY

M. Ellis and B. Stroustrup, *The Annotated C++ Reference Manual,* New York, Addison-Wesley, 1990.

D. Kapur, D. R. Musser, and A. A. Stepanov, "Tecton, A Language for Manipulating Generic Objects," *Proc. of Workshop on Program Specification,* Aarhus, Denmark, August 1981, *Lecture Notes in Computer Science,* Springer-Verlag, vol. 134, 1982.

D. Kapur, D. R. Musser, and A. A. Stepanov, "Operators and Algebraic Structures," *Proc. of the Conference on Functional Programming Languages and Computer Architecture,* Portsmouth, NH, October 1981.

A. Kershenbaum, D. R. Musser, and A. A. Stepanov, "Higher Order Imperative Programming," Technical Report 88-10, Rensselaer Polytechnic Institute, April 1988.

A. Koenig, "Associative arrays in C++," *Proc. USENIX Conference,* San Francisco, CA, June 1988.

A. Koenig, "Applicators, Manipulators, and Function Objects," *C++ Journal,* vol. 1, #1, Summer 1990.

D. R. Musser and A. A. Stepanov, "A Library of Generic Algorithms in Ada," *Proc. of 1987 ACM SIGAda International Conference,* Boston, December, 1987.

D. R. Musser and A. A. Stepanov, "Generic Programming," invited paper, in P. Gianni, ed., *ISSAC '88 Symbolic and Algebraic Computation Proceedings, Lecture Notes in Computer Science,* Springer-Verlag, vol. 358, 1989.

D. R. Musser and A. A. Stepanov, *Ada Generic Library,* Springer-Verlag, 1989.

D. R. Musser and A. A. Stepanov, "Algorithm-Oriented Generic Libraries," *Software Practice and Experience,* vol. 24(7), July 1994.

M. Stahl and U. Steinmüller, "Generic Dynamic Arrays," *The C++ Report,* October 1993.

J. E. Shopiro, "Strings and Lists for C++," *AT&T Bell Labs Internal Technical Memorandum,* July 1985.

A. A. Stepanov and M. Lee, "The Standard Template Library," Technical Report HPL-94-34, Hewlett-Packard Laboratories, April 1994.

B. Stroustrup, *The Design and Evolution of C++,* New York, Addison-Wesley, 1994.

# SYMBOLS

## Class Relationship Diagram Symbols

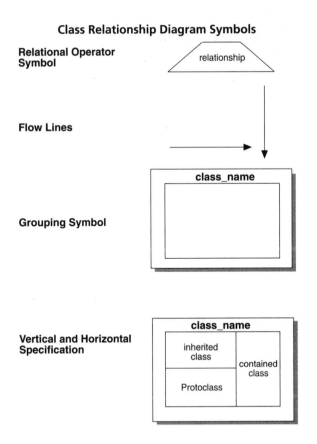

**Relational Operator
Symbol**

**Flow Lines**

**Grouping Symbol**

**Vertical and Horizontal
Specification**

## Program Flowchart Symbols

**Processing**
A group of program instructions which perform a processing function of the program.

**Input/Output**
Any function of an input/output device.

**Decision**
The decision function is used to document points in the program where a branch to alternate paths is possible based upon variable conditions.

**Preparation**
An instruction or group of instructions which changes the program.

**Predefined Process**
A group of operations not detailed in the particular set of flowcharts.

**Terminal**
The beginning, end, or a point of interruption in a program.

**Connector**
An entry from, or an exit to, another part of the program flowchart.

**Offpage Connector**
A connector used instead of the connector symbol to designate entry to or exit from a page.

**Flow Directions**
The direction of processing of data flow.

# System Flowchart Symbols

**Processing**
A major processing function.

**Input/Output**
Any type of medium or data.

**Punched card**
All varieties of punched cards including stubs.

**Punched tape**
Paper or plastic, chad or chadless.

**Document**
Paper documents and reports of all varieties.

**Transmittal Tape**
A proof or adding-machine tape or similar batch-control information.

**Magnetic tape**

**Offline storage**
Offline storage of either paper, cards, magnetic or perforated tape.

**Online storage**

**Display**
Information displayed by plotters or video devices.

**Collate**
Forming two or more sets of items from two or more other sets.

**Sorting**
An operation on sorting or collating equipment.

**Manual input**
A manual offline operation not requiring mechanical aid.

**Merge**
Combining two or more sets of items into one set.

**Manual Operation**
A manual offline operation not requiring mechanical aid.

**Auxillary Operation**
A machine operation supplementing the main processing function.

**Keying Operation**
An operation utilizing a key-driven device.

**Communication Link**
The automatic transmission of information from one location to another via communication lines.

**Flow**
The direction of processing of data flow.

# BIBLIOGRAPHY

Abel, Peter. 1991. *IBM PC Assembly Language and Programming,* 2nd ed. Englewood Cliffs, NJ: Prentice Hall.

Adams, Lee. 1988. *High-Performance Graphics in C Animation and Simulation.* Blue Ridge Summit, PA: Windcrest.

Aho, Alfred V., Ravi Sethi, and Jeffrey D. Ullman. 1986. *Compilers, Principles, Techniques and Tools.* Reading, MA: Addison-Wesley, 1986.

Andleigh, Prabhat K., and Michael R. Gretzinger. 1992. *Distributed Object-Oriented Data System Design.* Englewood Cliffs, NJ: Prentice Hall.

ANSI Committee Document, 1994. Doc No.X3J16/94-0027 W621/N0414.

Asante, Molefi Kete. 1990. *Kemet, Afrocentricity, and Knowledge.* Trenton, NJ: Africa World Press.

Baker, Louis. 1992. *C Mathematical Function Handbook.* New York: McGraw-Hill.

Banks, Michael A. 1991. *The Modem Reference,* 2nd ed. New York: Brady Books.

Barkakati, Nabajyoti. 1990. *The Waite Group's Turbo C++ Bible.* Indianapolis: SAMS.

Barr, Avron, and Edward A. Feigenbaum. 1982. *The Handbook of Artificial Intelligence.* Vols. I–II. Los Altos, CA: William Kaufman.

Behforooz, Ali, and Onkar P. Sharma. 1986. *An Introduction to Computer Science: A Structured Problem Solving Approach.* Englewood Cliffs, NJ: Prentice Hall.

Bekley, Edmund C., and Lawrence Wainwright. 1956. *Computers, Their Operations and Applications.* New York: Reinhold.

Benedikt, Michael, ed. 1982. *Cyberspace: First Steps.* 4th ed. Cambridge, MA: MIT Press.

Berger, Marc. 1986. *Computer Graphics with Pascal.* Menlo Park, CA: Benjamin Cummings.

Berry, John. 1988. *The Waite Group's C++ Programming.* Indianapolis: SAMS.

Blain, Derrel R., Kurt R. Delimon, and William J. English. 1994. *Real-World Programming for OS/2 2.11,* 2nd ed. Indianapolis: SAMS.

Blum, Adam. 1992. *Neural Networks In C++: An Object Oriented Framework for Building Connectionist Systems.* New York: John Wiley & Sons.

Bolon, Craig. 1986. *Mastering C.* Alameda, CA: Sybex, Inc.

Booch, Grady. 1994. *Object-Oriented Analysis and Design with Applications,* 2nd ed. Redwood City, CA: Benjamin Cummings.

Borger, Egon. 1988. *Trends in Theoretical Computer Science.* Rockville, MD: Computer Science Press.

Bruce, Philip, and Sam M. Pederson. 1982. *The Software Development Project Planning and Management.* New York: John Wiley & Sons.

Budd, Timothy A. 1994. *Classic Data Structures In C++.* Reading, MA: Addison-Wesley.

Campbell, Joe. 1987. *C Programmer's Guide to Serial Communications.* Indianapolis: SAMS.

Carroll, Martin D., and Margaret A. Ellis, 1995. *Designing and Coding Reusable C++.* Reading, MA: Addison-Wesley.

Chaitin, G. J. 1987. *Algorithmic Information Theory.* New York: Cambridge University Press.

Christian, Kaare. 1993. *Borland C++ Techniques and Utilities.* Emeryville, CA: Ziff Davis.

Clocksin, W. F., and C. S. Mellish. 1981. *Programming in Prolog,* 3rd ed. Berlin: Springer Verlag.

Conger, Jim. 1992. *Windows API Bible: The Definitive Programmer's Reference.* Corte Madera, CA: Waite Group.

Conger, Jim. 1993. *Windows New Testament.* Corte Madera, CA: Waite Group.

Conger, Jim. 1993. *Windows API New Testament.* Corte Madera, CA: Waite Group.

Covington, Michael A., Donald Nute, and André Vellino. *Prolog Programming in Depth.* Glenview, IL: Scott, Foresman.

Cox, Brad J. 1986. *Object-Oriented Programming: An Evolutionary Approach.* Reading, MA: Addison-Wesley.

Davis, Phillip J., and Reuben Hersh. 1981. *The Mathematical Experience.* Boston, MA: Houghton Mifflin.

Davis, William S. 1987. *Operating Systems: A Systematic View,* 3rd ed. Reading, MA: Addison-Wesley.

Dettman, Terry, Jim Kyle, and Marcus Johnson. 1992. *DOS Programmer's Reference,* 3rd ed. Carmel, IN: Que Corp.

Dilascia, Paul. 1992. *Windows ++: Writing Reusable Code in C++.* Reading, MA: Addison-Wesley.

Dorfman, Len. 1990. *Building C Libraries.* Blue Ridge Summit, PA: Windcrest Books.

Duncan, Ray, Charles Petzold, Andrew Schulman, M. Steven Baker, Ross P. Nelson, Stephen R. Davis, and Robert Moote. 1992. *Extending DOS: A Programmer's Guide to Protected-Mode DOS,* 2nd ed. Reading, MA: Addison-Wesley.

Eckel, Bruce. 1993. *C++ Inside and Out.* Berkeley, CA: Osborne McGraw-Hill.

Ellis, Margaret A., and Bjarne Stroustrup. 1990. *The Annotated C++ Reference Manual.* Reading, MA: Addison-Wesley.

Ellzey, Roy S. 1987. *Computer System Software: The Programmer/Machine Interface.* Chicago: SRA.

Ellzey, Roy S. 1982. *Data Structures for Computer Information Systems.* Chicago: Science Research Associates.

Elson, Mark. 1975. *Data Structures.* Chicago: Science Research Associates.

Emerson, Frances B. 1987. *Technical Writing.* Boston, MA: Houghton Mifflin.

Ezzel, Ben. 1990. *Graphics Programming in C++: An Object Oriented Approach.* Reading, MA: Addison-Wesley.

Feibel, Werner. 1995. *Complete Encyclopedia of Networking.* Alameda, CA: Novell Press.

Ferraro, Richard F. 1990. *Programmer's Guide to EGA and VGA Cards,* 2nd ed. Reading, MA: Addison-Wesley.

Finkbeiner, Daniel T., and Wendell D. Lindstrom. 1987. *A Primer of Discrete Mathematics.* New York: W. H. Freeman and Company.

Fischler, Martin A., and Oscar Firschein. 1987. *Intelligence, the Eye, the Brain, and the Computer.* Reading, MA: Addison-Wesley.

Gibbons, Alan. 1987. *Algorithmic Graph Theory.* New York: Cambridge University Press.

Gordon, Geoffrey. 1969. *System Simulation.* Englewood Cliffs, NJ: Prentice Hall.

Gorlen, Keith E., Sanford M. Orlow, and Perry Plexico. 1990. *Data Abstraction and Object-Oriented Programming in C++.* New York: John Wiley & Sons.

Harbison, Samuel P., and Guy L. Steele, Jr. 1991. *C Reference Manual,* 3rd ed. Englewood Cliffs, NJ: Prentice Hall.

Harmon, Paul, and David King. 1985. *Expert Systems.* New York: John Wiley & Sons.

Hashim, Safaa A. 1990. *Exploring Hypertext Programming: Writing Knowledge Representation and Problem Solving Programs.* Blue Ridge Summit, PA: Windcrest Books.

Heimlich, Richard, David M. Golden, Ivan Luk, and Peter M. Ridge. 1993. *Sound Blaster: The Official Book.* Berkeley, CA: Osborne McGraw-Hill.

Holub, Allen I. 1990. *Compiler Design in C.* Englewood Cliffs, NJ: Prentice Hall.

Hughes, Cameron, Thomas Hamilton, and Tracey Hughes. 1995. *Object-Oriented I/O Using C++ Iostreams.* New York: John Wiley & Sons.

IBM. 1989. *Object-Oriented Interface Design: IBM Common User Access Guidelines.* Carmel, IN: Que.

IBM. 1992. *OS/2 2.0 Presentation Manager Graphics Programming Guide.* Carmel, IN: Que.

IBM. 1992. *OS/2 2.0 Control Program Programming Guide.* Carmel, IN: Que.

Jacobson, Ivar, Magnus Christerson, Patrik Jonsson, and Gunar Overgaard. 1992. *Object-Oriented Software Engineering: A Use Case-Driven Approach.* Workingham, England: Addison-Wesley.

Jones, Capers. 1986. *Programming Productivity.* New York: McGraw-Hill.

Kaner, Cem. 1988. *Testing Computer Software.* Blue Ridge Summit, PA: Tab Books.

Kerninghan, Brian W., and Dennis M. Ritchie. 1978. *Programming in C.* Englewood Cliffs, NJ: Prentice Hall.

Kolatis, Maria Shopay. 1985. *Mathematics for Data Processing and Computing.* Reading, MA: Addison-Wesley.

Korsh, James F., and Leonard J. Garret. 1988. *Data Structures, Algorithms, and Program Style Using C.* Boston, MA: PWS-Kent.

Kowalski, Robert. 1979. *Logic for Problem Solving.* New York: Elsevier Science.

Lai, Robert S., and The Waite Group, 1992. *Writing MS-DOS Device Drivers,* 2nd ed. Reading, MA: Addison-Wesley.

LaQuey, Tracy, and Jeanne C. Ryer. 1993. *The Internet Companion: Beginner's Guide to Global Networking.* Reading, MA: Addison-Wesley.

Liebowitz, Jay, and Daniel A. De Salvo. 1989. *Structuring Expert Systems Domain, Design, and Development.* Englewood Cliffs, NJ: Prentice Hall.

Lindley, Craig A. 1991. *Practical Image Processing in C: Acquisition, Manipulation, and Storage.* New York: John Wiley & Sons.

Luse, Marv. 1993. *Bitmapped Graphics Programming in C++.* Reading, MA: Addison-Wesley.

Mandrioli, Dino, and Carlo Ghezzi. 1987. *Theoretical Foundations of Computer Science.* New York: John Wiley & Sons.

Matsumoto, Yoshihiro, and Yutaka Ohno. 1989. *Japanese Perspective in Software Engineering.* Singapore: Addison-Wesley.

McCracken, D. D. 1957. *Digital Computer Programming.* New York: John Wiley & Sons.

Mertin, James, and Kathleen Kavanagh Chapman. 1984. *Local Area Networks Architectures and Implementations.* Englewood Cliffs, NJ: Prentice Hall.

Meyer, Bertrand. 1988. *Object-Oriented Software Construction.* Englewood Cliffs, NJ: Prentice Hall.

Munnik, Josha, and Eric Oostendrop. 1994. *The Sound Blaster Book.* Alameda, CA: Sybex, Inc.

Murray, William D. 1990. *Computer and Digital System Architecture.* Englewood Cliffs, NJ: Prentice Hall.

Nance, Barry. 1990. *Network Programming in C.* Carmel, IN: Que Corp.

Norton, Peter, and Robert Jourdain. 1988. *The Hard Disk Companion.* New York: Brady Books.

Pagan, Frank G. 1991. *Partial Computation and the Construction of Language Processors.* Englewood Cliffs, NJ: Prentice Hall.

Panov, Kathleen, Larry Salomon, and Arthur Panov. 1993. *The Art of OS/2 2.1 C Programming.* Wellesley, MA: QED.

Patterson, David A., and John L. Henessy. 1994. *Computer Organization & Design: The Hardware/Software Interface.* San Mateo, CA: Morgan Kaufmann.

Peng, Yun, and James A. Reggia. 1990. *Abductive Inference Models for Diagnostic Problem-Solving.* New York: Springer Verlag.

Petzoid, Charles. 1994. *OS/2 Presentation Manager Programming.* Emeryville, CA: Ziff Davis.

Petzoid, Charles. 1992. *Programming Windows 3.1,* 3rd ed. Redmond, WA: Microsoft Press.

Pietrik, Matt. 1993. *Windows Intervals: The Implementation of the Windows Operating Environment.* Reading, MA: Addison-Wesley.

Plauger, P. J., and Jim Brodie. 1992. *ANSI and ISO Standard C Programmer's Reference.* Redmond, WA: Microsoft Press.

Plauger, P. J. 1992. *The Standard C Library.* Englewood Cliffs, NJ: Prentice Hall.

Purdin, Jack. 1992. *C Programmer's Toolkit,* 2nd ed. Carmel, IN: Que.

Reynolds, John C. 1981. *The Craft of Programming.* London: Prentice Hall.

Rimmer, Steve. 1992. *Supercharged Bitmapped Graphics.* Blue Ridge Summit, PA: Windcrest/McGraw-Hill Books.

Robinson, Phillip R. 1987. *Using Turbo Prolog.* Berkeley, CA: Osborne McGraw-Hill.

Rogers, Jean B. 1986. *A Prolog Primer.* Reading, MA: Addison-Wesley.

Rubin, Tony. 1988. *User Interface Design for Computer Systems.* New York: John Wiley & Sons.

Schildt, Herbert. 1987. *Artificial Intelligence Using C.* Berkeley, CA: Osborne McGraw-Hill.

Schildt, Herbert. 1990. *Using Turbo C++.* Berkeley, CA: Osborne McGraw-Hill.

Schildt, Herbert. 1992. *C Power User's Guide.* Berkeley, CA: Osborne McGraw-Hill.

Schildt, Herbert, and Robert Goosey. 1993. *OS/2 2.0 Programming.* Berkeley, CA: Osborne McGraw-Hill.

Schulmeyer, Gordon G., and James McManus. 1987. *Handbook Software Quality Assurance.* New York: Van Nostrand Reinhold.

Sedgewick, Robert. 1983. *Algorithms.* Reading, MA: Addison-Wesley.

Seyer, Martin D. 1991. *RS-232 Made Easy: Connecting Computers, Printers, Terminals, and Modems,* 2nd ed. Englewood Cliffs, NJ: Prentice Hall.

Sippl, Charles J. 1985. *Computer Dictionary.* 4th ed. Indianapolis: SAMS.

Smith, James T. 1991. *C++ for Scientists and Engineers.* New York: McGraw-Hill.

Soukup, Jiri. 1994. *Taming C++ Pattern Classes and Persistence for Large Projects.* Reading, MA: Addison-Wesley.

Staugaard, Andrew C., Jr. 1994. *Structuring Techniques: An Introduction Using C++.* Englewood Cliffs, NJ: Prentice Hall.

Sterling, Leon, and Ehud Shapiro. 1986. *The Art of Prolog.* Cambridge, MA: MIT Press.

Stitt, Martin. 1995. *Building Custom Software Tools and Libraries.* New York: John Wiley & Sons.

Stroustrup, Bjarne. 1991. *The C++ Programming Language.* 2nd ed. Reading, MA: Addison-Wesley.

Stroustrup, Bjarne. 1994. *The Design and Evolution of C++.* Reading, MA: Addison-Wesley.

Talman, Michael. 1992. *Understanding Presentation Graphics.* Alameda, CA: Sybex, Inc.

Teale, Steve. 1993. *C++ IOSTREAMS Handbook.* Reading, MA: Addison-Wesley.

Tenenbaum, Aaron M., Yedidyah Langsam, and Moshe J. Augenstein. 1992. *Data Structures Using C.* Englewood Cliffs, NJ: Prentice Hall.

Tenenbaum, Andrew S. 1987. *Operating Systems Design and Implementation.* Englewood Cliffs, NJ: Prentice Hall.

Thompson, William J. 1992. *Computing for Scientists and Engineers: A Workbook of Analysis, Numerics and Applications.* New York: John Wiley & Sons.

Tway, Linda. *Welcome to Multimedia.* New York: Management Information Sources.

Watt, Alan. 1989. *Fundamentals of Three-Dimensional Computer Graphics.* Workingham, England: Addison-Wesley.

Winston, Patrick Henry, Berthold Klaus, and Paul Horn. *LISP.* Reading, MA: Addison-Wesley.

# INDEX

## A

abstract base classes, 105
abstract classes, 63
abstract data types, classes as, 24–25
accessing objects. *See also* object visitation
    in deques, 274
    in sequence containers, 138–39
    from vectors, 251–54
access methods, 93
accumulate algorithm, 472–73
adaptors, 474–84
    binders, 482–83
    container, 158–61, 474–76
    defined, 158
    function, 165, 481–84
    inserter, 163–64
    insert iterator, 479–81
    iterator, 161, 163–64, 476–81
    negators, 481–82
    for pointers to functions, 483–84
    priority queue, 475
    queue, 475
    stack, 474–75
adding objects. *See also* insert() member
        functions
    to associative collections, 156
    to map collections, 312–13

to multimap collections, 321–22
to multiset collections, 212
to set collections, 193–95
to vector containers, 250–51
adjacent difference algorithm, 473–74
adjacent find algorithm, 458
aggregate classes, 64
algorithms, 114–24
    analysis of, 122–23
    basic requirements for, 116–19
    classic, 120
    components of, 122
    flowchart representation of, 116
    graph, 116
    member functions and, 119–20
    O notation and, 123–24
    pseudocode representation of, 115
    recursive, 121–22
    STL (Standard Template Library), 146,
        165, 168–77, 457–74
        accumulate, 472–73
        adjacent difference, 473–74
        adjacent find, 458
        binary searches, 466–67
        count, 458
        equal, 459

**497**

## B

# C

# D

# E

# F

# G

## H

## I

## L

## M

# N

# O

# P

## Q

## R

# S

# T